Integral Investing

Mariana Bozesan

Integral Investing

From Profit to Prosperity

Foreword by Ken Wilber

 Springer

A Report to the

World Academy of
Art and Science

Mariana Bozesan
AQAL Foundation
Munich, Germany

ISBN 978-3-030-54015-9   ISBN 978-3-030-54016-6   (eBook)
https://doi.org/10.1007/978-3-030-54016-6

This Springer imprint is published by the registered company Springer Nature Switzerland AG.
The registered company address is: Gewerbestrasse 11, 6330 Cham, Switzerland

Foreword

In this exciting and engaging book, Mariana says at one point, "In the early twenty-first century, Tom [her husband and collaborator] and I attended a personal development seminar led by Tony Robbins in a tent village in the Moroccan desert, and it was here that we discovered our ideal theoretical framework to facilitate our investment and company building activities: Ken Wilber's Integral Theory." Thus began Mariana and Tom's adventures in Integral Investing. In the following pages, Mariana (with occasional direct contributions from Tom) lays out what Integral Investing is, what it means, where it came from, why it's so important, and how to directly apply it yourself—and not just to your investment or company activities, but to your overall life, if you wish. *yuck*

Since I'm Ken Wilber, and I am indeed the principal architect of this integral framework, Mariana asked me to write a few words that might contextualize the material that follows. You'll learn a good deal about Integral Theory (or technically, integral metatheory) in the following pages. (It's primarily a metatheory because it looks at all of the various theories, maps, and models addressing a particular issue and then pulls together what appears to be the best elements of each.) Because of this very broad and intentionally synthesizing and integrating intent, I think you'll find this approach very fresh and interesting, and I hope that you will be able to see why many people consider it an invaluable guide or operating system for virtually any activity that you might want to undertake. In fact, to date, this integral framework has been applied to over 60 different disciplines and areas to create integral business, integral education, integral psychology, integral technology, integral leadership, integral medicine, integral marketing, integral counselling, integral ecology.... Well, I think you get the point, and this really is not meant to be a shout out list of integral's appeal. Rather, all that I want to do here is share with you how I stumbled on this integral approach myself, and how I increasingly came to see that it could have a very widespread application across a huge number of fields, all of them benefitting in very substantial ways. It was originally as much of a surprise to me as it might be to you, because, basically, nobody ever seems taught to do things this way.

I was completing my graduate studies in biochemistry when I became fascinated with the various types of self development courses that were increasingly available (this was back in the sixties, with the wildly explosive growth of the "human potential movement," much of which was narcissistic drivel from the "Me genera-tion," but some of which was pure gold and had never been seen in a Western culture before). These approaches had a staggering variety of names and claims, from achieving "full enlightenment" to "improving self confidence" to "emotional health in 1 hour"—and on and on. I began an obsessive study of these ideas, simply because there seemed to be some fairly important truths buried in all the outrageous claims. As I studied all of these—East and West, premodern and modern, Zen Buddhism to psychoanalysis, NLP to Gestalt Therapy—it soon became rather clear that, despite their enormous differences and disagreements, the ideas all fell into six or seven basic families. Ideas that could be clustered under the psychoanalysis related family, for instance, all agreed that emotional dysfunctions and symptoms often resulted from repressed shadow material, and that to cure the emotional symptom, a person had to reintegrate the shadow. The idea was to expand from a narrow and inaccurate self image (or "persona") to a whole and healthy "ego" or mind. But a very large and influential movement at that time (called Humanistic Existential, or The Third Force in Psychology—because it comes after the first two, more common forces of behaviorism and psychoanalysis) argued that the basic human problem is not that humans have an inaccurate self concept or ego mind, but that they tend to separate and split their mind from their body, and it's that dissociation, that fragmentation, that causes all the problems. The real aim should instead be to experience ourselves as a total and fully integrated organism, not one completely broken in half—the real aim was to expand from a dissociated mind to a full body/mind unity or total organism. To do so would release the incredible human potentials in every area of human activity.

Yet another family of these self improvement approaches—the Zen related family—was one whose principles were shared by deeply meditative or contempla-tive practices (East and West, Vedanta to Kabbalah to Sufism). They maintained that the human potentials approach wouldn't really work. The real problem, this family maintained, is not that the shadow is split from the ego mind, thus splintering it, nor that the ego mind is split from the body, thus fracturing the total organism; the real problem is that the total organism itself is split and fragmented from a deeply felt identity with the entire world. Until that split is fully let go of—in a type of "ultimate unity consciousness" or "being one with everything"—then a human being will necessarily be faced with suffering, dread, fear, and trembling.

And so went the battle of the self-improvement courses. On the one hand, most of them seemed to make at least some degree of sense, and I had deliberately sought out and was practicing versions of many of them, and they were all quite helpful. But on the other hand, they all disagreed with each other, sometimes vehemently, and the highly heated arguments between them were often taken up by the media. Happi-ness, for psychoanalysis and its family, aimed for the creation of a "whole and healthy ego," or what they called "ego strength." Zen and its family insisted that the ego is the cause of all suffering and you have to get rid of it entirely. Try fitting those two claims together.

This went on for several years, and I became rather obsessed with the desire to find a way to fit them together. Up to that point, particularly with my extensive training in the sciences, I had been operating with the idea that, based on actual evidence, one solution to a problem is generally right and its competing claims are wrong. I had no quarrel with that notion, but something seemed a little off about it when applied to all these competing claims of different world views (from psychoanalysis to humanistic to Zen). All the time I had been exploring six or seven different families of self-actualization, in the back of my mind was the idea that one of them was really, really the correct one, and that the others were all well intended but essentially wrong. And then what is perhaps the central integral insight occurred to me: "Everybody is right." As I saw it, no human brain is capable of producing 100% error (I'd joke: "Nobody is smart enough to be wrong all the time").

So essentially no idea, no matter how out there it seemed to be, was totally and completely wrong. Rather, it had at least a grain of truth. My aim was to find that grain—and then combine it with other grains, since each of them was true... albeit partially. Thus, attempting to integrate shadow material was not totally false but rather partially true. It needed to be supplemented with other truths. That would include not only uniting the broken persona with the repressed shadow to produce a whole and healthy ego mind but also going one step further and uniting the whole mind with the dissociated body to produce a felt unity with the total organism. That was also a true but partial idea. So that truth could be supplemented by going further yet, and uniting the separate and isolated total organism with the entire world to produce an "ultimate unity consciousness," a direct sense of "being one with everything" (a satori, Awakening, enlightenment, or Waking Up).

It turned out that those basic waves or levels of consciousness (along with three or four transitions between them) covered all of the major families of self-improvement that I had found. And they all fit together in a magnificent spectrum of consciousness, each of them being true but partially so, and each primarily addressing their own, quite different, but very real band or level in the spectrum. I wrote all of this up in my first book (called, no surprise, *The Spectrum of Consciousness*). I was 23 at the time, and I went on to write a book every 2 or 3 years for almost 50 years (and 30 books). But that discovery of the fact that we all have a very broad spectrum of consciousness or awareness, which includes numerous very real bands or colors or waves—each of which any of us can attain—was definitely news to me. And it became the first major ingredient of the integral framework, which would go on to include at least five major ingredients, virtually all of which were equally unknown to me (and most others) at the time. It is the awareness, and inclusion, of these little-known but profoundly important factors of our own being and awareness that got Integral Theory the reputation of being a genuinely comprehensive, inclusive, and—in the very best sense of the word—holistic framework.

A person certainly does not have to agree with all of the details that integral metatheory presents, and I certainly would not ask you to. Rather, it's the five major areas that are especially important. And I know of no other discipline of any type, anywhere in the world, that fully includes (or even seems to be aware of) all five of these fundamental areas. I'll simply give the technical names we often use for these five areas, and then very briefly explain what they mean. (Mariana introduces each of them in the following pages, and it will become very clear what they mean.) We call them quadrants, levels, lines, states, and types, and the general integral guideline is: If you want a truly comprehensive and effective approach to any area, make sure you include all of those elements, or you're leaving out something very real and very important—and this inadequacy will hobble your endeavors.

I'll run through some examples of this very quickly, starting with levels. The levels component involves the basic levels of consciousness that were the first components of integral (outlined in my first book). As I continued to study that developmental dimension of our being, it became clearer and clearer to me that there were at least two very different types of levels, or stages, or waves, or colors of the spectrum of consciousness—each of which could and did undergo a real development—and which I would call Growing Up and Waking Up. Growing Up referred to the standard maps and models of human growth and development created by research in fields such as developmental psychology. In fact, in a book called *Integral Psychology*, I analyzed over 100 different developmental models from around the world—including premodern, modern, and postmodern sources (I include charts of all 100 of them—again, this is primarily a metatheory or metamodel, in that it doesn't study so much facts as all the various maps and models and theories about those facts; the theories themselves try to fit various facts together, while a metatheory tries to fit the various theories together, which themselves fit the facts together, so everything gets covered in the end). The different models give anywhere from three to 20 different stages of growth, but on average they give around six to eight major stages or levels of growth and development that all human beings go through (some of these models have been tested in over 40 different cultures, and as far as we can tell, they really are multicultural). I often summarize these as four major levels: egocentric to ethnocentric to world-centric to integrated. But the point is, each and every one of us is on this astonishing path of Growing Up, and each of us can be at any of its stages or waves—which have vastly different views, values, and ethics. And yet most of us have no idea that this is occurring, or how profoundly it alters our needs, desires, morals, world views, and skills—not to mention how it will dramatically change how we look at literally any area at all, from our relationships to our investing to what we consider important in AI programming.

Why is this specifically important for something like business or investing? The research to support its importance is overwhelming (including that done by Harvard's Robert Kegan, Susanne Cook-Greuter, and William Torbert, among many others). If you look at the most successful CEOs and heads of business, the vast majority of them are in the upper stages of this development. This isn't an elitism; or if it is, it's an elitism to which all are invited, since these are stages available to everybody. It's just that the most successful business leaders are almost always at these higher stages, which gives them a phenomenal increase in their capacity for taking fresh perspectives, leadership, handling complexity, and balancing conflicting demands. As a simple glance at the 100 charts in Integral Psychology will demonstrate, there is a surprising agreement among researchers as to what these basic stages look like, and we also know a stunning amount about how to help individuals grow and develop through them more quickly and fully. It's just that virtually nobody knows about them.

Ask any college professor, "What are seven or eight of the major stages of human development that we all go through?" and they'll look at you with an utterly blank stare. As Mariana explains, these stages are today quite easily measured (and measuring them is part of her integral investment strategy). If I had eight major levels of my own growth and development available and I found out that I was presently at four, I would not really be satisfied or happy. Would you? What if you were considering investing in a company that was trying to go global and you found out its CEO was also at four? This is by no means the only factor that an integral approach considers (we have dozens of factors in at least these five different elements). But have you ever heard of an investment approach that even considers, or is aware of, such items? If you think about it, do you really want to support a company whose leadership is deeply at, say, an ethnocentric stage of development? No matter how much money it might make, does that really sound attractive? College protesters today often demonstrate because they want more "world-centric" values (which "treat everybody fairly, regardless of race, color, sex, gender, or creed")—and not "ethnocentric" values (which unduly favor one group), which is excellent. But I've never heard one of them explain the actual path a person must follow to get from ethnocentric to world-centric values. Well, it's called Growing Up, and we actually know a staggering amount about it.

I mentioned there were at least two very major, but quite different, types of stages or developmental pathways that humans have access to. One is Growing Up. The other is what I generically call Waking Up. It is true that at the very highest stages of Growing Up, those stages start to permanently include this type of Waking Up. But it turns out that, for the most part, these satori, or enlightenment, or awakening experiences are relatively independent states of consciousness, and a person can have a "peak experience" of virtually any of these unity states of Waking Up at almost any of their stages of Growing Up. This in itself was a very surprising discovery. But evidence continues to show that, although the percentage of the population permanently reaching the very highest stages of Growing Up is less than 1%, the percentage of the population having a "peak experience" of a state of Waking Up—where they report "an overwhelming feeling of being one with everything"—is well over 60%.

As for this type of Waking Up experience or "ultimate unity consciousness" itself, the evidence for its existence, like the existence all of the major elements of integral, is overwhelming. Jordan Peterson calls its existence "not disputable." In fact, Mariana herself deliberately undertook a post-graduate degree in this area to study the psychological history of very high net worth individuals. She found an enormous number of them had had these types of Waking Up experiences, and that they had profoundly and irrevocably changed their lives and their aspirations— forever. You can read about her research in the following pages. The important point

here is that if the phrase "spiritual but not religious" has any meaning, it applies to
these Waking Up experiences (even Sam Harris, noted member of the New Atheists,
recently wrote a book called Waking Up, and it's subtitled Spirituality without
Religion). These Waking Up experiences are not religious claims, or mythic literal
statements you are supposed to believe as a matter of faith (such as Moses parting the
Red Sea, Lot's wife being turned into a pillar of salt, Jesus Christ being born from a
biological virgin, and so on—those are actually the products of some of the earlier
stages of Growing Up, stages that James Fowler called "mythic literal"). Rather,
these Waking Up realizations are direct, first person, immediate, and reproducible
experiences or states of consciousness, and wherever they occur, they seem directly
plugged into—not this or that particular being—but rather a groundless Ground of
Being itself, which is one with absolutely everything, and thus when you experience
this yourself, you also feel "one with everything." This is not a fundamentalist
religious belief, or mythic fantasy, or opiate of the masses—although all of those
can indeed exist—but rather a direct awareness of an all-inclusive, all pervasive
reality whose experience is "not disputable."

Make of this what you will—and you are certainly welcome to not believe it. But
evidence for it—around the world and going back several thousand years—really is
astonishing. Wouldn't you at least want to make a little footnote of its possibility in
the back of your mind? Who knows? It might happen to you, and you don't want to
just think you're having a mental health issue. (Like near death experiences, these
spiritual peak experiences have no favorites—scientific materialists, religious fun-
damentalists, and prominent businesspeople have an absolutely equal chance of
having them.) What's more, there are actual practices that you can adopt to allow
you a direct experience of these states yourself. (This is the "states" part of "all
quadrants, all levels, all lines, all STATES, all types"—and discovering these higher
states in your own being we call "Waking Up.") You'll see how Mariana incorpo-
rates such practices in the following pages.

While you have access to these states of Waking Up, and to around six to eight
major stages of Growing Up, it's also true that through each of those stages or levels
of development or Growing Up, we find that there are numerous different lines of
development. In an individual, these are often called "multiple intelligences"—such
as cognitive intelligence, emotional intelligence, moral intelligence, verbal intelligence, interpersonal intelligence, and so on. (In the integral framework, this is the
"lines" part of "quadrants, levels, LINES, states, and types"). Even the developers of
Sofia, probably the world's best known robotic AI, have deliberately included all
nine typical multiple intelligences in their attempt to continue moving in the
direction of the creation of an artificial general intelligence, an intelligence that
will authentically duplicate (and likely surpass) actual human intelligence. Attempts
to include all of these multiple lines in any sort of AI is not something you would
have heard of several years ago—unless you were familiar with integral—but it has
begun to creep into the culture. We call acknowledging and opening up to these
multiple lines "Opening Up."

One of those lines that we all have is a line of defense mechanisms. This harks
back to psychoanalysis and shadow material, but an incredibly important discovery

made by post psychoanalytic researchers is that (1) there are many more (and higher) stages of development (or Growing Up) than Freud and the early therapeutic investigators believed, and (2) we can develop shadow material at any or all of them. This dramatically expands the reach of shadow therapeutic material—and the process of working with all that we call "Cleaning Up." Even brilliant CEOs who are at some of the highest stages of Growing Up and have had a profound Waking Up and are Opening Up to many of their multiple talents can (and often are) in serious need of Cleaning Up. This can especially show up in their work with groups or teams (and indeed, Mariana has found that, in terms of investing, something going wrong with teams can account for upwards of 80% of company failures, so this is clearly something an investor wants to keep a sharp eye out for—as well as would any of us in our own everyday lives).

Pulling all of these elements together are what we call the four quadrants. I'll just give some technical aspects of this factor (which at first might seem fairly jumbled), but what this all means will become very clear in the following pages. The four quadrants are simply some of the most elementary and fundamental dimensions that we are aware of. There are all sorts of variations on these, but usually they include the inside versus the outside—or the view from within and the view from without, or simply subject and object—and also the singular versus the plural, or the individual and the collective. If we put these all together, we get four views: the view from within the individual ("subjective"), the view from without or from the exterior of the individual ("objective"), the view from within the collective (the group seen from within, or "intersubjective"), and the view from without or from the exterior of the collective ("interobjective"). The inside and the outside of the individual and the collective—the four quadrants.

This seems very simple, even pedantic. But these fundamental dimensions or perspectives really are everywhere. (Note that the two "outside" dimensions are both "objective"—the exterior of the individual and the exterior of the collective—so they are often condensed to just "the objective, exterior world"—and when that happens, the four quadrants show up as "the Big Three.") But we see these in, for example, the three major perspectives of pronouns found in every sophisticated language the world over. There are the 1st-person (the person speaking—"I," "me," "mine"); the 2nd-person (the person being spoken to—"you," "your"); and 3rd-person (the person or thing being spoken about—"he," "she," "they," "them," "it," "its"). Notice that when you and I come together and discuss something, we form a "we," and this "we" includes your "I" and my "I" (which is why "we" is technically the 1st-person plural). If you and I did not form this "we" or mutual understanding (if we both spoke completely different languages, for example), we would not be genuine 2nd-persons for each other, we would be like rocks or carrots to each other—that is, nothing but 3rd-persons. The idea here is that any real 2nd-person perspective (or "you"), in order not to be just another 3rd-person "it," needs to come together into a genuine "we." So sometimes we refer to the Big Three as "I," "we," and "it," which is typically how these three dimensions appear in our awareness.

The Big Three are the four quadrants, with the two exterior or objective quadrants collapsed into one "it." The important point is that they are not just different perspectives, they represent ontologically real realities or genuine dimensions of existence, and they are accessed with different methodologies and different paradigms or exemplars. For example, the very well known trinity of "the Good, the True, and the Beautiful" is also precisely the Big Three. The "true" in that expression means "truth" in the standard, objective, scientific sense—any thing or event, individual or collective, looked at in an objective, exterior fashion ("the outside of the individual or collective"—a 3rd-person view). The "good"—ethics or morals— is not something that can be seen lying around "out there" like a tree or a mountain; it is the interior of any group. When you and I come together to form a "we," how should we treat each other (2nd-person ethics)? This is not something that is strictly "true" or "false," but rather "right" or "wrong," "good" or "evil," something that is the result of our shared values, meanings, and purposes—this is not "what is" (3rd-person science), but "what should be" (2nd-person morals). And then there is the "Beauty that is in the eye (and the 'I') of the beholder"—the interior of the individual (1st-person realities). So art, morals, and science; 1st, 2nd, and 3rd person; the Beautiful, the Good, and the True—and forward to Jürgen Habermas's three validity claims, Sir Karl Popper's three worlds, and on and on. These three (or four) quadrants really are everywhere.

What's not generally everywhere is the realization that all the quadrants are equally important. Genuinely including all of them is what Integral Theory calls "Showing Up"—this is to really show up for all of the utterly fundamental and deeply important realities of your own life and any activity you are engaged in. And yet, as unbelievably odd as it seems, by far the most common activity of any quadrant is spending much of its time trying to deny the real existence of all the others (we'll return to that in a moment).

As for whether there are really three or four of these dimensions, simply notice that, virtually from the start—and just within objective science itself—there has been an interminable debate over which type of material reality is the "really real" one: the whole system, or just the individual parts? Atomistic reductionists have a hard time seeing any reality for a wheel, and no matter how hard they stare at a wheel, they see only the individual spokes. Systems theorists, if anything, err in the opposite direction: the whole system is the real reality, and all individuals are just abstractions or fragmentations of the prior holistic reality. As for which one of these is correct, integral has always said, "Yes." That is, both represent very real perspectives (3rd-person singular and 3rd-person plural) that elicit very real dimensions (the individual looked at from without and the whole system looked at from without). Each represents very real and completely irreducible quadrants. But, as we were saying, not only are the quadrants actually everywhere, by far the most common action taken by those devoted to one of them is the denial of reality to all the others. Today's consciousness studies are only the most recent example. About half the theorists believe that consciousness is nothing but the 3rd-person "it" processes occurring in the physical brain and its neurological synapses and transmitters, while the other half believes that consciousness is a 1st-person reality that cannot be reduced to material entities no matter how complex. (Integral Theory again replies, "Yes.")

But whether we are talking about atomists or systems theorists, 1st-person consciousness advocates or 3rd-person advocates, virtually none of them make genuine room for the others—virtually none of them are truly Showing Up for the most important dimensions and perspectives of reality. And that ignorance, it seems to me, is exactly the problem with the major elements of Integral Theory itself. Whether we are looking at Showing Up (for all quadrants), Growing Up (through all levels), Opening Up (to all lines), Cleaning Up (our shadows), or Waking Up (to higher states including enlightenment), there are virtually no schools of thought anywhere in the world that fully acknowledge and embrace them all.

Now, the world today is facing any number of truly serious and deeply urgent problems. The smallest list would include climate change, pandemics, inequality, nuclear threat, geopolitical instabilities, the catastrophic possibilities of the first machine superintelligence, worldwide childhood immunization rates, economic factors, and sex and gender issues. You can take your pick as to which of those (or others) you believe are the most urgent. But one thing is undeniably certain: not one of those issues can be fully and adequately addressed without dealing with all of the elements that an integral framework embraces. Not one of them. That means that THE central and defining problem of our age is a less than integral or comprehensive approach to all of our other problems.

We keep scratching our heads about why progress dealing with so many of those issues seems to crawl along at agonizingly slow and even danger inviting rates. We are not fully Showing Up (the Good, the True, and the Beautiful are not being fully embraced), or Growing Up (most of us don't even know these stages exist, and alarmingly, some 60–70% of the world's population are at ethnocentric or lower waves), or Opening Up (of the dozen or so multiple intelligences, modern education systems narrowly train only two or three of them, usually cognitive and verbal), or Cleaning Up (we still project our shadows everywhere: "We're not racist, they are"), or Waking Up (what the hell is "enlightenment"?). And we wonder why we live in such a broken, fragmented, demented world—but what do we expect when we actively deny that much of truly existing reality?

Humanity will, in many ways, continue to make progress in virtually all areas of knowledge. Just as what we know today dwarfs what we knew just a 100 years ago, what we will know a 100 years from now will dwarf what we know today (and the future will look at us the way we look back at the past). But not being able to include that new knowledge is not what I mean by being "less than comprehensive" right now. The elements of integral that I have outlined do not depend on gaining new knowledge; these elements already have, right now, an overwhelming amount of evidence supporting them. And yet we are still taking woefully limited, fragmented, partial, and demonstrably broken approaches to virtually all of our affairs, right here and right now.

One of the main reasons that you have very probably not taken a fully integral approach to your life is not that you examined all these elements and decided not many of them have any reality; it's much more likely that nobody ever told you much about them. That blank stare in the typical college professor's face is the blank stare of our culture itself. The evidence for these realities makes all of them, in their own way, virtually "not disputable," but most of them are also "not heard of." On the other hand, when people do hear of them, a very large percentage of them—in no matter what field—get excited by them and start to include them in whatever approach they are engaged in (which is why over 60 different disciplines have created integral versions of their disciplines, see above).

So, welcome to Integral Investing. Mariana (and Tom) have done a wonderful job taking virtually all of the elements of integral metatheory and showing very directly how they each add something invaluable to a model of high impact, high return, self-actualizing, socially responsible, sustainable investing. Mariana calls it "the six P's": "the Parity of People, Planet, Profit—with Passion and Purpose." And that just refers to the major levels of Growing Up! You will also find quadrants, lines, shadows, states, and types all dealt with.

That's the fundamental point about integral. It does not itself claim to be or have any specific solution to any particular problem. It claims only to provide a framework that can be brought to any problem, with the major benefit being that, in offering a genuinely comprehensive and inclusive viewpoint through which to view the situation, it is much more likely to result in breakthrough resolutions. Mariana and Tom have been successfully using this framework to make sense of and guide their investment policies for several decades now, and they have the results to prove it. Mariana calls Integral Investing "the next paradigm in investing," and I think that's exactly right. I truly hope that you enjoy the following tour through this exciting new field! And welcome to a way of looking at things that probably nobody ever told you about before. . .

Denver, Colorado   Ken Wilber
Spring 2020

Preface

The current Industrial Revolution, called by some the Fourth Industrial Revolution, has catapulted us into an age of unprecedented exponentially growing technological disruption. That disruption is bringing with it significant consequences for all of us. They are impacting our entire existence, including how we work and do business with each other; how we educate ourselves and our children; how we take care of our health and wellbeing; and how we connect with each other. They are also constantly evolving, and we cannot know for sure how they will ultimately play out. While progress is triggering unprecedented prosperity for some, it is simultaneously threatening to drive increasing climate-related challenges, biodiversity loss, collective angst, techno-nationalism, protectionist techno-sovereignty, transparent citizenship, and the rise of digital governance.

The digitalization of technology can be traced back to the 1950s, but it essentially languished until the early 2000s. That's when the digitalization of the world came out of its *deceptive*, linear growth phase and went *exponential*, gradually disrupting most areas of our lives as it did so. Twenty years later, there is no escaping it; in fact, it's fair to say our future depends on it. That dependency has also put us at the center of a significant ethical challenge: Do we prioritize the solving of the global grand challenges led by climate change or the nurturing of exponential tech as our ultimate savior? Can we do both without sacrificing either one? I think it's entirely possible. It is an unarguably multifaceted challenge because of its exponential complexity and all-inclusive nature, but in this book, I explore how we could reconcile our competing demands in a constructive, empowering, and holistic way from an investment perspective.

Is it possible for us to continue benefiting from the exponential growth of technology without increasing the collateral damage? I believe we can—if we're willing to change. And when I say "change," I don't just mean change what we do. I also mean change how we think, and more importantly, change how we feel.

If we relied solely on current media reports to assess the state of the planet, we could easily slide into a mindset of resignation that our situation is hopeless. If we read more widely and deeply, though, another picture begins to emerge. In 2018, for example, the two co-presidents of the Club of Rome, Ernst von Weizsäcker and Anders Wijkman, together with several co-authors, issued warnings to humanity in *Come On!* Jorgen Randers et al. echoed those warnings in their *Transformation is Feasible* report to the Club of Rome, which was launched together with yet another call for action, the *Climate Emergency Plan* of the Club of Rome during their 50th anniversary celebrations on October 17, 2018, at the Vatican. But they all did more than warn. They also provided hope by showing *how* concrete actions could save us if only they were carried out in a timely manner. They made clear that our future is in our own hands, and that we can take ownership of change for the greater good.

On September 23, 2019, at the Climate Action Summit in New York, António Guterres, UN Secretary General, reinforced that mindset when he called on all world leaders to take substantive action to address climate change and to present workable plans on how to reach net-zero emissions by the mid-twenty-first century. He both acknowledged that his generation has failed in its responsibility to protect the Earth and also endorsed the work of several young climate activists, including 2019 Nobel Peace Prize nominee and Fridays for Future founder, Greta Thunberg of Sweden. The most dynamic responses to his call for climate action came from countries that are particularly vulnerable to the effects of climate change, such as island nations at risk of losing land to rising ocean levels. But we are all at risk unless we come together to use our combined passions, resources, intelligence, and creativity to move our global civilization toward holistic sustainability within planetary boundaries.

This book builds on earlier offerings of hope on both a practical and a theoretical level. I want not only to encourage a sense of optimism and confidence but also to present a path to concrete action to investors, financiers, entrepreneurs, business-people, and other stakeholders who care about our future and want to be active participants in taking ownership of change—without compromising on technological progress. As a member of the international Club of Rome and an avid exponential tech investor and Silicon Valley enthusiast, I am a particularly strong advocate for a balanced debate on the topic of exponential tech versus climate change and other global grand challenges because I am exposed to both sides of the argument. I frequently hear that we have all the technology we need to address the existential threats posed by climate change and that we must draw on all those available resources before we allow ourselves to pursue further disruptive exponential tech. No surprise there, I imagine.

But I equally frequently hear the contrary. Let me share a story that sums up that opposing opinion for me: At a private dinner on March 25, 2015, in London, I sat next to Kimbal Musk, the brother of Elon Musk, Tesla's co-founder and a committed environmentalist. At that dinner, Kimbal, a Silicon Valley tech investor, was raising money for his foundation Big Green, which essentially promotes food and health literacy among schoolchildren. I asked him how he was addressing climate change within the context of his work. To my great surprise he replied, "There is no climate change," and if in 100 years, "we should end up with one, then technology will have advanced far enough that it will provide us with the proper solutions to address it." I was rendered speechless by his answer, so I did not press the issue. However, not least for the sake of Big Green, I truly hope that Kimbal has since experienced a change of heart.

Kimbal Musk is not an outlier in terms of his response to my question about climate change. The belief that technology in and by itself will save us prevails in Silicon Valley and the tech world more broadly. Unfortunately, in general, the environment is low on the priority list and rarely addressed by tech people unless it is financially profitable. That mindset was a key driver behind my decision to place the debate concerning climate emergency and exponential technology center stage in this book. It is deeply connected with my own raison d'être and with how I show up in the world as a caring mother, wife, global citizen, investor, entrepreneur, and businesswoman. Therefore, beyond cultivating a sense of optimism, I hope to provide a platform to encourage leading-edge thought, discourse, and knowledge sharing to nurture individual passions and spark collective action.

According to various futurists including Raymond Kurzweil, we are heading toward a *technological singularity*, a point in human history where technological change occurs so fast that we cease to be able to predict what breakthrough will come next. The tech world may be striding into the future, but the regulators and financial systems are still mired in archaic, dysfunctional twentieth-century economic systems and mindsets and are not providing the requisite transformation leadership. This book seeks to fill a void by inviting high-net-worth individuals, investors, entrepreneurs, businesspeople, and other agents of transformation to come together in bypassing those outdated, pernicious systems and providing timely leadership to take us into a sustainable future. By embracing change, we have much to gain and nothing to lose that would not otherwise be taken away by our mother Earth should she finally lose patience with us.

But the ability to change on the outside requires a mind shift on the inside. This is the hardest change of all. Throughout the book, you will find boxes documenting mind shifts that my husband, Tom, and I have undergone. They are narratives that document personal experiences that we call *confessions*. These are meant to be the unvarnished recounting of Tom's and my evolution from being traditional investors with a money-only orientation to integral investors who embody the higher values characteristic of later stages of consciousness evolution. We have each experienced both significant personal growth and a mind shift, and we have witnessed similar transformations in our peers. Change is possible. We've observed it and lived it. And we are confident that the best is yet to come. We are convinced that a *collective* mind shift toward world-centric or even integral levels of consciousness (that is, mindset) would enable humanity's leaders and organizations to successfully address our global grand challenges (GGC). These are discussed in more detail later, but we should be particularly aware of the existential threats such as climate emergency, biological and thermonuclear weapons, and unsafe exponentially growing technologies, to name only a few. We believe that our current systems—political, economic, financial—reflect an outdated, ethnocentric mindset that has rendered us woefully ill-equipped to address the current threats. The COVID-19 crisis attests to that. Our leaders have not yet collectively acknowledged the severity of our situation, are not united in their opinions, and are not ready to take the type of action that our children are expecting from us. This is unfortunate, as time is of the essence—but we can make a difference if we all act now.

Tom and I are among a growing number of people who believe that *Transformation is Feasible*, and that the necessary resources, knowledge, technology, leadership, and capital exist to make it happen. In this book I show you how we as early-stage investors—and we are all investors in one way or another—and company builders can contribute toward safeguarding the future of life. In 2001, Tom and I radically changed our initial investment approach, which dated back to 1996, and built a model for doing so. We based it on Integral Theory by philosopher Ken Wilber and called it Integral Investing. I have chosen to share what we have learned as early-stage investors and company builders because it is time to correlate twenty-first-century investing with consciousness, leadership, and human evolution, and to focus all our available resources on solving the problems at hand without wasting time and energy on squabbling about which GGC is the most important or should be addressed first. They are *all* threatening our very existence, and our priority should establish *how* to solve them, not debating *whether* we should even try to solve them.

This book offers a snapshot of how early-stage investing and company building can play a role in solving the problems and, more importantly, the role that actors themselves, as investors, entrepreneurs, *stakeholders* can play. It is a handbook for Integral Investing in the twenty-first century that evolved as a response to innumerable requests from our peers, institutional investors, entrepreneurs, and other stakeholders. In these pages, I share our secrets, expertise, know-how, and processes of our integral investment model, and give you some of the tools you will need to find the answers to your own investment questions.

Chapter 1 presents an analysis of the exterior context in which investing, company building, finance, and economics are currently operating. Referencing a range of major thinkers, from Harvard professor Steven Pinker to exponential tech entrepreneurs from Silicon Valley, I look at our current challenges, including AI and the climate emergency, and try to answer the question of whether we are doomed to suffering because we underestimate "human stupidity," as Yuval Noah Harari argues, or are destined for total destruction and should thus prepare to colonize Mars to save ourselves, as Elon Musk is suggesting. Like Musk, I believe that humans are explorers and need a positive outlook on life. But before you start getting ready for Mars, I invite you to take a look at how evolutionary forces are currently at play in terms of past and future progress and how disruptive technologies, the compounded ingenuity of humanity's collective evolution, are currently contributing positively to our planet's health and humanity's wellbeing. Whether the context is health, mobility, transportation, the connected world, the Internet of Things (IoT), robotics, artificial intelligence, augmented intelligence, virtual reality (VR), augmented reality (AR), brain-computer interfaces, or the convergence of them all, I suspect you will consider the result of the analysis to be rather promising. Evolutionary forces have endowed humanity with the necessary resources, technological know-how, innovation, creativity, and capital to create mindboggling technology and evolving mindsets that can conspire to address existential threats.

If and how humanity could muster the necessary world-centric levels of consciousness to shift the current mindset to achieve the necessary transformations is the subject of Chap. 2. Scott Keller and Bill Schaninger of McKinsey wrote in an August 2019 article that "the need to shift mind-sets is the biggest block to successful transformations. The key lies in making the shift both individual and institutional—at the same time."[1] I agree that an "individual and institutional" mind shift is our secret weapon, but I opt for a much more differentiated analysis of what that means. Why? Because a simple mind shift from an infantile, and linearly thinking, egocentric mind set to an ethnocentric mind set, à la "make America great again," is not sufficient, whether it occurs in individuals or in institutions. We need a *world-centric shift* in mindsets because our problems are global and, like tech, growing exponentially. In Chap. 2, I dig deeper into the concept of mind shift by highlighting the hidden determinants and patterns of human evolution. I share the results of research that was triggered by my personal experiences (see my confessions in the boxes) and hypothesize that the great mind shift toward world-centric levels of consciousness I saw emerging in my research could represent an encouraging trend. I draw on established models and theories of consciousness evolution by Abraham Maslow, Clare Graves, Susanne Cook-Greuter, and Ken Wilber, among others, to lay the theoretical foundation of Tom's and my Integral Investing philosophy. I go deeper into human psychology in an attempt to show the way to personal liberation from scarcity thinking and our dependency on money and material things. I use Joseph Campbell's Hero's Journey to demonstrate how it is possible to achieve the kind of freedom that Nelson Mandela talked about when he said that people who take other people's freedom are not truly free because both are robbed of their humanity, and share how Tom and I keep the wheel of our lives in a healthy balance as the premise for making a continuous positive impact on the world.

Drawing on the premise that the best way to predict the future is to create it, in Chap. 3 I explain and illustrate the real-world application of investing within the exterior context presented in Chap. 1 and the hidden, interior transformation discussed in Chap. 2. I give examples (look for the boxes) of how we have successfully applied our investing model through the creation of integrally sustainable companies to show *how Transformation is Feasible* through early-stage investing. In Chap. 3 you will also learn why 80% of the investment risk lies with the team and key individuals and how to reduce that risk through the Theta Model, our due diligence process. Our Integral Investing model is summarized in 21 principles and serves as the manifesto for the Investment Turnaround, our moonshot. I encourage you to use these to think about and develop your own moonshot. I have also included references to some templates that you are free to apply to your own contexts, as well as a collection of further points to consider as you embark on your own transformation and self-actualization through investing.

---

[1] https://tinyurl.com/yaf2ksj2

There is hope. But we must step up and be agents for change. We can initiate the right planetary action on all existential threats, from climate change to unsafe AI to nuclear weapons. Or we can wait until we are forced to do so. I want to believe that the current COVID-19 pandemic presents a great opportunity, a dress rehearsal, for wise collective action. Are you ready?

Munich, Germany   Mariana Bozesan

Acknowledgments

This book would not have been possible had it not been for the many exceptional people who directly or indirectly contributed content, support, love, and encouragement. I sincerely wish I could name you all to give you the public thanks you deserve. Thank you, thank you, thank you.

First, I would like to express my deepest gratitude to Ken Wilber whom President Bill Clinton called "brilliant," Harvard professor Robert Kegan "a national treasure," and Roger Walsh "one of the greatest philosophers of this century and arguably the greatest theoretical psychologist of all time." I could not agree more. Your revolutionary philosophical work inspired me to go back to school and get my PhD in integral psychology so I could apply it in investing and entrepreneurship. Integral Theory became the theoretical foundation of Integral Investing and inspired me to build a comprehensive model that ensures the implementation of integral sustainability in early-stage investing. Integral Theory changed my life for the better and I will be forever grateful for that. Dear Ken, thank you also for being my biggest supporter from the very first moment we met in person in 2010 when we were introduced by our common friends Beena Sharma and Susanne Cook-Greuter. You have one of the most superb minds in the world today and most people celebrate that, of course. What is less known, however, is your highly developed open heart, sophisticated humor, innate joy, and generosity of spirit. Thank you for being there for me and for being who you are.

Lao Tzu said, "When the student is ready, the teacher appears." This became true for me when Harvard Professor Daniel P. Brown appeared in my life a few years ago. Dan, you became the best meditation teacher I have ever had during the past 4 decades. I am deeply grateful to you for seeing, encouraging, and helping me experience states of consciousness I never knew existed. Thank you to you and Gretchen for your friendship and, most of all, for being there for me when I lost both my parents within 8 months. Your open heart and support will never be forgotten.

Thank you, Susanne Cook-Greuter and Beena Sharma, for introducing me to Ken Wilber. Your seminal work on adult vertical development and leadership maturity have become an integral part of the Theta Model. A special thank-you goes to vertical leadership and sustainability expert Barrett Brown for your tireless and extremely professional support in applying the Theta Model in both our own organizations and our portfolio companies. I truly appreciate your ongoing guidance and unconditional friendship.

I am also deeply indebted to many of my fellow members in the international Club of Rome who believed in, trusted, and encouraged me to grow beyond my own field of expertise while writing this book. In no particular order, thank you, Wouter van Dieren, for your friendship, wisdom, and for always believing in me; without you, I would have not become a member of this extraordinary club of brilliant minds. Stefan Brunnhuber, thank you for sharing your ideas, wisdom, unconditional support, and authentic friendship with me. A special thank-you note goes to Ernst Ulrich von Weizsäcker and Anders Wijkman, who have been key in helping me grow beyond myself through this book. This work is much better because of how you have challenged me on various occasions. Thank you, Gunter Pauli, for your friendship and enthusiasm, for inspiring the world to become sustainable, and for the memorable hours spent listening to world-class music at the Salzburger Festspiele. Thank you, Johan Rockström, Jorgen Randers, et al., for your 2018 report to the Club of Rome, Transformation is Feasible. Your brilliant research and recommendations on how to transform existing systems have been crucial in defining our Integral Investing strategy for the coming decade. I would also like to take a moment to thank my new friends and fellows in the World Academy of Art and Science (WAAS), particularly Garry Jacobs, Mila Popovich, and Alberto Zucconi, but also Rodolfo Fiorini, Thomas Reuter, Vesna Vucinic, and Nebojsa Neskovic, to name only a few. Your selfless giving, trust, and friendship mean a lot to me. On the research front, my gratitude goes also to all the research participants and consciousness leaders who, despite your busy schedules, have been kind enough to participate in and contribute to my ongoing research. Without you, the Integral Investing model would not exist. I must not mention your names, but you know who you are, and I am deeply humbled by your presence in my life and your work in the world. My investment turnaround podcast contributors—too many to mention—also deserve a special thank-you note. I am honored to know you all, and I thank you from the depths of my heart for everything you are and do to make this world a better place.

Thank you, Candace Johnson, the amazing satellite woman and former president of the European Business Angel Network (EBAN). Your loving presence in my life has long been nectar for my soul. Without your caring embrace and trust, Integral Investing would have been a much bumpier ride. How can I ever truly express my endless gratitude for your becoming such an integral part of my life, dear sister that I never had? Thank you. Tess Mateo, Chantal Line Carpentier, Mary Ann Pierce, and Irene Natividad, you all deserve special thanks for believing in me and for inviting me to speak about Integral Investing and the impact of my work at the UN headquarters and numerous Global Summit of Women conferences. A big thank-you to you all amazing impact women including Paola Ferrari, Henrike von Platen, and many other Equality Moonshot sisters who are changing the world for the better. I am honored and privileged to call you my friends. Your presence in my life has helped make Integral Investing truly inclusive and diverse. I am especially grateful to my friend Elmas Durgun for your authentic friendship, unconditional love, and support. Thank you for taking care of me and for keeping me healthy, vital, and in good spirits. Without your loving support and shining presence in my life I would not have been able to finish this book in a timely fashion.

My gratitude goes also to all those extraordinary people who, despite their busy schedules, have been kind enough to endorse this book and have given me their constructive feedback. I am honored to know you and thank you from the depths of my heart. My profound appreciation goes also to my editors, Christian Rauscher of Springer and Lesley Cameron. Your thoroughness and endless patience are highly appreciated. For their presence in my life, as well as friendship, mentorship, encouragement, contributions, feedback, and ongoing direct or indirect support, I am deeply indebted to Marianne Williamson, Elon Musk, Peter Diamandis, Ray Kurzweil, Max Tegmark, Meia Chita-Tegmark, Tony Robbins, Deepak Chopra, Gaia Dempsey, Amita Kuttner, and many others whom space does not permit to mention. Thank you.

Last but not least, I would like to thank Tom Schulz, my husband and love of my life. Your unconditional love, curiosity, generosity, potentiating leadership, unique insights, and contributions as well as tireless support during some of the darkest hours of the writing process have given me the strength I needed to complete this journey. Without you and your unique investor and entrepreneurial skills, this book would simply not exist. Without you, I would still be researching new data. You have always believed in me more than I believed in myself. My gratitude to you is infinite. Endless thanks also go to our son, Albert Bozesan, who makes us both extremely proud. You are my best teacher and supporter. You have given me the love, room, and time to study and write. Your writing tips, unique creativity, innate joy, and ever-present humor have often inspired me and helped me reconnect with my true nature. Thank you. I love you both more than you will ever know.

Munich, Germany   Mariana Bozesan
Spring 2020

Endorsements

"On rare occasions a special book introduces vital new ideas to the public consciousness with no blindspot. This is one such book. Right now, we are at a tipping point in human history. The current pandemic crisis seems to have simultaneously initiated and corroborated a significant mind shift that is not only challenging but also actively starting to change outdated structures that cannot accommodate future human needs in the context of the new global reality. Years of massive change lie ahead. Either we learn to manage this change, or we allow it to control us and face devastating consequences. Mariana explains with clarity and precision the nature of the challenges we face and defines the thinking that will provide us with smart solutions to build a resilient and holistic sustainable future together. Reality comprises subjective, intersubjective, objective, and interobjective aspects. We can use our own life experiences to identify the purpose of our lives and find out what values inform the decisions we make as investors, entrepreneurs, businesspeople, parents, and caring human beings. Two particular aspects of the book merit comment. First, the sheer scope of the book and the way in which so many diverse ideas and examples are put together and effectively related to each other and to integral investing. Second, the way in which this book provides an extraordinary, optimistic, and empowering reference point for a feasible and convenient transition on a global scale. It is a ringing call for evolutionary integral investing practices with its pragmatic step-by-step Theta Model blueprint for active wisdom and wise action for the common wellbeing, empowering the science of decision making at new exponential heights to achieve significant integral return as measured by Mariana's 6Ps. Moreover, Mariana has recognized that the integral approach provides the ideal framework for achieving a clearer viewpoint on the relationships between AI and cognitive computing (CC). In fact, from a CC perspective, according to computational information conservation theory (CICT), the external and internal worldviews combine in a harmonic framework, with exact relationships in order to conserve information as much as possible, with an exponential gain if compared with all past and current reductionist approximations."

—Prof. Dr. Rodolfo A. Fiorini, *Department of Electronics, Information and Bioengineering (DEIB) Politecnico di Milano University & Fellow World Academy of Art and Science (WAAS), Italy*

"This is a remarkable book. In fact, it is three books in one, and with a crystal-clear message: The urgent need for a transformation to more sustainable, just and inclusive societies in response to a number of global challenges and existential threats.

The role of investment is crucial. For too long the financial sector has stayed under the radar. Dominated by short-term profit maximisation—as it is—in an economic system where producers do not pay the full cost of production and thus leave the consequences of pollution and social ills to society to pick up, the need for reform and transformation is paramount. Mariana presents a fascinating blue-print—built, among other things, on principles of ethics and, as well, on the careful selection of exponential technologies—for how to turn investing into a force for good.

Mariana is extremely gifted. Her knowledge about finance is top-notch. The same goes for methodologies on how to enhance consciousness and help people find a meaning and purpose in life. Her reference to Ken Wilber and his Integral AQAL Framework is convincing as well appealing.

What is equally important is Mariana's grasp of exponential (disruptive) technologies, not least AI. I may not be as convinced as she is that technology disruption will solve all the problems we are facing. I have my doubts on the concept of "abundance" as introduced by Peter Diamandis. But Mariana brings to the fore a great number of examples of technologies that have made a huge difference—both with regard to solving health problems and reducing carbon emissions. Handled with ethics and care, exponential technologies can and will help address many of the challenges we face.

This being said, Mariana's plea in the book for regulation of AI is spot on. Like Max Tegmark and other experts Mariana is convinced that AI can be and should be used for the common good. But we have no guarantees. Like all technology, AI can be used for good as well as for evil. Policymakers must learn about what is at stake and put in place policy frameworks that guide technology development in the right direction. All in all. A fascinating book. I can only hope it will be read by the many, not least policymakers, entrepreneurs, investors and financial operators.

—Dr. h. c. Anders Wijkman, *member of the Swedish Royal Academy of Sciences, former member of the European Parliament and Assistant Secretary-General of the United Nations and Policy Director of UNDP, Honorary President of the Club of Rome, Sweden*

"In this remarkable book, Dr. Mariana Bozesan addresses the most critical and important challenges of our time and gives solutions and answers. This book is a guide not only for investors to use their knowledge, experience, expertise, and money to bring about change but also for governments, corporations, and citizens the world over to approach the twenty-first century with a fresh perspective and to understand that the new paradigm brought about by the technological/industrial revolution brings new opportunities for each of us to bring about change. Yes! 'Transformation is feasible,' as Mariana boldly writes. And yes, it is important to have values to guide not only your everyday actions but also your investments in the future.

This is at once a scholarly work and a visionary one. It entices us to explore our most inner being and most external horizons. It does not accept 'No' for an answer, but rather urges us to 'never, never, never give in'—and rightly so.

Dr. Bozesan references Ken Wilber, her teacher, professor, and soulmate, to encourage us to recognize that the Spectrum of Consciousness brings about new insights that we cannot ignore. She then systematically analyzes and applies this Spectrum of Consciousness to a new way of investing, that of Integral Investing, a total system of self-actualization brought to bear for the improvement of the world, be it the UN's SDGs, the planetary boundaries, a local caregiver, or one of the world's largest corporations steered by Warren Buffett or Elon Musk.

I have had the privilege to know Dr. Mariana Bozesan for almost 10 years now. Her book reminds me of the many passionate discussions we have had in Germany, in France, and around the world—always illuminating, always enlightening. Enjoy, Learn, Apply, and Invest Integrally along Dr. Bozesan's principles, values, and guidelines. Your life will be richer and you will bring about real and positive change for our planet and universe."

—Dr. h. c. Candace Johnson, *Serial Satellite Investor and Entrepreneur, Founder of SES Astra, Vice Chair of NorthStar Earth and Space, Commander Luxembourg Order of Merit, Officer German Federal Order of Merit, and Officer Luxembourg Oak Leaf Crown, France*

"I am a fan of Mariana's integral approach to investment, which is very aligned with my own holistic thinking. While she enters through the doorway of Ken Wilber's integral theory, and I have entered through the door of holism and living systems science, our approaches are highly aligned, as one would expect from an 'integral' approach to anything. We are on a similar, and I believe important, search. And of course, Mariana's grasp of the *problématique* is fully developed. We share an understanding of the importance of investment, and in particular real investment in next-generation enterprises that reflect the ethos of the world emerging before our eyes. Such an integral approach to investing plays a vital role in helping to shift our economic system as a whole. I look forward to re-reading her work and learning anew how she has implemented such critical and forward-thinking conceptual clarity into the very practical, and often unforgiving, world of early-stage investing, and how it aligns with and enhances my own regenerative approach. No doubt indige-nous wisdom is common to both. It's one thing to imagine an integral approach to investment (and to all of economics). Putting it into practice with money on the line is where the real work begins, as I know only too well. Mariana is one of the few true courageous pioneers in the impact investment community, daring to move beyond conventional 'sustainable finance' thinking."

—John Fullerton, *founder of Capital Institute architect of Regenerative Economics, Member in the International Club of Rome, USA*

"Our current economic system is blind to many important aspects of life and society. In this comprehensive book, Mariana Bozesan is doing an excellent job of applying the Integral AQAL Framework in order to reintegrate many of these lost aspects into financial investment decisions. It is very encouraging to see how concepts like consciousness and personal inner growth, meaning and purpose, and social transformation can be introduced into financial decision making. This book is clearing the way for new economic thinking and perhaps even gives a direction for the necessary transformation of the global economic system."

—Tomas Björkman, *Founder of Ekskaret Foundation, Former Chair of EFG Investment Bank, Fellow of the Royal Swedish Academy of Engineering Sciences, Fellow of the World Academy of Art & Science (WAAS), and Member of the International Club of Rome, UK*

"*Integral Investing* by Mariana Bozesan is the most comprehensive guide so far to steer capital toward ethical and profitable investing by carefully choosing only those companies that address the real global challenges faced by our human family on our polluted and endangered planet. Mariana's investing philosophy goes far beyond current screening and social auditing models, and seeks moonshot technologies spearheaded by highly conscious, spiritually evolved, technologically competent, ethical global citizens. This kind of truly integral investing can help steer us toward restoring the natural abundance of our biosphere, harvesting its free daily photons from our Mother Star: the Sun."

—Dr. Hazel Henderson, *FRSA, Founder and CEO of Ethical Markets Media, and Honorary Member of the International Club of Rome, USA*

"I admire Mariana Bozesan. Ever since she joined the Club of Rome, she has been an inspiration. She shares her know-how and experience with great clarity and courage. She secures investments with ethics and morals that are unparalleled in the world of finance. I highly recommend her *Integral Investing* to anyone concerned about putting their money where their mouth is, especially to those early-stage investors and entrepreneurs who want to lead the transformation toward a truly Blue Economy: an economy that addresses the needs of all of us using what we have."

—Prof. Dr. h. c. Gunter Pauli, *Founder of Zero Emissions Research & Initiatives (Zeri), Executive Committee Member of the International Club of Rome, Fellow in the World Academy of Art and Science, Japan*

"Now is the time to accelerate the transition to the world we all want and need by achieving the UN's Sustainable Development Goals within planetary boundaries by 2050. Through her significant *Integral Investing* book, Mariana Bozesan paves the way to that goal through early-stage investing. Micro, Small, and Medium Enterprises (MSMEs) are the most important agents for the building of green, resilient, inclusive, and circular economies (GRIC), and Mariana's Theta Model demonstrates how capital can be optimally used to make transformation feasible. *Integral Investing* is a must-read for every impact investor and caring entrepreneur."

—Dr. Chantal Line Carpentier, *Chief New York Office of the Secretary-General, United Nations Conference on Trade and Development (UNCTAD), USA*

"When we published the Club of Rome report *Limits to Growth* in 1972, we had no clue about the crucial role of the financial sector. Our messages did not include analyses of and proposals about the major investment shifts that we did not know lay ahead of us. Mariana has bridged that gap in a fascinating way, connecting the predicament of man and planet with the refinement of advanced integral impact investment, and giving those of us who were pioneers a promising story that reads as a novel, even a thriller."

—Dr. J. Wouter van Dieren, *Officer of the Order of Orange Nassau, Recipient of the Rachel Carson Gold Medal (2006) and the Global Merit Award from the World Wildlife Fund (2012), Member of the International Club of Rome, Fellow of the World Academy of Art & Science (WAAS), The Netherlands*

"*Integral Investing* is a firework of entrepreneurial experience as well as a well-researched source of knowledge on how to apply exponentially growing technologies to implement the UN SDGs within planetary boundaries in early-stage investing. This handbook is a must read for anyone who wants to integrate investing, business and sustainability with the intention to ensure the future of life on our beautiful planet."

—Prof. Dr. Dr. Stefan Brunnhuber, *Medical Director and Chief Medical Officer Diakonie Hospital, Trustee, World Academy of Art and Science (WAAS), Member of the International Club of Rome, Germany*

"I find Mariana's book on *Integral Investing* fascinating and extremely relevant. It is thought provoking and an inspiring, albeit challenging, guidepost for all those who truly care about company building and early-stage investing in exponentially growing technologies with the intention to ensure our common future."

—Prof. Dr. Georgios Theodoropoulos, *Chair Professor in the Department of Computer Science and Engineering at the Southern University of Science and Technology, Shenzhen, Fellow of the World Academy of Art & Science (WAAS), China*

"Mariana Bozesan is one of the very few investors I have encountered who is truly concerned with an integral approach to investing based on full-spectrum economics that goes beyond both profit-only and EGS criteria."

—Prof. Dr. Christian Arnsperger, *Faculty of Geoscience and Environmental Studies (FGSE), University of Lausanne, Switzerland*

"This is an extraordinary and important book on early-stage investing with deep impact. Mariana's mastery of various interconnected fields is impressive, especially how she makes the case for the application of exponentially growing technologies to address existential threats—including climate change—in early-stage investing. A must read".
—Dr. Charly Kleissner, *Co-founder TONIIC & KL Foundation, Member of the International Club of Rome, USA*

"Mariana Bozesan is doing a terrific job of applying the Integral AQAL Framework to the difficult and delicate world of finances and investment. Recognizing that, for example, all four quadrants (the four basic ways that any phenomenon can be seen—from the interior and the exterior, and in the individual and collective forms) changes how we look at finances entirely, from something reflecting only the exterior individual and collective material capital of existence, to also reflecting individual and collective values, meanings, motivations, worldviews, and beliefs. All of these have a profound impact on finances, how they are seen, used, and developed; and using anything less than all those perspectives gives us a partial, fragmented, truncated, and broken view. Mariana is using these (and all of the other integral dimensions) to present a much more comprehensive, inclusive, and integral view. My deep thanks and highest congratulations to her!"
—Ken Wilber, *Founder Integral Institute & Integral Life, USA*

"Only occasionally do I come across a book that captures with acuity the essence of the 'spirit of the times,' as Carl Jung calls it, and more rarely still one that also channels a key message from the 'spirit of the depth,' the inner center where past and future merge and all true inspiration originates. Mariana Bozesan's latest work, *Integral Investing*, is such a book. It is certainly very timely in pointing to the urgent need for a massive transformation to more sustainable, inclusive societies in all parts of the world in response to the present planetary emergency. She accomplishes this by developing an innovative, integrated investment model. Why investment? As Mariana notes, we all invest our energy, money, and resources somewhere, and societal change is not possible without a collective shift in investment decisions. We face a stark choice today: invest for life and wellbeing in innovative ways or cling to profit-fixated or outdated impact-oriented modes of investment until the window of opportunity for saving our planet has closed forever. It is heartening to learn that we even have such a choice, and that transformation is possible. As this book convincingly argues, the technology is either already there or rapidly emerging, and there is no shortage of capital and resources—it is 'just' a matter of allocation. Resource allocation is the central purpose of an economic system, and how allocation happens defines such systems. Therein lies the deeper problem: A profound mind shift is needed to revolutionize the prevailing allocation process; a complete re-set of our engrained and still dominant and deeply reductionist cultural perspective on life under late consumer capitalism. To facilitate this shift, the author delves deep into the fear-based psychology of the outmoded profit-focused model and replaces it with a more integral model, based on the philosophy of Ken Wilber, wherein conscious investment becomes a path to self-actualization, personal growth, and holistic wellbeing. This book is thus a profoundly usable, hands-on guide for a new generation of world-centric investors. The authenticity and value of this guide lie in the author's many decades of practical experience as an investor and entrepreneur and her deep knowledge of the latest trends in technology."

—Prof. Dr. Thomas Reuter, *Asia Institute, University of Melbourne, Board and Executive Committee Member of the World Academy of Arts and Science (WAAS), Australia*

"*Integral Investing* is a tour de force of brilliant integration, seemingly straight out of the future. It synthesizes the finest minds and biggest hearts in impact investing, global sustainability, psychology, and exponential technologies, wisely guiding us toward a world that works for all. Mariana Bozesan embodies the future of investing. She has persistently and humbly probed to deeply understand the vast investing landscape, the wild world of artificial intelligence, the bewildering terrain of social and environmental change, and our ever-mysterious inner domains. She has walked the halls of power on multiple continents, jointly built highly successful businesses, bravely fought her own dragons, and literally transformed herself through decades of personal practice. In this book, Mariana snaps us out of modern investment delusions with an edifying, shamanic shout and radically reorients our investing philosophy for exponential impact. Be forewarned: If you read these pages, there's no going back to how you saw the world before. Some visions cannot be unseen, and hers is a formidable beauty to behold. Her maps are psychoactive, showing us who we need to become to scale transformational change through investing. Her approach is grounded and proven, and it will inoculate us from the incessant volatility and increasing complexity ahead. Most importantly, this work empowers us to serve at scale, enabling us to massively leverage our privilege to help eradicate poverty, heal the environment, and make right the dark injustices that have plagued us. An unprecedented flourishing of humanity and nature is possible, and *Integral Investing* is an undeniable and vital contribution to help us get there."

—Dr. Barrett C. Brown, *Executive Coach, Founder and Managing Director of Apheno Advisory, USA*

"Ken Wilber, the great philosopher, offers an introduction to the famous quadrants, each of which begins 'simple' and culminates as 'integral.' 'Integral' presents a huge challenge for investors. Old civilizations could afford to limit their scope to local affairs, perhaps venturing as far as national ones. In the Anthropocene, this is no longer an option. Humanity dominates and tortures the planet. *Integral Investing*, according to Mariana Bozesan, is perhaps our best answer to the challenges we face. I am very happy to see this book published, and I hope that the investors' community will adopt it as their new guideline."

—Prof. Dr. Ernst Ulrich von Weizsäcker, *Honorary President of the International Club of Rome, Fellow of the World Academy of Art & Science, Germany*

"Holistic, long term, balanced, ethical, successful: These characteristics of *Integral Investing* are vital for investors and companies, but also for politics, macroeconomics, and financial institutions in general. Without this type of approach, the financial markets will continue to stagger and stumble from crisis to crisis, and the UN Sustainable Development Goals will remain out of reach. Having worked for the past four decades on sustainable development and values-driven investing, I can say that the sustainable investment paradigm is only slowly entering the mainstream consciousness—and only verbally, which includes green-washing, at that. Short-term profit maximization must be replaced by long-term profit optimization to ensure the prosperity and wellbeing of all creation. *Integral Investing* also means investing with integrity. I congratulate Mariana Bozesan for this timely and very important, encouraging, and holistic guide!"

—Prof Dr. h.c. Christoph Stückelberger, *Founder and President of Globethics.net, Switzerland*

"*Integral Investing* is a thought-provoking book that is equally inspiring and stimulating for all who truly care about becoming successful impact investors or entrepreneurs. Mariana walks her talk and speaks from personal experience as a serial entrepreneur turned investor. She offers a proven, yet challenging, investment template against which we can judge our own expectations for the future of life in this century. Her integrating call to action aims at eliminating current silos, unifying competing mindsets, giving tremendous hope, and providing concrete direction."

—Dr. Andreas Rickert, *Co-founder and CEO of Phineo gAG, Germany*

"No matter who we are, where we live, what kind of work we do, or how much power or money we have, we must choose whether we want to be part of the problem or part of the solution. The right choice, however, depends on our level of awareness. Do we see the world from an egocentric perspective in which everything must serve our own ego, or are we able to also care about our children, other people's children, and the world around us? Mariana has made her choice and has now written a groundbreaking book, *Integral Investing: From Profit to Prosperity,* on how to use capital to build sustainable companies, create jobs, and ensure the future of life on this planet. I highly recommend her book to anybody interested in understanding the complexity and interconnectedness of the formidable challenges we face and who decides to either start a company to address them or to invest in companies that will succeed. As Mariana rightly points out, the premise for success is the need to grow our consciousness. We must begin to understand that the reality in which every person lives, loves, and works is a social construct, the so-called consensual reality. This reality represents the narrative of our own culture that in many cases prevents us from seeing the deeper, much more important determinants that are responsible for the cultural and social constructs within which we live. The sooner we become aware of these constructs and how they impact our sense of right and wrong, of equality and dignity, the sooner we will begin to grow our human potential. This new awareness unleashes our creativity, resilience, and sense of wellbeing, which can then create sustainable and true prosperity for ourselves and our communities.

Mariana is a very courageous and aware woman whose inspiring life story is a very good example of how to become a consciousness leader and a change maker. Her Integral Investing model attests to the fact that companies and systems in which everybody wins can be successfully created. The world needs many more leaders like Mariana who are walking examples of what it means to share, to contribute, and to protect both human and natural capital. Thank you, Mariana, for your unique contributions toward creating a more equitable, sustainable, and prosperous society through *Integral Investing*."

    —Prof. Dr. Alberto Zucconi, *Co-founder (with Carl Rogers) & President Person-Centered Approach Institute (IACP), Chair and Board of Trustees World Academy of Art and Science (WAAS) Secretary General, World University Consortium (WUC), Italy*

"This book fills an important gap in the sustainable investment landscape. Investors focus mostly on business plans, market outlook, or teams' skill sets and much less on individual interior perspectives, individual mindsets, or the interplay within them. By referring to a number of showcases, *Integral Investing* demonstrates why such ignorance can become momentous. Quite often, such "soft factors" cause a start-up to fail. Mariana's Theta-Model offers a systematic and consistent method to assess these factors and integrate them in the due diligence process. Several decades of successful impact investing seem to be a solid proof point for the validity of this method.

Beyond the specific investors' community, this book does also entail a general message for any sustainability transformation. The world of systems, theories, and doctrines must be rooted and backed by personal behavior. A stronger focus on the latter will be needed if we want to facilitate the much-needed sustainability transformation."

    —Prof. Dr. Christian Berg, *Member in the International Club of Rome, Germany*

Introduction

This is a book written primarily for entrepreneurs and investors seeking sustainable prosperity during these turbulent times. But it also carries precious insights and an important message for every thinking individual seeking solutions to the pressing challenges confronting humanity today. It is set in the context of revolutionary global events; an outdated, unsustainable economic system that is widening inequalities while straining planetary boundaries; the ongoing climate emergency that compels us to make an urgent transition from fossil fuels; an exponential revolution in disruptive technologies that are multiplying security risks and investment opportunities; and the multidimensional threats to human security generated by the most serious pandemic in a century.

We live today in a world whose political, economic, educational, scientific, technological, and social ideas, institutions, and activities are grossly inadequate to cope with the speed, complexity, and uncertainty generated by rapid social evolution. Humanity is confronted by a loss of faith in our institutions of governance, a loss of trust in the media, a polarization of societies and retreat from democracy, rising levels of inequality and economic vulnerabilities, and a return to strident nationalism and geopolitical tensions at precisely a time when humanity's collective scientific, technological, and institutional capacity for peace, prosperity, and inclusive progress for all has never been greater. These problems are rooted in failed ideas, theories, institutions, and policies, all of which are unable to show us a viable way forward.

The quality of our actions depends on the quality of our thinking and our decisions. The world needs new leadership in thought that leads to action. Reliable action depends on reliable knowledge of our lived reality. *Integral Investing* is based on a way of thinking that is at once human-centered and value-based. It encompasses and integrates all aspects of our lives within a comprehensive perspective. It includes and harmonizes the objective and subjective dimensions of both our individual and our collective existence—our inner thoughts and feelings as well as the external world and conditions in which we live. It views the evolutionary currents and creative forces that are moving us forward. It seeks to lead us away from the fragmented way of thinking and acting that characterizes the world of today to an integral way of knowing and doing rooted in universal values.

This is an eminently practical and useful book that is also mentally exhilarating and spiritually inspiring. It is based on the author's personal quest for growth in consciousness and for a higher knowledge with the power to change the world. It traces the stages and steps of her search for personal meaning and effective action in the real world. It reconciles the highest universal values with the scientific evidence and empirical methods needed to translate high principles into concrete material results. It explores hidden dimensions of our lives wherein lies the power to rapidly and dramatically transform the outer world we inhabit.

Integral Investing presents cogent arguments with theoretical coherence, intellectual clarity, and scientific evidence backed by real-world accomplishments. It challenges the limitations and blind spots generated by simplistic linear thinking, a reductionist mindset that focuses on the parts but misses the whole, a scientific materialism that reduces everything to external factors while ignoring the creative inner core of our beings, and a mechanistic dualism that reduces everything to process and forgets the person—the individual—and the central place of our inner consciousness and experience as determinates of the outer world we create and live in.

Mariana is a highly successful serial entrepreneur and an accomplished angel investor committed to generating sustainable prosperity for the companies she works with and the world she lives in. My own experience as an international business consultant fully confirms the power of the core strategies she advocates. She is a hugely accomplished computer scientist, psychologist, and evolutionary integral thinker, whose analysis and methodology are profoundly rational, comprehensive, and organic. Based on my own research as a transdisciplinary social scientist, I deeply value the clarity of her thinking and depth of her insights. She is also a Fellow of the World Academy of Art & Science and a member of the International Club of Rome working to address the pressing social and ecological challenges that threaten the future of our planet and our civilization. The moonshot she and Tom have embraced to implement the SDGs within planetary boundaries by 2050 testifies to the seriousness of their commitment. As a member of both organizations, I take great pleasure in knowing her and deeply value her contribution to our collective work for the world. Mariana is a pure soul traversing her path to self-actualization and spiritual growth. I share her joyous wonder on that ultimate adventure of consciousness.

The World Academy of Art & Science was founded in 1960 by eminent scientists, statesmen, and intellectuals dedicated to reliable knowledge to promote the common good of all humanity. WAAS is pleased and proud to accept Mariana Bozesan's *Integral Investing* as a Report to the Academy. It exemplifies the kind of value-based thinking and integral knowledge the world needs to weather the challenges we face and seize the emerging opportunities that lie before us.

The World Academy of Art & Science   Garry Jacobs
(WAAS), Pondicherry, India
August, 2020

Contents

About the Author

Dr. Mariana Bozesan was named *Europe's Female Angel Investor of 2019* by the German Business Angel Network (BAND) and Business Angels Europe (BAE), as well as *Best European Early Stage Investor of the Year 2017* by the European Business Angels Network (EBAN).

She is best known as an integral investor and serial entrepreneur. She focuses on exponentially growing technologies with the intention to address climate change and other existential threats, and to accelerate the implementation of the UN SDGs within planetary boundaries.

Dr. Bozesan was awarded full membership in the international Club of Rome, where she co-authored the 2017 bestseller and Club of Rome report "Come on: Capitalism, Short-termism, Population and the Destruction of the Planet." She is also a Fellow in the World Academy of Art and Science (WAAS) and was National Advisory Board Member for the G8/G20 Social Impact Investment Task Force. Furthermore, she serves as a strategic advisor on safe AI as well as ethical and integral finance and sustainability to various organizations, businesses, and governmental as well as non-governmental bodies. She is also a futurist, published researcher and author, environmentalist, and human rights activist. As a prominent keynote speaker and an inspiring lecturer on the future of investing, business, and finance, she lectured at prestigious organizations including Stanford, Oxford, and INSEAD as well as the United Nations, TEDx and RIO+20.

Dr. Bozesan has an outstanding track record as an integral investor by de-risking early early-stage investments in exponential technologies using the Theta Model, which she developed based on Ken Wilber's Integral Theory. Her investment portfolio includes more than 40 successful investments.

As a philanthropist, she supports more than 38 humanitarian organizations. Together with the co-presidents and other members of the Club of Rome, she launched the Investment Turnaround and was joined by numerous like-minded investors. She is the founder of several organizations including AQAL Capital, a single-family office, and the AQAL Foundation. Educated at Stanford University and KIT (Karlsruhe Institute of Technology), Dr. Bozesan earned an MSc (Dipl.-Inform.) in Artificial Intelligence and Computer Science from KIT and a PhD in Psychology.

Chapter 1
The Context of Investing

1.1 COVID-19: Evolutionary Dress Rehearsal or Autocratic Regression?

During the final stages of writing this book, COVID-19 was declared a global pandemic[1] and is now forcing us to question existing systems. Governments around the world took action, much of it unprecedented, to contain the virus—including closing borders, enforcing social distancing, and imposing lockdowns and other restrictions on movement. It is only 2020 and already we are on the fourth pandemic of the century: COVID-19 was preceded by SARS in 2001–2004; H1N1, known colloquially as the swine flu, in 2009; and Ebola in 2014–2016. All four were zoonotic—that is, they were transmitted from animals to humans. Such diseases are more common than you might imagine, which is the reason why Bill Gates has warned us for many years, most eloquently in a 2015 TED talk,[2] about our collective vulnerability in the face of a pandemic.[3] Few listened, as was demonstrated by the general lack of preparation in the face of the COVID-19 outbreak.

The American Centers for Disease Control and Prevention (CDC) estimates that 75% of new diseases that infect humans are spread via animals. The prevalence of such diseases seems likely to increase given that a combination of natural disasters and irresponsible human behaviors is inflicting ongoing damage to the quality and quantity of wild animals' habitats, and forcing animals into urban areas. As both climate change and the global population continue to grow, so too do the extent and scope of the crisis.[4] I suspect that all goes without saying. One related danger that is frequently overlooked, however, is that how we respond nationally and internationally to this and similar crises could determine the future of democracy.

---

[1]An earlier version of this section was published on medium.com, see Bozesan (31 March 2020).
[2]https://tinyurl.com/t8lcmc6
[3]https://www.gatesnotes.com/Health/Pandemic-Innovation
[4]https://tinyurl.com/u2uupjm and https://tinyurl.com/uy48874

© Springer Nature Switzerland AG 2020
M. Bozesan, *Integral Investing*, https://doi.org/10.1007/978-3-030-54016-6_1

Is Democracy in Danger?

Alex Gladstein, Chief Strategy Officer at the Human Rights Foundation, argues that open democracies are more likely to respond in a competent manner to COVID-19 than are authoritarian regimes (such as those in Iran, North Korea, or Syria) whose actions are directed by the interests of the ruling classes rather than public well-being. And while he believes that the delayed response to the pandemic by the Trump administration in the United States and the Johnson government in the United Kingdom is a sign of incompetence rather than a failed democracy,[5] democracies could indeed fail if they do not take this opportunity to prove themselves more competent than authoritarian regimes. For example, let us take a look at restrictions on freedom of movement, a literally foreign concept in many Western democracies. Times of crisis such as pandemics may require temporary restrictions on freedom of movement: witness the introduction of social distancing and lockdowns in democracies across the globe in 2020. As responsible citizens, we can accept such temporary aberrations because they are for the greater good—but we must protect democracy by making sure those restrictions do not extend beyond the lifetime of the crisis that triggered them.

The USA PATRIOT Act passed after the 9/11 terrorist attacks is only one example of restrictions that have been imposed with good intentions at the time but are still active.[6] In Hungary, where democracy has long been a fragile concept, extraordinary measures were implemented to grant Prime Minister Viktor Orbán "sweeping powers" to deal with the COVID-19 crisis. Most significantly, there are no clauses in the legislation that granted these "sweeping powers" to spell out when and how they will come to an end.[7] No matter where we are, as soon as life returns to normal, we must insist on regaining our civil liberties, even if we have to take to the streets in protest. Of course, because we live in a technologically advanced era, those civil liberties extend to our digital lives. If data have been collected for scientific purposes, for example, they must have an expiration date and be anonymized; they must not be used against citizens; and there must be democratic accountability attached to their harvesting, use, and storage.

Exponential Tech: A Threat or a Blessing?

The current situation almost encapsulates the inherently contradictory nature of life in the exponential tech age. And the initial response, or lack thereof, in some countries including the United Kingdom and parts of the United States, could be seen as an assault on Enlightenment. Social media quickly turned into a breeding ground for COVID-19 fake news and misinformation on the one hand, and a source of life-saving information on the other, with hashtags such as #FlattenTheCurve and #StayHomeAndSaveLives on Twitter going viral and subsequently helping to educate people on the importance of respecting social distancing and other scientifically

---

[5]https://tinyurl.com/urzk5dd min. 20:51

[6]https://tinyurl.com/j8b5tt8 and https://tinyurl.com/uc5mtn5

[7]https://tinyurl.com/rgxhpx9

robust measures crucial for survival.[8] In Italy, where more than 6000 people died of the virus in a single month, respirator valves were 3D-printed after a hospital in Brescia reported that the lives of hundreds of people were at risk because they had run out.[9] Italian engineers Cristian Fracassi and Alessandro Romaioli asked the manufacturer to provide the blueprints of the valves so they could print replicas on their start-up company's 3D printer, but their request was denied. Undaunted, the engineers looked at the design of the original valve and developed three prototypes of these life-saving devices in only a couple of hours. They transformed a common snorkeling mask into an emergency respiratory mask and printed 100 devices within 24 h for less than €1 (just over US$1.00 at time of writing) per piece (compared with the regular price per valve of around €11,000) and had saved the lives of at least 10 patients by late March 2020. At the time of writing, the researchers were working for free, and this could have been an amazing example of people before profits were it not for the patent owner and manufacturer of the valve threatening to sue because of patent infringement.[10] This highlights the question of ethics and morals when it comes to the value of a human life compared with the financial gain derived from a patent.

As the call for social distancing increased and more people were required to self-isolate or self-quarantine, organizations encouraged many workers to work from home. This would not have been possible before the Internet age, and we can now fully appreciate the importance of digitalization (in fact, of all the 6Ds, which we will discuss later), including the necessity for high-quality global Internet access, which means that social distancing does not have to mean social isolation. We have now seen in real terms how exponentially growing technologies (discussed below) and platforms (Netflix, Amazon Prime Video, Slack, Google Suite, Alibaba's Ding Talk, or Microsoft Office 365) can be applied to maintain some semblance of normality during a crisis. While we cannot know what the long-term economic effects will be, the short-term pain is being at least partially eased in some sectors by remote working, access to free online learning options,[11] and even remote graduation.[12] Some gyms and yoga studios are looking after their clients' physical and mental wellbeing by offering online classes, often by donation so that they continue to look after their instructors as well. Videoconferencing tools such as Skype and Zoom have played a significant role in the current need to live virtually, and Zoom even experienced a financial boost, as their stock more than doubled after January 2020.[13] AI is also playing a central role in the management of this crisis. In an IEEE Spectrum article, Megan Scudelari discusses how five companies are currently using deep learning models to find new drugs that might successfully treat

---

[8]https://tinyurl.com/thf7flm

[9]https://tinyurl.com/vkgmnb3

[10]https://tinyurl.com/w4pzpbb

[11]See, for example, free Ivy League courses at https://tinyurl.com/yx4quugj

[12]https://tinyurl.com/wxoltz2

[13]https://tinyurl.com/vpmr6uh

COVID-19.[14] These companies have opened their platforms to allow scientists around the world to leverage their collective intelligence to expedite the development of antiviral drugs and a vaccine.

The need for self-sufficiency at home has never been more apparent, and I am positive that this experience will encourage the construction of sustainable housing and zero-energy buildings, and the retrofitting of existing homes with renewable technologies in the near future. From solar panels to solar tiles, power walls, energy storage, home automation, and even vertical farming at home, to name only a few initiatives, the necessary technologies are available and could be successfully and effectively applied with proper legislation and government support. One exponential technology that is currently still a work in progress but that will ultimately prove its value in any future time of social distancing is autonomous service robots powered by neural networks that can be used to remotely deliver food, medication, and other supplies to people in quarantine. For now, though, food delivery companies such as Deliveroo and Glovo have switched to contactless delivery.[15] To date, many large organizations have displayed a people-first mindset. Online retail platforms such as Amazon and Kijiji canceled the accounts of people who had bought up essential supplies to sell for inflated prices online.[16] And many supermarkets not only imposed limits on the number of items customers could buy at any one time but also had designated hours (usually the first business hour of the day) for seniors and high-risk members of the community. Some also offered free delivery. But let us not get ahead of ourselves.

Systemic Evolution or the Collapse of Civilization?
As I write these words, things are still changing—sometimes by the hour. By the time this book goes to print, the pandemic may have peaked, and life may be returning to normal for most people. But there will be consequences, both long-term and short-term. The implications are not only medical and biological, or social, cultural, and political—they are not even only economic. If pandemics really are increasing in frequency and impact—and remember, we are on our fourth pandemic of the twenty-first century and it is only 2020—they are also fundamentally existential. We can see the current situation as an opportunity to evolve to the next stage of human civilization and not only prevent the collapse of democratic societies but evolve them, or we can regress to nationalism, populism, and dictatorship either through incompetence or out of fear. We will see how resilient the various forms of government and governance are and how we can make them more resilient in the future. Thus far, individual governments around the world are taking historic measures to stop the spread of the pandemic and to prop up the economy during

---

[14]Scudelari (19 March 2020).

[15]https://tinyurl.com/s82h9ff

[16]https://tinyurl.com/tc67bn6

its reign. Unfortunately, there is little to no collective activity to help countries such as Iran, North Korea, or Syria.[17]

Current responses are only highlighting how helpless and disunited we are in the face of COVID-19 which, like climate change, does not respect national borders.

Can the European Union Become a Beacon of Light in the Darkness?
Systemic change is nonnegotiable if we want to protect democracy. Yanis Varoufakis, a former economic minister of Greece, is convinced that "Europe is unprepared for the COVID-19 recession,"[18] and that current stimulus packages will do little to counteract it. He is comparing the current stimulus packages with those issued in 2008 in response to the financial crisis that provided liquidity to an already bankrupted financial system without changing it at its core—such packages were essentially fiscal enablers. In his view, the COVID-19 crisis is only resurrecting the problem, and so he is calling for systemic changes. First, he called for solidarity to be a priority for the European Union, which has never been weaker than now. "Europe is only as healthy as its sickest resident and only as strong as its most bankrupted nation," and the price the EU will pay for a lack of united action threatens to be the "disintegration of the union itself,"[19] which would bring its own terrible consequences. Varoufakis has led the Democracy in Europe Movement 2025 toward proposing the following 3-point plan for addressing the COVID-19 depression and creating more resilient systems in the process[20]:

- Issue €1 trillion Eurobond by the European Central Bank (ECB).
- Inject a €2000 European Solidarity Cash Payment (UBI-like).
- Introduce a European Green Recovery and Investment Program to ensure the future of jobs, public health, public education, and the green transition (while getting rid of the old trickle-down recovery packages that did not work in the past).

This would require a democratically elected European government, a treasury that raises taxes to ensure the repayment of the Eurobonds in a timely fashion, and a green recovery agency. New systems will have to replace fossil fuel-based, free-market economies that are not sustainable in the long term with wellbeing economies fueled by zero-greenhouse gas emissions and ensure that small and medium enterprises, which create a large percentage of common prosperity in most nations, maintain their diversity, creativity, innovation, and resilience through massive amounts of capital made available to them. This capital must serve the greater good, be patient (long-term), be properly de-risked, and enable the development of integrally sustainable companies (see Chap. 3). But we can only achieve what we measure. This is why we must move beyond traditional GDP (for profit-only) criteria

---

[17]https://tinyurl.com/v2ojcmg

[18]https://tinyurl.com/saa7hmw

[19]Yanis Varoufakis, minute 0:47–1:16. Viewed at https://www.youtube.com/watch?v=jm97g0RqYGM

[20]https://tinyurl.com/yd62jjjf

for success and include integral sustainability metrics such as the parity of people, planet, and prosperity.

I am confident we can collectively learn from our COVID-19 experience and apply the lessons learned to protect ourselves and our planet. At an individual level, if we are healthy and have been lucky enough to either not be affected by the virus or have overcome it, we have an opportunity to grow beyond ourselves and become a source of support for those in need and to avoid fear from becoming a hidden pandemic. Times of crisis remind us that we cannot control the outside world, we cannot control what other people do, we cannot control the weather—and we certainly cannot control a virus. But we can control our psychological state, what we think, how we behave, and who we become in a crisis. We have choices. We can move into a state of desperation, panic-buying, and depriving our friends and neighbors of the basic supplies they need, or we can become an inspiration and a force for good for ourselves and others. We can grow emotionally and be there for those in need, or we can regress, feel sorry for ourselves, and become a burden, in every sense of the word, to those around us. Our mindset will determine whether we choose misery or happiness, and only we can define that mindset for ourselves (see Chap. 2).

1.2 A Challenged World

My past had convinced me that Soviet-type communism did not work (see box Confessions: From Communism to Capitalism), but once I was living in the West, I had a new question to ponder: Does capitalism really work better?

Often disguised as democracy and claiming to be built on values such as individual freedom, brotherhood and equality, and the promise of abundance for all,[21] capitalism can easily fool us into believing that it is the better path to follow, that it offers more opportunities to thrive and escape unacceptable circumstances. Yet, capitalism, in its current global manifestation, is holding the whole world hostage not only through staggering and ever-increasing levels of inequality but also through short-term profit maximization, the latter of which has in turn sparked human-caused planetary crises of unprecedented proportions.[22] In its 2020 global risk report,[23] the World Economic Forum highlights five areas of major concern:

- *Environmental fragilities* caused by climate action failure, human-made environmental and natural disasters, extreme weather, and accelerated loss of biodiversity whereby "the rate of extinction is tens to hundreds of times higher than the average over the past ten million years" (p. 7). Climate change is hitting us harder

---

[21]Diamandis and Kottler (2012), Pinker (2011 & 2018).

[22]See, for example, Stiglitz (2010) & Stiglitz (May 2011); Vollmann (2018a) & (2018b), von Weizsäcker and Wijkman (2018).

[23]World Economic Forum (2020).

and faster than expected, with the last 5 years being the warmest on record and pointing toward a 3 °C increase by the end of this century and planetary emergencies of unprecedented proportions.

- *Technological instabilities* due to the breakdown of information infrastructure, cyberattacks, adverse technological advances, and data fraud or theft undoing the remarkable economic and social benefits initially created by technological digitalization.
- *Societal and political strains* caused by pandemics and other infectious diseases, food and water crises, involuntary migration, and failure to pursue appropriate urban planning and ensure social instability.
- *Geopolitical tensions* caused by weapons of mass destruction, terrorist attacks, state collapse, interstate conflicts, global governance failure, and national governance failure.
- *Economic vulnerabilities* due to financial failure and fiscal crises caused by deflation and/or unmanageable inflation, asset bubbles, unemployment, energy price shocks, illicit trade, and failure to build critical infrastructure.

The post-COVID-19 era will be different from its predecessor, just as it ought to be. The data from the pre-COVID-19 era showed quite clearly that we had an outdated, unsustainable economic system. Despite its weaknesses, however, it was supported by a majority of investors, financiers, and businesspeople. For example, an investors' poll published in December 2019 by the Global Sustainable Investment Alliance shows that "only 16% of total respondents are already reporting in line with" (p. 8) climate-related financial risk disclosures in their mainstream financial reports.[24] The reason for that seems to stem from the fear of impacting economic growth, and even many academics such as William Nordhaus, recipient of the 2018 Nobel Prize in economic sciences, continue to be outspoken advocates of traditional economic growth.[25] Tax havens such as the Cayman Islands and Panama have encouraged indiscriminate economic growth at the expense of nature, people, and Earth's resources, which has contributed to the growth of destructive business practices. We are so enamored with growth that we did everything possible to prevent the underlying financial systems from going bankrupt during and after the 2007/2008 financial crisis. The stimulus packages, quantitative easing, issued in response to it continued to provide enormous liquidity to the bankrupted banks just to keep the illusion of growth alive. In *Tax Havens and Global Environmental Degradation*, Victor Galaz et al.[26] establish a clear link between tax havens, deforestation—for example, 68% of all scrutinized foreign capital was associated with the deforestation of the Amazon—and illegal fishing—for example, 70% of ships associated with illegal fishing were registered in tax haven countries. They, therefore, posit that lost tax revenue ought to be considered an indirect subsidy to

---

[24] Global Sustainable Investment Alliance (December 2019).

[25] See, for example, https://www.nobelprize.org/prizes/economic-sciences/2018/nordhaus/facts/ and https://news.yale.edu/2018/10/08/cheers-and-roses-undergrads-yales-latest-nobel-laureate

[26] Galaz et al. (2018).

economic activities with disastrous environmental, and eventually tragic social, consequences, and that the elimination of tax heavens be added to the UN's sustainability agenda.

Confessions: From Communism to Capitalism

During my childhood in Romania, hunger, cold, misery, and shortages of just about anything you can imagine were part of my daily life. My crooked toes and feet are a daily reminder of those difficult times. My feet grew as fast as any child's feet grow, but my parents could afford to buy me shoes only once a year. For that, they borrowed money, which they paid back during the following 12 months. But deprivation was not shared equally: while I went short of food, some of my classmates ate strawberries in the middle of winter; while we had an outhouse in the backyard, no bathroom or running water, and a coal oven for heating, a lucky few families enjoyed both indoor toilets and bathrooms, complete with running water and central heating. As far back as I remember, I was determined to escape poverty and enjoy strawberries whenever I felt like them. I realized early on that to do this, I would have to use my brain, the only thing I had that gave me any kind of advantage over my strawberry-eating schoolmates. This way of thinking also happened to reflect the party line, in which I deeply believed, although my parents gradually became disillusioned by it. My father was born in 1934 to hardworking but poverty-stricken farmers in Transylvania, in northern Romania. Like me, my father was a communist in his youth and thus a great believer in equality, freedom, and social justice; and like so many other idealists, he eagerly adopted Karl Marx's now-infamous idea that the class struggle inevitably leads to the dictatorship of the proletariat, which in itself represents only a transition to a classless society without the exploitation of people by people. As a young adult, he was a devoted party secretary, determined to make the theory work for the underprivileged, whom he represented. The Hungarian uprising of 1956 gave him his first hint that he may have been deceived. A few years later, he knew for sure that nothing had changed for the better. In fact, things were worse than ever. For people like him, poverty was a fact of life. He became disillusioned, although he recognized the danger to which this exposed him. Until we emigrated to West Germany, he faced the constant threat of rotting in prison like so many of his idealist friends, but even so, he continued fighting—not so much communism but human foolishness. He was too much of a warrior to give in, and he used the system to fight the system, but he remained mired in poverty. He believed in revolution, equality, ethics, and other communist ideals, and he never tired of fighting corruption, bigotry, and ignorance. However, while the conformists were doing rather well, we as a family were dirt poor. Things improved a little when my mother began working as a baker—not because of the extra money (although that certainly

(continued)

helped) but because, like so many other decent people in corrupt societies, she turned her back on her principles and began stealing food from work. And so, for the 11 years leading up to our emigration to West Germany, we did not starve.

My parents may have been completely disillusioned by communism, but they were smart enough to not put me or themselves in danger by disclosing their political opinions. Thus, I toed the party line and became a great believer in the communist ideology. I never questioned the system, for it never occurred to me there could be anything to question. I was living under a regime that encouraged education and learning; provided outstanding free education in sciences and free healthcare; and promoted equality between men and women, as well as perseverance and the prospect of achievement through hard work independent of any religious indoctrination. I learned to believe in my own abilities and what I could achieve through my intellectual skills alone. My hopes for a better future were high, and I worked hard to try to make them a reality. I truly believed that if I worked hard and studied, I would eventually escape poverty. This belief that I could achieve virtually anything if I only worked hard enough would become a guiding force for the rest of my life. And I did get out of poverty—but not in Romania. I only escaped poverty because we left the so-called "communist" society (Karl Marx would turn in his grave if he could see what people made of his philosophy)—and all it offered, negative and positive—to move to the capitalist West, which had been presented to me for so long as the ideological root of all evil. Our emigration to West Germany in 1974 improved not only our material circumstances but also my view of the world. Once I was in the West, the brainwashing I had experienced while living under communism became obvious to me, and I decided that I would never again become a member of any political, or religious, organization. I would never again be blindsided by any type of dogma. Letting go of the "communist" doctrine was easy for me because I had seen for myself that it did not work—unless working meant keeping millions of people oppressed, poor, and miserable, in which case it was very effective. Thirty years after the fall of the Berlin Wall, as I look at current realities, I wonder, does capitalism truly work better?

If we are not to self-destruct as a species, taking down the planet as we go, we must face the fact that the time has come for a radical transformation in our attitudes to life. But we must act carefully, *responding* rather than *reacting* so that we do not simply swap one harmful ideology for another. To do that, we must understand the full complexity of the greater context in which we operate, including its hidden determinants. At the center of those hidden determinants is mindset, human psychology, and trust in both the individual and the collective. The current Edelman Trust Barometer, for example, shows an epochal lack of trust in "the four societal

institutions that the study measures—government, business, NGOs and media."[27]
Therefore, as we analyze the context in which capital, investing, and businesses
operate, we need to stand guard at the door of our minds and make sure that we do
not fall into the traps of either exaggerated pessimism dominated by
"progressophobia"[28] or inflated, naïve confidence. Wise optimism should be our
guiding light.

1.2.1   Planetary Emergencies

The COVID-19 pandemic has amplified our economic vulnerabilities and demonstrated that they stem not only from the increased volatility in the financial markets
but also from the fact that they lack sustainability, solidarity, social and ecological
orientation; disregard our global interdependence; are decoupled from nature and the
real economy; and are measured by a single factor: GDP. Additional contributing
factors to economic vulnerability are (1) the global debt, which at around 225% of
GDP is significantly higher than before the 2008 global financial crisis and which is
increasing daily as governments are forced to mitigate the COVID-19 crisis, and
(2) the constriction of global financial circumstances, which is imposing burdens on
countries that built up dollar-based liabilities while interest rates were low. While
these factors pose serious threats to the world economy when paired with geopolitical and societal tensions, it is significant to note that the picture changes significantly if we analyze how these risks have changed over the past 10 years.[29] In 2009,
the top risks were seen to be mostly economic in nature (the collapse of asset prices,
retrenchment from globalization, fossil fuel price spikes, fiscal crises), followed by
chronic disease, pandemics, and gaps in global governance. In 2020, however, the
top existential threats are:

- *Ongoing climate emergency*, manifested by extreme weather events, natural
  disasters including unexpected pandemics such as COVID-19, critical sea level
  rises, water crises, and the failure to mitigate and adapt to climate change
- *Nuclear threat*, including weapons of mass destruction, exacerbated by the
  withdrawal from and termination of the INF Treaty by the United States followed
  by Russia[30]
- *Unsafe AI and cyber criminality*, including data fraud, data theft, and cyber
  attacks

In *Call to Action from the Planetary Emergency Partnership,* an open letter to
global leaders, the Club of Rome warns decision-makers that "how leaders decide to

---

[27]See, for example, the Edelman Trust Barometer (2019) at https://tinyurl.com/t9kutqv
[28]Pinker (2018, p. 39).
[29]World Economic Forum (2020, Figure IV, p. 8).
[30]https://tinyurl.com/ua45n9d

stimulate the economy in response to the corona crisis will either amplify global threats or mitigate them, so they need to choose wisely."[31] As a collective, we may be tempted to do anything we can to mitigate the fallout from the pandemic so we can get back to business as usual as fast as possible. But we have a real opportunity now to transform our systems (economics, financial, governance, education, etc.) and make them more sustainable.[32] This means that those who care most about their economic future must address existential threats.

1.2.2   The Speed of Change

The current warnings about climate change are not new, but they have become increasingly relevant. The COVID-19 crisis showed us in no uncertain terms that if we are to overcome climate change challenges, our leaders must trust in science and recognize the value of foresight, prevention strategies, and wide-scale disaster preparation. One of the first—and certainly the most remarkable—forewarnings came via *The Limits to Growth*,[33] the groundbreaking 1972 report to the Club of Rome. It sold more than 9 million copies and put the impact of exponential economic and population growth on a finite planet on the world agenda thanks to the shocking wake-up call it sounded. It alerted the public to the potentially disastrous results of ongoing resource depletion, uncontrolled population and food production growth, as well as a growing carbon footprint. The environmental consequences would be dire and the social implications massive if business were to continue as usual. Unfortunately, few people truly accepted or took to heart, let alone acted upon, the recommendations of the report—and look where we are now. William Nordhaus was far from alone in his nonresponse to the warnings, and I believe that he and his ilk must accept much responsibility for our current precarious situation.

The MIT researchers who wrote *The Limits to Growth* modeled its now-famous 12 scenarios using the WORLD3 system dynamics of their eminent professor of engineering Jay Forrester. They created a model for the computer simulation of physical growth, including interactions between population growth, industrial growth, food production, and ecological limits on a finite planet. The scenarios in the report represented the options global society could choose to take between 1970 and 2100. Some were optimistic and indicated where the potential collapse could be averted through a deliberate reduction in population as well as systematic CO_2 footprint reduction per person. Others were pessimistic and simulated pollution crises, demonstrating what could—and in fact, as we now know, *did*—go wrong due to resource depletion, excessive pollution, and an increased decline in well-being through population explosion, a growing human footprint, and resource scarcity. Although the report *did not predict* which of the 12 scenarios was most

---

[31] https://tinyurl.com/rl2ty86

[32] https://tinyurl.com/saa7hmw

[33] Meadows et al. (1972).

likely to happen, it encouraged sustainable development within planetary boundaries. It was also perceived as unnecessarily alarmist. It was heavily criticized by some economists,[34] and in 1992, economist Wilfred Beckerman even observed that "the best—and probably the only—way to attain a decent environment in most countries is to become rich."[35]

In 2008, Paul Krugman, a Nobel Prize laureate in economics, even disparaged the group's endeavors as "hard-science arrogance" and Jay Forrester's system dynamics model "a classic case of garbage-in-garbage-out: [insinuating that] Forrester didn't know anything about the empirical evidence on economic growth or the history of past modeling efforts."[36] Economists, in general, were offended by the report and held firm to the belief that something that must not happen will not happen. Their resistance emphasizes, however, the ubiquitous tension between the current climate emergency and the "crucial roles played by exploration and discovery, technological progress, and substitution."[37]

My own involvement in climate emergency action began in 2003 at the Alliance for a New Humanity conference in Puerto Rico, which my husband, Tom, and I co-sponsored. The keynote speaker was Vice President Al Gore, and for several days we had the opportunity to discuss in depth his concerns about climate change. At that time, I was already a big fan of Gore, having listened to his 1992 audiobook, *Earth in the Balance: Ecology and the Human Spirit*.[38] I believed he genuinely cared about people and the future of our planet. During the first conference dinner, Gore shared with us how he was desperately trying to get important countries including Russia and the United States to ratify the Kyoto Protocol, and what we could all do to support his efforts. That was when it became obvious to me that we investors had to redirect our investments, resources, focus, and activities toward averting human-caused climate change, AKA the biggest threat to Earth and humanity in recent history. I realized that we could and should balance our ongoing needs as investors with the long-term needs of the planet. The two motivations were not mutually exclusive. In fact, by switching our investing behaviors, we could make a positive difference to the health and future of the planet. However, Tom and I were in the minority at that point.

"The Kyoto Protocol is an international treaty which extends the 1992 United Nations Framework Convention on Climate Change (UNFCCC) that commits state parties to reduce greenhouse gas emissions, based on the scientific consensus that (part one) global warming is occurring and (part two) it is

(continued)

---

[34]See, for example, Beckerman (1972); Nordhaus (1973); Nordhaus et al. (1973).

[35]Beckerman (1992, p. 482).

[36]https://krugman.blogs.nytimes.com/2008/04/22/limits-to-growth-and-related-stuff/

[37]Nordhaus (1992, p. 45).

[38]Gore (1992).

extremely likely that human-made CO_2 emissions have predominantly caused it. The Kyoto Protocol was adopted in Kyoto, Japan, on 11 December 1997."[39]

1.2.3   Accepting the Challenge

The 2006 Academy Award conferred on Gore's documentary, *An Inconvenient Truth*, brought climate change into the mainstream and pushed home the point that the time for procrastinating is over. Like *The Limits to Growth*, *An Inconvenient Truth* was heavily criticized and accused of exaggerating the problem and being gloomy and disempowering. When the 2007 Nobel Peace Prize was jointly awarded to the Intergovernmental Panel on Climate Change (IPCC) and Gore for their research on and dissemination of knowledge about human-made climate change, we heard yet another wake-up call. Or we ought to have. Instead, business continued—indeed, continues—as usual, with little significant action having been taken to date by regulators, governments, or industry. The result: global CO_2 emissions continue to rise unimpeded. According to data provided by the Copernicus Climate Change Service of the European Centre for Medium-Range Weather Forecasts, the global average temperature for June 2019 was the highest since records began.[40]

Of course, reducing CO_2 emissions is a fraught business, but perhaps if we understand why nations are reluctant to even discuss such reductions, we will be better placed to understand how we could make changes. Figure 1.1 illustrates why negotiations between nations about reducing CO_2 emissions are so difficult.

Every year, the International Energy Agency (IEA) publishes its statistics on worldwide CO_2 emissions in an attempt to show clearly why the global community must reduce the total amount of CO_2 being released into the atmosphere.[41] But *who should do the reducing?* CO_2 emissions present a particular global challenge, for they do not halt at the border of the country emitting them, and there is no world government to legislate on behalf of the planet to reduce them. We, therefore, depend on each individual national government to do the right thing and advocate for our planet.

To identify the source of emissions, my husband, Tom, developed a variwide chart (Fig. 1.1) that uses 2017 data (published in 2019) from the International Energy Agency.[42] The vertical axis shows CO_2 emissions per capita and the horizontal axis population data per country or continent. While emissions vary widely from one

---

[39]Viewed July 5, 2019 at https://en.wikipedia.org/wiki/Kyoto_Protocol

[40]https://climate.copernicus.eu/record-breaking-temperatures-june

[41]See, for example, IPCC (2020).

[42]International Energy Agency (2018).

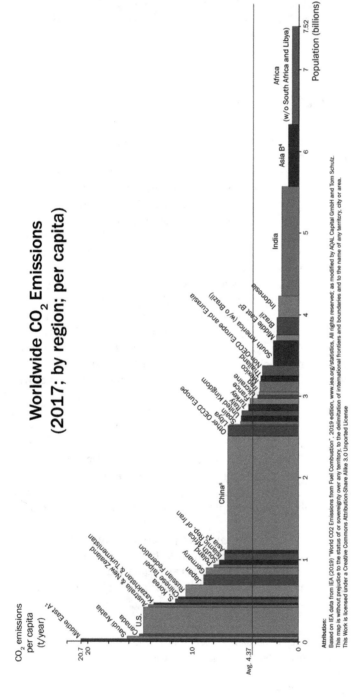

Fig. 1.1 2017 worldwide CO_2 emissions per capita and country. (Source: Schulz (2019))

Attribution:
Based on IEA data from IEA (2019) "World CO2 Emissions from Fuel Combustion", 2019 edition, www.iea.org/statistics, All rights reserved; as modified by AQAL Capital GmbH and Tom Schulz.
This map is without prejudice to the status of or sovereignty over any territory, to the delimitation of international frontiers and boundaries and to the name of any territory, city or area.
This Work is licensed under a Creative Commons Attribution-Share Alike 3.0 Unported License

Notes:
Energy-related CO2 emissions only; no other greenhouse gases
[1] Middle East A: Bahrain, Oman, Kuwait, Qatar, United Arab Emirates
[2] Middle East B: Israel, Jordan, Lebanon, Syrian Arab Republic, Yemen
[3] Asia A: Brunei Darussalam, Malaysia, Mongolia, Singapore
[4] Asia B: Asia w/o Asia A, China, India, Thailand, Chinese Taipei, Indonesia, Korea, Japan
[5] China: People's Rep. of China, Hong Kong
Version: 17-Dec-2019 by AQAL Capital GmbH (https://aqalcapital.com) and Tom Schulz

region to the next, the world average is 4.35 metric tons per capita. Most industrialized nations range between 4 and 15 metric tons of CO_2 emissions per capita. The total CO_2 emissions of a region are represented through a rectangular area. The *height* of each rectangle is proportional to the CO_2 emissions per capita and the *width* is proportional to the population of the represented region. The regions are sorted by CO_2 emissions per capita, from highest to lowest, and are a mix of countries and continents.

When you look at this chart, it becomes evident that Earth will not be able to absorb additional greenhouse gas emissions to make room for developing nations to "catch up" by increasing their per capita emissions to match the current average. Yes, developed countries are responsible for the current misery, but the fate of Earth will essentially be decided by what occurs in developing nations from this point on. The future of life depends on their not building an economy based on fossil fuels at any cost and instead "leapfrogging" the use of renewable energy sources, thus joining those awakened souls and climate activists behind the Paris Agreement on Climate Change[43] and the adoption of Agenda 2030 with its Sustainable Development Goals (SDGs) in 2015.[44] Nevertheless, there continues to be not only little obvious appreciation of the sense of urgency but also insufficient commitment or regulatory action to address the current climate emergency. In fact, in 2017, one of the world's greatest polluters per capita, the United States (see Fig. 1.1) decided to withdraw from the Paris Agreement,[45] with President Trump stating that "the concept of global warming was created by and for the Chinese in order to make U.S. manufacturing non-competitive."[46] Some people watching the temporary drop in global emissions due to COVID-19 lockdowns and reduced economic activity may be tempted to believe that no additional climate action may be needed in the aftermath of the pandemic. This belief could not be further from the truth. Climate change is the result of 100 years of global emissions into the atmosphere; it is not going to be turned around in only a few weeks.[47]

Investors and entrepreneurs are very pragmatic, and in order to assess whether or not something is sustainable within planetary boundaries, we need not only a definition of sustainability within planetary boundaries but also metrics to help measure and deliver the outcome. One of the first definitions of sustainable development was published in *Our Common Future*, a 1987 report by the United Nations World Commission on Environment and Development.[48] Known as the *Brundtland Report*, in honor of former Norwegian Prime Minister Gro Harlem Brundtland, who chaired the commission at the time, it defined "sustainable development as the development that meets the needs of the present without compromising the ability

[43]https://unfccc.int/process-and-meetings/the-paris-agreement/what-is-the-paris-agreement

[44]https://sustainabledevelopment.un.org/post2015/transformingourworld

[45]See, for example, https://fas.org/sgp/crs/misc/IF10668.pdf

[46]https://twitter.com/realdonaldtrump/status/265895292191248385?lang=en

[47]https://tinyurl.com/rm3whvq and https://tinyurl.com/rz9m5zr

[48]World Commission on Environment and Development (2009, p. 43).

of future generations to meet their own needs." Since then, we have made much progress through the ratification of Agenda 2030 of the UN in 2015 with its 17 Sustainable Development Goals[49] and 230 individual indicators.[50] However, we are still a long way away from being able to provide a clear and implementable blueprint for investors, business people, and other stakeholders. This is particularly significant because the UN SDGs are inspirational goals that at times contradict each other. For example, if we keep focusing on goal number 1—end poverty in all its forms everywhere—and try to implement it regardless of other considerations, we will continue to burn fossil fuels to lift people out of poverty, and thus violate goal number 13—take urgent action to combat climate change and its impacts. This is why we must ensure the UN SDGs are implemented within planetary boundaries, the constraints dictated by our planet's operating system.

"The planetary boundaries concept presents a set of nine planetary boundaries (Fig. 1.2) within which humanity can continue to develop and thrive for generations to come."[51] The nine factors covered by them concern the regulation of the stability of Earth's operating system and include, for example, biosphere integrity, freshwater use, ocean acidification, ozone depletion, and climate change.

Humanity is continuing to operate in a twentieth-century type of business-as-usual scenario—the very scenario that took us into in the yellow zones in the first place. If we are to ensure a safe operating environment and also implement the Paris Agreement, we must get back into the green zones. Unfortunately, we are currently hurtling toward breaking through the orange boundary, which could have irreversible consequences.[52] As discussed at length by Ernst von Weizsäcker and Anders Wijkman in *Come On!*,[53] their 2018 report to the Club of Rome, current financial, economic, and governance systems are not sustainable in terms of the above requirements. Most governments promote gross domestic product (GDP) to enhance job creation, safeguard tax revenue, and increase overall prosperity whereby prosperity is defined in a narrow, local, and mostly financial-only sense at the expense of both the UN's SDGs and our planetary boundaries.[54] The price for this short termist approach to prosperity will be paid by future generations through subsidies for fossil fuels such as coal, tar sands, and natural gas, as well as nuclear energy.[55] The result

---

[49]https://sustainabledevelopment.un.org/

[50]https://sustainabledevelopment.un.org/content/documents/11803Official-List-of-Proposed-SDG-Indicators.pdf

[51]https://www.stockholmresilience.org/research/planetary-boundaries.html

[52]Randers et al. (2018); Rockström et al. (2009).

[53]Von Weizsäcker and Wijkman (2018).

[54]Pinker (2011); Stiglitz et al. (2018).

[55]Vollmann (2018a) & (2018b).

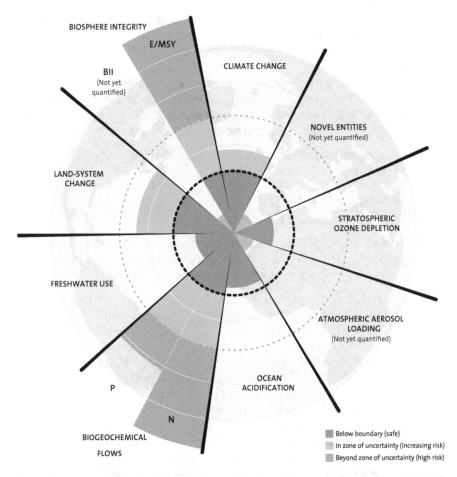

BIOSPHERE INTEGRITY

E/MSY

BII
(Not yet
quantified)

CLIMATE CHANGE

NOVEL ENTITIES
(Not yet quantified)

LAND-SYSTEM
CHANGE

STRATOSPHERIC
OZONE DEPLETION

FRESHWATER USE

ATMOSPHERIC AEROSOL
LOADING
(Not yet quantified)

OCEAN
ACIDIFICATION

P

N

BIOGEOCHEMICAL

FLOWS

Below boundary (safe)
In zone of uncertainty (increasing risk)
Beyond zone of uncertainty (high risk)

Fig. 1.2 Earth's planetary boundaries. (Source: J. Lokrantz/Azote based on Steffen et al. 2015. Planetary Boundaries: Guiding human development on a changing planet. Science, 347(6223). Printed with permission)

will be not only climate devastation and record biodiversity loss[56] but also global inequality of unprecedented proportions.[57] Since November 2007, the European Commission, European Parliament, Club of Rome, OECD, WWF, and several other major organizations have been collaborating in an attempt to change this outdated approach to measurement criteria, albeit without much global success to date.[58] In terms of accounting practices, the same approach is taken in corporate accounting, which is not required to take into account environmental degradation,

---

[56] Martin (2015).

[57] Dorling (2014); Stiglitz (2011).

[58] Stiglitz et al. (2018).

social, or governance issues. Thus, the sole measurement criterion on which we currently rely is short-term profit at the expense of long-term financial sustainability, as well as the security of people and the planet.

However, there is hope. The European Commission recently defined a 10-step action plan[59] aimed at implementing sustainable finance with the intention of transforming the EU economy in order to meet the goals of the Paris Agreement and Agenda 2030. This long-term strategy intends to achieve carbon neutrality by 2050 and is accompanied by several key pieces of documentation[60]:

- Financing a Sustainable European Economy: Taxonomy Technical Report, published in June 2019 by the Technical Expert Group (TEG) on Sustainable Finance
- Sustainability-related Disclosures
- Climate Benchmarks and ESG Disclosures

As investors who care about the future and want to win "the race of our lives" against the destruction of our planet, we need to keep a close eye on these developments and begin to change our own investment practices to:

- Move beyond a short-term, financial, profit-only approach by making long-term investments in companies that renounce short-term profitability and quarterly benchmarking, and assess the degree to which companies weaken their long-term investments by not including UN SDG criteria in their strategies and tactics.
- Build robust measurement criteria that include integrated UN SDG metrics within planetary boundaries that drive sustainable performance and demonstrate reliably the value of nonfinancial information. The investment products currently available rarely go beyond the negative screening of particular sectors. We must, therefore, develop more attractive investment mandates, benchmarks, portfolio turnovers, and performance fees and metrics.
- Eliminate investments in extremely complex investment structures with increasing complexity of products and services that encourage speculative trading and are disconnected from the comforts, needs, and expectations of the primary beneficiaries.
- Simplify investments and eliminate intermediary agents and money managers with expensive lifestyles that make them dependent on high earnings—and can lead to their taking inappropriately high risks.
- Stop investing in financial products whose incentive structures are predominantly influenced by short-term financial performance, market indices, benchmarks, market share, personal security, success, and reputation, as well as short-term regulatory compliance. Such incentives encourage unsustainable behaviors in the participating agents and can lead to a lack of alignment of goals, a culture of fear, growing self-interest, and high levels of remuneration linked to short-term profits.

---

[59]https://ec.europa.eu/info/publications/180308-action-plan-sustainable-growth_en

[60]See, for example, https://tinyurl.com/y2qq6syw, https://tinyurl.com/rkz92zx, and https://tinyurl.com/tfkv6cd

- Seek out or develop your own portfolio structures and strategic asset allocation by exploring new approaches that ensure sustainable investments.
- Encourage the development of sustainable financial markets by contributing to the development of better risk-management tools, especially for the "too big to fail" organizations. Work with regulators for the introduction of better regulatory systems that help implement Agenda 2030 within planetary boundaries to serve the interests of long-term investors.
- Support transparency and corporate disclosure by investing in companies that already have—or want to introduce—voluntary and regulatory disclosure practices for all information pertaining to long-term value creation.
- Help finance the development of circular and full-spectrum economies, thus facilitating the aggregation of the necessary capital to address the Paris Agreement and Agenda 2030.

The implementation of these measures is a gargantuan task, and so it inevitably leaves unanswered many questions pertaining to proper measurements, regulations, and capital. But we know that we have to act soon—and we cannot risk waiting for governments or regulators to act on our behalf. So, what to do?

In Jorgen Randers's opinion, capitalism in its current form cannot provide the necessary paradigm shift, because it is designed to allocate money to what is profitable in the short term and not to what society and/or the planet need in the long term.[61] Furthermore, several experts are united in their opinion that democratic parliaments are unlikely to pass new regulations in time to save us out of fear of losing voters who could presumably be against solutions that require, for example, higher taxes and more expensive gasoline and/or electricity in the short term.[62] Thus, democratic bodies are not only barely meeting the needs of the current generation but also compromising the ability of future generations to meet their needs. Democratic governments appear rather overwhelmed by the complexity of the problems—the prevalence of short-term thinking, profit-only orientation, outdated measurement criteria, old dogmas, lack of understanding of exponential growth, inertia, and lack of a unified political will. Moreover, because of the lack of legislative incentives and proper measurement criteria, the private sector is moving too slowly toward a sustainable financial and economic system.

My question is: What can we as individual investors do to avert the worst within the 10-year window of opportunity given by the Paris Agreement and Agenda 2030? Before diving deeper into possible solutions from an investors' perspective, let us take a look at another global context in which we are currently operating, one that will continue to influence and disrupt our lives more than anything else in the history of humanity: exponentially growing technologies.

---

[61]Randers et al. (2018); Randers (2012).

[62]See, for example, Gore (2006, 2011); Krugman (2012); Randers et al. (2018); Randers (2012); Sachs (2008).

1.3   Exponentially Growing Technologies

1.3.1   Evolution of Evolution

Despite the current assortment of challenges, humanity as a whole is on average better off today than 50 years ago.[63] We live in some of the most peaceful, progressive, and exciting times in human history,[64] and, despite the unprecedented population growth,[65] life expectancy keeps increasing,[66] the average standard of living is improving,[67] and famine has largely been conquered.[68] Today, people have a greater chance of digging their graves with their own teeth through unhealthy lifestyle choices that lead to noncommunicable, lifestyle-related diseases or dying through suicide or of old age than from starvation, terrorism, war, or communicable diseases.[69] Poverty has been reduced from 94% at the dawn of the First Industrial Revolution around 1820 to 9.6% in 2015,[70] the average global income has increased tenfold,[71] and global child mortality rates have fallen from 18.2% in 1960 to 4.3% in 2015. According to Max Roser, "over the last 200 years people in all countries in the world achieved impressive progress in health that lead to increases in life expectancy."[72] In South Korea, for example, life expectancy at birth grew from an average of 25 years in 1800 to above 80 in 2012, surpassing even German and the United States life expectancy.

Literacy rates have also increased—from 12% in 1820 to 87% in 2014[73]—and most countries in the world now have democracy as their form of government—in 1799, there were no democratically governed nations; in 2019, 96 out of 167 countries with more than 0.5 million inhabitants were democracies.[74] It is a relatively undisputed fact that this could only have been accomplished through technology, exploitation of fossil fuels, and modern agriculture practices that enabled the production of significantly more food per hectare of land. This productivity increase both reduced the amount of agricultural land necessary to feed populations (on a per capita basis) and the number of people working in agriculture and freed the labor force to move into manufacturing and other types of employment.[75] As a result, the

---

[63]Rosling et al. (2018, pp. 27–39).

[64]Roser (2018), & (2018e).

[65]Roser and Ortiz-Ospina (2017a/2013) & 2017b/2013).

[66]Roser (2018a) & (2018c).

[67]Roser (2018b); Roser and Ortiz-Ospina (2018)

[68]Ritchie and Roser (2018).

[69]http://ghdx.healthdata.org/gbd-results-tool

[70]Roser and Ortiz-Ospina (2017a/2013a).

[71]Roser (2018b). Viewed 5 July 2019 at https://ourworldindata.org/economic-growth

[72]Roser (2018a), https://tinyurl.com/y7lq78m2

[73]Roser and Ortiz-Ospina (2018).

[74]Roser (2018d); https://www.pewresearch.org/fact-tank/2019/05/14/more-than-half-of-countries-are-democratic/

[75]Roser and Ritchie (2018a, b).

number and severity of famines have been significantly reduced,[76] as have food costs.[77] Today, the majority of people in the world have a standard of living that is comparable to that of people in the West in the 1950s.[78] None of this progress would have been possible without human curiosity, ingenuity, determination, a willingness to grow beyond oneself, a sense of wonder and purpose—and, of course, ongoing developments in technology.

Whether we call the current era the Second Machine Age, as Eric Brynjolfsson and Andrew McAfee from the MIT Center for Digital Business do,[79] the Third Industrial Revolution, the term preferred by Jeremy Rifkin,[80] or even the Fourth Industrial Revolution, as Klaus Schwab, founder of the World Economic Forum,[81] will have it, research shows that we are living in an era of massive transformations driven by double exponentially growing technologies.[82] But what does this really mean for us as individuals, investors, business people, and people who care?

1.3.2 The Role of Exponentials

After seeing Mosaic, the groundbreaking Internet browser, Tom and I returned from California to Germany in 1994, ready to ride the Internet wave. We knew that it was taking off because the growth of the Internet was exponential (Fig. 1.3), as was the exponential growth of the underlying computation power, which had become both affordable and powerful enough to enable such applications such as the Internet. But the Internet is just one manifestation of the exponential tech boom.

Our plan was to start a technology transfer business to help companies build their Internet presence using Java-based application servers, and so we founded Infobahn International in Munich, Germany. However, 12 months down the road, we had a rude awakening: the few businesspeople in Germany who had even heard of the Internet had no interest in building an Internet presence. We experienced not only ignorance of its existence and potential, but also actual hostility toward it. Most people to whom we talked felt that the Internet had come out of nowhere. They did not understand the extraordinary opportunity it was offering because it was a paradigm changer challenging the entire business-as-usual attitude. No one seemed to know quite how to classify it. For example, the banks we asked for funding referred us to movie subsidy and film financing organizations. For me, the most disturbing fact was that even high-tech executives who should have known better did

---

[76]Hasell and Roser (2018).

[77]Roser and Ritchie (2018a, b).

[78]Rosling et al. (2018, pp. 27–39).

[79]Brynjolfsson and McAfee (2014)

[80]Rifkin (2011).

[81]Schwab (2016).

[82]Kurzweil (2005, p. 67).

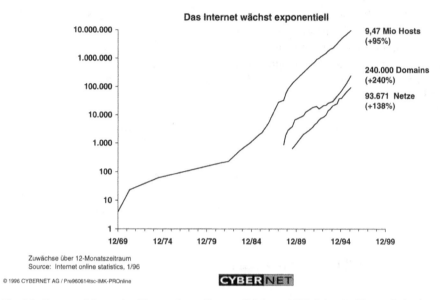

Fig. 1.3 Exponential growth of Internet hosts (Source: Cybernet, 1996. Printed with permission by co-founder of Cybernet Tom Schulz) (This is an original slide from Cybernet that only exists in German. It shows how the Internet was growing exponentially between 1969 and 1999)

not get it. I remember vividly how the head of Oracle Germany, my indirect boss at the time, went against founder Larry Ellison's directive to begin selling Oracle's products online, stating during an internal company meeting, I heard him say: "solange ich bei Oracle bin, ist Internet kein Thema" ("as long as I am at Oracle [Germany], Internet is a non-issue"). As a consequence, I quit Oracle and focused on growing Infobahn International, while Tom co-founded Cybernet to give companies access to and push the adoption of the Internet. In our fundraising efforts, we repeatedly showed the immense Internet infrastructure implementation curves—represented logarithmically in a linear fashion in Fig. 1.3—dating back to 1969. Like every exponential curve, in the beginning, it looked and felt linear.

As a species, we have been conditioned to think linearly and locally because for millennia we lived our lives mostly in a limited geographic area, lived on average a relatively short time, and performed mostly the same jobs in the same ways as our ancestors did. Our lives were fairly predictable. It was only through accelerated technology growth that our *linear* and *local* way of thinking began to be challenged.

Throughout the history of humankind, technological progress evolved not only slowly but also exponentially (see the orange curve in Fig. 1.4). The COVID-19 pandemic provided a real-life example of how difficult it is for most people (world leaders are no exception) to wrap their minds around exponential curves—not least because the past few years have seen an increasing misuse of the word "exponential" to mean "lots" or even "accordingly" (as in, "if we need more staff, the costs will increase exponentially"), so there is a general fuzziness about what the concept and the related curves all mean. In times of crisis, this is particularly problematic, as it

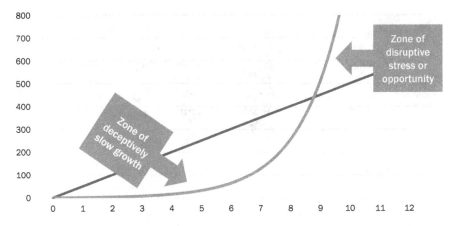

Fig. 1.4 Exponential versus linear growth

means that people—governments as well as the general public—do not see the doublings coming and thus do not respond either adequately or in a timely fashion. This also partially explains why many governments have a hard time reacting to advice from the science community on what measures are required to save people's lives. The numbers and growth are difficult to process and therefore difficult to believe.

Within the context of exponential growth, Ray Kurzweil and others in the exponential tech movement use the term "intuitive linear" to refer to the habitual human pattern of thinking locally and linearly without actually defining the term "intuition."[83] From the perspective of the continuum of consciousness and the nature of the mind, which we will briefly discuss within the context of Integral Theory in Chap. 2, researchers such as psychiatrist Arthur Deikman differentiate between lower-order intuition, which might apply within the context of linear/habitual thinking, and "higher intuition as a direct knowing of non-dual realities," which allows for human perceptions to extend beyond the boundaries of time and space.[84] Therefore, I recommend avoiding the term "intuition" unless its intended meaning is clearly defined.

John von Neumann, inventor of the von Neumann machine, one of the first computer architectures, recognized the impact of exponential growth and its acceleration of technology toward *singularity*—a term we will discuss later—as early as the 1950s.[85] Humanity is now at that seminal point of technological evolution where its exponential growth is becoming explosive and massively disruptive. Thus, if we want not only to survive but also to thrive in the twenty-first century, we must learn to think, and most important to *act*, *exponentially* and *globally*.

---

[83] Kurzweil (2005, p. 11).

[84] Deikman (1998).

[85] Oxtoby et al. (May 1958).

The Fun Game of Exponentials
To see just how few of us truly understand exponentials, try this game with your children or friends. Ask them what they would prefer: a dollar a day for the next 30 days or a penny on the first day, two pennies on the second, four on the third, and so on until the end of the 30 days. Their answer will tell you if they have the foresight to see the difference between $30 for the first choice and $10 million for the second.

I speak frequently at a variety of events, and in my presentations, I sometimes ask people if they understand exponential growth as a premise for surviving and thriving in this century. Without exception, there are people who roll their eyes, bored by my question, and I get it. Yet, when I have a chance to speak to them afterward, nine times out of ten I realize that they did not internalize exponentials, or if they did, they did not do so in mathematical terms. They seem oblivious to how rapidly exponential tech is going to change their own lives in the coming decades. It is difficult for most people to see that we are doubling the rate of technological progress every decade, which means that we can expect to see in 25 years—at today's rate—the same technological achievements that previously took us 100 years to make.[86] For example, assuming 1 step = 1 meter, 30 linear steps would take us 30 meters. Thirty exponential steps, however, would take us 1 meter for the first, 2 meters for the second, 4 meters for the third, and so on. By the time we had completed 30 exponential steps, we would have walked 1,073,741,824 meters. That is 26 times around the earth! Every exponential step is double the length of the preceding one. This is why exponential growth is so deceptive. No matter how fast a linear curve grows (see the green line in Fig. 1.4) it can never catch up with an exponential one once it has passed its deceptive phase at the knee of the curve. It becomes *disruptive*—and this is what we are currently experiencing in many areas of our global lives, from climate change through exponential growth of CO_2 emissions, to population growth or even exponential technology growth. As with the COVID-19 response, the sooner we understand this phenomenon, the sooner we can turn this challenge into an opportunity for us all by addressing climate change and creating collective abundance within planetary boundaries. *This is the caveat: We must ensure that exponential tech growth is guided to respect the limits of the physical context of Earth.*

If we do not observe the planetary boundaries, that growth threatens to destroy us, because it will exacerbate our current challenges. We must leverage our intelligence now to avoid making things worse—something we have not managed to date. Will we be able to use the double exponential growth in technology to address our challenges? Or, to paraphrase Ray Kurzweil: How can an intelligence create an intelligence more intelligent than itself within planetary boundaries?[87] To get closer

---

[86]Kurzweil (2005, p. 11).

[87]Kurzweil asks on p. 46 of The Age of Spiritual Machines (1999), "Can an intelligence create an intelligence more intelligent than itself?"

to an answer, let us continue to develop our understanding of exponentials and their potentially positive implications for our future. The following story might add to your understanding of the impact of exponentials—but if you are already bored with this, you may want to skip the next two paragraphs and go straight to the game you could play with your friends to see how well they understand exponentials.

The King and the Sage

According to an ancient legend, an Indian king who was a renowned chess lover often challenged visitors to his land to a game of chess. One day, the king challenged a traveling sage to a game and offered him any reward of his choice, should he win. The sage modestly asked only for a few grains of rice that should be counted in the following manner: Place a single grain of rice on the first chess square and double the number of grains on every subsequent square. The king agreed. When he lost the game, the king, a man of his word, ordered a sack of rice to be delivered so he could pay his dues. Then he had the rice grains placed according to the agreement: 1 grain on the first square, 2 on the second, 4 on the third, 8 on the fourth, and so on. The rice payment, as you can see, was based on exponential growth, and the king quickly realized that he was unable to pay his debt. On the 30th square, he would have had to put 1,000,000,000 grains of rice, and finally, on the 64th square, he would have had to place more than 18,000,000,000,000,000,000 grains of rice. The total debt equaled 210 billion tons of rice, enough to cover today's India with a one-meter-thick layer of rice.

We must never lose sight of the power of doubling: one doubling leads to 2 items, 10 doublings to 1,000 items, 20 to 1 million, and 30 to 1 billion. While we might still be able to make sense of the billion, the doublings on the second half of the chessboard result in almost inconceivable figures!

The story of the chessboard sums up why it is important to understand not only how technology has evolved throughout the history of humankind but, more importantly, how it will continue to drive progress with a double exponential acceleration. The key to this progress is the underlying force of evolution (see below). For now, let us focus on the exterior aspects of "evolution as a process of creating patterns of increasing order"[88] that goes through various stages and will ultimately function as a premise for the universe "to Wake Up" as Ray Kurzweil would say.[89]

---

[88] Kurzweil (2005, p. 14).

[89] Kurzweil (2005, p. 21).

1.3.3   Stages of Evolution

In *Life 3.0: Being Human in the Age of Artificial Intelligence*, MIT professor Max Tegmark defined life broadly as a "process that can retain its complexity and replicate."[90] While physicists still do not know what caused the Big Bang—or even if that really did trigger the beginning of our universe—there is a relatively strong consensus on what has occurred since the Big Bang. Understanding what occurred is extremely relevant in the context of this book because it helps us:

- Grasp the meaning of the exponentially growing complexity in which we live
- Prepare for this complexity
- Influence our future in the universe

So, please join me in the "most important conversation of our time"[91] as I unveil Kurzweil's six epochs of evolution and Tegmark's three lives.[92]

Epoch 1: *Physics and Chemistry* of evolution, as Kurzweil named it, occurred when the first atomic structures were built during the first few hundred thousand years after the Big Bang due to electrons that became trapped gravitating around nuclei made of protons and neutrons. In his view, "evolution works through indirection [because] it creates a capability and then uses that capability to evolve the next stage:"[93]

Epoch 2: *Biology and DNA.* Three and a half billion years ago, the first signs of life appeared when the first prokaryotic life structures developed after molecules were "born" through atoms that came together to build much more stable structures. They were simple life-forms that kept reproducing and evolving to build more complex biological systems, such as eukaryotic cells, that contained DNA and RNA molecules as information-storing structures and mechanisms, as well as cell membranes and nucleus membranes, mitochondria, and so on that enabled them to store energy and process information more efficiently. This was the first indication of how evolution rewards the ever-growing complexity of life. A billion years later, multicellular life-forms developed and began cooperating in large numbers to build multicellular organisms. Tegmark calls this Life 1.0 (biological stage) and says that it occurred as the "self-replicating information processing system whose information (software) determines both its behavior and the blueprints for its hardware." Note the distinction Tegmark makes between *hardware* (atoms and molecules) and *software* (DNA and RNA as the blueprint for atoms and molecules). It will be useful to you when we move on to exponentially growing information technology.

---

[90]Tegmark (2017, p. 48).

[91]Tegmark (2017, p. 22).

[92]Tegmark (2017, pp. 22–48).

[93]Kurzweil (2005, p. 15).

Epoch 3: *Brains* evolution began when early life-forms began to recognize patterns that were stored as information in specialized neural cells that enabled the building of intelligent life forms, from fish to *Homo sapiens.* Sticking with computer terminology, Tegmark sees this as the onset of Life 2.0 (cultural stage), when the hardware—atoms, molecules, cells, and organisms—has evolved somewhat without explicit influence from their participants, but—and this the crucial difference—the "software is largely designed"[94] through neural patterns, or learning. Humans are an example of Life 2.0 because we can create abstract models and redesign our world in our brains before transforming the world around us. This sets us apart from bacteria, for example, which are still in the Life 1.0 stage.

Epoch 4: *Technology* is the apogee of the ability of humans to influence the world through intelligence. For example, it took biological evolution 2 billion years from the creation of the first life-form to move on to the creation of the next paradigm, cells.[95] The technological evolution, however, needed only 14 years to move from the invention of the first personal computer,[96] in 1975, to the creation of the next paradigm, the World Wide Web.[97] Biological evolution ultimately led to extraordinary technological evolution, and we are just at the beginning of its exponential acceleration.

Epoch 5: *The Merger of Human Technology with Human Intelligence.* This epoch has already started and will continue to lead us toward the predicted *singularity* "with biological evolution leading directly to human-directed development"[98] and beyond. It is expected to eventually enable us to transcend the limitations of our biology, including our brains, through technology. For many of us, our smartphones have already become our "extended memory," our access to others, our business, our knowledge base. The expectation is that we will continue to enhance our human intelligence by exploiting the potential offered by that very intelligence.[99] However, we must learn to control our negative human tendencies, especially through the evolution of AI and the development of Life 3.0 (technological stage), as Tegmark called it. This is expected to occur within the next 100 years, with the expectation being that life will design not only its hardware but also its software.

Epoch 6: *The Universe Wakes Up.* In a far-off future, "intelligence, derived from its biological origins in human brains and its technological origins in human ingenuity, will begin to saturate the matter and energy"[100] and could circumvent the speed of light as a limiting factor on the transference of information to help the universe Wake

---

[94]Tegmark (2017, p. 26).

[95]Kurzweil (2005, p. 15).

[96]https://en.wikipedia.org/wiki/History_of_personal_computers

[97]https://webfoundation.org/about/vision/history-of-the-web/

[98]Kurzweil (2005, p. 17)

[99]Brynjolfsson and McAfee (2014); Kelly (2016).

[100]Kurzweil (2005, p. 21).

Up by evolving into "exquisitely sublime forms of intelligence." This is, of course, very speculative at this point, and we will leave it at that for now, keeping in mind that double exponential growth applies not only to the exterior, the physical part, of the world but also to the interior, the consciousness and the unconsciousness part of being.

We humans have set ourselves up to become increasingly intelligent as we merge with technology to the point where we will combine biological thinking with technological "thinking." But have we already arrived at the end of our biological evolution? Or are we not even close? Only the future will tell. As an AI-trained investor, I agree with Tegmark that we cannot completely eliminate the thought that humans may eventually build human-level artificial general intelligence (AGI) or even superintelligence[101]—a discussion we will have later. Tegmark goes beyond the possibility of superintelligence creation, stating, "Since we humans have managed to dominate Earth's other life forms by outsmarting them, it's plausible that we could be similarly outsmarted and dominated by superintelligence"[102]—a statement to which I would add the hope that we manage to avoid self-caused extinction in the process.

If we cannot decide for sure that superintelligence is unlikely, we had better get very smart very soon, understand it deeply, and begin taking safety precautions to prevent undesirable outcomes. This is why Tegmark founded the Future of Life Institute together with other concerned scientists including the late Stephen Hawking, Ray Kurzweil, and Dennis Hassabis, and serial entrepreneur Elon Musk. The institute came up with 23 Asilomar AI Principles.[103] These have been adopted by thousands of AI researchers, concerned scientists, and business and industry people, including Tom and me. Safety engineering for AI means preparing by envisioning what could go wrong to make sure we get it right. This is why I am also involved with the augmented intelligence[104] efforts of the institute.

1.3.4 Stages of Technology Acceleration

Within the context of technological evolution (Fig. 1.5), the majority of people generally think of Moore's Law, named after Intel's founder Geoffrey Moore by his friend Carver Mead, of Cal Tech.[105]

But Moore's Law refers to integrated circuits *only* and is the *fifth* in a lineup of technological evolutions after the mechanical calculators of the 1890s, Alan Turing's relays, the vacuum tube, and transistor-based computers. The twentieth century was

---

[101]Bostrom (2014).

[102]Tegmark (2017, p. 135).

[103]https://futureoflife.org/ai-principles/

[104]https://futureoflife.org/augmented-intelligence-summit-2019-2/

[105]Moore (1965).

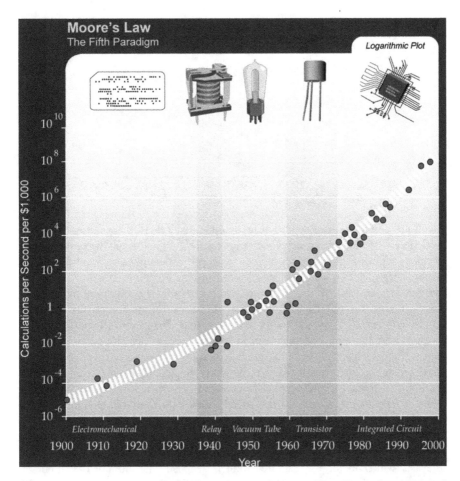

Fig. 1.5 Moore's Law: The fifth paradigm. (Source: Courtesy of Ray Kurzweil and Kurzweil Technologies Inc.)

one of the cruelest centuries in human history, with two world wars and tens of millions of casualties, not to mention numerous other, more localized conflicts, but it was also one of the most radical in terms of human achievement. The data relating to the exponential technology growth represented in Fig. 1.5 show only progress; there is no hint of that progress being negatively affected by concurrent existential threats.

Kurzweil calls this type of evolution the Law of Accelerating Returns[106]: the returns, such as the speed, massive cost reduction, or supremacy, of the evolutionary process, which explode exponentially over time. Within this context, it is important to note that Moore's Law and the Law of Accelerated Returns are brilliantly recognized evidence of a technological reality that describes certain regularities,

---

[106]Kurzweil (7 March 2001) & (2005, p. 35).

Fig. 1.6 The S-curve of
technological evolution

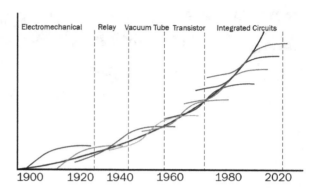

directions, and patterns of evolution in the digitalization era. They are not the same
types of laws we find in physics, for example, such as Newtonian laws or the laws of
thermodynamics, which described how our world works until they were challenged
by new laws such as quantum mechanics or Einstein's theory of relativity. What we
can expect, however, is that the next S-curve in Fig. 1.6 representing the next
paradigm in technology has already started, but because it is deceptively flat at the
beginning of the "S," it would barely be on our radar. The curve will undergo a rapid
phase of adoption and improvement, in which the tech that the curve represents
becomes more powerful while the price of that technology drops. When the technology matures, it reaches its apogee, the curve begins to flatten out, and the next
paradigm emerges. I cannot emphasize enough the importance of these S-curves in
terms of reflecting the reality of fast-paced technology adoption. Due to the exponential nature of the curves and our human inability to interpret them properly,
mainstream analysts have constantly misunderstood them and consequently did not
forecast technology evolution accurately. They relied on their traditional linear
forecasts, which do not fully capture exponential speed. The adoption of cell phones
and the proliferation of photovoltaic solar panels are two everyday real-life examples
that challenged the authority of linear forecasting.

When all the paradigms are stacked on top of each other as in Fig. 1.6, we can
clearly see that the rate of technological advancement occurs at an accelerated pace
alongside an exponential curve. This explains how our physical world is amplified
by the digital world, which itself is colliding with, for example, artificial intelligence,
blockchain, robotics, Internet of Things (IoT), neurotechnology, nanotechnology,
bioinformatics, advanced material, robotics, quantum computing, and 3D printing.
One exponential growth that is mentioned less often, but is not less relevant,
occurred even faster than that of computation: growth in telecommunication technology for data transmission. Its explosive advance—due to accelerating developments in improved optical switches, electromagnetic technologies, and fiber
optics—made the proliferation of today's applications possible. Overall, I agree
with Peter Diamandis that "tomorrow's speed of change will make today look like

we're crawling,"[107] because evolution applies positive feedback in such a manner that more evolved forms from a previous stage of development are used to create the next stage. Thus, the next stage both transcends and includes the previous stage and the exponential growth progresses over time in such a manner that *the rate of exponential growth itself grows exponentially.* So, if you feel that the world is accelerating and getting more complex every day, or that you are struggling to keep up, never mind catch up, with the avalanche of information or emails, or the explosion of technological advances from autonomous cars to genetic engineering, 3D printing, or robotics, you are right. Why? Because *the rate of exponential growth itself grows exponentially* and the way in which it acts upon us means we can no longer see it. Furthermore, we are only at the *beginning* of these exponential curves, and the speed of progress will only increase if nothing happens to interrupt it. As we saw earlier, both the biological evolution and the technological evolution are examples of exponentially accelerating processes whereby the technological evolution has evolved to support the biological evolution. The key to technological evolution has been, and continues to be, the ongoing aggregation of humanity's collective intelligence over millennia. The importance of grasping the full significance of the double exponential growth in technology therefore cannot be overstated, for it has the potential to help us overcome our global great challenges if properly leveraged and steered in the right direction. The nature of evolution will eventually flatten out Moore's Law, but Kurzweil's Law of Accelerating Returns forecasts the emergence of the next paradigm that will continue to drive exponential growth.

To understand this at a deeper level, let us take the time to look at it step by step and see (1) how accelerated computation brought us to where we are today and (2) how we can prepare for tomorrow.

Exponential investors, entrepreneurs, and other progressive stakeholders use the 6Ds of acceleration as a technological road map to predict future technologies and when and how to capitalize on the opportunities giving them an advantage over those who do not understand the implications of those new technologies. The 6Ds were popularized by Peter Diamandis and Steve Kotler in their book *Bold: How to Go Big, Create wealth, and Impact the World,*[108] as a roadmap to show what can happen when an exponential technology is born and to help prepare for it, because technology never goes back and it provides opportunities to impact the lives of millions of people:

1. *Digitalization* is the logical consequence of the Law of Accelerating Returns. It enables technology to turn every product or service into "1's and 0's." For example, music CDs followed analog vinyl albums and turned them into digital and thus, for most people, much better-quality music. From IBM to Google to Amazon, data center construction is mushrooming, yet those of us who invest in sustainable data centers clearly see how it is still normal in the construction

---

[107]https://tinyurl.com/rnbcc27

[108]Diamandis and Kotler (2015).

industry to work with pen and paper, and that the industry as a whole is having a hard time adapting to digitalization or adopting new technologies to scale production. A *Harvard Business Review* article from April 2016 noted that construction came second only to agriculture, out of 22 sectors covered in the article, in terms of being a late adopter of digitalization.[109] This reluctance to embrace digitalization is not sustainable from a business perspective. Once something becomes digitalized, it becomes subject to exponential growth and the Law of Accelerating Returns. Thus, it becomes easily and ubiquitously accessible. We will see later how entire professions from legal clerks to radiologists will be transformed, even eliminated, through AI systems that are much faster and more accurate than humans. Now ask yourself: How are you digitalizing your investment processes and businesses?

2. *Deception*: As illustrated in the king and the sage story and in Fig. 1.4, in the early stages of digitalization, the process of doubling is deceptive, for we barely register its impact until we get to the second half of the metaphorical chessboard. And in Fig. 1.3, we saw how, at the dawn of the Internet boom, people in Germany did not see the same potential in the Internet that my husband and I saw. And look at CDs. They were sold for more than 10 years until the music industry began taking notice, at which point they finally became profitable. The German automobile industry, which still builds mainly combustion engines, is a contemporary example of the impact of deception. It was not until Tesla threatened the big players in that market, from Mercedes to BMW to Audi/VW, that they began to react. Rumor has it that the Quandt family built the electric cars i3 and i8 on their own, despite extreme internal opposition from their own company, BMW. Now ask yourself: What trends do you not see that may disrupt your investments and businesses?

One of my personal experiences of deception comes from the summer of 1985 when Tom and I were exchange students at Stanford. At that time, Ken Olsen, founder of Digital Equipment Corporation (DEC, the second-largest computer company worldwide at the time after IBM), decided not to productize the RISC-based (Reduced Instruction Set Computing) workstations that were leading-edge technology at the time and had been developed in his own company at DEC's Western Research Lab in Palo Alto, by a team led by Stanford Professor Forrest Basket. Olsen was so blinded ("deceived") by his own old, proprietary hardware VAX and PDP/11 and operating system VAX/VMS that he refused to productize the modern RISC computer technology using Unix, the new operating system.

I remember as if it were yesterday how the RISC developers left the conference room weeping about the management decision from the east

(continued)

---

[109]https://hbr.org/2016/04/a-chart-that-shows-which-industries-are-the-most-digital-and-why

coast where DEC was headquartered. In our view, that incident was one of many similar ones that marked the beginning of the end for DEC. Within days, most RISC developers had left DEC and started their own companies, with Forrest Basket who co-founded Silicon Graphics being one of the most prominent. The rest is history.

3. *Disruption*: When the Internet became mainstream through the World Wide Web as technology that allowed us to share large amounts of data faster and cheaper, old business models were massively disrupted. The iPhone is the best example of this disruption, and not only in the context of the phone industry but also the camera, music, computer, and GPS industries, to name but four. But as we saw earlier, disruption is not a new phenomenon. Ken Olsen did not only not productize at the time the RISC computing technology; he also repeated his mistake with the PC and even AI, despite DEC being a market leader in the sector at the time with their Expert Systems. Olsen is also credited as having said, "There is no reason for any individual to have a computer in his home."[110] Eventually, DEC was acquired first by Compaq, a workstation newcomer, and then by Hewlett-Packard. DEC had everything those companies needed to lead the world of computing at the time, but Olsen was somewhat deceived by his previous successes. I worked in his organization, so I knew that he did not listen to those who saw the need for change—that is, until DEC was literally disrupted. This simple example shows that disruption must be recognized and acted upon early to prevent destruction rather than disruption. According to research by McKinsey & Company, digitalization is high on the agendas of top CEOs and boards in order to prevent disruption that could lead to massive reductions in corporate profits globally from 10% of global GDP right now to less than 8% in 2025, offsetting the gains of the past three decades.[111] But the question remains: How to implement an exponential jump in a global world with a linear and local mindset? Digital transformation means not only technology adoption and transformation but also a psychological mind shift, as well as behavioral change and adaptive processes (see below). Now ask yourself: What trends are there that will disrupt your investments and businesses? How might you or your life change when a certain product or service that you care about becomes disruptive?

4. *Demonetization*: I mentioned earlier that Moore's Law is the fifth paradigm in technological evolution (Fig. 1.5) after the development of the electrotechnical, relay, vacuum tube, and transistor paradigms. It refers to the density of integrated circuits (IC), which has doubled every 18–24 months for more than 50 years now, leading to extraordinary computing power. It can be expected that this paradigm will eventually be replaced by the next one, which could very well be quantum

---

[110]https://en.wikiquote.org/wiki/Ken_Olsen

[111]https://tinyurl.com/ybtk4nxx

computing,[112] but that is beyond the scope of this book. The result of Moore's Law, however, has extended beyond an exponential increase in computation power; it has also led to massive cost reductions, or demonetization, as the cost of computer memory imploded and the communication bandwidth exploded. Once a device or application has been developed, the cost of replicating it is essentially zero. One current example of demonetization and dematerialization (see below) that I can relate to on a personal–professional level is data centers, which are springing up around the world as a result of digitization. According to the 2019 report by the Global Alliance for Buildings and Construction, IEA, and UNEP, the buildings and construction sector together account for "almost 40% of [global] energy- and process-related emissions" making "climate action in buildings and construction [as] among the most cost-effective" measures we could take.[113] However, the report continues, "the sector is not on track with the level of climate action necessary. On the contrary, final energy demand in buildings in 2018 rose 1% from 2017, and 7% from 2010." Now ask yourself: What trends will demonetize the products and services in which you have invested and/or built a business around? How might you or your work change when a certain product or service that you care about becomes *demonetized*?

Investment Example: Ultra Energy Efficient Data Centers

As our contribution toward reducing CO_2 emissions and to avoid building stranded assets for future generations, Tom and I invest in ultra-energy-efficient green data centers that use water-cooling rather than air-cooling technologies and thus can reduce construction costs and operating costs by up to 50%.[114] This way we can begin to decouple the increasing need for IT capacity from resource consumption. The greatest challenge we face when doing this is finding architects and construction companies that can build data centers using digital technologies so we can serve the accelerating demand and scale fast. In other words, we are positively disrupting these industries through the application of software within architecture design, vertical team development, paperless construction sites, and so on.

5. *Dematerialization*: CDs and CD players replaced analog records and record players. However, with exponential growth in computation power and communication bandwidth, as well as significant reductions in storage costs, CD technology was in turn eventually *dematerialized* and eliminated all together. Today we download music and video files from one device to another in no time and at virtually zero cost (the ethics, copyright, and moral rights implications of this are outside the scope of this book). This is another everyday example of how

---

[112]https://tinyurl.com/y9q8yg5q

[113]Global Alliance for Buildings and Construction, IEA and UNEP (2019, p. 3).

[114]https://www.ta.hu-berlin.de/res/co.php?id=14935

exponential technology can turn material things into digital applications. We no longer carry around separate heavy GPS equipment, cameras, or video or audio recorders. These devices were *dematerialized* within only a few years and became an app on our smartphones at no additional cost to users—and the environmental bonus is that we have fewer pieces of equipment to dispose of when we want to upgrade to newer and better versions. Now ask yourself: How will *dematerialization* affect your own investments, products, or services? Are there any components that would become obsolete? How can you prepare for that?

6. *Democratization*: Technology has always had a massive impact on society, but it is only when it leads to *democratization*, or availability at massive scale, that we see how it can also lead to abundance for all. The Internet and mobile communication are prime examples of this. Once products and services are digitalized, they are globally available and thus become ubiquitous. For example, in 2016, 4.8 billion people—two-thirds of the world's population—had access to mobile communication. This has had a remarkable transformative impact on all our lives. We have transformed how we work and do business with each other, how we connect, and how we entertain or educate ourselves. We raise and educate our children in a different way than we were raised and educated, and we connect with each other differently. Moreover, how we invest our talents, time, money, and resources is changing in significant ways too. Humans are explorers, and we now have the opportunity to become a multiplanetary species, as Elon Musk and other space investors such as Richard Branson, Peter Diamandis, and Jeff Bezos are trying to demonstrate.[115] Now ask yourself: How might your product or service become easily available globally without barriers? What benefits and challenges could arise with the democratization of your products?

Now that we have a deeper understanding of the hidden determinants of technological acceleration, the 6Ds, let us take a closer look at how their manifestation increases that acceleration even more, especially as we embark on the Fourth Industrial Revolution. We will also take a closer look at various applications of exponentially growing technologies, from healthcare to entertainment, to better understand why these sectors are so attractive to investors and entrepreneurs. Moreover, we will look at what we can do to leverage these technologies to address the grand global challenges (GGCs).

---

[115]https://www.ft.com/content/fcb1f970-031c-11e9-9d01-cd4d49afbbe3

1.4 Disruptive Technologies and the Grand Global Challenges

The First Industrial Revolution[116] was initiated in the eighteenth century through the invention of the water wheel and the steam engine, which enabled human civilization to move from being an agrarian and rural society to being a largely industrialized and urban society. The Second Industrial Revolution occurred between 1870 and 1914 through electrification, telephony, the phonograph, and light bulbs. It enabled the mass production of consumer goods and the invention of the internal combustion engine and marked the beginning of the massive growth society. The Third Industrial Revolution, also called the Digital Revolution, dates from the second half of the twentieth century, a time that saw wide-scale use of computers—including PCs—by the average person in their own home, general access to the Internet, and the overall development of information and communication technology (ICT). In *The Third Industrial Revolution: How Lateral Power Is Transforming Energy, the Economy, and the World*, published in 2013, Jeremy Rifkin argues that technological advances have the potential to help us make our society a sustainable one through the large-scale development and deployment of renewable energy, the Internet of Things (IoT), and autonomous transportation. In his view, a circular economy, logistics, communication, and information management are key factors that can take us closer to such deep transformations. Rifkin was basically setting the scene for the Fourth Industrial Revolution, which builds on its predecessor and relies on the exponential development of technology that has, in turn, led to the development of a number of new fields, including AI, robotics, nanotechnology, biotechnology, quantum computing, 3D printing, and autonomous vehicles.

No matter what we do personally or professionally, we are all investors. We cannot not invest. Whether we have disposable income and decide to make a living out of investing per se, or we simply drive a car, or go shopping for food, clothing, or furniture, we are investors. As a species, we invest our time and money, one way or another, and thus influence the economy, politics, the environment, and the state of our planet. Investing is a very personal endeavor. Those of us who are professional investors and company builders are first and foremost human beings with their own preferences, knowledge, and expertise. This is why most investors focus their investment activities on what is immediately important and interesting and brings reward, joy, and fulfillment to them. As you read through this chapter, you will see that it is absolutely possible and realistic to leverage the incontrovertible power of capital to balance your goals as an investor with the goal of addressing the grand global challenges (GGCs).

---

[116]Schwab (2016).

1.4.1 Human Health and Longevity

What if we could eradicate diseases like Parkinson's, Alzheimer's, or ALS (amyotrophic lateral sclerosis, also known as Lou Gehrig's disease), the progressive neurodegenerative illness that gradually paralyzed eminent physicist Stephen Hawking over the decades? What if we could eradicate the flu and deadly viruses such as HIV or eliminate pain for good? Would we do it? And if we did, who would decide who gets access to treatment? Governments, regulators, scientists, doctors, corporate leaders, individuals, parents? What if only the rich could afford it?

> My beloved mother passed away after a decade of suffering from Parkinson's disease. My father died of bladder cancer, my mother-in-law died of pancreatic cancer, and my father-in-law died of prostate cancer. This is why Tom and I are both deeply interested in alleviating suffering and have a history of investing in medical advances and healthcare in general. We view this as our humble contribution to the integral impact.

We already have ante-natal screening techniques such as amniocentesis that can detect genetic abnormalities in a fetus, and in jurisdictions where women have the right to choose, a fetus with genetic abnormalities may be aborted. Who decides what behavior is ethical and what is unethical? And what of gene editing? There is a growing fear among many people about the implications of gene editing not just for ourselves but also for future generations.

In the context of cancer, for example, the prospect of using gene editing to cure it would most likely be perceived as a positive use of the science, but what if people wanted to have their genes edited to look better or be better at sports? What about bio-engineering an unborn child to have blue eyes, blond hair, or athletic prowess? Should bio-engineering be globally outlawed? What if a country did not comply? Doping is already a serious problem in sport. What would global acceptance of gene editing mean for the Olympic Games? Or the Tour de France? Would all sports competitions become meaningless? What if some people could afford to bio-engineer their bodies to double their life expectancy while others could not afford to eat? The emerging field of digital and synthetic biology raises monumental issues, but it could also solve monumental problems while forcing humanity to come up with better global governance.[117]

The DNA of living organisms changes on an ongoing basis. It always has. Humans have been genetically modifying organisms for the past 10,000 years by, for example, crossing and selectively breeding new crops and new varieties of dogs and/or other domesticated animals; and viruses and bacteria have been performing

---

[117]https://tinyurl.com/y36zkoku

this kind of "gene swapping" for millennia.[118] But researchers have only been able to sequence the human genome and develop the tools to help them change genomes relatively inexpensively in order to achieve specific, desired outcomes since research from the Human Genome Project,[119] launched in 1990 and completed in 2003, became available. DNA editing and gene therapies have changed and will continue to change, life as we know it forever. According to experts, of 50,000 currently known genetic diseases that affect humans, simply swapping one base pair of genes for another in the genetic code has the ability to heal such 32,000 of them.[120] CRISPR (Clustered Regularly Interspaced Short Palindromic Repeats), for example, may allow us to beat diseases such as cancer and tumors, sickle cell anemia, and cystic fibrosis, to name only a few.[121] By inserting designed molecules into cells, CRISPR changes the existing DNA sequence in that cell precisely, permanently, and relatively inexpensively. This gene-editing technology makes it possible to take a gene inside a virus and use that virus as a vehicle to inject the gene into target cells. It is groundbreaking, it is occurring now, and it has become extremely important in addressing pandemics such as COVID-19. We can use CRISPR-edited genes offer the prospect of allowing us to:

- *Develop proper tests for viruses* such as COVID-19, as soon as their viral sequence has been identified.[122]
- *Genetically alter species of mosquitoes* in order to stop the spread of malaria, which is responsible for over 400,000 deaths each year.[123]
- *Genetically engineer animals* such as horses to have higher muscle mass[124] or cure muscular dystrophy in dogs.[125]
- *Enable same-sex healthy female mice to give birth* to mice that are then able to have babies on their own.[126]
- *Begin to end addiction.*[127]

If we can heal muscular dystrophy in dogs, imagine what possibilities lie ahead for humans. We have already seen the use of CRISPR-edited genes in China to enable the birth of baby girls Lulu and Nana, who underwent gene editing while they were single-cell embryos to protect them from HIV.[128] Another gene therapy has

---

[118]Robinson and Dunning Hotopp (1 October 2016).

[119]https://www.genome.gov/human-genome-project

[120]https://www.sciencedaily.com/releases/2017/10/171025140532.htm

[121]https://www.cell.com/nucleus-CRISPR

[122]https://tinyurl.com/rhfqvuc viewed 3 April 2020.

[123]Poinar et al. (2019).

[124]Rooney et al. (2018).

[125]Regalado (24 August 2018).

[126]Li et al. (2019), https://tinyurl.com/ycctkyg3

[127]Li et al. (2019), https://tinyurl.com/ycctkyg3

[128]Cyranoski and Ledford (26 November 2018) and YouTube video https://tinyurl.com/qrkpf2b

been shown capable of altering and/or correcting vision in patients with a rare genetic cause of blindness called choroideremia.[129]

These developments have unarguably offered hope to many of us, but they have also created major ethical and moral dilemmas, and 18 leading researchers, including some of the original developers of CRISPR/Cas9, recently called for a moratorium on editing human genes that can be passed on to the next generation.[130]

As investors, we can use our capital to get directly involved in, influence, invest in, and potentially accelerate the development of such treatments and cures. The air travel analogy of securing your own oxygen mask in an emergency before helping others is sliding into cliché (not to mention bordering on ironic in the context of grand global challenges), but we cannot effectively address problems such as climate change if we are too unhealthy to function well. In other words, step one should be to address our own health problems, and we can do that through emerging technologies. For example, companies such as Human Longevity, BenevolentAI, Futura Genetics, and Stealth BioTherapeutics, to name only four,[131] can help identify, and are increasingly able to address, individual genetic predispositions by leveraging advances in cell-therapy diagnostics, AI for medicine, genomic analysis, or mitochondrial dysfunction, and other health-related areas. Another area that Tom and I and other investors are watching closely is the field of stem cell research. Potential applications of human stem cells are to (a) help the 1.2 million people who await yearly an organ transplant by growing transplantable autologous human organs within the embryos of other mammals as an alternative to xenotransplantation (transplanting animal organs into humans)[132] and (b) naturally regenerate human joints, thus omitting the need to transplant artificial ones.[133] From an exponential investor's perspective, the fascinating thing is that future solutions in healthcare are likely to come from US tech giants such as Apple, Amazon, Google, and IBM, as well as Asian tech companies such as Alibaba, Samsung, and Tencent. Apple CEO Tim Cook corroborated this when he said that "Apple's greatest contribution to mankind" will be the empowerment of "the individual to manage their health."[134]

And let us not forget bacteria. Bacteria have evolved over millennia to be able to react to chemicals in the environment, and that characteristic is being exploited now for the greater good. FREDsense,[135] for example, is a Canadian company that embeds small DNA circuits in bacteria to program them to monitor water quality, produce clean water, and treat wastewater. The signals produced by the bacteria are quantitative and highly accurate and can be picked up in real time by FRED (Field

---

[129]Xue et al. (2018).

[130]Lander et al. (2019).

[131]https://www.humanlongevity.com/; https://benevolent.ai/; https://www.futuragenetics.com/en/; https://www.stealthbt.com/

[132]Yamaguchi et al. (9 February 2017).

[133]Oberbauer et al. (2015).

[134]https://mashable.com/article/tim-cook-apple-health/?europe=true#2_RYZocC7kqU

[135]https://www.fredsense.com/

Fig. 1.7 Protein bar made
from dehydrated
cultured meat

Ready Electrochemical Detector), which will know instantaneously if a water supply is contaminated. FRED could be used to monitor all sorts of water supplies, including those in the mining, pharmaceutical, or sewage treatment industry. And because it is cost-effective, it could be used to transform water quality globally.

Bacteria can be bio-engineered for a number of other uses as well. Cambrian Innovations,[136] for example, a company that was recognized in 2019 by the World Economic Forum as the circular economy tech disruptor, is using electrically functional microbes to produce electricity, heat, and clean water from sewage. And a team of researchers from the United Kingdom and Finland made headlines in the science world when they modified *E.coli* bacteria to produce engine-ready propane, thus rendering fracking obsolete.[137]

Moving up the evolution tree from single-cell bacteria, companies such as Modern Meadow[138] are experimenting with higher life-forms by altering DNA and injecting it into living cells to grow collagen, an animal protein. That collagen is then used to bio-fabricate leather. It leaves a smaller planetary footprint than raising animals to do so. Several companies are also making progress in the production of meat protein without exploiting animals.[139] The photograph below, which I took at the BIOTOPIA Eat Festival[140] in Munich, Germany, shows a mock-up of protein bars made of dehydrated cultured meat that are grown in a laboratory (Fig. 1.7).

[136]https://cambrianinnovation.com/

[137]https://labiotech.eu/industrial/imperial-turku-escherichia-coli-propane-biofuels/

[138]http://www.modernmeadow.com/

[139]https://www.scientificamerican.com/article/lab-grown-meat/

[140]https://www.biotopia.net/en/ and https://www.biotopia.net/de/events/biotopiafestival

Memphis Meats[141] is a start-up that is producing meat from meat cells instead of animals. It cooks and tastes like regular meat and produces significantly smaller amounts of greenhouse gas emissions than traditional meat production—and there is no slaughter involved.

Organovo, which in 2009 became the first company to receive an NIH grant to create bio-printed blood vessels,[142] has reproduced human tissue through bio-printing. 3D tissues can be used to study diseases and develop new drugs. Eventually, this bio-printing process could lead to printing tissues and organs for human transplant—a prospect that may sound far-fetched but was demonstrated on April 15, 2019, by Israeli scientists who successfully 3D-printed the first heart using a patient's own cells.[143]

These developments are all extremely promising and exciting. We are already using our smartphones, computers, and the Internet to extend our memories, knowledge, and communication skills; and we are fast approaching the point where we take for granted the practice of replacing various body parts with nonbiological materials such as titanium. This all suggests that we are moving from our biological-only evolution toward a hybrid construct that combines both biological and nonbiological elements, such as those that exist today, and will eventually include nanobots—also called nano-robots—that will enter our bodies at nanoscale. We would appear to be on the cusp of the next paradigm shift in human life, moving from biohumanism to neurohumanism to posthumanism.[144]

Four Bridges for the Future of Healthcare

In *Fantastic Voyage: Live Long Enough to Live Forever*, Ray Kurzweil and Terry Grossman[145] envision three bridges that could lead to radical life extension in humans between now and 2045:

- Bridge One (now) consists of today's antiaging therapies and health advice found in mainstream culture and literature; for example, articles about healthy eating habits, the benefits of regular exercise, meditation, supplements, and the pursuit of a meaningful life.[146] (In their 2009 sequel to Fantastic Voyage, Transcendence: Nine Steps to Living Well Forever, they provide a detailed guide to Bridge One.[147]) The intention of Bridge One is to help slow the aging process until Bridge Two becomes available.
- Bridge Two (envisioned for 2025–2030) will draw on advances made during the biotechnology revolution and use antiaging knowledge harvested from decoding the biology of the human genetic and protein codes. Its goal is "understanding and

---

[141]https://www.memphismeats.com/

[142]https://organovo.com/

[143]https://www.engadget.com/2019/04/15/tel-aviv-university-3d-printed-heart/

[144]See https://transcend.me/pages/three-bridges-to-immortality

[145]Kurzweil and Grossman (2004).

[146]Kurzweil and Grossman (2004).

[147]Kurzweil and Grossman (2009).

reprogramming the outdated software of life."[148] This could occur, for example, through genetically re-engineering DNA damage,[149] by growing new organs,[150] or by mending a heart after a heart attack.[151]

- Bridge Three (2045–The Singularity) consists of the nanotechnology revolution and AI, which Durairaj et al. expect to help rebuild our bodies at the molecular level through the use of medical nano-robots.[152] Nano-robots—also known as nanoids, nanites, or nanomites—are rather hypothetical devices that can range in size between 0.1 and 10 micrometers and are made up of nanoscale or molecular components. They are intended to perform microsurgery, nano dentistry, diagnosis and testing, gene therapy, and cancer detection and treatment, and thus heal disease.[153]

Kurzweil and Grossman concluded that these three bridges might eventually lead to a tipping point in human existence,[154] which Aubrey de Grey[155] called the "longevity escape velocity"—the point when we should be able to stop and eventually reverse the aging process. In 2018, Kurzweil stated that humanity could possibly reach the "longevity escape velocity" around 2030.[156] That would then induce Bridge Four, which would consist of the human ability to back ourselves up just as computers, smartphones, and other devices currently do. In other words, we could, in theory, encode our knowledge, skills, and personality in the form of data that could be uploaded and backed up in the cloud. In his view, "part of our thinking will be non-biological ... [which] will be able to grow exponentially so it will ultimately predominate ... That part will ultimately be so smart that it will be able to back up our biological part as well."[157]

1.4.2   In Service of Our Planet's Health

Living in a solar-powered age is no longer a dream, because technology—note, not governments—is coming online to address the health of our planet. In 2018, reports showed that the United Kingdom was leading the way in solar power with a record weekly production of 533 gigawatt hours (GWh) of solar power displacing natural

---

[148]See Kurzweil quote from video at minute 17:30. Viewed 5 August 2018 at https://tinyurl.com/ued3sfn

[149]Perera et al. (2016).

[150]https://www.livescience.com/59675-body-parts-grown-in-lab.html

[151]http://news.mit.edu/2015/laurie-boyer-mending-broken-heart-0803

[152]Durairaj et al. (2012).

[153]Cavalcanti et al. (2008).

[154]Kurzweil and Grossman (2009, pp. 403–406).

[155]De Grey and Rae (2007).

[156]https://www.youtube.com/watch?v=_ryxuehnp8k&feature=youtu.be

[157]https://www.youtube.com/watch?v=_ryxuehnp8k&feature=youtu.be

gas as the number one energy source between June 21 and 28, 2018. Germany also achieved a new record that year, with a monthly production of 6.17 terawatt hours (TWh), and Denmark had a record 361 h of sun in May, leading to a 33% increase in solar electricity production.[158] While governments of developed nations with strong economies appear to be slow to change—for example, Germany's government decided to phase out coal only by 2038,[159] and the United States' current government denies the very possibility of human-caused climate change—developing countries are actively moving toward the normalization of sustainable energy sources nationwide. Egypt, for example, is currently building the Benban Solar Park that will be the world's fourth-largest solar power plant and will produce approximately 3.8 TWh per annum.[160] The island nation of Palau, like the Maldives, Indonesia, and many other island nations, is under threat from rising sea levels due to climate change. Palau's government has therefore pledged to move away from deriving 90% of the country's current energy from diesel to using 100% renewable energy by the end of this decade. This transition will come at no cost to the government, as it has decided to use technology such as predictive analysis and AI to build not only a digital market place for solar panel manufacturers but also massive storage capacity to initiate the first and fastest shift to 100% renewable energy use.[161] And things are happening in the private sector too. In an effort to capture a larger portion of the sun's electromagnetic spectrum and to yield a 90% more efficient solar cell than traditional modules, NovaSolix, which focuses on renewable solar energy, announced in November 2018 its intention to use carbon nanotubes—which will cost 10% of the price of traditional solar modules—for its technology. The company plans to deliver electricity for 0.3 cents/kilowatt hour (kWh), making it cheaper to build new wind and solar power plants than to run existing, and subsidized, coal and gas plants: the "unsubsidized cost to build new utility wind and solar facilities is equal to, and often less than running already-built fossil facilities."[162] This is extremely significant, because now the market, not slow regulators, will dictate reasonable behavior in terms of addressing climate change.

Technology is also critical for the unmanned aerial vehicles (UAVs), solar cars, and other electric vehicles that aim to replace current fossil fuel-based transportation and help soothe some of our planet's pain. For example, Gen4solar, the world-record holder for single-junction solar cell efficiency, has improved the weight-to-power ratio of its solar cell by 160%.[163] The intention is to accelerate the adoption of autonomous electric vehicles that can recharge while in use, to extend their

---

[158]http://www.solarpowereurope.org/looking-back-on-a-record-breaking-solar-summer/

[159]Commission on Growth, Structural Change and Employment-Final Report. Viewed 6 July 2019 at https://tinyurl.com/y49xcs8s

[160]https://en.wikipedia.org/wiki/Benban_Solar_Park

[161]https://www.fastcompany.com/90203041/this-island-nation-is-making-the-fastest-ever-shift-to-renewables

[162]https://pv-magazine-usa.com/2018/11/23/all-i-want-for-christmas-is-a-90-efficient-solar-panel/

[163]https://tinyurl.com/uo5q2cr

endurance, and to keep the impact on aerodynamics and design to a minimum. Solar energy must be stored somewhere, of course, and technology is also helping improve storage capacity.

Energy and storage are crucial for digitalizing sustainable mobility. The solutions currently available can only benefit from further development, and this in turn will require the development of new materials. BP and Daimler have both invested in Storedot, which develops modern materials through a combination of nanotechnology and new organic compounds. Storedot has developed technologies for optimized, fast-charging batteries for mobile devices and lithium-ion batteries that can be charged in 5 minutes and have a 500-kilometer range,[164] and WiTricity,[165] a Massachusetts-based company, is working on a cordless technology that should deliver power to car batteries in a wireless manner using magnetic resonance. WiTricity's technology has the potential to make charging car batteries simpler than filling up your car at the pump in the traditional (that is to say, current) way.

The price of lithium-ion batteries has dropped by an average of 20% per annum since 2010, further contributing to the accessibility factor.[166] Battery technologies are a good example of the challenges we face in balancing the requirements of the SDGs and respecting planetary boundaries. There is significant room for improvement with respect to their environmental and social friendliness,[167] but they are a move in the right direction and, with the proper mindset, we have the potential to overcome their current drawbacks. The important part is the storage aspect. The Tesla Gigafactory 1 is delivering an annualized run rate of approximately 20 GWh, which makes it the highest-volume battery plant in the world. It "produces more batteries in terms of kWh than all other carmakers combined."[168] Tesla is planning to build an additional 10 Gigafactories worldwide after its Buffalo, NY, and Shanghai, China, plants have been completed in order to accelerate the adoption of renewable power technology and help us break free of the current fossil-fueled economy that is so damaging to the planet.[169]

These technologies are already marking the beginning of the end for coal, gas, and diesel, and they are contributing significantly to the implementation of the Paris Agreement, because while solar energy may not be subsidized, it makes more economic sense to use it rather than energy produced through subsidized coal power plants. According to research by Carbon Tracker,[170] 42% of coal plants are running at a loss today. This is predicted to increase to 96% by 2030, making coal-produced energy financially not viable. In the words of Peter Diamandis, "we no

---

[164]https://www.store-dot.com/

[165]http://witricity.com/

[166]https://tinyurl.com/ybvoq6tg

[167]Korthauer (2018).

[168]Tesla SEC filing. Viewed 12 March 2019 at http://ir.tesla.com/node/18941/html

[169]https://en.wikipedia.org/wiki/Gigafactory_1

[170]See 42% of Global Coal Power Plants Run at a Loss, Finds World-first Study (30 November 2018). Viewed 3 April 2020 at https://tinyurl.com/vwzf47j

longer kill whales to light our night and we will stop ravaging mountain sides as well."[171]

1.4.3   Food and Water

A January 2019 EAT-*Lancet* Commission report titled *Food in the Anthropocene: The EAT-Lancet Commission on Healthy Diets from Sustainable Food Systems* declared 2019 the year of nutrition and confirmed that food production is the largest source of environmental degradation.[172] With the world's population expected to reach 10 billion by 2050,[173] an overhaul of current food production systems is key to the successful implementation of the Paris Agreement and Agenda 2030. Whether we act as individuals or corporate entities, we can all help to make food production sustainable by:

- *Eliminating fossil fuels use*, thus turning land use into a net carbon sink
- *Stopping net expansion of cropland* by optimizing current land use for food production
- *Significantly reducing water use*
- *Improving fertilizer technologies*
- *Changing our eating habits*
- *Reducing food waste*

What is the state of the art in terms of technology-driven, sustainable food production and water supplies, and how do we repair a damaged environment? In the immediate term, vertical agriculture could hold the key to sustainable food production in urban areas. A large percentage of the growing population will live in megacities, and urban farming offers a way to provide them with fresh food sourced locally, making it both cheaper and environmentally more responsible thanks to the reduced need for transportation to market. AeroFarms, for example, is a mission-driven, certified B (benefit) corporation that uses a patented aeroponic technology to grow plants that need less than 95% of the water generally needed in a conventional outdoor farm, no sunlight, and no soil or pesticides.[174] It operates all-year-round inside a former steel mill and paintball arena in Newark, New Jersey, and annually yields approximately 39 times more food per square meter than a traditional farm—and with minimal environmental impact. ("A benefit corporation is a new legal tool that creates a solid foundation for long term mission alignment and value creation. It protects mission through capital raises and leadership changes, creates

---

[171]From the Abundance 360 conference 2019 introduction https://tinyurl.com/y2trxgxf

[172]Willett (19 January 2019). See https://tinyurl.com/sublssc and https://tinyurl.com/t3huy2c

[173]Roser and Ortiz-Ospina (2017a/2013).

[174]https://aerofarms.com/

more flexibility when evaluating potential sale and liquidity options, and prepares businesses to lead a mission-driven life.")[175]

Iron Ox, a fully automated farm, is dedicated to addressing multiple grand global challenges, including climate change, by eliminating food waste and providing food security for our ever-growing population through sustainable and scalable food production. It operates inside a former commercial warehouse in San Carlos, Silicon Valley, and uses robots to grow green leafy foods. Its "hydroponic growing system uses 90% less water over traditional farming while growing 30 times the amount of crops" on the same amount of cultivated land.[176]

A particularly notable development in this arena occurred on November 1, 2018, when Spread Co., the world's largest automated vertical farm organization, started shipping leafy lettuce from its Techno Farm Keihanna in Kyoto, Japan.[177] The Kyoto farm is the world's largest in a series of robotic vegetable farms with a production capacity of approximately 30,000 heads of lettuce per day. It is slated to expand to more than 100 locations through a franchise model. Spread Co. uses specialized LED lights designed for vertical farming as well as IoT/AI technologies and self-contained robots. The company has been able to reduce its energy use by 30% and water use by 98% through recycling and does not use any pesticides. The indoor hydroponic lettuce are planted on shelves that are stacked vertically (as the farm category name suggests). This approach allows island nations like Japan to become more self-sufficient in their food production while significantly reducing their land use.

All these technologies offer hope for the future of sustainable agriculture, but it will take time for them to be scaled globally. And of course, while more automated farms could help address climate change, they could also lead to job losses for workers whose livelihoods are currently dependent on agriculture. The future of work is one of the most complex topics that must be addressed within the context of the exponential technology evolution and that I discuss throughout this book. Retraining programs and a universal basic income, also known as guaranteed minimum income, and other initiatives could help address equity imbalances.

Water

Technologists are also working on solutions to meet the increasing need for potable water on our climate change-stricken planet. In October 2018, the Water Abundance XPRIZE awarded its grand prize of US$1.5 million to the Skysource/Skywater Alliance for accomplishing a true moonshot (see the moonshot section in Chap. 3) by developing in a 2-year competition a technology to "harvest water out of thin air" using energy-efficient technologies.[178] The high-volume water generator can be used anywhere, including disaster areas, and can extract a minimum of 2000 liters

---

[175]https://benefitcorp.net/what-is-a-benefit-corporation

[176]http://ironox.com/

[177]http://spread.co.jp/en/

[178]http://www.skysource.org/

of potable water per day out of the atmosphere by using 100% renewable energy for less than US$0.02 per liter. Another XPRIZE was awarded to 10 finalists in the global US$20 million NRG Cosia Carbon Prize[179] for developing technologies within the CarbonCure global impact effort to profitably sequester and transform CO_2 emissions from a gas or coal plant into useful products whose value exceeded the cost of extracting the CO_2. These products could be, for example, nanoparticles that enhance green concrete, plastics, or batteries.

Lab-Grown Meats and Plant-Based Burgers

Personally, I have kept meat out of my diet for four decades now. However, on August 14, 2018, I could not resist trying my first meat analogue hamburger, when Jamis McNiven, the owner of the legendary Buck's of Woodside Restaurant in California convinced Tom and me to try his Impossible Burger, a plant-based protein burger. As a non-meat eater, I was not really in a position to judge its quality, but Tom, a confirmed carnivore, loved it—and we were both thrilled to read in the Buck's menu: "The future is here" from the perspective of addressing world hunger.

Biotechnology can be used to produce environmentally friendly lab-grown meats through in vitro cultivation of animal cells, a process that uses the extraction and proliferation of animal stem cells to create another product (it is uncannily similar to beer brewing). Livestock in the meat industry are estimated to devour 30% of the world's grain, account for 25% of land use, and are chief contributors to CO_2 emissions. This is why Just Inc., a Silicon Valley-based start-up that made its name by making vegan eggs from mung beans, later partnered with Japanese company Toriyama to produce Wagyu beef from cell lines. However, just like one of its main competitors, Aleph Farms in Israel, Just Inc. expects it will be a couple of years before it can deliver the first cell-based steak.[180]

Although companies producing lab-grown meat have attracted significant private investments, some scientists criticize the fact that the acquired knowledge is often protected as trade secrets, and furthermore, progress has not been fast enough to date to make artificial meat widely available to address hunger and poverty.[181] A new grant of US$3 million, made available in February 2019 by the Good Food Institute,[182] a think tank in Washington, DC, could help change that, but the grant money is rather a drop in the ocean compared with the tens of millions of dollars invested in Memphis Meats alone over the last 2 years by Bill Gates and Richard Branson. The Good Food Institute grant money will be split between six lab-grown meat and eight plant-based protein projects that hope to shorten the time from lab to market. These synthetic meats could ultimately provide a viable solution to global hunger by using less energy, less land, and less water. However, there is still uncertainty around greenhouse gas emission levels. The extant research suggests clean meat could lead

---

[179]https://carbon.xprize.org/prizes/carbon/teams

[180]https://en.wikipedia.org/wiki/Aleph_Farms

[181]https://tinyurl.com/y3el5vhm

[182]https://www.gfi.org/gfi-research-grant-winners-2019

to reduced global warming in the short term because its production does not generate the potent methane that cows do, but the large-scale production process of synthetic meat does result in CO_2 emissions, which in the long term—1000 years or more— could become significant.[183]

Addressing the Plastics Problem

There is optimism in some quarters that we may eventually be able to address the plastic soup in our oceans.[184] In a classic example of why we should never underestimate the power of one, in 2013, 16-year-old Boyan Slat studied the problem of plastic in the ocean for a school science project. Two years later, he founded The Ocean Cleanup to address the problem.[185] Today, The Ocean Cleanup is close to rolling out an autonomous, solar energy–powered and scalable system to allow us to clean up ocean plastic before it breaks down into microplastics. Despite continued technological setbacks, the company is aiming for a plastic-free ocean by 2050. In a similar vein, scientists at the US National Renewable Energy Laboratory (NREL) recently encountered a transmuted enzyme that eats plastic,[186] although more research is required to make it deployable at large scale. Hope comes also from the traditional chemical industry, which finally seems to be realizing that recycling plastics could become an important profit source as the "global plastics-waste volumes [c]ould grow from 260 million tons per year in 2016 to 460 million tons per year by 2030."[187] Furthermore, as Arnout de Pee et al. noted in a 2018 article for McKinsey & Company, major players in the chemical industry have begun to recognize that "ammonia, cement, ethylene, and steel companies can reduce their carbon-dioxide (CO_2) emissions to almost zero with energy-efficiency improvements, the electric production of heat, the use of hydrogen and biomass as feedstock or fuel, and carbon capture."[188] De Pee et al. noted in the same article that half of global CO_2 emissions result from the manufacturing of ammonia, cement, ethylene, and steel and that the "decarbonization of these sectors will cost [investors, regulators, and businesses] between $11 trillion and $21 trillion through 2050." In a 2018 report for McKinsey & Company, the same authors observed that "industrial companies can reduce CO_2 emissions in various ways, with the optimum local mix depending on the availability of biomass, carbon-storage capacity and low-cost zero-carbon electricity and hydrogen, as well as projected changes in production capacity."[189]

All the developments discussed above offer tremendous hope because they confirm that humanity has the ability to address major issues such as decarbonization

---

[183]Lynch and Pierrehumbert (2019).

[184]Moore and Phillips (2012).

[185]https://www.theoceancleanup.com/

[186]Austin et al. (2018).

[187]Hundertmark et al. (2018).

[188]De Pee et al. (June 2018, p. 7).

[189]De Pee et al. (June 2018, p. 7).

of industry, solving the plastic soup problem, and carbon sequestration—we just need to adjust our mindset and focus on solving them.

1.4.4 On Mobility and Transportation

According to a 2019 Morgan Stanley report, internal combustion engines (ICE)) are expected to be outnumbered by battery-powered electric vehicles (BEVs) before 2050, as the number of electric vehicles is growing exponentially worldwide and is expected to reach 1 billion by 2050, or as much as 90% of all vehicle sales.[190] This development, if it can occur sustainably within the limits of the planetary boundaries, will most likely be fueled less by traditional car manufacturers such as General Motors, Daimler, Porsche, or VW, which currently manufacture expensive BEVs and autonomous vehicles (AVs), and more by arrivistes such as Great Wall Motors, a Chinese company that is, at time of writing, selling an electric car with a 350-kilometer battery range for only US$8680.[191] Morgan Stanley expects that four out of five cars sold worldwide in 2050 will be BEVs. This shift will disrupt not only the traditional auto manufacturers, but also the automotive supply chain, components suppliers, semiconductor manufacturers, chemical producers, and other players in auto-related capital goods.

Like BEVs, AVs could become an essential factor in decreasing pollution worldwide. Tom and I believe that the transition toward using both BEVs and AVs will occur much faster than is currently estimated by linear-thinking analysts, although the high purchase price, limited range of a single charge, limited access to plug-in stations, and limited battery life might slow their adoption in the early stages. Nevertheless, a self-driving future is most definitely in sight, as numerous companies are already testing self-driving cars in California alone. On January 30, 2019, Argo AI, an AV start-up in which Ford invested US$1 billion in 2017, became the 62nd company to be granted a testing permit for autonomous vehicles by the California Department of Motor Vehicles, following in the footsteps of Bosch, Honda, Tesla, VW, Waymo, and Apple, to name but six.[192] Amazon is said to be testing autonomous trucks by Embark to deliver goods to their customers, and in October 2018, the US National Highway Transportation Safety Administration issued an updated AV policy in anticipation of further developments.[193] Other AV initiatives are being launched in heavily polluted countries like China, which is on track to become the first country to deploy AVs at large scale, despite its need to source some fundamental components such as drivetrains, semiconductor chips, and advanced battery technology. According to a report by Roland Berger, a German consultancy, this is

---

[190]https://www.morganstanley.com/ideas/electric-car-supply-chain

[191]https://electrek.co/2018/12/27/great-wall-motor-ora-r1-all-electric-urban-car

[192]https://tinyurl.com/y29tgcdw

[193]See https://www.nhtsa.gov/vehicle-manufacturers/automated-driving-systems

not only due to the techno-utilitarian attitude of the Chinese government, which favors exponential technologies, but also to the openness of Chinese market, which absorbed more than half of the electric vehicles sold worldwide, and a global network of clients who are open to adopting new technologies in the auto sector.[194] Moreover, the Chinese authorities relaxed their regulatory guidelines for AVs, gave permission to non-Chinese manufacturers such as Daimler and BMW to test their AVs in cities like Beijing and Shanghai, doubled the installed base of their battery-charging infrastructure, ended the ban on ownership of electric vehicles made by foreign manufacturers, and introduced limits on registrations for traditional cars (i.e., ICEs).

Eventually, current transportation systems will be expanded by regulators to address the micro-mobility market as well and will include drones and smaller delivery vehicles which, within the context of the current COVID-19, have gained increased attention.[195] With US$5.7 billion in start-up investments since 2015, the micro-mobility market has also been growing two to three times faster than the car-sharing or ride-hailing markets.[196] More than 85% of those investments targeted China, and several micro-mobility start-ups, such as e-scooter manufacturers Bird and Lime, have amassed valuations estimated at more than US$1 billion.[197]

Another relevant development is LiDAR technology.[198] LiDAR is a surveying method that helps determine the 3D representations of a target, as well as the distances and angles between them. It is the central technology used in autonomous vehicles (with the exception of Tesla vehicles, which use only cameras, radar, and ultrasonic sensors) and works by illuminating a target with a pulsed laser light and measuring the reflected pulses with a sensor. It is a prime example of the massive demonetization process of exponential tech at work: The price of one LiDAR device dropped from about US$80,000 in 2007 to a few thousand dollars at the time of writing,[199] and it is likely to drop even further to only a few dollars once it becomes available on a chip.

In June 2017, Tom and I attended the annual gathering of Toniic, one of the largest global private impact investors networks, in Berlin. While there, I had the opportunity to meet, and listen to a report by, fellow exponential investor Jamie Arbib. We were shocked and dumbfounded by the groundbreaking research results published in his paper.[200] Arbib and his co-researcher, Tony Seba, collected research data and fed it into a systems dynamics model that they had developed. In their report, *Rethinking Transportation 2020–2030: The Disruption of Transportation and the Collapse of the Internal-Combustion Vehicle and Oil Industries*, they draw

---

[194]Berret (1 October 2018).

[195]https://tinyurl.com/yxaqwdrd

[196]Heineke et al. (January 2019).

[197]https://techcrunch.com/2018/12/03/will-uber-gobble-up-lime-or-fly-off-with-bird/

[198]https://oceanservice.noaa.gov/facts/lidar.html

[199]Lee T. (2018b).

[200]Arbib and Seba (2017).

on their results to argue that humanity is currently embarking exponentially rapidly on the most disruptive era in the history of transportation. According to the World Health Organization, the number of yearly fatalities due to traffic-related incidents throughout the world is 1.25 million.[201] Arbib and Seba showed that within 10 years of regulatory approval of AVs, this death toll could be avoided.

The driverless car era has already begun. Waymo, the driverless car subsidiary of Alphabet, had approval to build an AV factory in Michigan by January 2019.[202] Current expectations are that 95% of the population in the United States will eventually use, or at the very least have access to, on-demand electric AVs. These AVs will not be owned by individuals, says Arbib, but by savvy business people who will build entire fleets to service the population. In the beginning, existing ride-hailing companies such as Uber, Lyft, and Didi will probably try to grab large portions of the new market and newcomers will require large amounts of capital investments for market entry. Arbib calls this emerging type of business Transportation as a Service (TaaS).

A switch to TaaS could have a tremendous impact on consumer spending, as it would mean that the average American family would no longer need to own their own cars and could, for example, save up to US$5600 per annum in transportation costs, which is the equivalent of receiving a 10% net salary increase. As soon as AVs are approved, electric AVs are likely to replace human-driven ICEs due to their lower maintenance, energy, and insurance costs, and as demand for oil drops, oil prices are expected to tumble, along with their entire value chains. In addition, utilization rates for AVs are expected to be 10 times higher than for ICEs, with up to 1 million kilometers driven per vehicle lifetime by 2030. The TaaS business model could mean the driving cost per kilometer could be as much as 90% cheaper compared with the cost of buying a new, traditional car and, in terms of operating costs, could be half the cost of driving a regular ICE.

The Future Is Closer Than You Might Think
Google's Waymo launched its driverless ride-share and the world's first self-driving taxi service in December 2018 in the suburbs of Phoenix, Arizona. In March 2018, it started to offer test rides to regular—that is, not research participants—people.[203] We may be riding a robot taxi soon, a fact that has become particularly relevant within the context of the COVID-19 pandemic and our need for social distancing.

Working on the assumption that the driverless car phenomenon truly takes off, McKinsey substantiates Arbib's findings in a recent report[204] by emphasizing the

---

[201] https://www.who.int/gho/road_safety/mortality/traffic_deaths_number/en/

[202] https://futurism.com/waymo-approval-open-driverless-car-factory-michigan

[203] https://futurism.com/report-waymo-unveil-first-driverless-rideshare

[204] Pizzuto L et al. (2019).

role China will play within this arena, a role expected to catapult it into a market leadership position that could transform "mobility" (the term McKinsey uses in reference to transportation) in a fundamental way. McKinsey expects a substantial share of the mobility market value to shift within a 9- to 10-year time frame away from car purchasing toward a mobility-as-a-service (MaaS—in essence, another expression for TaaS) business model whereby clients will pay per driven kilometer and not per car ownership. New business models will emerge and be driven, as it were, by software and data through a convergence of various disparate industries including the automotive, transportation, software and hardware, and data services industries. Technology players such as Baidu, Tencent, and Waymo are already building or buying AVs to provide transport/mobility services to clients. Waymo, for example, has already decided to transform a factory in Detroit, Michigan, into an autonomous vehicle manufacturing facility. It will work with traditional car manu-facturers to add autonomous hardware to existing designs such as Chrysler Pacifica Hybrid Minivans and Jaguar Pace SUVs.[205] And automaker Byton is vertically integrating its vehicles to create "electric cars that are smart, connected, and auton-omous. The car will become a platform—a smart device on wheels."[206] Carsten Breitfeld, founder of Byton, insists that in order to survive in the transport market of the future, organizations need both a mindset and a culture that are more about "consumer electronics and software and the internet and less about the car indus-try."[207] Breitfeld considers China to be the perfect country to determine the future of transport because:

- *It is the world's largest automotive market*, with more than 30 million cars sold annually.
- *The speed of growth is swift in all areas.*
- *There is plenty of capital available*, and investors are flexible and willing to invest not only in early-stage companies but also in teams and ideas only.
- *There is strong political will* to support future developments in all areas, but especially smart electric transportation.

Byton was able to raise US$240 million for its A-round based only on the company's design, team, and business plan. Tesla decided to go much further, announcing on April 24, 2019, its intention to roll out its Robo-Taxis plans, which it hopes will address climate change, the future of car ownership, and the future of work, and show how Tesla owners can become ridesharing entrepreneurs and financially independent, making up to US$30,000 per year. In 2020, Tesla plans to have overcome the current massive regulatory hurdles and have 1 million Robo-Taxis on the road in order to disrupt the disruptors—that is, the ride-sharing

---

[205]https://tinyurl.com/y4t5otpt

[206]Byton founder Carsten Breitfeld. Viewed 17 March 2019 at https://tinyurl.com/y2xgblcj

[207]Carsten Breitfeld. Viewed 17 March 2019 at https://tinyurl.com/y2xgblcj

companies Lyft and Uber, whose market capitalizations are US$16 billion and an expected US$90 billion, respectively.[208]

Electric Aircraft

A particularly radical departure from traditional transport systems, and one with growing significance, is the use of electric aircraft systems such as unmanned drones and vertically lifting aerial vehicles. These are revolutionizing the future of transport and mobility, democratizing the sky, and enabling new participants to join in. Drones supported by advanced data analytics become geospatial tools. Equipped with high-resolution cameras and detailed sensors, drones have already become indispensable in e-agriculture and are revolutionizing precision agriculture.[209] By embedding new technology into agricultural processes, they can contribute to increased crop yields and optimize crop and land surveillance, which will all combine to provide food security for this century's predicted world population of 10 billion.[210] And because they have freedom of movement in the sky, drones can deliver medicine to hazardous or otherwise inaccessible areas, making life safer for those with dangerous jobs—for example, roofers, toxic chemical workers, electrical power installers, and tree surgeons—and providing a lifeline for people living in remote areas or trapped in disaster areas.

Drones are also disrupting current modes of transport. German company Lilium, for example, created the world's first electric vertical take-off and landing jet (eVTOL) and is in the process of creating the first electric air taxi, which will radically alter how we travel.[211] The air taxi is not a flying car but it could become one. Uber revealed in 2018 its drone-like flying vehicle prototype for an aerial taxi service as part of UberAIR. It also announced plans to test these vehicles in Dallas and Los Angeles by 2020 and hopes to ultimately operate what it calls skyports. The Uber electric flying taxi will be manufactured by Bell Helicopter, is scheduled to be operational by 2023, and will be a combination of a "traditional helicopter, a light aircraft, and a passenger-carrying drone."[212] The requisite air traffic systems will be developed in partnership with NASA. In January 2019, Boeing NeXt completed the first flight of its autonomous passenger air vehicle (PAV), which is 9-meters long, can carry up to 227 kilograms, and has a range of 80 kilometers.[213] Also in January 2019, Bell introduced eVTOL, an urban hybrid-electric flying taxi that should be in service in the mid-2020s and will use Uber's own air traffic system, currently under development.[214]

---

[208]https://tinyurl.com/y6nrcbs6

[209]Adamchuck (2013).

[210]Sylvester (2018).

[211]https://lilium.com/

[212]https://tinyurl.com/y8edxska

[213]https://tinyurl.com/ydbjrc5a

[214]https://www.theverge.com/2019/1/7/18168814/bell-air-taxi-nexus-uber-flying-car-hybrid-ces-2019

In a classic display of capitalist anticipation, some developers are already constructing luxury apartment buildings with landing pads on their rooftops.[215] And in capital-abundant cities such as Dubai, police are testing Hoverbikes in an effort to be ready for the introduction of aerial vehicles by 2020.[216]

In a slight twist to the transportation story, when Tesla founder Elon Musk decided to do something about the "soul-destroying" traffic in Los Angeles, he opted to do something that was, compared to his previous ideas such as Tesla and SpaceX, "boring." He announced that he wanted to build an underground transport system whereby people and cars would be taken off regular roads and shuttled around at high speed on electric drivetrains. Thus the Boring Company was born, and in December 2018, the first test tunnel was unveiled in Hawthorne, California.[217] Musk hopes to be able to construct his tunnels at an all-inclusive, final price of US$10 million per mile—which sounds like a lot if you do not know that the current price per mile for a regular highway system is US$200 million–US$500 million.

Managing the Change

Despite their advantages and their ability to address societal challenges worldwide by transforming business models, governments and regulators are still struggling to find a balance between encouraging innovation and attracting further investments and developing policies on data ownership, infrastructure growth, community safety, security, privacy, and airspace management, all while winning and maintaining public confidence. The environmental impact of TaaS (or MaaS) is expected to be dramatic: current estimates are that it will cut air pollution and greenhouse gas emissions by up to 90% and energy demand by 80%. As solar and wind technology are also expected to disrupt the current electricity infrastructure at the same time, we may even have a carbon-free road transportation infrastructure by 2030.[218] Furthermore, James Arbib and Tony Seba predict that the geopolitical significance of oil will vastly weaken, potentially leading to the destabilization of OPEC countries unless they diversify and/or accelerate their move toward the solar age. Conversely, lithium-based geopolitics will develop, as lithium, nickel, cobalt, and cadmium are (at least currently, but who knows what discoveries lie ahead) needed to manufacture batteries. However, the dependency upon these materials is neither comparable to nor as critical as our dependency on oil, because they are needed to build the batteries for the vehicles, are recyclable, and still have 80% capacity when they are taken for recycling. Compare this with the characteristics of fossil fuels.

[215]https://therealdeal.com/miami/2018/12/08/luxury-condo-developers-in-miami-add-landing-pads-for-flying-cars/

[216]https://gulfnews.com/uae/crime/video-cops-on-flying-bikes-to-patrol-dubai-by-2020-1.60260681

[217]https://www.youtube.com/watch?v=6t8BiLK0mbE

[218]Arbib and Seba (2017).

The social and economic impact of TaaS is likely to be very significant. On the one hand, the time gained from being driven rather than driving could lead to a GDP increase of an additional US$1 trillion by 2030 in the United States alone; on the other hand, it will reduce the number of jobs in all disrupted areas. Arbib and Seba are quite clear about the fact that in the United States, there will be job losses of up to 3% of the workforce through the introduction and normalization of AVs, which could amount to a drop in income of US$200 billion. However, some new jobs such as robot repair technicians (see Sect. 1.5, Artificial Intelligence: Revolution, Emergency, Salvation? for more on this) will also be created and mobility will increase, especially in urban areas. According to a UN report, about 23% of the world's population lived in a city with at least 1 million inhabitants in 2016.[219] By 2030 this number is expected to reach 27%, adding to the already dire traffic situation.

Sustainable investors, therefore, have a rather significant market opportunity to make a huge holistic impact. For example, Munich, Germany, a rather conservative city, has already started to implement a smart city initiative together with 11 partners from the business and academic worlds. The project district is called Neuaubing-Westkreuz/Freiham, and its 30,000 residents' quality of life should be improved in a sustainable manner once the project has been finalized. By applying exponential tech and intelligent use of data, the project intends to reduce fossil fuel consumption and CO_2 emissions by more than 20%, while energy efficiency and the use of renewable energy are both expected to increase by more than 20%. The goal is to create a completely CO_2-neutral city by 2050. In order to achieve all that, the city plans to invest around 20 million Euro in the 350-hectare wide district, with 6.85 million Euro of that coming from the EU.[220]

1.4.5 Convergence of the Internet of Things

The Internet is already connecting billions of us on and off the planet every day, and 5 billion more people are expected to come online over the next decade. The benefits of being connected are accompanied by a whole host of privacy and security issues, because every single device that comes online is vulnerable to being hacked, an issue that I will touch on briefly at the end of this chapter. Within 5 years there will be potentially 20–30 billion new devices connected with one another. This translates as two to three connected devices for every human on Earth, whether those devices are in our homes, cars, businesses, pets, even our own bodies.

The Connected World
Exponentially growing technology plays a key role in the transition from an analog world to a digitalized one, with the ultimate goal being a planetary nervous system in

---

[219]https://tinyurl.com/zz3t9y9

[220]https://www.smarter-together.eu/cities/munich-/

which every single person and thing can be connected. In 2017, the Internet access rate worldwide was estimated at 48%, with 81% access in developed countries and 41.3% in emerging markets.[221] By 2020, Internet use is predicted to reach 5 billion users worldwide,[222] and the 5G network with 10 Gbps will be key to that. The 5G network is the manifestation of exponential growth in telecommunication: from 3G (384 kbps in 2001) to 4G (100 Mbps) to 5G networks, whose first licenses are being sold as time of writing. With 5G, it will be possible to download a 1.5 Gb movie in 0.2 seconds. Google's sister company Loon, a network of tens of thousands of giant balloons floating 20,000 kilometers above us, will provide balloon-powered Internet to many inaccessible parts of the world; by 2018 it had already partnered with Telkom Kenya to bring connectivity rural Kenya.[223] However, it is imperative to ensure that Internet connectivity, in general, is not monopolized by only a few providers. As exponential investors, we can get involved to make sure this technology is also affordable and opens up access to education, business opportunities, and thus abundance for the people at the bottom of the pyramid.

But the progress of exponential tech does not stop at a few balloons in our atmosphere. The race for satellite supremacy has just begun. OneWeb and Airbus, for example, teamed up to launch a 900-satellite constellation to provide affordable, high-speed Internet network coverage across the world. The first satellites, each of which weighs 150 kilograms, were launched at the end of February 2019,[224] and the plan is to produce three satellites per day until all 900 are up and running. Shanghai-based LinkSure Network is planning to challenge Google and SpaceX through its *free* global WiFi service. It plans to be using 272 satellites by 2026, beginning with 10 satellites in 2020.[225] But all of these plans and developments pale in comparison when we look at SpaceX Services. On February 1, 2019, the company requested permission from the Federal Communication Commission to launch 1 million Earth stations in addition to the 11,943 low-Earth Starlink orbit satellite constellation they had previously deployed.[226]

Of course, we cannot talk about an interconnected world without talking about the astounding growth of the mobile phone industry. For 2020, it is estimated there will be 6.95 billion connected people, with more than 50% of them being smartphone users; for 2022, global mobile phone penetration is forecast to be 7.26 billion people.[227] As mobile phone owners, we have also intentionally or unintentionally decided to adopt our first *wearable*. Our phones have numerous

---

[221] https://www.statista.com/statistics/209096/share-of-internet-users-in-the-total-world-population-since-2006/

[222] https://www.futuretimeline.net/21stcentury/2020.htm#internet-2020

[223] https://www.bbc.com/news/technology-44886803

[224] https://tinyurl.com/y7gqd35r

[225] https://tinyurl.com/yd4nkqbq

[226] https://tinyurl.com/yydk29qq

[227] https://www.statista.com/statistics/218984/number-of-global-mobile-users-since-2010/

sensors that provide economic, social, health, and cultural benefits. They also remove our anonymity. (More on that later.)

But it is not only phones that connect us. Cars too are getting smarter and more connected. The digitalization process started in the late 1960s, at the onset of the oil crisis, when car manufacturers began building in electronic processors to help increase fuel efficiency. Since then, the number of built-in sensors per car has grown to an average of 60—used for ABS, cruise control, airbags, parking assist, etc.—and is expected to hit more than 200 in the foreseeable future. This will translate into 22 billion car sensors being used in the automobile industry by 2020.[228] A side effect of this will be the increasing interconnectedness between vehicles. Tesla, for example, likely has the most sophisticated technology needed to control and self-drive a car. Its autopilot system is self-learning and, since all Tesla cars are interconnected, the entire Tesla self-driving fleet becomes one exponentially learning self-driving system. Consequently, if one car learns something new, all Tesla cars will learn it and integrate it into their own systems within seconds. As more of us begin to rely on fleets of self-driving and self-learning cars, we may never want to own a car again.

Beyond smartphones and cars, more and more objects in our lives will become more intelligent and self-learning. Even the clothes we wear are changing. Google's Jacquard project[229] integrates interactive fabrics using conductive yarn to let you answer your phone with a tap on your sleeve. We are moving into a world where your sweater has a touch screen, your shirts monitor your health, and your jacket can access your electronic wallet. We will be able to access our world in whole new ways through flexible microchips and skin patches that can be attached to our skin to monitor our heart, brain, and muscle activity. They will measure our blood pressure and eye pressure and help us sleep better. And what if you could monitor your sun exposure through a skin patch that communicates with your smartphone app? In February 2019, L'Oréal made this possible. Representing the convergence of cutting-edge consumer electronics and the skincare industry,[230] their app is an AI-powered skin diagnostic service based on scientific research into skin aging. Even more exciting, researchers at Ohio State University Wexner Medical Center developed a computer chip that was then planted in the brain of a man who had been paralyzed in an accident. The chip essentially simulated a neurological bypass and the man regained functional control of his hand.[231]

On a lighter note, not having to use your car key is already a reality in many traditional cars, but not having to use your home keys ever again or going to a gym where each training device has information on your fitness progress—just like your doctor does—is closer than many of us realize. Microchips and objects are turning

---

[228]http://www.automotivesensors2017.com/

[229]https://atap.google.com/jacquard/

[230]https://tinyurl.com/yyh5gxdt

[231]https://www.sciencedaily.com/releases/2016/04/160413140118.htm

into everyday enabled sources of data, not only through the Internet of Things but the convergence thereof.

Wearables and Precision Medicine

Sensors will be instrumental in opening up access to better healthcare data, leap-frogging developments in improved precision medicine, supporting clinical trials, and enabling access to better health through innovation and significant price reductions. They will be the vector for input from wearables such as an Apple watch, Oura ring,[232] or implanted chip, all of which monitor their wearers' vital signs, thus helping empower wearers to take responsibility for their health and wellbeing. Some wearables' sensors can detect falls and issue a call for help, and others can detect atrial fibrillation (thus helping reduce the risk of strokes and heart failure). An ECG feature on wearables not only monitors the wearer's heart rate but also sends the data directly to their physician; other features measure body temperature, provide GPS information or WiFi functionality, work as pedometers or altimeters, or provide optical heartrate information; and smart bands,[233] such as the biosensor developed by the University of Texas at Dallas, use sweat to measure blood sugar, stress,[234] and even blood alcohol content levels, performing better in this last task than a traditional Breathalyzer.[235] The Tufts University School of Engineering developed a tooth-mounted sensor that monitors in real time what is happening in and around our bodies and provides invaluable healthcare information, including data on glucose, salt, and alcohol intake, via WiFi.[236] An additional breakthrough in wearable sensor technology for medical diagnostics was the development of a portable ultrasound sensor that can be powered by a smartphone, developed by engineers at the University of British Columbia, BC, Canada. It is the size of a standard Band-Aid, could reduce the cost of an ultrasound scanner to about US$100, and could mean the difference between life and death in disaster and remote areas.[237]

Brain–Computer Interfaces

If you could connect your thoughts, moods, and brain functions to a computer, would you want to do that? If yes, what benefits would you like to experience? What downsides could you imagine for this kind of technology?

I have practiced meditation since 1980, and I am curious about any technology, technique, or teaching that could enhance my meditation experience. Therefore, a couple of years ago, I purchased Muse,[238] a headband designed to leverage electro-encephalography (EEG) to detect electrical activity in a meditator's brain to enhance the meditative experience and facilitate and expedite the transition into an altered

---

[232]https://ouraring.com/

[233]https://tinyurl.com/y6p9md33

[234]https://tinyurl.com/y4ep2mfv

[235]https://en.wikipedia.org/wiki/Breathalyzer

[236]Gerardo et al. (2018).

[237]https://tinyurl.com/y4tec3or

[238]https://tinyurl.com/y2uyj3py

state. I liked Muse, and I certainly experienced altered states of consciousness when using it while meditating. However, I also have four decades of meditation training, which may have influenced my experience. Suffice to say, I was initially pleased with my purchase. But shortly after I bought it, I discovered that my brainwaves, my experiences, were being shared with Muse, the company, without my consent. This was—is—not acceptable to me. They were using my data, my brainwaves, without my approval. I felt my privacy had been deeply invaded, and I was not offered the choice to opt out. Technology is advancing increasingly rapidly, and we must keep up the pace to protect our data and have a say in who has access to it. Should we decide to give businesses access to it, I believe we should also benefit from it, financially or otherwise.

We can also harness the benefits of technology through swallowables. Some of these, such as gastroenterological biosensors,[239] can fulfill important healing and diagnostic functions. Gastroenterological biosensors are devices that travel through the body collecting data and detecting warning signs of pathogens or illness such as internal bleeding or cancer. And new brain–machine interfaces allow brain signals to control devices outside the body such as bionic arms.[240]

Such devices, whether they are wearables, swallowables, or anything else, can serve important functions and shift the boundaries between humans and technology. Of course, we already have both brain–computer interfaces and implantable technologies, even though we may not think of them in this way. The brain–computer interface I now have is my hands. With them I use my computer, iPhone, or iPad—but I am very much looking forward to welcoming better interfaces that support my brain function and help me thrive as I grow older. I have three dental implants and am very grateful for them. Have they changed how I feel about what it means to be human? No, I do not define myself through my physical body or my mind. Therefore, I am very much looking forward to enhancing the foundation of the temple of my soul as long as it occurs within a democratic context that recognizes my personal boundaries.

We are on the cusp of significant breakthroughs that could offer a better approach to screening, diagnostics, and treatment to improve outcomes and significantly lower healthcare costs. By leveraging our capital, exponential investors can play a major role in guiding all stakeholders—including those from academia, government, and business—toward a collaboration that would enable the whole of society to benefit from these rapid advances in technology and medicine.

Robotics

When we think of robots, many of us will think immediately of the friendly R2D2, of the *Star Wars* movies, or with a life-threatening, humanoid robot called Terminator. But in the real world, household robots like the Roomba vacuum cleaner, which I love, have entered our daily lives and are hard to think away. Some people even

---

[239]https://tinyurl.com/yyfhvj5p
[240]https://openbionics.com/hero-arm/

predict a future when we will prefer a robot over a human because of the superior quality of work delivered by a robot. Today's robots, which are still automatons (repeating pre-programmed tasks) rather than autonomous (making independent decisions based on shifting circumstances), are taking on a variety of activities with various degrees of complexity and jobs that converge at the intersection between computing, sensors, AI, material science, augmented reality, and 3D printing. For many years we gave robots the dirty, dull, and uninteresting jobs like cleaning our floors, mowing our lawns, or stacking boxes in a warehouse. As robots became more "intelligent" through machine learning, smaller, faster, and more adaptive to new and unstructured conditions, we began to give them more dangerous tasks to perform, such as cleaning up in disaster areas like Chernobyl or disposing of bombs and mines in war zones. Following the Fukushima Daiichi nuclear disaster in March 2011, DARPA, the US Defense Advanced Research Projects Agency, initiated a robotics challenge[241] to develop machines that can respond to various challenges, including driving a car, removing debris, or opening a door. One of the teams that rose to the challenge was Boston Dynamics, a very successful MIT spin-off now owned by the Japanese conglomerate SoftBank Group. Boston Dynamics developed Atlas, a bipedal, high-mobility humanoid robot that can walk on two legs in outdoor terrain, leaving the arms free for other tasks, and perform an entire parcours without errors.[242] Atlas was a product of improved computational power, advances in robotics technology, improved sensors, improved and more adaptable materials, and exponentially smaller, faster, and generally better technology than was available to earlier robots. All of those advances, paired with rapid prototyping methods and 3D printing, enabled increased innovation and much better results.

Of course, technology keeps evolving. RHex, for example, designed by the University of Pennsylvania Kod*Lab,[243] can access difficult terrain and so support research in challenging environments such as desert areas. It has six springing legs and can flip, jump, and pull itself up. The modular snake robot, designed by Carnegie Mellon University Robotics Institute,[244] is a legless robot that moves like a snake, can squeeze into tight spaces and can climb by mimicking the movements of animals. Harvard University's Octobot[245] was inspired by an octopus. The first entirely soft, 3D-printed robot with no electronics or skeleton, it has increased flexibility to wrap itself around objects. The open-source movement in robotics is in full swing and is now supported also by Amazon's AWS Robomaker and Google's Cloud Robotics Platform. The latter recently announced its cloud robot services to promote the sharing of ideas and enhance the development of the Robot Operating System (ROS), which simplifies the programming of robots.[246]

---

[241] https://www.darpa.mil/program/darpa-robotics-challenge

[242] https://www.bostondynamics.com/atlas

[243] https://kodlab.seas.upenn.edu/

[244] https://www.ri.cmu.edu/

[245] https://www.seas.harvard.edu/news/2016/08/first-autonomous-entirely-soft-robot

[246] http://www.ros.org/

Within the working environment, robots are exceptional at performing repetitive tasks, can work around the clock without a break, and do not need unions to protect their interests. (Again, the detailed ethical aspects of those points are outside the scope of this book.) Since 2014, 505 factories across Dongguan, in China's Guangdong province, have invested heavily in robot technology.[247] As a result, in May 2016, FoxCon, an Apple and Samsung supplier, replaced 60,000 factory workers with robots.[248] These robots are performing noncomplex tasks. As they become more cost-efficient and more effective than humans over time, they will displace even more humans. *Artificial Intelligence, Automation, and the Economy*, a report prepared for and delivered to the Obama administration in December 2016, predicted that 6–9% of jobs globally will be automated and 47% of jobs in the United States are at risk of becoming obsolete due to automation within the next 20 years.[249]

Using robots rather than humans does not always pose a threat to jobs and/or the workforce, though. In societies like Japan, where the mortality rate is higher than the fertility rate, there is a great need for people in the workforce, and robots are therefore playing an increasingly significant role. The Japanese retailer Uniqlo, for example, replaced 90% of its warehouse staff with robots, thus increasing the potential pool of workers for other sectors.[250] Although the Chinese do not (yet!) have that problem, the state-owned, Beijing-based First Bank opened in May 2018 its first, entirely human-free, robot-operated office in Shanghai.[251] And can you imagine coming home from work to a perfectly home-cooked meal? Imagine no more, because Japanese technology is about to make it a reality. Miso Robotics, for example, has created Flippy, a robot that helps commercial cooks make food at an affordable price.[252] The Alibaba Group owns automated grocery stores, such as Hema, as well as restaurants such as the Freshippo Robot restaurant chains where robots, supported by a few humans, prepare and serve your food, and clean up after you once you have eaten.[253] Other companies, such as Alibaba's direct competitor JD.com, have launched similar initiatives.

Needless to say, for an exponential investor, robotics—and all other exponential technologies, for that matter—is also closely connected to addressing the *future of life*, a term I prefer over the more commonly heard "future of work" This is already influencing *who we are as human beings* and *how we want to live* (see the section on Artificial Intelligence).

---

[247]https://tinyurl.com/y86gro75

[248]https://www.bbc.com/news/technology-36376966

[249]https://tinyurl.com/hwvoxrk

[250]https://www.dailydot.com/debug/uniqlo-replaced-tokyo-warehouse-staff-robots/

[251]https://www.youtube.com/watch?v=cMQyZAyP228

[252]https://misorobotics.com/

[253]https://www.youtube.com/watch?v=FFCPKmLAZb4

3D Printing

In 2008, while still living in Silicon Valley, I went to my dentist because of a painful molar. My dentist had just purchased a new device and wanted me to be the first patient to receive the gift of a 3D carved molar. I accepted without hesitation, and 12 years later the crown is still working. Dentists in general, but especially those in Silicon Valley, have been early adopters of 3D imaging and 3D printing; since the late 2000s, sales of in-office 3D printers in the dentistry industry have skyrocketed, and they are expected to reach US$3.7 billion by 2021.[254] The adoption of this technology means that dental implants, crowns, dentures, and night guards can be made not only more cheaply but also more accurately by being customized through 3D scanning and high-quality printing materials.

The aerospace industry was another early adopter of the 3D-printing technology, using it for prototyping simple 3D-printed plastic models of parts. Authentise, an additive manufacturing automation company, has already 3D-printed and delivered not only various metal parts for the Airbus A350, but also footwear for Adidas, Nike, and New Balance, and taillights for Bugatti Chiron.[255] Now, that is versatility in action.

Now that many of the 3D-printing technology patents are expiring and the cost of printers has dropped significantly, we are set to experience an entire revolution in 3D printing that will create a whole new world in digital manufacturing and the supply chain industry. To be cost-effective, traditional manufacturing counts on the fact that products must be manufactured on a large scale in big factories. Disruption is in plain sight, though. From houses to airplane engines, portable 3D-printer technology enables the creation of objects in a precise and efficient manner—and virtually without waste. The 3D printers are better, smarter, faster, and more efficient at producing high-quality objects than traditional methods. The range of materials used for 3D printing now is vast, running the gamut from various plastics to thermoplastics, from waxes and rubbers to metals and ceramics, and from chocolates to sugars. This opens up the possibility of printing food, complex integrated circuits, or a simple door handle.[256] Lowe Innovation Labs, for example, is helping clients create a digital file for the on-demand 3D printing of virtually anything in and at their home.[257]

Even though this technology is still evolving, it is already possible to make a social impact with it: a 60-square-meter house can be 3D-printed in less than 24 h for under US$4000.[258] The house contains a living room, a small office space, one bedroom, one bathroom, and all the necessary plumbing, windows, doors, and electrical systems. Hadrian-X, the brick-laying robot from Fastbricks Robotics, for example, can "print" a house with three bedrooms and two bathrooms within

[254]https://www.smartechanalysis.com/reports/3d-printing-dentistry-2016/

[255]https://authentise.com/news

[256]https://tinyurl.com/y4wlcap9

[257]http://www.lowesinnovationlabs.com/bespoke-designs

[258]https://www.youtube.com/watch?v=wCzS2FZoB-I&t=4s

72 h.[259] The environmental upsides require further research, but the reduced energy demands and reduced pollution due to less transportation needs are rather obvious benefits.

The humanitarian benefits will be hugely significant. Digital manufacturing enables immediate delivery virtually anywhere, and 3D-printed humanitarian aid—from disposable medical solutions to housing, shelter, and sanitation equipment—is already being provided in disaster areas by companies such as Field Ready.[260] An additional benefit is that they bring local manufacturing to disaster zones, bypassing huge supply chains to offer new solutions that are better, faster, and cheaper from concept to the final products needed on the ground, and so they are essentially extending the reach of the aid they offer.

In this new digital manufacturing world, inventory will be less necessary, which is likely to result in the virtual elimination of shipping, and perhaps even of the factory itself, thus significantly reducing CO_2 emissions. Instead of shipping raw materials and finished products around the world, we will send digital designs that our clients can 3D print themselves. We are entering a world where products will be designed and only the design will be marketed. From auto parts to fast fashion, 3D printing on demand has the potential to reduce waste, produce a smaller carbon footprint, eliminate sweatshops, and offer fair treatment and quality pay for quality work. Furthermore, digital manufacturing addresses not only the freedom of design[261] but also the redesign of the entire business model whereby the design itself is sold or licensed and not the entire production and supply chain. This is a good example of the *democratization* of a traditional industry such as manufacturing in the same way that YouTube democratized video. Anyone with talent, some equipment, and Internet access will be able to create, share, and sell designs easily. However, as manufacturers will eventually simply send digital designs to any user, they will also need to address and prevent piracy. This means finding ways to protect intellectual property rights and introducing patent protection and cybersecurity laws that can be enforced globally and consistently. As 3D printing occurs in real time, designers may find themselves responsible for monitoring the process to ensure that the expected standards are fulfilled and that the design does not get copied and/or stolen.

Even as I have been writing this book, 3D-printing technology has been evolving. In a January 2019 article in *Science*, Brett Kelly et al.[262] described a new 3D-printing technology, which they nicknamed the "replicator," that can create an object using multiple images of the object to be printed rather than adding layer on layer. The system works like a reverse computer tomography scan. And there is another bonus: "'Our technique generates almost no material waste and the uncured material is

---

[259]https://www.fbr.com.au/view/hadrian-x

[260]https://www.fieldready.org/

[261]https://www.stratasys.com/resources/search/white-papers/design-for-ddm

[262]Kelly et al. (2019, January).

100% reusable,' said Hossein Heidari, a graduate student in Taylor's lab at UC Berkeley and co-first author of the work."[263]

From Augmented Reality to Virtual Reality

I rarely forget a face, but I have always had a hard time remembering names. This is why I was thrilled when, in 2014, Google announced Google Glass, its, ultimately unsuccessful, attempt to augment our experience of the regular world by providing additional, digital information to overlay the real world by using smart glasses. Google Glass tried to help people like me, for example, remember names and faces by delivering information and pictures from its camera via an eyeball-level LED. It is a prime example of augmented reality (AR), which has been around for quite some time now. AR becomes our new reality the moment we enhance any sensory experience with computer-generated sounds or visuals via a headset, phone, computer, or other devices. It permits us to interact with our world in entirely new ways. For example, Magic Leap is creating a new world in which these realities seamlessly blend together to enable extraordinary new experiences (when I first read about it, it reminded me of the movie *Minority Report*). Magic Leap's intention is to create virtual images that are indistinguishable from the real world and place them there for us to use, integrate, and enjoy.

In the healthcare context, both virtual reality (VR) and AR are bringing relief to people with PTSD by helping them recreate and relive traumatic experiences in a safe environment in an attempt to reduce their trauma, and doctors are finding both AR and VR useful for practicing surgery.[264] (AR differs from VR in that it consists of digital images being added to or superimposed on your real-world surroundings. (At its most basic this would be using something like a Snapchat lens.) With VR, you are cut off from the real world. It is a little like being transported directly into the game world, for example.)

The possibilities are virtually endless. Imagine test driving a car in VR, or using VR to experience the beauty of this planet without trampling over the Great Barrier Reef or contributing to the chaos and clutter on Everest. Imagine learning to become more empathic with people and other cultures by using VR to "walk in somebody else's shoes." Imagine journalists, for example, going into war zones without risking their lives, or low-income students being able to travel the world.

We still do not know how these technologies will affect us, of course. Standard market projections focus on how AR will become smaller and faster, but past technology disruptions show that this view could be too narrow and overlooks the impact of converging technologies—for example, in the way mobile technology has converged with the Internet. AR, and to some extent VR, is on a collision course with other emerging exponential technologies—for example, the Internet of Things (IoT), 3D printing, and machine learning, to name only a few.

---

[263]https://www.sciencedaily.com/releases/2019/01/190131143330.htm

[264]See, for example, https://hbr.org/2018/03/how-augmented-reality-will-make-surgery-safer

Blockchain: Truth Defender or Environmental Disaster?

Blockchain is a mathematical, decentralized, public, virtual structure (a chain of blocks), based on distributed ledger technology (DLT), that was built to create a shared and cryptographically secured database of digital transactions.[265] It is a collective, perpetual, append-only (unchangeable and only extendable entries) general ledger with virtually "unbreakable" (using current computing technology) database entries. Could it be both a workable replacement for our current, outdated financial systems and an answer to the grand global challenges?

The first blockchain application was Bitcoin, a cryptocurrency mined in 2009 by a programmer who called himself Satoshi Nakamoto and whose true identity remains unknown. Apart from having developed the technology, Nakamoto's principle achievement consists in convincing the participating agents, who do not necessarily trust each other, to agree that a distributed, "unbreakable," and shared accounting ledger gives a truthful reflection of all transactions and thus can be trusted. That agreement eliminates the need for a centrally regulated authority (for example, a bank in the case of cryptocurrency) to provide oversight. This is extremely significant because it shakes the foundations of our current financial and economic systems.

Trust is a treasured human value. It is fundamental to feeling safe and secure and has always been key to the healthy functioning of any society. It is, therefore, also a guarantor for the peaceful and secure exchange of valuable goods. However, securing trust has been challenging since the beginning of human civilization. This is one of the reasons why writing, mathematics, and ledgers were invented: they document the ownership of property as well as the exchange thereof. For example, Christine Proust, a researcher of economic archives who has documented old Babylonian mathematical tablets, has demonstrated that metrology and value notation was already being taught in Mesopotamia by the end of the third millennium BC.[266] Such ledgers (often double entry) were originally made of bone, stone, and later paper and served to document value transactions including money, which was invented to simplify the exchange of goods.

In more recent history, governments tried to secure trust through centralized and regulated banks as well as armies of accountants and auditors, all of which contribute significantly to the various dimensions of the *cost of trust*. The financial crisis of 2007/08 showed us in no uncertain terms that when things go wrong, the cost of trust may be higher than we could have imagined. That crisis nearly destroyed the global economic system, with US$25 trillion being obliterated from the value of the stock markets by October 2008.[267] It also revealed how easy it was for major financial organizations to ignore and bypass governmental regulations.[268] What started as a liquidity crunch evolved into:

---

[265]Orcutt (2018, p. 18).

[266]Proust (2009).

[267]Naudé (January 2009).

[268]Casey and Vigna (2018, pp. 10–16).

- A disruption of capital flows
- A flood of currency crises
- The total breakdown of some of the largest financial institutions in the world, including Lehman Brothers, which in 2007 had reported record revenues and profits, all of which were endorsed by Ernst & Young, the company's auditor
- The bailout of "too big to fail" governmental institutions such as Fannie Mae and Freddie Mac
- Severe downturns in global stock markets
- The failure of major businesses and the weakening of economic activity, which led to the 2008–2012 global recession, including the European sovereign-debt crisis[269]

As we know now, Lehman Brothers was not the only institution to inflate its balance sheets. From Barclays to Washington Mutual Bank to Deutsche Bank, major banks were fined hundreds of billions of dollars for being dishonest.[270] This crisis demonstrated the true *cost of trust*. No wonder many people were demanding and actively looking for better options. Nakamoto eventually came up with one that avoided human participation and relied instead on mathematics and impenetrable cryptography. Blockchain became the technology and Bitcoin, the resulting cryptocurrency. Beyond tracking monetary transactions that represented until recently more than 90% of all transactions, blockchain can be an immensely disruptive force for various industries, permitting secure record-keeping and peer-to-peer transactions, reducing the risk of corruption, minimizing transaction friction, and allowing for a secure exchange of patented products. It could disrupt the financial system and eventually render centralized authorities and systems, such as banks or other intermediaries, obsolete. Therefore, it is not surprising that these previously unchallenged major players are getting nervous.[271] Their main point of criticism is the use of blockchain for money laundering and other illegal, thus not transparent, transactions that cannot be supervised in order to avoid fraud.

There is another side to the blockchain, one that is rarely considered but is important from the perspective of an integral investor. Michael Casey and Paul Vigna note that there are also social implications of using blockchain for the 2 billion people on the planet who are considered too poor to be trusted with a bank account.[272] *Lack of trust* prevents them from having a bank account and thus from participating in and benefitting from the global economy. They are therefore essentially locked into poverty. Blockchain allows this group of people to override those restrictions. It enables participants to wire money anonymously and perform secure transactions without involving intermediaries, such as a notary, clerks, or lawyers whose costs (*cost of trust*) are not insignificant. Some blockchain start-ups, including

---

[269]Krugman (2009) & (2012); Stiglitz (2010).

[270]Allen (2013).

[271]https://tinyurl.com/yd8lxdzk

[272]Casey and Vigna (2018, pp. 10–16).

the Finnish fintech MONI, provide refugees with access to funds through DLT-secured transactions. MONI has been working with the Finnish Immigration Services since 2015 to give qualified refugees a prepaid credit card, secured by a digital ID number stored on a blockchain, that gives the cardholder access to government benefits.[273]

Another important social application of blockchain could be the control and administration of legal identities, especially for the 1.1 billion people in the world who, according to the World Bank, are "invisible" because they cannot prove their identity and lack any official recognition (ID) of their existence.[274] As a consequence, they struggle to access social services. Given that these services include access to vaccinations, the implications are dire not only for the 33% of this group who are children under 5 years old but also for their wider communities. ID2020 is a private-public partnership digital identity alliance that aims to use DLT technology to change this.[275]

In addition to highlighting the *need for trust*, the *cost of trust*, and the *dependence* on intermediaries, Casey and Vigna, point to tech giants like Amazon, Google, and Facebook, which have built right under our noses new centralized monopolies using "the most important *currency* in the world: our digital data."[276] By controlling our digital data, they are now able to control us. This is why, Casey and Vigna say, it is in our collective interest to "overturn this entrenched, centralized system" by securing our data using blockchain. Increased awareness of this application of blockchain may explain, at least in part, what Casey and Vigna describe as the "gold-rush-like scene in the crypto-token market, with its soaring yet volatile prices."[277]

A further benefit of blockchain technology could be the *transference of physical possessions into cyberspace*, the ability to possess a *digital asset*. Because copying digital products such as software, music, or e-books is easy, licensing regulations and safeguards have not proven effective. Blockchain and bitcoin make the ownership of a digital asset through a unique verification code possible. Because nobody can "alter the ledger and double-spend," or duplicate, a bitcoin, it can be conceived of as a unique "thing" or asset."[278] Therefore, a new economy could be created around these digitized assets that would be managed by blockchain-encrypted software. Regular money is independent of its usage. Through the application of blockchain technology, it can become programmable. According to Casey and Vigna, this could translate as follows:

---

[273]https://moni.com/

[274]https://tinyurl.com/yxnxtfhh

[275]https://id2020.org/

[276]Casey and Vigna (2018, p. 14).

[277]Ibid.

[278]Ibid.

- The contract representing the transfer of ownership of goods between the partic-
  ipants becomes "smart," not only automated in the context of banks and money
  owners.
- The contract-executing computers are monitored by a decentralized and distrib-
  uted network of blockchains.
- All participants in the "smart contract" ensure a fair transaction.
- There is no need for a third party/intermediaries.
- Open relationships at global scale are possible.
- Communities can begin to self-govern because programmable money (tokens)
  and smart contracts provide a secure and trustworthy foundation.

It also means that, in theory, decentralized economies could become possible
through this kind of "token" economy, although there are several downsides that
would need to be addressed (see below).

In his forthcoming white paper *The Role of a Parallel Digital Blockchain
Associated Currency to Finance Our Sustainable Development Goals (UN SDG)*
Stefan Brunnhuber presents a 30-step guideline for major stakeholders on how
blockchain (DLT) technology could be used to implement the 17 UN SDGs globally. Brunnhuber estimates the implementation cost at around US$5 trillion annually
over the next 20 years and deems traditional financing models unfit to provide the
necessary funding. He, therefore, suggests a parallel, blockchain-secured, electronic
currency that could provide the necessary means, finances, and actions to make it
happen while benefitting from the distributed ledger technology and its "traceability,
trust, and transparency, lower transaction costs, reduce additional energy consumption, and enable business automation, cross-organizational harmonization, authori-
zation, accountability and authentication."[279] Such a program could take advantage
of the built-in social contract of DLT and help reduce corruption while increasing the
efficiency of each transaction and the overall decentralized economy built with and
through it. The devil is in the detail, of course. If such ideas could be implemented,
they could both revolutionize and disturb the global economy as well as our current
financial systems.

Meanwhile, regulators all over the world are regarding the cryptobubble and
cryptocurrencies, such as "permissionless" blockchains Bitcoin or Ethereum, that
have been issued through Initial Coin Offerings[280] (an ICO is the rough equivalent of
an Initial Public Offering (IPO) in the regular investment world) as relatively easy
ways to avoid security laws and as new, speculative money-making schemes. The
author of the bestselling book *The Wisdom of Crowds*, James Surowiecki, even goes
as far as to call Bitcoin "a calamity, not an economy."[281] In an *MIT Technology
Review* article from May 2018, Surowiecki emphasizes the important role of governments in regulating our economic and financial systems through the central

---

[279]Brunnhuber (2019, pp. 10–11).

[280]https://papers.ssrn.com/sol3/papers.cfm?abstract_id=3080098

[281]Surowiecki (May/June 2018, p. 28).

banks' control of various currencies. By being able to issue debt in the local currency, governments can also help manage business cycles, combat unemployment, and address financial crises. Cryptocurrencies would create "a more volatile and harsher economy, in which the government would have limited tools to fight recessions and where financial panics, once started, would be hard to stop."[282] Only the future will show what will happen, but by 2018 the Chinese government, for example, had already imposed an official ban on ICOs and cryptocurrency-based crowdfunding and advertising schemes.[283] Twitter, Facebook, and Google did likewise,[284] although the latter rolled them partially back only a few months later.[285] Of course, change is constant. Facebook, for example, announced on June 18, 2019, a white paper in which it revealed details about its own cryptocurrency, Libra, which is expected to become available during the first half of 2020.[286] People could use their regular money to purchase Libra (so-called stable) coins and spend them either by buying things or transferring them to other people. Libra's "mission is to enable a simple [digital] global currency and financial infrastructure that empowers billions of people," especially the unbanked, by removing transaction fees common to regular credit cards and (international) money transfers. Needless to say, Facebook's declaration shocked the international finance world, particularly the central banks that, due to lack of cryptocurrency regulations, feel their national currency sovereignty is being threatened by Facebook's growing monopoly. Others regard it not only as a major disruption but also as the potential beginning of an international cryptocurrency race that could weaken and undermine the global economy. Although it has tightened cryptocurrency regulations, China's central bank has been working on a digital yuan since 2014 and is presumably planning to launch it through several organizations, including Tencent's WeChat Pay and Alibaba's Alipay.[287] Its digital currency may become China's key vehicle for enhancing its global economic position in the midst of the current trade war with the United States and, who knows, Libra could become a major ally.

But how secure is blockchain really? A closer analysis induces major doubt. For example, a 2016 attack that targeted Ethereum's blockchain was able to lift 3.6 million Ether, approximately US$80 million worth, from the Decentralized Autonomous Organization (DAO), a blockchain-based investment fund.[288] Luckily, the theft was "undone" through the application of a software update (called a *hard fork*) which essentially created a different history in the blockchain in which the money was not stolen. A much larger theft, however, took place in January 2018: US$523 million worth of the digital currency NEM disappeared from Coincheck, a Japanese

[282]Surowiecki (May/June 2018, p. 30).

[283]https://www.loc.gov/law/help/cryptocurrency/china.php

[284]https://support.google.com/adspolicy/answer/2464998

[285]https://tinyurl.com/ybt6wfck

[286]https://libra.org/en-US/white-paper/

[287]https://tinyurl.com/y3sa3mt6

[288]https://en.wikipedia.org/wiki/The_DAO_(organization)

cryptocurrency exchange.[289] The NEMs were stolen by hackers, who may never be identified, and the funds seem gone forever. This demonstrates that what is supposed to make the blockchain secure—namely (a) the *cryptographic fingerprint* (called *hash*) that is unique to each block in the chain, (b) the *consensus protocol* by which all participants/computers in the network (called *nodes* whose owners are called *miners*) agree on the common history, and (c) the *links* between the blockchain that include the previous hashes making it extremely difficult to retroactively change a previous entry—is not secure after all.

Another major downside is the extraordinary amount of computer power (including cooling requirements) and thus the energy required for the mining of new, encrypted blocks that can be added to the blockchain to secure new transactions. Current implementations are extremely energy-hungry and consume vast amounts of electricity, which translates into a significant carbon footprint. In a paper published by the MIT Center for Energy and Environmental Policy Research in November 2018, researchers showed that the energy consumption of Bitcoin per annum was around 48 TWh. They estimated that the annual carbon emissions from Bitcoin production range between 21.5 and 53.6 Mt. CO_2 and therefore called for regulatory intervention.[290] According to journalist Kathryn Miles, "Bitcoin is wrecking the environment" because of the currently used "energy-devouring proof-of-work approach" by blockchains that have been mined thus far mostly in China and Romania where there was little regulation and plenty of energy.[291] A less energy-hungry alternative could become the proof-of-stake system, which requires capital as a guarantee. However, the implementation of such systems has turned out to be rather complex and thus not much better than the inefficient, slow, and hardly scalable proof-of-work approach.

This all may change with the onset of quantum computing as the most evolved computation technology, a paradigm change, that enables the most advanced form of cryptography using quantum theory as suggested by Russian researchers Aleksey Fedorov, Evgeniy Kiktenko, and Alexander Lvovsky. In their article "Quantum Computers Put Blockchain Security at Risk,"[292] Fedorov et al. note that up to 10% of the global GDP will most likely be stored in blockchains by 2025 but encourage all blockchain tech users—for example, the finance, healthcare, and manufacturing sectors, but especially cryptocurrency issuers like Bitcoin—to integrate quantum technology if they want to survive. The authors consider the overall blockchain encrypted market to be worth more than US$150 billion and request increased data security, accountability, and transparency, particularly when the protected information is currency. They think that quantum computers "will be able to break a blockchain's cryptographic codes," based on their single line of defense (traditional cryptographic algorithms that issue digital signatures), within the next 10 years,

---

[289]https://tinyurl.com/ya8wznee & https://tinyurl.com/y5sv8smf
[290]Stoll et al. (December 2018).
[291]Miles (May/June 2018, p. 33).
[292]Fedorov et al. (19 November 2018).

rendering them obsolete. At the same time, quantum computers, once available, should be able to provide the solution to this problem by issuing quantum signatures through quantum cryptography using quantum Internet, and so on.[293] The conversation around blockchain remains exciting but is less existential than the one about the potential threat already arising out of the artificial intelligence (AI) revolution. MIT physicist Max Tegmark calls that "the most important conversation of our time."[294]

1.5 Artificial Intelligence: Revolution, Emergency, Salvation?

The general enthusiasm about AI that erupted in 1956 was soon followed by the AI winter.[295] That winter dawned not only because of lack of funding but also because of insufficient data, networking ability, and computing power to fulfill its promises. At the time, these promises included applications in computer vision, natural language processing, robotics, machine learning (particularly neural networks), and, my personal favorite, expert systems—knowledge-based systems that were trying to replicate human decision-making using object-oriented programming and rule-based inference machines. Today's resurgence of AI is basically due to the exponential growth in computing power (see Chap. 2) and the massive amounts of data now available, both of which fed the technological development of neural networks and their ability to mimic the qualities of the human brain. The purpose of this chapter, however, is not to add to the myriad books defining and explaining the extremely complex field of AI. My intention is instead to provide investors and company builders with enough knowledge to help them apply AI technologies to address current existential threats, particularly climate change, and, more crucially, understand the pitfalls to which AI development, if left unchecked, could lead. It is my conviction that AI is on its way to becoming a serious exponential threat itself.

AI Changed My Life in 1983
Originally, I wanted to study mathematics, but by the time I was ready to enroll at university, computer science had emerged and with it the opportunity to make math more practical, an idea that appealed to me. I, therefore, enrolled in computer science at the Karlsruhe Institute of Technology (KIT) in 1979. I loved the math classes and electronics classes, but I did not particularly enjoy

(continued)

---

[293]https://tinyurl.com/y37e4wzb
[294]Tegmark (2017, p. 22).
[295]https://en.wikipedia.org/wiki/AI_winter

the programming languages. From Assembly 8080 to Pascal, I found them rather cumbersome appropriations of human thinking, and it was not until I came across the field of artificial intelligence (AI), in particular expert systems, that my interest in AI was ignited. That occurred in 1983, when I attended the International Joint Conference on AI (IJCAI) in Karlsruhe, my university town. That conference set the course of my life, thanks to two significant decisions I made. One was to listen to a presentation by Stanford Professor John McCarthy, who coined the term AI in 1955[296] with the intention of recreating human intelligence in a computer and invented LISP, a practical mathematical notation, programming language, particularly to support AI programming, in 1958.[297] The second decision was to find out more about Knowledge Engineering Environment (KEE), a programming environment developed using LISP by IntelliCorp,[298] an AI software supplier founded by Stanford Professor Ed Feigenbaum,[299] Dr. Thomas P. Kehler, and others. I was thrilled. Using LISP and KEE, I could write code in a similar way to how I thought as a human being without having to twist my mind around to fit the syntax of traditional programming languages like Pascal, Fortran, or COBOL. Less than a year later, I was an exchange student at Stanford University, where I attended John McCarthy's AI classes. In 1986, after completing my diploma thesis on Expert Systems for VLSI Design at KIT, I joined IntelliCorp.

1.5.1   AI Is Not a Substitute for Human Stupidity

Climate change and nuclear threat are not the only existential threats we are facing. AI poses a third significant threat, particularly if it evolves to superintelligence, "a challenge for which we are not ready now," says Oxford philosopher Nick Bostrom.[300] Bostrom echoes the thoughts of many, including Max Tegmark, Edward Snowden, and Yuval Harari, with the latter insisting we should never underestimate "human stupidity."[301] Almost daily, we are confronted with news, and sometimes warnings, about how various forms of AI algorithms and applications are increasingly taking control of our lives.[302] These warnings have increased since some AI implementations began outperforming human intelligence in domains as

---

[296]http://www-formal.stanford.edu/jmc//reviews/bloomfield/bloomfield.html

[297]https://en.wikipedia.org/wiki/Lisp_(programming_language)

[298]https://en.wikipedia.org/wiki/IntelliCorp_(software)

[299]https://tinyurl.com/y6xlqndc

[300]Bostrom (2014, p. 259).

[301]Harari (2018, p. 179); Snowden (2019); Tegmark (2017).

[302]https://tinyurl.com/yyj5abwn & https://tinyurl.com/y6eo852a

diverse as poker and chess games to the game of Go.[303] For example, AlphaGo Zero, an application developed by British company DeepMind, surpassed the capabilities of its previous version AlphaGo, which was the first AI to defeat the human world Go champion. AlphaGo Zero "achieved superhuman performance, winning 100–0 against the previously published, champion-defeating [its predecessor] AlphaGo" by training itself.[304]

More recently, Google Assistant used Duplex, Google's current AI voice application, to make a phone call to schedule a haircut appointment in a salon without anyone realizing it was an AI.[305] Despite this success, Duplex did not pass the Turing test, named after Alan Turing, the British mathematician/computer scientist who decoded Enigma, the famous German encryption machine during World War II. Turing developed the test in 1950 to establish a computer's ability to display intelligent behavior similar to that of humans so that it could pass as a human.

The potential of AlphaGo Zero, Duplex, and similar AI applications is so significant that AI expert and venture capitalist Kai-Fu Lee puts AI at the center of the political fight for the "new world order."[306] In his book AI Superpowers, Lee estimates that by 2023, the AI battle between the United States and China will most likely be won by China, which "seems poised to seize global leadership"[307] in most of the following four AI waves:

1. *Internet AI* is ubiquitous in and controls people's lives through applications such as Netflix, YouTube videos, and platforms such as Amazon, Facebook, Alibaba, Baidu, and Google that already seem to "know" our preferences, interests, and shopping patterns. Those applications use algorithms to learn more about, label, optimize, and manipulate people. The significance of *Internet AI* applications became obvious when Cambridge Analytica purchased and used Facebook data to understand, target, and manipulate American voters during the 2016 presidential election.[308] Lee sees China at a 60–40 advantage over the rest of the world for three reasons: (a) its total number of Internet is higher than those of the United States and Europe combined, (b) its frictionless payment ability, and (c) its online-to-offline platforms (that "turn online actions to offline services,"[309] essentially navigating online users to brick-and-mortar service providers), which breed innovative AI applications.

[303]Bostrom (2014, pp. 12–13).

[304]Silver et al. (19 October 2017, p. 354).

[305]https://tinyurl.com/yasguzo5 & https://tinyurl.com/y2hgdg5w & https://tinyurl.com/yxcfoyh4

[306]Lee, K.-F. (2018a). Refer to page 136 for a "balance of capabilities between the United States and China across the four waves of AI, currently and estimated for 5 years in the future." For a more recent comparison by Lee, see his presentation during the a360 (Abundance 360) conference from January 2019. Viewed October 17, 2019 at https://tinyurl.com/yyh9h9a6

[307]Lee, K.-F. (2018a, p. 139).

[308]Nadler et al. (2018).

[309]Lee, K.-F. (2018a, p. 68).

2. *Business AI* is the second wave that uses AI technology to take advantage of and mine massive amounts of well-structured corporate databases and conventional enterprise software (legacy systems). These are available in more traditional companies such as insurance companies, banks, law offices, and hospitals, which have used human experts to categorize, search, and label their data for many decades. AI can now help humans make better sense of data and so make better decisions. For example, businesses can develop complex neural networks using IBM Watson,[310] a deep-learning service that helps data scientists design their own AI-based decision-making systems to provide better correlations between the available data for accounting, inventory, or management purposes. One of the more promising applications of *business AI* seems to lie in the healthcare field, particularly in terms of predictive medicine and diagnosis, but also for knowledge dissemination. For example, Jim Wang, CEO of NovaVision Group, a Chinese healthcare conglomerate, thinks that AI could level the playing field regarding the quality of healthcare provided in rural and urban areas in China.[311] Lee considers that the United States is currently leading (US 90–China 10) in *business AI* simply because of the historical development of legacy systems. He considers that China is likely to take the lead in public services in the future.

3. *Perception AI* is the third wave. It takes advantage of audio, visual, and other sensory intelligence to feed and run AI algorithms. For example, Amazon Echo and Alexa devices are digitizing the audio environment through voice recognition and natural language processing, Alibaba's City Brain[312] parses information from cameras in order to digitize traffic flows, and Apple's iPhone X uses computer vision and object recognition to safeguard mobile devices. Lee calls this merging of the online and offline worlds that *perception AI* facilitates OMO (online-merge-offline). This integrated environment driven and controlled by *perception AI* will, according to Lee, make, for example, pay-with-your-face, robot-assisted shopping, and individually tailored education, possible and accessible to users. The convenience of such OMO systems presupposes, of course, the user's permission not only for face and voice recognition purposes but also for accessing personal banking data and individual preferences and habits. Culturally, there are, however, huge differences at play. Lee asserts that the Chinese are more willing to trade their privacy for convenience than the Americans and Europeans, who are accustomed to and value democracy, privacy, and freedom. Lee gives China a clear advantage over the United States on *perception AI* simply because of its headstart on privacy elimination and the massive amount of data available from the country's large network of cameras and sensors in public areas. The crucial battle for privacy protection as a basic human right has just begun. (See below for more on this.)

---

[310]https://tinyurl.com/y3kcjdcm

[311]https://tinyurl.com/y7agxhmj

[312]https://www.alibabacloud.com/et/city

4. *Autonomous AI* "represents the integration and culmination of the three preceding waves," states Lee. He believes that "combining these superhuman powers yields machines that don't just understand the world around them—they shape it."[313] The premise for *autonomous AI* is the ability of machines to see, hear, sense, and optimize the massive amounts of data they collect and that will eventually render them autonomous. Lee considers the United States to currently be in the "commanding lead (90–10)," but "in 5 years' time [he gives] the United States and China even odds of leading the world in self-driving cars, with China having the edge in hardware-intensive applications such as autonomous drones."[314] (In earlier chapters we talked about the ongoing emergence of self-driving cars, autonomous robots, and autonomous drone technology. Once these are legally accepted they will all be examples of autonomous AI. For now, they are classified as automated, not autonomous: autonomous AI is allowed to make decisions and improvise as conditions change.)

Only the future will tell who leads the world in AI technologies. What we know for now is that China has understood the importance of AI development for its future position in the world and has "spurred myriad policies and billions of dollars of investment in research and development from ministries, provincial governments and private companies."[315] China is leading the world in solutions for natural language processing, computer vision, and robotics, and the average citations for AI papers authored by Chinese researchers are above the world average, albeit still lower than those of their US counterparts, who currently represent the largest AI talent pool. Before going deeper into the changes, challenges, and impact AI developments could have for societies and cultures around the world, let us get a better understanding of the current state of AI technology.

1.5.2 Demystifying AI

Two major technological advances in the mid-2000s brought an end to the AI winter: (1) the exponential growth in computing technology discussed earlier (Fig. 1.5) and (2) the increasing availability of data.

Both were crucial for the progress of neural networks with machine learning and deep learning (Fig. 1.8).

The learning technology embedded in neural networks was originally brought to the wider public in 1986 when researchers David Rumelhart, Geoffrey Hinton, and Ronald Williams published a paper describing "a new learning procedure, back-propagation, for networks of neuron-like units... [that] repeatedly adjusts the

---

[313]Lee, K.-F. (2018a, p. 128).

[314]Lee, K.-F. (2018a, p. 136).

[315]O'Meara (21 August 2019).

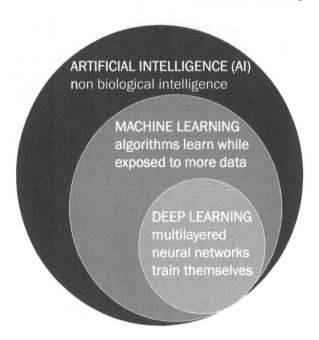

weights of the connections in the network" and helps train the neural network more efficiently.[316] However, the deep learning revolution was unleashed on the world through a paper by Alex Krizhevsky, Ilya Sutskever, and Geoffrey Hinton titled *ImageNet Classification with Deep Convolutional Neural Networks*.[317] The paper won the ImageNet competition[318] and revolutionized computer vision in 2012. Figure 1.8 shows the correlation between AI (also dubbed GOFAI for Good Old-Fashioned AI), machine learning, and deep learning.

Machine learning is a subset of AI, the algorithmic process through which AI creates nonbiological intelligence by analyzing and learning from large amounts of data in order to develop and adapt its own algorithms without external instructions.

Deep learning, on the other hand, tries to imitate the deep neural networks of the human brain. It gets increasingly better at recognizing and emulating humans' decision-making patterns and enables allows computers to understand ever-higher concepts from low-level data. For example, in order to win the game of Go, players have to use their own intuition to make their moves. Trying all possible solutions, even through the use of a computer, would be virtually impossible because the number of potential combinations is larger than the number of atoms in the universe.[319] Thus, AlphaGo, an application developed British company DeepMind, now owned by Google, is a deep learning AI that somehow developed its own

---

[316]Rumelhart et al. (9 October 1986).

[317]Krizhevsky et al. (3 December 2012).

[318]https://en.wikipedia.org/wiki/ImageNet#ImageNet_Challenge

[319]Tegmark (2017, pp. 86–89).

intuition and beat Lee Sedol, the world's Go champion in March 2016. This is a development that many AI experts said would not happen for at least another decade, although in 2015 Volodymyr Mnih et al. had published a paper titled *Human-Level Control through Deep-Reinforcement Learning*[320] in which they revealed how they applied behaviorist psychology techniques with positive reinforcement to classic machine learning. The reinforcement process allows AIs to become increasingly better at making predictions and to eventually make decisions without human intervention. For example, AlphaGo Zero surpassed the capabilities of its previous version, AlphaGo, achieved superhuman performance levels, and won 100–0 against AlphaGo by training *itself* and therefore "no longer [being] constrained by the limits of human knowledge," said DeepMind co-founder Demis Hassabis.[321] Based on sophisticated algorithms called (artificial) neural networks, deep learning is behind the radical technology advances we can find today in, for example, MRIs, satellite photography, facial recognition, language understanding, and simultaneous translation, to name only a few. Thanks to deep learning, self-driving cars could become safer, more reliable, and eventually better drivers than some humans (see the section on the Evolution of Mobility and Transportation).

Defining Intuition

The Cambridge dictionary defines intuition as "(knowledge from) an ability to understand or know something immediately based on your feelings rather than facts: Often there's no clear evidence one way or the other and you just have to base your judgment on intuition" (retrieved October 21, 2019, from https://dictionary.cambridge.org/dictionary/english/intuition). I personally consider most definitions of intuition restrictive because they tend to reduce humans to either cognitive and/or emotional beings. I, therefore, subscribe to a multi-perspectival, more integral view, and mode of knowing described in more detail through Ken Wilber's Integral Theory[322] (see Chap. 2).

An additional example of an application of AI that benefits humanity is the integration of collective intelligence and AI technology within the area of faulty protein folding as it occurs in illnesses such as Parkinson's and Alzheimer's disease.[323] Proteins are key building blocks of biology, and their shapes, which define their function, depend on the sequence of their amino acids. Under normal circumstances, proteins take the most energy-efficient shape, but sometimes they can become tangled and fold in an unhealthy way, leading to disease. Some scientists have been using custom computer programs on supercomputers to try to understand and predict how a protein unfolds, although success has been limited to date.

---

[320]Mnih et al. (26 February 2015).

[321]https://tinyurl.com/y39f8hyg

[322]Wilber (2000).

[323]Agbas (30 August 2018).

However, there have been some successes from possibly unlikely quarters. FoldIt is a crowdsourced protein folding prediction computer game conceived by computer science professor David Salesin and biochemistry professor David Baker, both of the University of Washington, and developed by a team under Zoran Popovic, an associate professor of computer graphics, also at the University of Washington.[324] The combination of computing power and gamers' intuition turned out to be a very powerful one. In 2011, it proved key to a victory in the fight against HIV/AIDS.[325] But these advances did not stop at supercomputing or crowdsourcing. In December 2018, Google's DeepMind introduced the world to AlphaFold,[326] a deep learning application based on neural networks for predicting protein folding to accelerate drug research. AlphaFold is, however, only the beginning of AI's ability to make a real impact in the realm of disease treatment and medical breakthroughs. These distinctions lead us to another way of classifying AI, namely:

Narrow AI (also known as *ANI: Artificial Narrow Intelligence*), called "'weak AI'—the variety devoted to providing aids to human thought" by Nils Nilsson,[327] is the kind of AI available today and includes the examples mentioned thus (e.g., facial recognition, natural language processing, machine translation, data-driven decision-making, and self-driving vehicles). *Narrow AI* is not even close to matching human intelligence. It lacks consciousness, self-awareness, and emotions, but it is able to learn and to enhance itself (e.g., DeepMind AlphaGo and DeepMind AlphaGo Zero).

General AI (also known as *AGI: Artificial General Intelligence*), or what Nilsson calls "'strong AI'—[as] the variety that attempts to mechanize human intelligence"[328] whereby intelligence is defined by Max Tegmark as "maximally broad" (as opposed to *narrow* AI) and has the "ability to achieve complex goals."[329] *AGI* is anticipated to perform high-level reasoning, solve complex problems, learn, plan, think in an abstract manner, strategize, innovate, create, and make judgments based on uncertainty. According to Hans Moravec, however, "it is comparatively easy to make computers exhibit adult level performance on intelligence tests or playing checkers, and difficult or impossible to give them the skills of a one-year-old when it comes to perception and mobility."[330] This observation is called Moravec's paradox.[331] It is expected that human-level AGI should be able to accomplish any goal at least as well as a human so that it can pass the Turing test and become a universal Turing machine. However, in order to

[324]https://fold.it/portal/info/about

[325]https://www.scientificamerican.com/article/foldit-gamers-solve-riddle/

[326]https://deepmind.com/blog/alphafold/

[327]Nilsson (2009, p. 319).

[328]Nilsson (2009, p. 319).

[329]Tegmark (2017, p. 50).

[330]Moravec (1992/1988, p. 15).

[331]https://en.wikipedia.org/wiki/Moravec%27s_paradox#CITEREFMoravec1988

achieve that, AGI should experience consciousness, empathy, and sentience; the ability to perceive, feel, and subjectively experience something. Tegmark believes that "there's a non-negligible possibility that AGI progress will proceed to human levels and beyond,"[332] which could lead to an intelligence explosion, the *singularity*, with the creation of superintelligence and beyond.

Super AI, also known as *ASI (Artificial Super Intelligence)*, is defined as an AI that uses AGI to become superintelligent. Oxford philosopher Nick Bostrom defines superintelligence as an intellect that outperforms "the best current human minds across many very general cognitive domains."[333] He posits that ASI could emerge within 30 years of AGI, which, according to various sources, could occur by 2075 with a probability of 90%.[334]

How far we really are from achieving AGI or superintelligence is subject to much speculation and discussion.[335] However, we cannot afford not to be part of further developments in this field, because they can turn into an existential risk for humanity if left unchecked. According to Bostrom, "superintelligence is a challenge for which we are not ready" and "some little idiot is bound to press the ignite button just to see what happens."[336] Needless to say, we must do whatever is required to prevent that from happening, and in the next section, we will take a closer look at the potential and challenges of AI, particularly from the perspective of investing and company building.

1.5.3   Why AI Must Be Regulated

Elon Musk is a well-known critic of unsafe and unethical AI. He argues that, if we do not pay attention, the percentage of nonhuman intelligence (i.e., AI) on our planet will continue to grow until it supersedes human intelligence, with potentially dire consequences.[337] Echoing the words of the late Stephen Hawking, Musk warned about the dangers of AI in saying, "We need to be super careful with AI. Potentially more dangerous than nukes"[338] while expressing his frustration about his futile efforts to get governments to regulate it.[339] During a panel with Alibaba's founder Jack Ma at the 2019 World Artificial Intelligence Conference, Musk stated, "Most people underestimate the capability of AI" and "the biggest mistake AI researchers

---

[332]Tegmark (2017, p. 133).

[333]Bostrom (2014, p. 52).

[334]Bostrom (2014, pp. 18–21).

[335]Bostrom (2014); Kurzweil (1999) & (2001); Tegmark (2017).

[336]Bostrom (2014, p. 259).

[337]https://tinyurl.com/y6nzdoyx

[338]https://tinyurl.com/y2x4ba7j

[339]https://www.youtube.com/watch?v=5taE_br3Vr8

are making is to assume that they are intelligent."[340] In his view, the difference between AI and humans in the future will be like the difference between current humans and chimpanzees. Counteracting Musk's assessment, Ma argues that "only college people are scared of AI, street-smart people [like him] are not," because once people begin to understand themselves better, they can improve the world. Musk jokingly called Ma's statement "famous last words" and argued for the importance of fighting for the preservation of human consciousness. Musk added, "If you can't beat them, join them" which is one of the reasons he invested in Neuralink, a company that creates brain–machine interfaces aiming to enhance the bandwidth and other capabilities of the human brain. This is obviously an emotive topic. In order to understand what "join[ing] them" means, we must understand what is at stake, what we are trying to preserve, what we are fighting for, what consciousness is, and what human intelligence is. More importantly, we must understand what AI is, the dangers associated with its development (starting with AGI and ASI), and what the rest of us, particularly investors and company builders, can individually do to "secure the future of consciousness such that the light of consciousness is not extinguished" without going to Mars.[341]

As in so many other areas, Musk has shown us the way. In January 2015, he donated US$10 million to the Future of Life Institute, an organization founded by Max Tegmark, Jaan Tallinn, Anthony Aguire, et al., to keep "AI beneficial for humanity," jumpstart AI safety research, and make sure AI is regulated before it spirals out of control.[342] After agreeing that superintelligence presents a clear and present danger to humanity, in January 2015 the "world's top artificial intelligence developers sign[ed an] open letter calling for AI-safety research," which on January 6, 2017, led to the development and adoption of the 23 Asilomar AI Principles.[343] These principles acknowledge the benefits of AI without being blinded by them. I have also signed them, and I encourage everyone to do the same and to adhere to them. They are clustered under the headings of research issues, ethics and values, and longer-term issues.

Several other initiatives have since been launched. For example:

- OpenAI, a nonprofit organization in San Francisco (https://openai.com)
- The Machine Intelligence Research Institute (MIRI) in Berkeley, California (https://intelligence.org)
- The Leverhulme Center for the Future of Intelligence in Cambridge, UK (www.lcfi.ac.uk)
- The K&L Gates Endowment for Ethics and Computational Technologies at Carnegie Mellon University in Pittsburg, Pennsylvania (https://www.cmu.edu/ethics-ai/)

---

[340]https://www.youtube.com/watch?v=f3lUEnMaiAU

[341]Musk (2019, Minute 12:19). Viewed 25 October 2019 at https://www.youtube.com/watch?v=f3lUEnMaiAU

[342]https://tinyurl.com/y8xvrp6s

[343]https://tinyurl.com/y42nlfrp & https://futureoflife.org/ai-principles/

- The Future of Humanity Institute in Oxford, UK (https://www.fhi.ox.ac.uk).
- The Center for the Study of Existential Risk in Cambridge, UK (https://www.cser.ac.uk)
- The industry partnership for beneficial AI between Amazon, DeepMind, Facebook, Google, IBM and Microsoft (https://www.partnershiponai.org)

But what exactly are the traps and dangers of AI?

1.5.4 Intelligence and Consciousness

Earlier I discussed the stages of evolution and referred to Tegmark's definition of life as "a process that can retain its complexity and replicate"[344] while evolving from:

- A simple biological stage, Life 1.0, to
- A cultural stage, Life 2.0, to
- A technological stage, Life 3.0, where it can design both its software and hardware and can take control over its own future.

Life 3.0 is what AGI could achieve in the twenty-first century. However, there are some dissenters from this opinion. First, there are the "techno sceptics" who believe that AGI will not occur for several hundreds of years. Then there are the "digital utopians," including Google's co-founder Larry Page, one of "the most influential exponent(s)" of a digital life as the next step in cosmic evolution. According to Tegmark, Page is convinced that the outcome of Life 3.0 would most certainly be good. Page insists we should let go of "AI paranoia," as it could delay the further evolution of digital life, thus causing "a military takeover of AI."[345] Tegmark has become a proponent of the third alternative, the "beneficial-AI movement." This possibility could eventually also enable Life 3.0 in this century, but its "good" outcome must be enforced through hard work and global cooperation—and as we have seen, he is not alone in this opinion.

Addressing these significant topics will take time and require a major collective effort at national and international levels. From an investor's perspective, we can only aim at gaining a clearer idea about the various issues at hand so we can take informed decisions on how to contribute to the future of life in a way that benefits us all in an integrally sustainable fashion. So, let us continue to understand the terms artificial intelligence, intelligence, and consciousness before moving on to highlighting the potential dangers of an unchecked AGI.

In *Life 3.0*, Tegmark defines AI as "non-biological intelligence," intelligence as the "ability to accomplish complex goals," and AGI as the "ability to accomplish any

---

[344]Tegmark (2017, p. 48).
[345]Tegmark (2017, p. 32).

cognitive task at least as well as humans."[346] He also acknowledges that "there is no undisputed definition of consciousness" and uses the "broad and non-anthropocentric definition *consciousness = subjective experience*" without going too deep into philosophical discussions surrounding the "*hard* problem" of consciousness that debates whether or not matter has consciousness.[347] In simple terms, humans are using their natural intelligence, including their various levels of consciousness/awareness, to build AI machines that should eventually able to complete any job as well as their human builders. The thorniest conversation would arise if AIs eventually became conscious, had feelings, and subsequently were entitled to rights. We must look at the ethical considerations of this potential eventuality before it is too late, but because we are at the very beginning of this change, we do not recognize and are therefore ignoring the double exponential growth of the technology evolution. Not only are we prey to Moravec's paradox, but, as Elon Musk noted, we have not yet developed the required sense of urgency to protect ourselves. Moreover, if we are to build artificially intelligent systems, we must understand intelligence first, and to date, we have only a partial understanding of it.

One concept that I deem extremely important within the context of AI, but which is rarely discussed, is that of human mindset evolution. During the course of our lives, we can grow and develop our mindsets, our human software as Tegmark calls it, and have the opportunity to acquire wisdom and virtues and grow to later stages of consciousness evolution (see Chap. 2 for more on this). If left unchecked, this growth could actually lead to AI programmers building their own biases into the AI applications they develop, which in turn would lead to unethical and unsafe AIs. For example, shortly after Google launched with great fanfare their AI-driven machine learning software Google Photos, it emerged that it was identifying Black people as "gorillas."[348] While this was later acknowledged to be a major mistake, it is symptomatic of the very real risks of programmers building their own biases into AIs—for example, biased views on gender or racial bias in healthcare algorithms.[349] (Remember GIGO: garbage in, garbage out? Personal bias, especially bias that programmers are blissfully oblivious to, creates a similar type of challenge.)

While such biases are likely to be more or less accidental, due to the programmers' lack of awareness, some AI algorithms have been deliberately and specifically designed to keep users glued to certain platforms such as Facebook, Amazon, or YouTube in order to increase revenues.[350] In a 2019 article for the *MIT Technology Review*, Karen Hao writes about how Google is enhancing its YouTube machine learning algorithms. A tiny increase of 0.24% in user engagement can translate into

---

[346]Tegmark (2017, p. 39).

[347]Tegmark (2017, p. 315).

[348]https://www.bbc.com/news/technology-33347866

[349]https://tinyurl.com/y6aqj56d and https://tinyurl.com/yyjtgc62

[350]https://tinyurl.com/y2ez4c2y

millions of dollars in additional revenue for the company.[351] A more sinister example of this occurred on February 17, 2019, when a YouTuber exposed a so-called wormhole that facilitates the exploitation and monetization of child pornography.[352]

1.5.5 Data Hunger, Privacy Violation, and Ethical Implications

AI algorithms are data-hungry because without data they cannot function. Their main purpose is to collect massive amounts of data to improve themselves, which in turn translates into higher revenues for their operators. Before Google went global and made billions of dollars selling our information, for example, nobody thought much about its vehicle driving through our streets and taking pictures of our houses, cars, gardens, and yards. Before it become known that Facebook, to give another example, illegally sold millions of personal data sets to the UK-based Cambridge Analytica, thus enabling Russian hackers to target and significantly influence American voters during the 2016 election, few people either took AI algorithms seriously or considered them dangerous.[353] In fact, few people think twice about the fact that Facebook, Amazon, Alibaba, or Google, etc., are using their clients' private information to make millions of dollars by selling that information without the owners' explicit permission. At the time of writing, no one has yet asked for a share of the revenue derived from their data, although it would seem only fair to do so.

When I ask people about their opinions about privacy, most say they have nothing to hide. But "saying that you don't care about privacy because you have nothing to hide is no different from saying that you don't care about freedom of speech because you have nothing to say," states whistleblower Edward Snowden in his 2019 book *Permanent Record*.[354] In other words, if we care about preserving our democracies along with *all* our precious human rights—equality, freedom, and liberty—we must think again, and more deeply. Why? Because our freedom is priceless, and it is certainly not up for grabs. "Just because this or that freedom might not have meaning to you today doesn't mean that it doesn't or won't have meaning tomorrow, to you, or to your neighbor."[355] I grew up in Romania under Ceausescu's dictatorship fully aware that "walls have ears." I remember vividly how my parents and I always lowered our voices when we talked about something vital, such as our plans to emigrate to West Germany in 1973. In fact, we continued to lower our voices for many years after we relocated to Germany. Today, I am being reminded of the lack

---

[351] https://tinyurl.com/y2tooww6

[352] https://tinyurl.com/y5bdh946

[353] https://tinyurl.com/y9rorxln

[354] Snowden (2019, p. 208).

[355] Snowden (2019, p. 209).

of freedom I experienced during my childhood and I am worried. I am worried because we all carry potential surveillance devices with us. We keep them in our homes, trusting that they serve us rather than spy on us. But we must not be naïve. To keep our democratic freedoms, we, as investors and company builders, must act decisively before it is too late. Existing AIs have already begun penetrating our world, presenting us with distinctive and significant ethical questions, and we currently lack precise and stable answers for them. This became more obvious to me during my participation in the Augmented Intelligence Summit, held and organized by the Future of Life Institute in March 2019.[356] We discussed various topics related to beneficial AI, including the future of healthcare, work, criminal justice, and ethics. The conversations were informed by an excellent paper titled "AI Policy: A Primer and Roadmap" by law professor Ryan Calo, who does not think that AI presents an existential threat to humanity in the foreseeable future.[357] He insists, however, that the conversation around AI ethics needs not only simple ethical standards but also policy and binding rules to enforce it. In his view, these policies should address the following questions:

- *Justice and equality* through "the capacity of algorithms or trained systems to reflect human values such as fairness, accountability, and transparency ('FAT'),"[358] which would include bias and material decisions with respect to financial, health, and liberty outcomes.
- *Use of force* as a special case of AI-enabled decision-making (that bears the responsibility for the choices made by machines) and consensus about meaningful human control, especially with respect to decisions to go to war.
- *Safety, certification, and cybersecurity*, especially with respect to autonomous systems, such as in cars, robots, but also in airplanes (e.g., the 2019 Boeing 737 Max scandal).[359]
- *Privacy and power*, as discussed above within the context of data hunger and its ownership, as consumer privacy has become increasingly under siege with citizens having little or no ability to avoid various forms of surveillance.
- *Various cross-cutting questions* that would make sure that, because of its complex and novel nature, the topic of safe and beneficial AI is addressed as a whole and not in bits and pieces. In general, law and technology are seen as too slow to react to one another. That could backfire in this case, given the exponentially growing nature of AI technology and the lack of expertise at the policy level, to name a few issues.
- *Taxation and displacement of labor*, which is concerned with the prospect of AIs displacing jobs currently performed by humans (e.g., through autonomous

---

[356]https://futureoflife.org/augmented-intelligence-summit-2019-2/

[357]https://lawreview.law.ucdavis.edu/issues/51/2/Symposium/51-2_Calo.pdf

[358]Calo (2017, p. 9).

[359]https://www.theguardian.com/business/2019/oct/23/boeing-profits-737-max-mcas-scandal

vehicles), providing universal basic income by imposing taxes on AIs (i.e., robots), or taxing innovation and progress.

AIs cannot advance without automatically learning from an ever-increasing amount of data. However, the most important issue regarding data regulation is not about what to do with data and how to handle it once it has been collected. We must focus instead on the *prevention of data collection* in the first place. Data should not be collected without the explicit consent of data owners—in other words, us. (A further distinction must be made with respect to the legality or illegality aspect of data collection, discussed below.)

At the EU level, there are several activities taking place around General Data Protection Regulations (GDPR), a legislation that passed in April 2016 and was enforced in May 2018.[360] The GDPR aims at protecting the data privacy of each EU citizen, including those in the European Economic Area, by giving individuals control over their own data, forcing data collectors to disclose their data collection practice, and limiting the data retention time. (When you are asked to give your consent to a website regarding its cookie practice, know that this is the result of this or similar laws.) In June 2019, the European Commission published a detailed OECD report, *Artificial Intelligence in Society*, that looks at and assesses policy and governance interventions on how the acceleration of AI development is affecting global economies and societies.[361] The report honors the importance of AI applications in myriad areas including mobility, healthcare, criminal justice, marketing, security, and safety. Under the guidance of a high-level, multistakeholder group of experts, the OECD also developed the first international AI standards, including its own AI Principles, agreed on by multiple governments. Furthermore, on April 8, 2019, the European Commission published its "Ethics Guidelines for Trustworthy AI."[362] According to these guidelines, trustworthy AI must be:

- "Lawful" in accordance with existing laws and regulations
- "Ethical" with respect to ethical principles and regulations
- "Robust" with respect to both technology and the social environment

It must also obey human agency and oversight, privacy and data governance, transparency, diversity and fairness, accountability and responsibility, and human and environmental wellbeing standards, and be technically robust and safe. Does this all mean that the NSA, Facebook, Amazon, YouTube, and Google have stopped illegally collecting data from Europeans? Well, no. It means that we, the people, have begun to fight back, watch what is going on, and act. This is an important first step in the age of exponentially growing technologies (where we are subject to

---

[360]https://tinyurl.com/y2wpcvc3

[361]https://ec.europa.eu/jrc/communities/sites/jrccties/files/eedfee77-en.pdf

[362]https://tinyurl.com/y6e9okmz and https://tinyurl.com/y5b44wef

various types of hacking from AI to biotech, a separate topic that is beyond the scope of this book).[363]

We must also be aware of the *legality issue*. Why? Because legality does not always equate to democratic law. Since Snowden's whistleblowing in 2013, we have learned that numerous governmental organizations are collaborating with major telecommunications and technology companies to access our data, invade our privacy, and exercise power and control over us under the pretext of national security.[364] According to information made available to the German newspaper *Süddeutsche Zeitung*, major politicians such as German Chancellor Angela Merkel, ex-Italian Prime Minister Sergio Berlusconi, and former UN General Secretary Ban Ki-Moon are subject to surveillance and privacy invasion. All three have had confidential phone conversations intercepted.[365] Snowden has also alerted us something even more disturbing: hacking our privacy—even hacking the American constitution—is sometimes perfectly *legal*.[366] We should, therefore, be deeply concerned about how some governments are changing the law to fit their need for surveillance under the pretext of terrorism investigation without a court order. For example, the US PRISM program "enabled the NSA to routinely collect data from Microsoft, Yahoo!, Google, Facebook, Paltalk, YouTube, Skype, AOL, and Apple, including email, photos, video and audio chats . . . transforming the companies into witting coconspirators."[367]

Stuart Russell, UC Berkeley professor and author of *Human Compliance: Artificial Intelligence and the Problem of Control,* and one of the speakers at the 2019 Augmented Intelligence Summit, confirms what Bostrom, Musk, Harari, and Tegmark have been saying all along: "We must plan for the possibility that machines will far exceed the human capacity for decision making in the real world" by creating and gaining access to a superintelligence, which could be the biggest but also "the last event in human history"[368] (by which he implies that humans may not have a future thereafter). I am mindfully optimistic that we will succeed because there are many ways to avoid disaster. Like Isaak Asimov, who devised the three laws of robotics,[369] Russell specifies three principles for "provably beneficial" machines/AI that could help humanity steer toward the future we want[370]:

- The only objective of machines is "to maximize the realization of human preferences."
- The "machine is initially uncertain about what those preferences are."

---

[363]Harari (2017).

[364]https://en.wikipedia.org/wiki/Edward_Snowden

[365]https://tinyurl.com/yyxf4vjf

[366]Snowden (2019, p. 223).

[367]Snowden (2019, pp. 223–224).

[368]Russell (2019, p. xi).

[369]Chase (2015, p. 164).

[370]Russell (2019, p.173).

- The "ultimate source of information about human preferences is human behavior," whereby preferences are individually defined, are all-encompassing, and address everything humans might ever care about.

Asimov's Three Laws of Robotics
1. A robot may not injure a human being or, through inaction, allow a human being to come to harm.
2. A robot must obey the orders given it by human beings except where such orders would conflict with the First Law.
3. A robot must protect its own existence as long as such protection does not conflict with the First or Second Law.

Like Russell, world-renowned Stanford teacher and Baidu chief scientist Andrew Ng thinks AI will transform every possible industry "just as electricity transformed almost everything 100 years ago"[371] and that we must assess the vital role of AI in our everyday life, address our security needs, take advantage of untapped data sources to inform our AI algorithms, and find out how we can disrupt ourselves before it disrupts us.

As a trained AI and computer scientist, I have learned to live with the idea that this extraordinary technology can be used to do both good and bad. This is why I have chosen to stay alert, become deeply involved with it, and be right there at the forefront of the development, ready to act for the greater good using my investing and company-building skills. While I want to feel protected by my own country and its government, especially in a global world that is not always ruled by democracy, I also want to have sovereignty over my own data. Therefore, I do not agree with either governments or companies legally or illegally invading our privacy and collecting our data to exercise power or control. Moreover, I do not think it is right for companies to collect our data to enhance their AI algorithms without our consent. This is as much a governance and policy issue as it is an issue of values, ethics, and morals that should be sourced at the highest possible levels of consciousness (world-centric or Kosmos-centric). Rather than worry about being subjugated by out-of-control AIs, I would rather leverage the benefits of exponentially growing technologies to solve the current climate and myriad other crises plaguing us globally and locally. On a round planet, there is no choosing upsides.

Moving forward, the vital question should no longer be whether "AI is more dangerous than nukes," because we can establish with certitude that AIs can become more dangerous. The potential danger becomes perfectly obvious once we begin to understand what is truly possible. Thus, the question is not about whether an autonomous car is more dangerous than a horse carriage or a metal knife more dangerous than fire. No, we must go well beyond these superficial conversations,

---

[371]https://www.gsb.stanford.edu/insights/andrew-ng-why-ai-new-electricity

because technology development is part of our human journey through time and space. We must not only make sure we keep AIs under control but also go much deeper to truly understand the bigger picture. We must begin to understand ourselves, our place in the universe, and within the bigger picture of evolution—but not only evolution, also its underlying feature, namely exponential growth. No matter how educated we are, our minds cannot truly comprehend, let alone address, exponential growth, because we are linear thinkers by nature. Yet in the light of AI progress, we can, and must, make this quantum leap in evolution and take control. We must grow and reach higher levels of consciousness so we can imbue our AIs with wisdom and a mindset that rests in the later stages of consciousness (see Chap. 2). If we do not, we risk being eliminated by the very AIs we are developing.

According to Kurzweil's Law of Accelerating Returns, the speed, cost-effectiveness, and power of the evolutionary process increase exponentially over time. That could eventually render traditional humans obsolete. In Chap. 2, I discuss Ken Wilber's Integral Theory and how evolution applies positive feedback. This process results in exponential growth over time so that *the rate of exponential growth itself grows exponentially*, which is even more difficult for humans to understand. Technological evolution has evolved to support our biological evolution. The next paradigm shift is already occurring from biological thinking to a hybrid construct that combines both biological and nonbiological thinking such as smartphones, computers, nanobots, and so on, moving from biohumanism to neurohumanism to posthumanism.[372] I am cautiously optimistic that we can create a truly inspiring future if we win the race between the growing power of AI and other technologies and the wisdom with which we manage them. To win this race, we must adopt a different strategy than our old one, which allowed us to learn from our mistakes as we explored the creation and use of fire, combustion engines, even atomic power. Within the context of AGI, synthetic biology, or an AGI-driven nuclear arms race, we must get it right from the start by making it safe, because these technologies could obliterate us. We *must* take control of what future AIs are allowed to do. Because there are different levels of consciousness, we must ensure that wise democracies from world-centric levels of consciousness drive our decision-making. We must ensure that a Gandhi-type, not a Hitler-type, informs our decisions (see Chap. 2). Only if we understand and honor the existence of different stages of consciousness evolution will we be in a position to create beneficial AIs. Will these AIs be driven by an egocentric or ethnocentric mindset that would create separation and nationalistic tendencies, or will we make sure that our AIs are implementing a world-centric or even Kosmos-centric level of consciousness for us all? The decision is ours to make. We will see in Chap. 2 and Chap. 3 how a more holistic approach to investing has a role to play in such decision-making.

---

[372]Kurzweil (2005).

1.6 Summary of Chapter 1

Thus far, we have looked at some of the most important contexts in which humanity operates these days and which are relevant from the perspective of an investor who wants to have a positive impact in the disruption era. We live in exciting, and fast-changing, times. The remarkable advancements in technology and the capital flowing into its ongoing development could give techno-enthusiasts like me a reason to believe that progress will continue at the current, exponential pace, largely uninhibited by the current climate emergency, the vulnerability created by our current outdated financial systems, or as yet unknown other challenges, and that technology—including AIs—will eventually solve our current issues before it is too late to reverse the damage our species has inflicted on ourselves and our planet. For many, it appears to be a zero-sum game whereby we put all our eggs into the technological basket. The "race of our lives" would then be defined by free-market mechanisms that eventually bring us to a safe place where we all win within a *business as usual* scenario and hope reigns supreme. Hope is, however, a good student but a very bad master. What could be a better master? Von Weizsäcker and Wijkman in *Come On!,* Pope Francis in his encyclical *Laudato Si',*[373] and Steven Pinker in *Enlightenment Now,*[374] have all called for a new Enlightenment.[375] But why do we need a new Enlightenment? What is wrong with the old one? Von Weizsäcker and Wijkman agree that in order to be able to address the global challenges, a new Enlightenment must:

- *Be world-centric* rather than Eurocentric
- *Go well beyond individual freedoms* and the separation of state and Church
- *Address the current philosophical crises* mainly caused by the current destructive practices of modern capitalism

Enlightenment 2.0, say von Weizsäcker and Wijkman, ought to be wisdom-driven, a balance between nature and humanity, short- and long-term goals, acceleration, and steadiness, and the private and public realms. It should also encourage achievement and reward justice and equity. But there is also a new dimension that we must realize, namely what Maja Göpel calls The Great Mindshift.[376] In order to implement such a new global, wisdom-driven model for thriving on our blue planet, however, we must dig deeper and look well beyond the *external* manifestations of applying a technological, regulatory, scientific, social, or environmental lens. We must take a closer look at the *source of wisdom and virtue*. We must look within at the *hidden determinants* of such exterior transformation—*our interiors both individual and collective*. This is what we will do next.

---

[373]Pope Francis (2015).

[374]Pinker (2018).

[375]Von Weizsäcker and Wijkman (2018).

[376]Göpel (2016).

References

Adamchuck V (2013) Precision agriculture and food security in bringing space down to earth. 13 March 2015 (16–20). By the world economic Forum's global agenda council on space security. Viewed 26 April 2020 at https://tinyurl.com/ybrmxp35

Agbas A (2018, 30 August) Trends of protein aggregation in neurodegenerative diseases. Viewed 21 October 2019 at https://www.intechopen.com/online-first/trends-of-protein-aggregation-in-neurodegenerative-diseases

Allen L (2013) The global economic crisis: a chronology. Reaktion Books, London

Arbib J, Seba T (2017) Rethinking transportation 2020–2030. The disruption of transportation and the collapse of the internal-combustion vehicle and oli industries. A RethinkX sector disruption project. Viewed 16 March 2019 at https://tinyurl.com/y7nr4k95

Austin HP et al. (2018) Characterization and engineering if a plastic-degrading aromatic polyesterase. PNAS, 115(19), E4350-E4357; published ahead of print 17 April 2018. https://doi.org/10.1073/pnas.1718804115 Viewed 15 March 2019 at https://www.pnas.org/content/115/19/E4350

Beckerman W (1972) Economists, scientists, and environmental catastrophe. Oxf Econ Pap 24 (3):327–344

Beckerman W (1992) Economic growth and the environment: whose growth? Whose environment? World Dev 20(4):481–489

Berret M (2018, 1 October) New mobility trends: China is driving away from the competition. A Roland Berger report. Viewed 3 April 2020 at https://tinyurl.com/y6wmggra

Bostrom N (2014) Superintelligence: paths, dangers, strategies. Oxford University Press, Oxford

Bozesan (2020, 31 March) What follows COVID-19: Democratic evolution or regression toward autocracy. An earlier version of this section was published on medium.com on 31 March 2020, at https://tinyurl.com/uxnbm9v

Brunnhuber S (2019) Forthcoming book The Tao of finance. PDF made available through personal email exchange with Stefan Brunnhuber, 2 October 2019

Brynjolfsson E, McAfee A (2014) The second machine age: work, progress, and prosperity in a time of brilliant technologies. W.W. Norton & Company, New York, London

Calo R (2017) Artificial intelligence policy: a primer and roadmap. Univ Calif Davies 51:399. Viewed 26 October 2019 at https://lawreview.law.ucdavis.edu/issues/51/2/Symposium/51-2_Calo.pdf

Casey MJ, Vigna P (2018, May/June) In blockchain we trust. MIT Rev 121(3):10–16

Cavalcanti A, Shirinzadeh B, Zhang M, Kretly LC (2008) Nanorobot hardware architecture for medical defense. Sensors 2008(8):2932–2958. https://doi.org/10.3390/s8052932. Viewed 3 April 2020 at https://www.ncbi.nlm.nih.gov/pmc/articles/PMC3675524/

Chase C (2015) Surviving AI: the promise and peril of artificial intelligence. The Three Cs Publishing [city of publication not identified]

Cyranoski D, Ledford H (2018, 26 November) Genome-edited baby claim provokes international outcry. Viewed 3 April 2020 at https://tinyurl.com/y8gyk2yb

De Grey A, Rae M (2007) Ending aging: the rejuvenation breakthroughs that could reverse human aging in our lifetime. St. Martin's Press, New York

De Pee A, Pinner D, Roelofsen O, Somers K, Spleeman E, Wittleveen M (2018, June) Decarbonization of industrial sectors: the next frontier. Viewed 3 April 2020 at https://tinyurl.com/y4p4rkxy

Deikman A (1998) Intuition. In: Palmer H (ed) Inner knowing: consciousness, creativity, insight, intuition. Jeremy P. Tarcher, New York, pp 177–185

Diamandis PH, Kotler S (2012) Abundance: the future is better than you think. Free Press, New York

Diamandis PH, Kotler S (2015) Bold: how to go big, create wealth, and impact the world. Simon & Schuster, New York

Dorling D (2014) Inequality and the 1%. Verso, London, New York

Durairaj RB, Shanker J, Sivasankar M (2012) Nano robots in bio medical application in proceedings of IEEE-international conference on advances in engineering, science and management (ICAESM–2012), Nagapattinam, Tamil Nadu, 2012, pp. 67–72. Viewed 3 April 2020 at https://tinyurl.com/sb4juq8

Edelman Trust Barometer (2019) 19th Annual global report. Viewed 14 March 2020 at https://tinyurl.com/ulzekno

Fedorov AK, Kiktenko EO, Lvovsky AI (2018, 19 November) Quantum computers put blockchain security a risk. Nature 563(7732):465–467. Viewed 28 April 2020 at https://tinyurl.com/ybt6wfck

Galaz W, Crona B, Dauriach A, Jouffray J-B, Österblom H, Fichter J (2018, 13 August) Tax havens and global environmental degradation. Nat Ecol Evol 2:1352–1357. Viewed 12 March 2020 at https://www.nature.com/articles/s41559-018-0497-3

Gerardo CD, Cretu E, Rohling R (2018, 29 August) Fabrication and testing of polymer-based capacitive micromachines ultrasound transducers for medical imaging. Macrosyst Nanoeng 4:19. Viewed 27 April 2020 at https://tinyurl.com/y45deyzq

Global Alliance for Buildings and Construction, IEA and UNEP (2019) 2019 global status report for buildings and construction: Towards a zero-emission, efficient and resilient buildings and construction sector. Viewed 2 April 2020 at https://tinyurl.com/yx3xzrtg

Global Sustainable Investment Alliance (2019, December) Sustainable investor poll on TCFD implementation. Viewed 14 March 2020 at https://tinyurl.com/u3g7tx9

Göpel M (2016) The great mind shift: how new economic paradigm and sustainability transformations go hand in hand. SpringerOpen, Berlin

Gore A (1992) Earth in the balance: ecology and the human spirit. Dove Audio Cassettes, Santa Monica, CA

Gore A (2006) An inconvenient truth: the planetary emergency of global warming and what we can do about it. Rodale, New York

Gore, A. (2011, June) Climate of denial [Electronic version]. Rolling Stones, 22 June 2011. Viewed 27 April 2020 at https://tinyurl.com/3cbjx4g

Harari NY (2017) Homo Deus. A brief history of tomorrow. Harper Collins, New York

Harari NY (2018) 21 lessons for the 21st century. Jonathan Cape, London

Hasell J, Roser M (2018) Famines. OurWorldInData.Org. Viewed 16 July 2018 at https://ourworldindata.org/famines

Heineke K, Kloss B, Scurtu D, Weig F (2019, January) Micromobility's 15,00-mile check-up. Viewed 31 January 2019 at https://tinyurl.com/y95ymw6m

Hundertmark T, Mayer M, McNally C, Simons TJ, Witte C (2018, December) How plastics waste recycling could transform the chemical industry. McKinsey Company. Viewed 27 April 2020 at https://tinyurl.com/y6vropvd

International Energy Agency (IEA) (2018) CO_2 emissions from fuel combustion. Viewed 5 March 2019 at https://webstore.iea.org/co2-emissions-from-fuel-combustion-2018

IPCC (2020) Special report on climate change and land. Viewed 2 April 2020 at https://www.ipcc.ch/site/assets/uploads/sites/4/2020/02/SPM_Updated-Jan20.pdf

Kelly K (2016) The inevitable: understanding the 12 technological forces that will shape our future. Viking, New York

Kelly BE, Bhattacharya I, Heidari H, Shusteff M, Spadaccini CM, Taylor HK (2019, January) Volumetric additive manufacturing via tomographic reconstruction science. Science 363 (6431):1075–1079. https://doi.org/10.1126/science.aau7114. Viewed 5 May 2019

Korthauer R (ed) (2018) Lithium-ion batteries: basics and applications. Springer, Berlin

Krizhevsky A, Sutskever I, Hinton GE (2012, 3 December) ImageNet classification with deep convolutional neural networks. In Nips' 12 Proceedings of the 25th International Conference on Neural Information Processing Systems – Volume 1. Curran Associates Inc., 1097–1105. Viewed 20 October 2019 at https://dl.acm.org/citation.cfm?id=2999134.2999257

Krugman P (2009) The return of depression economics and the crisis of 2008. Norton, New York & London

Krugman P (2012) End this depression now! Norton, New York, London

Kurzweil R (1999) The age of spiritual machines: when computers exceed human intelligence. Penguin Books, London

Kurzweil R (2001, 7 March) The law of accelerated returns. Viewed 3 April 2020 at http://www.kurzweilai.net/the-law-of-accelerating-returns

Kurzweil R (2005) The singularity is near: when humans transcend biology. Viking Penguin, New York

Kurzweil R, Grossman T (2004) Fantastic voyage: live long enough to live forever. Rodale, New York

Kurzweil R, Grossman T (2009) Transcend: nine steps to living forever. Rodale, New York

Lander E, Baylis F, Zhang F, Charpentier E, Berg P (2019) Adopt a moratorium on heritable genome editing. Viewed 3 April 2020 at https://tinyurl.com/y4ts35ue

Lee K-F (2018a) AI superpowers: China, Silicon Valley and the new world order. HMH, New York, Boston

Lee T (2018b) Why experts believe cheaper, better lidar is right around the corner. Viewed 3 April 2020 at https://tinyurl.com/y39nmno9

Li Y, et al. (2019) Genome-edited skin epidermal stem cells protect mice from cocaine-seeking behaviour and cocaine overdose. Nat Biomed Eng 3:105–113. Viewed 10 March 2019 at https://www.nature.com/articles/s41551-018-0293-z

Lynch J, Pierrehumbert R (2019,19 February) Climate impacts of cultured meat and beef cattle. Frontiers in sustainable food systems. https://doi.org/10.3389/fsufs.2019.00005. Viewed 14 March 2019 at https://www.frontiersin.org/articles/10.3389/fsufs.2019.00005/full

Martin C (2015) On the edge: the state and fate of the world's tropical rainforests. Report to the Club of Rome. Greystone Books, Vancouver

Meadows D, Meadows D, Randers J, Behrens W III (1972) The limits to growth. Universe Books, New York

Miles K (2018, May/June) The little coin that ate Quebec. MIT Technol Rev, 121(3), 33–39

Mnih V, Kavukcuoglu K, Silver D, Rusu AA, Veness J, Bellemare MG, Graves A, Riedmiller M, Fidjeland A, Ostrovski G et al. (2015, February 26) Human-level control through deep-reinforcement learning. Nature, 518(740), 529–533 Viewed 21 October 2019 at https://tinyurl.com/tk2v327

Moore GE (1965, 19 April) Cramming more components into integrated circuits. Electronics, 38 (8):114. Viewed 20 December 2018 at https://tinyurl.com/u5l4uco

Moore C, Phillips C (2012) Plastic ocean. Avery, New York

Moravec H (1992/1988) Mind children: the future of robot and human intelligence. Harvard University Press, Boston

Musk E, Neuralink (2019, 16 July) An integrated brain-machine interface platform with thousands of channels. White paper retrieved https://tinyurl.com/y5kd42fu

Nadler A, Crain M, Donovan J (2018) Weaponizing the digital influence machine: the political perils of online ad tech. Viewed 20 October 2019 at https://datasociety.net/wp-content/uploads/2018/10/DS_Digital_Influence_Machine.pdf

Naudé W (2009, January) The financial crisis of 2008 and the developing countries. Discussion paper no. 2009/01. United Nations University, world Institute for Development, Economics Research. Viewed 3 April 2020 at https://www.wider.unu.edu/sites/default/files/dp2009-01.pdf

Nilsson N (2009) The quest for artificial intelligence: a history of ideas and achievements. Cambridge University Press, New York

Nordhaus WD (1973) World dynamics: measurement without data. Econ J 83(332):1156–1183. https://doi.org/10.2307/2230846

Nordhaus WD (1992) Lethal model 2: the limits of growth revisited. Brookings Pap Econ Act. 1992 (2):1–59. Viewed 26 April 2020 at https://tinyurl.com/ycqbuhja

Nordhaus WD, Houthakker H, Solow R (1973) The allocation of energy resources. Brookings Pap Econ Act 4(3):529–576. Viewed 25 June 2019 at https://www.jstor.org/stable/2534202?seq=1#page_scan_tab_contents

O'Meara S (2019, 21 August) Will China lead the world in AI by 2030? Nature 572 (7770):427–428. Viewed 23 October 2019 at https://tinyurl.com/y5wqdtee

Oberbauer E, Steffenhagen C, Wurzer C, Gabriel C, Redl H, Wolbank S (2015) Enzymatic and non-enzymatic isolation systems for adipose tissue-derived cells: current state of the art. Cell Regen, 4(7). https://doi.org/10.1186/s13619-015-0020-0. Viewed 11 March 2019 at https://www.ncbi.nlm.nih.gov/pubmed/26435835

Orcutt M (2018, May/June) Blockchain. MIT Technology Review, 121(3)

Oxtoby JC, Pettis BJ, Price G B, von Neumann J (1958, May) Bulletin of the American Mathematical Society, 64(3), part 2 (whole no. 654). Viewed 25 February 2019 at https://tinyurl.com/wcn7elh

Perera D, Poulos RC, Shah A, Beck D, Pimanda JE, Wong JWH (2016) Differential DNA repair underlies mutation hotspots at active promoters in cancer genomes. Nature 532(7598):259. https://doi.org/10.1038/nature17437. Viewed 3 April 2020 at https://www.nature.com/articles/nature17437

Pinker S (2011) The better angels of our nature: the decline of violence in history and its causes. Allen Lane, London

Pinker S (2018) Enlightenment now: the case for reason, science, humanism, and progress. Viking, New York

Pizzuto L, Thomas C, Wang A, Wo T (2019, January) How China will help fuel the revolution in autonomous vehicles. Viewed 28 April 2020 at https://tinyurl.com/y45deyzq

Poinar G, Thomas J, Zavortink TJ, Brown A (2019) Priscoculex burmanicus n. gen. Et sp. (Diptera: Culicidae: Anophelinae) from mid-cretaceous Myanmar amber. Historical Biology, 2019:1. https://doi.org/10.1080/08912963.2019.1570185. Viewed 10 March 2019 at https://www.sciencedaily.com/releases/2019/02/190211163959.htm

Pope Francis (2015) Laudato Si' on care for our common home. Our Sunday Visitor, Huntington, IN

Proust C (2009) Numerical and metrological graphemes: from cuneiform to translation. Cuneiform Digital Library J, 2009:1. Viewed September 27, 2019 https://cdli.ucla.edu/pubs/cdlj/2009/cdlj2009_001.html

Randers J (2012) 2052: a global forecast for the next forty years. Chelsea Green, White River Junction, Vermont

Randers J, Rockström J, Stoknes PE, Golücke U, Collste D, Cornell S (2018) Transformation is feasible. How to achieve sustainable development goals within planetary boundaries. A report to the Club of Rome, for its 50th anniversary, 17 October 2018. Stockholm resilience center. Viewed 3 April 2020 at https://tinyurl.com/y9epzlmk

Regalado A (2018, 24 August) A CRISPR cure for Duchenne muscular dystrophy is closer after a trial in dogs. Viewed 10 March 2019 at https://www.technologyreview.com/s/611940/a-crispr-cure-for-duchenne-muscular-dystrophy-trial-in-dogs-exonics/

Rifkin J (2011) The third industrial revolution: how lateral power is transforming energy, the economy, and the world. St. Martin's Press, New York

Ritchie M, Roser M (2018) Causes of death. Viewed 12 July 2019 at https://ourworldindata.org/causes-of-death

Robinson K, Dunning Hotopp J (2016, 1 October) Bacteria and humans have been swapping DNA for millennia. The Scientist, October:46–51. Viewed 6 July 2019 at https://tinyurl.com/y47wje94

Rockström J, Steffen WL, Noone K, Persson Å, Chapin FS III, Lambin EF, Lenton TM, Scheffer M et al (2009) Planetary boundaries: exploring the safe operating space for humanity. Ecol Soc 14 (2):32

Rooney MF, Hill EW, Kelly VP, Porter RK (2018, 31 October) The "speed gene" effect of myostatin arises in thoroughbred horses due to a promoter proximal SINE insertion. PLoS ONE 13(10): e0205664. https://doi.org/10.1371/journal.pone.0205664. Viewed 10 March 2019 at https://www.ncbi.nlm.nih.gov/pmc/articles/PMC6209199/

Roser M (2018a) Life expectancy. OurWorldInData.Org.Viewed 12 July 2018 at https://ourworldindata.org/life-expectancy

Roser M (2018b) Economic growth. OurWorldInData.Org. Viewed 12 July 2018 at https://ourworldindata.org/economic-growth

Roser M (2018c) Child mortality. OurWorldInData.Org. Viewed 17 February 2018 at https://ourworldindata.org/child-mortality

Roser M (2018d) Democracy. OurWorldInData.Org. Viewed 17 February 2018 at https://ourworldindata.org/democracy

Roser M (2018e) War and peace. OurWorldInData.Org. Viewed 17 February 2018 at https://ourworldindata.org/war-and-peace

Roser M, Ortiz-Ospina E (2017a) World population growth. OurWorldInData.Org. Viewed 12 July 2018 at https://ourworldindata.org/world-population-growth

Roser M, Ortiz-Ospina E (2017b) Global extreme poverty. OurWorldInData.Org. Viewed 27 April 2020 at https://ourworldindata.org/extreme-poverty

Roser M, Ortiz-Ospina E (2018) Literacy. OurWorldInData.Org. Viewed 13 July 2018 at https://ourworldindata.org/literacy

Roser M, Ritchie H (2018a) Yields and land use in agriculture. OurWorldInData.Org. Viewed 16 July 2018 at https://ourworldindata.org/yields-and-land-use-in-agriculture

Roser M, Ritchie H (2018b) Food prices. OurWorldInData.Org. Viewed 16 July 2018 at https://ourworldindata.org/food-prices

Rosling H, Rosling O, Rosling Rönnlund A (2018) Factfulness. Ten reasons we're wrong about the world—and why things are better than you think. Sceptre, London

Rumelhart D, Hinton G, Williams R (1986, October 9) Learning representations by back-propagation errors. Nature 323(6088):533–536. Viewed 20 October 2019 at https://www.nature.com/articles/323533a0

Russell S (2019) Human compliance: artificial intelligence and the problem of control. Viking, New York

Sachs JD (2008) Common wealth: economics for a crowded planet. Penguin, New York

Schulz T (2019) 2017 worldwide CO_2 emissions per capita and country. Viewed 2 April 2020 at https://tinyurl.com/vnkqum6

Schwab K (2016) The fourth industrial revolution. Crown Business, New York

Scudelari M (2020, March 19) Five companies using AI to fight coronavirus: Deep learning models predict old and new drugs that might successfully treat COVID-19. Viewed 30 March 2020 at https://tinyurl.com/wlhpvkc

Silver D, Schrittwieser J, Simonyan K, Antonoglou I, Huang A, Guez A, Hubert T, Baker L, Lai M, Bolton A, Chen Y, Lillicrap T, Hui F, Sifre L, van den Driessche G, Graepel T, Hassabis D (2017, 19 October) Mastering the game of go without human knowledge. Nature 550 (7676):354–359. Viewed 18 October 2019 at https://discovery.ucl.ac.uk/id/eprint/10045895/1/agz_unformatted_nature.pdf

Snowden E (2019) Permanent record. Macmillan, London

Steffen W, Richardson K, Rockström J, Cornell SE, Fetzer I, Bennett EM et al (2015, 13 February) Planetary boundaries: guiding human development on a changing planet. Science 347 (6223):1259855. https://doi.org/10.1126/science.1259855. Viewed 12 August 2020 at https://science.sciencemag.org/content/347/6223/1259855

Stiglitz J (2010) Freefall: America, free markets, and the sinking of the world economy. Norton, New York, London

Stiglitz J (2011, May) Of the 1%, by the 1%, for the 1%. Vanity fair May 2011. Viewed 3 April 2020 at http://www.vanityfair.com/society/features/2011/05/top-one-percent-201105

Stiglitz J, Fitoussi J, Durand M (2018) Beyond GDP: measuring what counts for economic and social performance. OECD, Paris. Viewed 19 February 2019 at https://read.oecd-ilibrary.org/economics/beyond-gdp_9789264307292-en

Stoll C, Klaassen L, Gallersdoerfer U (2018, December) The carbon footprint of Bitcoin. MIT Center for energy and environmental policy research. Viewed 3 April 2020 at http://ceepr.mit.edu/files/papers/2018-018.pdf

Surowiecki J (2018, May/June) Bitcoin would be a calamity, not an economy. MIT Technol Rev, 121(3):28–31

Sylvester G (ed.) (2018) E-agriculture in action: drones for agriculture. Food and Agriculture Organization of the United Nations and International Telecommunication Union, Rome. Viewed 3 April 2020 at http://www.fao.org/3/i8494en/i8494en.pdf

Tegmark M (2017) Life 3.0: being human in the age of artificial intelligence. Allan lane, London

Vollmann T (2018a) No immediate danger. Volume one of carbon ideologies. Viking, New York

Vollmann T (2018b) No good alternative. Volume two of carbon ideologies. Viking, New York

Von Weizsäcker EU, Wijkman A (2018) Come on! Capitalism, short-termism, population and the destruction of the planet – a report to the Club of Rome. Springer Nature, New York

Wilber K (2000) A theory of everything: an integral vision for business, politics, science, and spirituality. Shambhala, Boston

Willett W (2019, 16 January) Food in the Anthropocene: the EAT-lancet commission on healthy diets from sustainable food systems. The Lancet 393(10168):P200. Viewed 12 March 2019 at https://tinyurl.com/scz3w9o

World Commission on Environment and Development (2009/1987) Our common future. Oxford University Press, Oxford

World Economic Forum (2020) The global risks report 2020, (15th edn.) Insight report. World Economic Forum, Cologny. Viewed 14 March 2020 at http://www3.weforum.org/docs/WEF_Global_Risk_Report_2020.pdf

Xue K, Kanmin Xue, Jolly JK, Barnard AR, Rudenko A, Salvetti AP et al. (2018) Beneficial effects of vision in patients undergoing retinal gene therapy for choroideremia. Nature Medicine 24:1507–1512. Viewed 10 March 2019 at https://www.nature.com/articles/s41591-018-0185-5

Yamaguchi T, Sato H, Kato-Itoh M, Goto T, Hara H, Sanbo M, et al. (2017, February 9), Interspecies organogenesis generates autologous functional islets. Nature 542:191–196. Viewed 3 April 2020 at https://www.nature.com/articles/nature21070

Chapter 2
Hidden Dimensions and the Search for Meaning

Jim hae, so now what the fuck do J do? Clean up the residue, J guess

At the peak of his brilliant high-tech career, AI authority, bestselling author of multiple books, including *AI Superpowers*, and mega venture capitalist Kai-Fu Lee was forced to face his own mortality following a diagnosis of lymphoma. Lee wrote his Ph.D. dissertation on AI in the 1980s and contributed to this exciting field through brilliant ideas such as the "quantification of the human thinking process, [and] the explication of human behavior." Thirty-five years later, as he fought for his life, he made an unexpected, and arguably uncharacteristic, comment about his life: "Instead of seeking to outperform the human brain, I should have sought to understand the human heart."[1] A man who had spent his entire career living like a "supercharged productivity machine," and encouraging the rest of the world to do the same, had now turned his "egocentric wallowing inside out."[2]

Was this a classic case of someone rethinking their life when confronted by death? Or was it something bigger, something we could conceivably regard as being part of a global trend? My own research[3] tells me his change in mindset is not unique. In fact, I would suggest that such mind shifts are increasing in a significant way, and may even explain current trends toward systemic transformations, be it in investing, business, politics, or economics.

When Silicon Valley companies like Google and Salesforce offer free meditation to their employees[4] and major players, authors, and business drivers like Lee begin to speak of *love* as the underlying force that should drive the global "new world order," it is time to take a closer, deeper look at what is happening to uncover the hidden determinants behind what Ernst von Weizsäcker and Anders Wijkman described as "the call for a new enlightenment" (see Chap. 1).[5] Why? Because the

---

[1]Lee (2018, p. 231).

[2]Lee (2018, pp. 180–185).

[3]Bozesan (2016).

[4]See, for example Schoenberg et al. (2018); Brodwin (24 August 2017).

[5]Von Weizsäcker and Wijkman (2018).

© Springer Nature Switzerland AG 2020
M. Bozesan, *Integral Investing*, https://doi.org/10.1007/978-3-030-54016-6_2

more I look around me, the more evident it seems to me that our current problems are not only environmental, political, social, or even, dare I say, technological. They are also systemic and holistic.[6] In other words, they are *integral*. They do not seem to relate only to the exterior—the objective or conscious dimensions of reality. Their true nature appears to be also related to the interior—the mindset, the subjective, and the unconscious dimensions such as the interior individual and interior collective, the cultural. They are emotional and psycho-spiritual. As we contemplate the evolution of the current enlightenment toward its next stage, Enlightenment 2.0, we should be alert to the possibility that we ought to be contemplating aspects of the human psyche that have never previously been on our radar.

2.1   What Is the Purpose of Your Life?

Astrobiologists Michael Russell and Isik Kanik argue that the purpose of life is "the hydrogenation of carbon dioxide."[7] You are free to adopt this as the purpose of your own life. Indeed, I have many friends who do. Personally, I am not convinced. I believe that we would be misguided if we allowed the purpose of our lives to be reduced to carbon, or quarks, or whatever else scientists are bound to discover next—but I am a scientist myself, so I am open to being proven wrong about this at some point in the future. Russell and Kanik look at life from a thermodynamic point of view and theorize that it "evolves to maximize entropy and attempts to reach this state as rapidly as possible."[8] And within the context of the evolution of life being key for building AI-based systems, it behooves us to remember that Richard Dawkins described DNA as "a set of instructions for how to make a body."[9] If we are truly nothing more than the sum total of our genes, once the technology is available to us, we will be able to download ourselves into a robot and live forever. But can life—*can humans*—really be reduced to a genetic code that could be completely replicated and eventually downloaded into sophisticated AIs in order to perpetuate, broaden, enhance, and expand life beyond Earth as the transhumanist movements intend?[10] It is a fascinating—and for some of us, even the scientists among us, disturbing—prospect. Only time will tell if it is also realistic. However, when Lee wrote that "instead of seeking to outperform the human brain, [he] should have sought to understand the human heart" and that he had not previously recognized "that something far more meaningful and far more human lay in the hearts of the family members," he did not refer to the heart as a collection of carbon atoms whose purpose is to maximize entropy. No, he talked about love: that inexplicable, illogical

---

[6]Vollmann T (2018a) & (2018b).

[7]Russel and Kanik (2010, p. 1012).

[8]Russel and Kanik (2010, p. 1015).

[9]Dawkins (1976, p. 23).

[10]Bostrom (2005).

it comes back around to the Church,

feeling that is bigger than our physical selves. It is possibly the very factor that makes us human, and it cannot be squeezed into a single gene sequence, no matter how hard we try—or how much we would like it to be possible.

To deepen our understanding of the purpose of life and our understanding of matter, the mind, and consciousness, we could participate in the centuries-old but ongoing debate between mechanistic dualists, scientific materialists, cognitive psychologists, and panpsychist philosophers, to name only a few. (See the box below for an explanation of these.)

Mechanistic dualism, or the mind–body dualism, is also called Cartesian dualism, after French philosopher René Descartes, who regarded matter as unconscious and soul as immaterial. With his famous utterance "I think, therefore I am,"[11] Descartes expressed his thought that "the whole essence of nature… is simply to think." However, the soul–body or mind–brain relationship, the "hard problem of consciousness," is still with us and will probably stay with us until we are finally able to explain how and why sentient beings have phenomenal experiences.

Scientific materialists such as Daniel Dennett and Richard Dawkins[12] reject the mind–body dualism and notions like consciousness or purpose because of the subjective nature of such phenomena. They insist there is no purpose to life.

Cognitive psychology[13] is interested not in the structure of conscious experience but in higher mental processes such as decision-making, thinking, and knowing. It is a form of scientific materialism that investigates human cognition and tends to treat mental activity like a software that runs on a computer. In cognitive psychology, sentient beings are regarded as conscious machines with feelings that are generated through brain activities. Consciousness is therefore understood to be like a simulation by the brain. Drawing on these reductionist theories, scientists such as Dietrich Dörner,[14] author of *Bauplan für eine Seele* (literally, *Blueprint for a Soul*), have been instrumental in the current development of artificial intelligence applications.

Panpsychism[15] is one of the oldest forms of philosophical theories. Its influence can be found in philosophies and belief systems all over the world, from Taoism in China to Platonism in Greece, and Vedanta in India. It fell out of favor in the mid-twentieth century, when logical positivism ruled the day but is currently enjoying something of a revival through scientists such as

(continued)

---

[11]Descartes (1998/1637, pp. 18–19).

[12]Dennett (2006); Dawkins (2006).

[13]Davis and Palladino (2005/1995).

[14]Dörner (2008/1998).

[15]Kelly et al. (Eds.) (2015).

> Thomas Nagel, who in his book *Mind & Cosmos* has researched "why the materialist neo-Darwinian conception of nature is almost certainly false."[16]

Going deeper is beyond the scope of this book. Instead, I invite you to take a simpler approach: Stay open-minded and maybe begin to take a multi-perspectival view of the world. I say this because we can use our own life experiences to identify the purpose of our lives and find out what values inform the decisions we make as investors, entrepreneurs, businesspeople, parents, and caring human beings.

I underwent a whole series of personal awakening and transformations several decades ago. Afterward, I realized not only that I was not alone but also that there was a mind shift occurring across the planet, a *collective awakening*, if you like. With hindsight, it seems to me that the birth of initiatives such as the UN's Millennium Development Goals (MDGs),[17] impact investing,[18] and conscious capitalism,[19] to name only three, were born through mind shifts and interior transformations of people whom Paul Ray and Sherry Anderson called the Cultural Creatives. These were a group of awakened leaders who brought higher standards of ethics and morals, as well as a social and environmental mindset, into the business world and began transforming it in the late 1960s.[20] When Ray and Anderson published *The Cultural Creatives: How 50 Million People Are Changing the World* in 2000, they estimated that the mindset of the Cultural Creatives had penetrated between 25% and 30% of the Western population. A new market comprising consumers interested in personal health and a more natural lifestyle, eco-tourism, alternative energy, alternative vehicles, and green buildings began to emerge in tandem. That market, named the LOHAS (Lifestyle of Health and Sustainability) segment in 1999, had a market share of US$290 billion in 2017.[21]

Authenticity Rules the World of LOHAS
LOHAS are seriously critical to anything that may be labeled as "fake." They are the ones that read the small prints; look up brands on Internet forums and like staying informed by unbiased reviews. To appeal to LOHAS brands need to be genuine and trustworthy, from the inside out. LOHAS individuals tend to perceive brands as authentic when things are done exceptionally well,

(continued)

---

[16]Nagel (2012).
[17]See https://www.un.org/millenniumgoals
[18]https://en.wikipedia.org/wiki/Impact_investing and https://thegiin.org/impact-investing/need-to-know/#what-is-impact-investing
[19]https://www.consciouscapitalism.org
[20]Ray and Anderson (2000).
[21]https://blog.ethos-marketing.com/blog/lohas-marketing-strategic-guide

executed individually, and extraordinarily produced by someone demonstrating human care. Originality in design or being first of its kind is also reinforcing authenticity. Artificial, synthetic run of the mill products are rejected, as well as imitations and products made by an exploited workforce or from abused animals. (From the LOHAS Sweden website: lohas.se/about-lohas)

I became so intrigued by this emerging mindset change, and its potential impact, that I enrolled in a doctoral program to research it more thoroughly. My aim was to find out whether it was an anomaly or a trend. Before I share my findings with you, I would like to direct your attention to the section entitled Confessions: The Involuntary Awakening of a Marxist. It is the story of my own awakening from being a young Marxist who grew up in a communist country to becoming a world citizen who lives in the free world and has a greater understanding of my own place in the universe. Note that when I talk about Karl Marx, I am referring to him in his politically purest form: the humanist, as opposed to the sham created by the communist governments of the former Eastern Bloc and the Soviet Union. The communism endemic in those regions had absolutely nothing to do with Marx's ideals, which when implemented as intended could actually have resulted in a well-functioning democracy. As a young Marxist with little experience of the world, I not only was impressionable but I also unquestioningly accepted his ideals with all the naivety of one who does not yet understand that humanity as a whole is not ready to turn them into reality. However, I gradually began to question the entire concept of communism, even before my family and I managed to emigrate to West Germany. As I grew up and learned more about the world on both an academic and personal level, I found myself questioning standards, concepts, aims, and ideals more and more. I learned to trust in myself as a physical, thinking being. And I eventually underwent my own mind shift—a mind shift that propelled me to integral thinking. Intrigued? (For a more detailed description of my own journey toward Waking Up see my *Confessions: The Involuntary Awakening of a Marxist* in Sect. 2.2.2, Waking Up).

2.2   Mind Shift as a Trend

As a species, we appear to rule the world and are living in relatively unchallenging times, even when you factor in the current COVID-19 pandemic or the looming threats posed by the grand global challenges, and yet we are still troubled. Otto Scharmer of MIT has written that we are currently experiencing a consciousness crisis because we are dealing with an "intellectual bankruptcy" whereby "the blind spot of economics and economic theory is our own *consciousness*."[22] This crisis seems to have initiated a significant mind shift[23] that is not only challenging but also actively starting to change outdated structures that cannot accommodate the needs of the new global reality. A host of leaders from all areas of life, including high-net-worth and ultra-high-net-worth individuals, have emerged as major players in this shift. Spurred into action by both personal crises and major global emergencies, they have begun to act more daringly.[24] As a result, new structures and new measurement criteria in the areas of investing, philanthropy, business, and finance are mushrooming, resulting in reforming banks such as the GLS Bank in Germany, the TRIODOS Bank in The Netherlands, and the Crédit Coopératif in France to name only a few. At the time of writing, 59 financial institutions, four associate banks, and 16 partners had joined together to form the Global Alliance for Banking on Values (GABV) to serve close to 60 million clients worldwide.[25] In their 2019 annual report,[26] the GABV:

- Challenge the myth that sustainable investments yield lower returns
- Show that sustainable banks have significantly higher levels of growth in deposits and loans than traditional banks
- Demonstrate higher and better-quality inflows of capital
- Reveal that sustainable banks are investing more successfully in a greener and fairer society
- Show that their business model is more robust and resilient than that of traditional banks

Furthermore, we continue to witness the emergence of progressive organizations such as SOCAP,[27] the Social Venture Circle,[28] the UN PRI (Principles of Responsible Investing of the UN),[29] the Global Impact Investing Network (GIIN),[30] the Giving Pledge,[31] and the Toniic investors network,[32] to name only a few again. Some were started by ultra-high-net-worth individuals such as Richard Branson, Warren Buffett, Bill Gates, Al Gore, George Soros, and Elon Musk, who apparently use investing in reformist institutions as a self-actualizing vehicle that aims to guide humanity toward a better future. But research by, for example, Christian

---

[22]Scharmer (2010, p. 17) & (2013).

[23]Göpel (2016).

[24]See, for example, Balandina (2011) & (2016); Bozesan (2016); Giving Pledge (2020); Godeke et al. (2009); Soros (2008); Strong (2009).

[25]http://www.gabv.org/

[26]https://issuu.com/bankingonvalues/docs/annual_report_2019_en

[27]SOCAP (2012); https://socialcapitalmarkets.net/

[28]Social Venture Circle (2020); www.svcimpact.org

[29]https://www.unpri.org/

[30]https://thegiin.org/

[31]https://givingpledge.org/

[32]https://www.toniic.com/100-impact-network/

Arnsperger,[33] Julia Balandina-Jacquier,[34] Antony Bugg-Levine and Jed Emerson,[35] Hal Brill et al.,[36] Cathy Clark et al.,[37] Edward Kelly and Bill Torbert,[38] Peter Senge et al.,[39] and Rajendra Sisodia et al.[40] supports the view that an increasing number of regular wealth owners have *awakened to later stages of consciousness*, driving them toward transformation referred to as *integral,*[41] *second tier, yellow meme,*[42] or *strategist*[43] (see below for more on this).

When we look more closely at this phenomenon, it appears to be a trend toward personal growth.[44] It seems to me that the desired changes toward sustainability are taking place within a rather complex context, comprising changes not only in environmental, financial, economic, and social perspectives but also in individual behaviors. What Nobel Prize laureate Paul Krugman called "obsolete doctrines that clutter the minds of men"[45] are actually sociopolitical and interobjective rules, circumstances, and regulations that often impede transformation, but also contain culturally interior, intersubjective, and deeply ingrained norms, such as ethics and morals,[46] that heavily influence both our individual and our collective behaviors.

Transformations in consciousness are not a new phenomenon. They have evolved over thousands of years[47] and, in relatively recent times, have been represented by Abraham Maslow in his hierarchy of needs,[48] Jean Gebser in his structures of human consciousness,[49] and Robert Kegan in his order of consciousness models,[50] to name only three of the most commonly known and discussed. While these models help us make sense of the trajectories of human evolution, phenomenological investigation into the interior transformation of the participating agents has been relatively scant,

---

[33] Arnsperger (2010).

[34] Balandina (2011) & (2016).

[35] Bugg-Levine and Emerson (2011).

[36] Brill et al. (1999) & (2015).

[37] Clark et al. (2015).

[38] Torbert and Kelly (2013).

[39] Senge et al. (2005).

[40] Sisodia et al. (2007).

[41] Arnsperger (2010).

[42] Beck and Cowan (1996).

[43] Cook-Greuter (2004) & (2005) & (2008) & (2013).

[44] See for example, Aburdene (2005); Adams (2005); Boyatzis and McKee (2005); Cook-Greuter (2013); Goleman et al. (2002); Hendricks and Ludeman (1996); Jaworski (1996); Kelly (2011); Marques et al. (2007); Mitroff and Denton (1999); Ray and Anderson (2000); Rooke and Torbert (2005); Senge et al. (2005).

[45] Krugman (2012, p. 191).

[46] Stückelberger and Duggal (2018).

[47] Wilber (1998) & (2000b) & (2000c) & (2017).

[48] Maslow et al. (1998).

[49] Gebser (1984).

[50] Kegan (1982) & (1994).

despite increasing occurrences of individual dissatisfaction within the financial and business worlds.[51] Money appears to have stopped providing the security it has promised since its invention, and a growing number of people are becoming aware of the schism between the material world and a life of meaning.[52] Financial abundance is no longer the ultimate goal for these individuals because material prosperity has not brought them the happiness they anticipated.[53] In fact, if anything, the opposite appears to be true.[54] Moreover, the overall dissatisfaction appears to be rooted in the fact that the majority of today's institutions are still operating primarily via outdated corporate values,[55] short-term monetary and profit-only orientation,[56] bitter competition,[57] mostly hierarchical organization structures with controlling management styles,[58] disrespect for individual values,[59] and an inability and/or unwillingness to acknowledge, let alone prevent, negative action,[60] and anxiety and mistrust.[61]

2.2.1 Researching the Mind Shift

In 2001, I began to interview and collect data from global investors between the ages of 30 and 70 for my Ph.D. research (Note: by 2020 I have researched 138 subjects). My research subjects were independently wealthy individuals who worked as angel investors or venture capitalists or company builders—including presidents of Fortune 500 companies—Wall Street financiers, serial entrepreneurs, and also musicians, lawyers, artists, medical doctors, and business owners in the context of the entertainment business. They all held doctorates, master's degrees in science, or MBAs from the world's elite universities. My research, which was published in 2010,[62] was centered on identifying and analyzing the transformational experiences of high-net-worth individuals, all of whom had faced various personal and professional crises at various points in their lives in addition to what are, in a global finance context, relatively common financial crises. I wanted to uncover the most significant emotional, physical, cognitive, spiritual, and other experiences that had resulted in

---

[51]Kofman (2006); Ray and Rinzler (Eds.) (1993); Secretan (2006).

[52]Klein and Izzo (1999).

[53]Ricard (2003).

[54]Blanchflower and Oswald (2004).

[55]Kofman (2006).

[56]Collins and Lazier (1992).

[57]Collins (2001).

[58]Eisler (2007) and Smith (2007) & (2008).

[59]Toms (1997).

[60]Senge et al. (2005).

[61]Secretan (2006).

[62]Bozesan (2010).

an interior transformation that made these individuals move from having an ego-centric to a world-centric world view. I also wanted to know:

- What were the triggers, context, and process of their transformation
- What were the factors that facilitated or inhibited the change of their minds
- What ensured the continuity and longevity of their transformation, especially as it may have occurred in a hostile, litigation-friendly environment dominated by less-conscious investors, peers, and money managers
- How they created new investing structures in the light of the current global contexts
- How they saw the future of investing, capitalism, business, and philanthropy within the context of global challenges

I used a research method called heuristic structuralism and developed it as a pluralistic mode of inquiry in which each point of view is respected as a potential source of insight. My approach was a combination of Clark Moustakas's in-depth heuristic method[63] and Ken Wilber's integral methodological pluralism, which contains "at least eight fundamental and apparently irreducible methodologies, injunctions, or paradigms for gaining reproducible knowledge or verifiable repeatable experiences."[64] I shared my findings using mythologist Joseph Campbell's Hero's Journey[65] as a demonstration vehicle. I chose this over more advanced evolutionary models such as Clare Graves's[66] evolution of human values, Lawrence Kohlberg's[67] and Carol Gilligan's[68] moral development, Jane Loevinger's[69] and Susanne Cook-Greuter's[70] ego development, Robert Kegan's[71] self-development, or Wilber's[72] Integral Theory of evolution because of the general popularity of the Hero's Journey, which has been applied in various legends, myths, and tales, as well as in Hollywood movies such as *The Lion King, Star Wars,* and the *Matrix Trilogy.*[73] (Note that some portions of the following research summary and feedback have previously been published.[74]).

---

[63]Moustakas (1990).

[64]Wilber (2006, p. 33).

[65]Campbell (1968/1949).

[66]Beck and Cowan (1996).

[67]Kohlberg and Ryncarz (1990).

[68]Gilligan (1993/1982).

[69]Loevinger (1977).

[70]Cook-Greuter (2005).

[71]Kegan (1982); Scotton et al. (Eds.) (1996).

[72]Wilber (2000b)

[73]For more detail, see Bozesan (2010) & (2016).

[74]For example, Bozesan (2010) & (2013, June) & (2016), to name only three.

Fig. 2.1 The hero's journey toward awakening

2.2.2   Waking Up: The Hero's Journey Toward Awakening

My research subjects were competitive, highly intelligent high-achievers, driven to work hard in order to fulfill their maximum human potential, and powered by innate curiosity and creativity. Their exceptional material and financial abundance was openly displayed and confirmed their original self-reinforcing mentality that success is measured by extrinsic metrics—the house, the vacation home, the luxury car, the yacht, for example—rather than intrinsic metrics, such as a deep-seated, self-defined feeling of self-worth. The visible, outward signs of success seemed to solidify their belief that their actions had led directly to personal happiness. This belief helped them achieve high social status, build exceptional reputations, accumulate remarkable wealth, and create strong egos. They truly believed that they were in control of their own lives. They were, in eighties parlance, the masters of the universe.

For example, one research subject, the former president of one of the largest beverage companies in the world, told me, "I built the myth of myself that I was better [...] than anyone else ... I was ego-driven, totally externally oriented, manipulative in dealing with human beings, not open to feedback ... All that mattered was outcomes... [I was] very intense, very driven, never present in any conversation." His success appeared secure—until it was not. At the peak of his brilliant career, he became aware not only of his own physical and emotional challenges but also of the futility of climbing the corporate ladder. He recognized that there were "fewer jobs left" in the world that could potentially give him the satisfaction he sought. He *Woke Up* to the fact that he "was getting to the point of diminishing returns" and that something was missing. He would later realize that the "something" he was missing was authentic happiness. He said, "If I didn't get my result, I wasn't happy. If I got my result, I wasn't happy." Extrinsic success had lost its meaning for him, because "the next gold ring was less meaningful ... than the previous one." When "a number of peers who were in similar positions in other companies ... died [of stress] in their 40s at their desks," my friend realized that he "wasn't manifesting" why he "was here" and asked himself the key question: Is this it?

His *Journey* toward *Awakening* had begun (Fig. 2.1).

The research subjects' egocentric view of the world began to crumble as they became tortured by dreadful pain of various kinds, which challenged their common belief of always being in control. Their source of pain was often physical (*Body Awakening*) and manifested in the beginning as simple "colds and sore throats," "heart hurting," "back problems," weight gain, "migraines," or food allergies. Other times, the pain was emotional in nature and was triggered by a "horrible divorce," death of a "mother," a "terrible financial loss," not getting a dream job, or being "fired" from an important position.

The emotional pain manifested as "heartbreak," a "high degree of anxiety," "worry and fear," "grief," tension between "fear and desire," the "need" to be accepted by the outside world, and "frustration." The result was a "feeling of helplessness," "unhappiness," "deep sadness and almost shame," lack of fulfillment, lack of "joy," lack of "love," "unrest," and lack of "trust." Most of the investors who participated in my research did not initially understand the message their physical being was sending them; they essentially remained in denial and changed nothing. Sure, they began taking better care of their bodies through improved nutrition, exercise, and massages, but as soon as the pain diminished, they went back to their old behaviors—until the next painful encounter. They fell into the trap of addressing their agony by using the same cognitive abilities and talents that had made them successful, including an ability to control people and outcomes. Some of them noted that they became "a control freak," some "closed down" to "never" be emotionally available again, others began wearing "a coat of armor." Eventually, both the physical and emotional pain increased so severely that they hit a *tipping point* and were forced to Wake Up and face their "worst nightmare": the shadow of their egos. Once they were willing to *cross the threshold,* a term used by Campbell to describe this process, and relinquish control, they opened the door to higher levels of consciousness and were liberated.

Each individual demonstrated a different ability and approach to face their own shadows, ranging from the decision to experience the "dark night of the soul" through holotropic breathwork and a willingness to face the "worst [emotional] pain," to participating in meditation retreats, personal-growth seminars, or "vision quests." The sum result of such a journey is known as Maslow's *peak* experiences,[75] meditative or contemplative experiences, *near-death experiences, out of body experiences*, experiences of *flow*, state or *unity consciousness* experiences, *exceptional human experiences, transpersonal* experiences, or other spiritual emergencies.[76]

One research participant, for example, described his experience as a "lightning bolt [that] moved through" his body and caused a feeling "so powerfully strong that it was almost to the point where I couldn't walk." Others expressed having witnessed their extraordinary states as a "mystical experience," "divine light," or "divine intelligence." One investor described his experience as a feeling in which the

---

[75]Maslow (1999/1968).

[76]Alexander and Langer (Eds.) (1990); Commons et al. (Eds.) (1984); Cook-Greuter (2005); Csikszentmihalyi (1990).

"heart was exploding with love" and the "body turned into an intense beam of light" that opened his heart completely. Remember: The people making these comments were non-religious, had high-level science educations, and had built tremendously successful careers. At the time of their first experience of this kind, most of them had neither the framework nor the language to interpret or articulate what they were experiencing. Their entire world view was shattered as soon as they gave up control and surrendered to the "unknown," the "unbearable fear," and the "terrible pain" they were experiencing. It was the beginning of a "major shift," called by some a "quantum leap in consciousness." Neuroscience research indicates that such exceptional human experiences can contribute to the achievement of higher levels of personal integration and move an individual to later stages of ego development.[77] Having decided to embark on a healing journey through shadow work, the participants then entered the next phase of the Hero's Journey: the *Initiation* phase.

Confessions: The Involuntary Awakening of a Marxist

It was a beautiful sunny day in the summer of 2000. I had been fasting for 5 days when I met my colleague Larissa for lunch in downtown Palo Alto, California. Although I was not physically hungry, my eyes devoured the spicy kale with tofu and the organic Brussels sprouts mixed into a bouquet of red bell pepper with sprouted pine nuts in Larissa's lunch. The juicy carrot salad with raisins and the smell of freshly baked bread made my mouth water and reminded me of the pleasure of eating a good, healthy meal. I found myself thinking about all the times I had gone to school on an empty stomach and how grateful I was that my life was so different now. As we chatted, Larissa asked me about my childhood. As I related my tale of poverty and privation, Larissa looked at me in disbelief, asking how I had been able to study on an empty stomach. "Common knowledge," she said, "maintains that people cannot study on an empty stomach." What had kept me going, she wanted to know—but truly, I had never thought about what kept me going. I knew simply that I must not only go on but also do well. We were taught that we had the power to make a better world for ourselves through hard work, learning, and sacrifice. Before I was 9-years old, I had already adopted Lenin's mantra, which my father taught me: "Learn, learn, and learn." I believed that in order to get what I wanted in life, I would have to work hard, which for me meant being a good student. I was told this by my parents, and I, therefore, believed that hard work was my ticket to a better life— despite seeing my parents' hard work not pay off in this way. An empty stomach did not sway my certainty that a better future would be mine.

We were poor, life was hard, and money was tight, so I grew up appreciating everything that came my way. Two memories, in particular, will stay with me forever: (1) getting my first doll when I was 7 years old, and (2) receiving a little parcel with beautiful clothes from our relatives in Canada following the terrible

---

[77]See, for example, Alexander and Langer (Eds.) (1990); Beauregard and O'Leary D (2007); Commons et al. (Eds.) (1984) & (1990); Cook-Greuter (2005) & (2008); Damasio (2006); Goleman (2000); Goleman et al. (2002); Kegan et al. (1990); Koplowitz (1984) & (1990); McCraty (2001); Newberg and Lee (2005); Vaughan (2000) & (2005); Walsh and Vaughan (1993); Wilber (2000b).

Romanian floods from 1971. So, overall, despite the poverty, I grew up believing that bad times always turned into good ones because people care. Subconsciously, I chose early on to be very grateful for my little fortunes and learned to focus on the things that gave me great inner satisfaction.

It was around this time that I identified a world that gave me great pleasure and a sense of control in an uncertain world: the world of math and science. "Why science?" Larissa wanted to know. Again, I had to admit that I had never given this much thought, but even as I voiced this confession, the answer came to me: "I get a deep sense of fulfillment from solving a difficult math problem that has kept my mind busy for a long time," I said to Larissa. I continued to explain how I love the feeling when, after long hours or sometimes days of thinking about it, I suddenly and seemingly out of the blue find the solution to a difficult problem regardless of where I am physically. When you live in a society where everybody lacks so many things, people become manipulative in order to survive. But math could not be manipulated. Unlike many other subjects, it was deterministic and not a matter of interpretation or control. Coming from a blue-collar family, I had neither the means nor the money to bribe anybody to receive good grades in school as so many other people did. Therefore, I had to be self-reliant. I owe much of my academic achievement to my remarkable middle-school math teacher. Mrs. Fotache, who showed me how I could succeed if I only worked hard enough. And I did work hard. And I was rewarded many times over. At age 14, I left the ranks of the young Pioneers and joined the Young Communists. But even at that young age, my enthusiasm for the communist society I was living in had already begun to wane. I began to see that we were not equal after all. No matter how hard I worked, it seemed likely I would still not enjoy the standard of living that many people around me did. One of my girlfriends, for example, had poorer grades than I did but ate strawberries in the middle of the winter, while we had hardly anything to eat even though I was a high achiever in school and both my parents worked very hard. But even as my idealism began to fade, I still hoped for better times. Not so my parents. While they retained their belief in the principles of communism, they were done hoping that Romania would ever change into a genuinely communist society as envisioned by Karl Marx. It was time to make a change. Without discussing politics, they started the process of emigrating to West Germany on the grounds of family reunification, as my mother was of German heritage.

After World War II, West Germany experienced the economic miracle known as the *Wirtschaftswunder*, and recruited workers from Greece, Italy, Turkey, and what was then Yugoslavia. However, reuniting displaced Germans from the Soviet Union and Eastern Europe with their families in the West was preferable in terms of cultural integration. My father listened daily (and secretly) to both Radio Free Europe and The Voice of America and knew that the West German government was willing to pay Ceausescu a fair amount of money for every worker of German heritage who was allowed to leave Romania to go work in West Germany. My mother's immediate family already lived there and visited us every year, so we asked for an invitation to join them, painfully aware that the approval process might take up to 13 years. But we were lucky. We lived in Moldova, where there were few German nationals and willing potential emigrants, and in less than 5 months, we received permission to leave. On Halloween 1974, at age 16, I boarded the plane to leave Romania with my parents. Life would never be the same again. We did not know what would happen to us, but we had faith. Not in God—God was never in the picture for committed communists like us—but in the West German government and in ourselves and our own ability to work hard to prove that we would be willing to do anything and everything to earn not only a living but also respect for our work and integrity. We had nothing to lose at that point. The future could only be better.

And it was.

My parents had no expectations beyond the hope that our relatives would give us a bed to sleep in and that they would find jobs quickly. But things turned out much better. The Germans were extremely good to us. From lodging, to food, to job hunting for my parents and schooling for me, they took care of absolutely everything, including paying for German classes for my father who, like me, did not speak German. We were ecstatic and deeply grateful. My parents found work and I went to high school. Four years later I became a student in computer science and mathematics at KIT, the Karlsruhe Institute of Technology. I loved my life and enjoyed being a university student. And then I started to have inexplicable stomach pain. Before midday, every day, my stomach would start burning and I would have to go home to bed. One day, as I lay in bed in my dormitory, I thought to myself that going to the doctor would be useless. He would just prescribe me antacids. The doctor had diagnosed stress as the cause of my condition and called my pain psychosomatic, so I now had a label for my discomfort, but it did not tell me anything about how to get rid of it or why I was stressed when my life seemed to be going so well. Eventually, I remembered a somewhat similar situation from a few years earlier when my doctor had prescribed cough syrup although I had spots on my lungs. I had an ongoing dry coughing condition, not a cold. I was curious, to say the least. The doctors I had consulted were loving, caring people, but I would not feel totally happy again until I knew more about my condition and treatment. I needed more information. Not knowing what else to do in those pre-Internet years, I went to a bookstore. After browsing through several medical books, I learned that I had chronic bronchitis caused by a flu in my youth from which I had not fully recovered—thanks to a childhood passion for ice-skating. The dry coughs were my body's attempts to rid itself of the mucus from my damaged bronchi and not caused by the TBC I had had in my preschool years. The books advised participating in sports regularly to aid this process. That would relieve me of the dry coughs. Now I had some answers. Why in the world, I wondered, did not the doctors tell me that? Were they lacking time to explain, or did they think I would not understand? Whatever it was, it did not matter. At 17, I had learned a big lesson about having faith in my body's natural tendency to heal and in taking responsibility to address my own ignorance, even with respect to complicated medical issues.

So here I was, 4 years later, in a similar situation with my stomach problems. As I reflected on my past experience, I took one more antacid and decided to take responsibility for my health again by learning what was going on and how I could treat myself. After a couple of hours' research in a bookstore, I came out with a book on autogenic training and one on fasting. I followed the exercises recommended in the bioenergetics book and calmed my mind and body so well that my stomach pain disappeared completely within a couple of days—with no recurrence since then. I was amazed at how positively my body responded to the simple relaxation exercises. In addition, my mood improved. I practiced the visualizations and began meditating daily and felt as fresh and recovered as after a good night's sleep.

For the first time in my life, I was learning that I was not my thoughts but that I had thoughts. I became conscious of the power that my mind had over my body. Until then, I had treated my body like a machine that had to obey my will. When my body revolted, I was surprised and upset at the same time. I had lost control and did not understand why. My mantra that everything was possible if I only wanted it enough and put in enough effort no longer worked. My body obviously had a different agenda. All I wanted was to get back to my old routine in life. Little did I know that this would not be an option.

I had learned to derive great satisfaction from math and science, and I loved both subjects. But my ultimate motivation was the promise of a better life by escaping poverty through material gain. I now lived in a free country and I had the intellectual capacity to achieve such a life. I believed that while the road to financial independence was indeed paved with sacrifice, eventually I would be happy. I had no reason to question my modus vivendi, because it seemed to work. And it did work—until it did not. Until my body rebelled, my life had had but one dimension: the thinking mind inside a machine that was my body. I defined myself as the person in here looking to the outside world for approval, for a place in the world, for extrinsic recognition. My joy and satisfaction depended on it. My orientation was outward and linear. It was me in relation to those on whom I depended. I did not exist without the outside world.

Triggered first by physical pain and then by the eventual relief from that pain, I started thinking, for the first time in my life, about the beautiful miracle that is the human body. I realized that I had taken my body for granted my whole life. I took a shower daily and brushed my teeth twice a day, but it never occurred to me that an internal cleanse might be required. The book on fasting revealed how I could take an internal "shower" to do just that. It made so much sense (although I was painfully aware of the irony of fasting as an adult after a childhood in which the only thing I experienced in abundance was deprivation). For the first time in my life, I began to look within. After the third day of my first fast, I started feeling light and weightless. My mind was pure and lucid. My thoughts were quiet and clear. My skin looked bright and almost translucent. I had more energy than ever, needed less sleep, and preferred quietude and contemplation over chatter. I became more tranquil and in touch with some part of me that I had never known existed. Thinking, my endless internal chatter, was replaced with total awareness. I was grateful to be alive. I felt blissful and fulfilled. I was serene. Now I finally understood—no, I viscerally *felt it at the level of my soul, not in my physical body*—what Erich Fromm meant in his book *To Have or to Be*. Fromm thought that the needs of the human soul must be fulfilled if we are to free ourselves from the shackles of consumerism. I now understood what he meant. As a scientist, I had been spiritually deprived because of my scientific mindset. Now, for the first time in my life, I felt I had a soul. I noticed that I was happy just because I existed, regardless of what I did or owned. I felt pure happiness without doing anything. I noticed a deep quality of being that came from within. I had a sense of security and absolute trust in the future. I *felt* the absolute and unconditional love about which Fromm talked: the experience of loving, of joy, of grasping a truth does not happen in time, but in the here and now. "*The here and now is eternity*, that is, timelessness."[78]

The sound of a glass shattering as it hit the floor wrenched me away from my thoughts and back into the room. I had gotten so carried away by my story that I saw with a start that Larissa had finished her meal. Her beautiful eyes and spirit had been supporting me throughout, enabling me to forget where I was. "Keep going," she smiled, as we prepared to go our separate ways. "The initiation of your soul is very beautiful. You were spiritually deprived, and you did not know it. Now you know that you are not a human being having a spiritual experience but the other way around."

My inner journey had begun with that wake-up call in 1980, but my atheist upbringing, my Marxist convictions, and my scientific mindset allowed me to trust in, and then embrace, my physical, emotional, and other experiences only after several more years of serious scientific research and further personal growth and development. Without realizing it, I had become a player in a mind shift trend that was still in its embryonic stage.

2.2.3 Cleaning Up and Embarking on Vertical Growth

The research participants perceived their experiences as ultimately tremendously healing. They gave the participants a glimpse of the hidden dimensions of their inner reality and encouraged them to pursue further inner transformation with the same devotion with which they had developed their professional lives. They hired some of the best available resources, including teachers, counselors, coaches, and psychotherapists. Their pain, both physical and emotional, diminished and the quality of their lives improved. They lived for a time like "closet mystics" (I did) and "spiritual dilettantes" as they exposed themselves to a host of techniques, philosophies, and teachings that ran counter to their scientific predispositions and training and, it could be argued, would have challenged their credibility as business people and scientists in their regular circles. Some discovered a certain teacher and/or method that worked well for them and stayed with that teacher or method, sometimes for several decades. I was interested to note that all the research participants expressed an inner yearning

---

[78]Fromm (1983/1976, p. 125). From the German original Haben oder Sein "das Erlebnis des Liebens, der Freude, des Erfassens einer Wahrheit geschieht nicht in der Zeit, sondern im Hier und Jetzt. Das *Hier und Jetzt ist Ewigkeit*, das heißt Zeitlosigkeit" (my emphasis).

for a "common sense spirituality" that explicated their mystical experiences and transcended traditional religious norms, which they all refused to accept.

In the beginning, the *Initiation* phase, their extraordinary experiences conflicted with their scientific education and knowledge, which could not explain those experiences. But by using an approach they were comfortable with—studying the research data[79]—they were able to integrate their newly discovered mystical selves with their former, pragmatic selves. One research participant described his Initiation phase as "like drinking out of a fire hose. In this area, MIT and Stanford Business School were like drinking out of a fire hose for academic and business issues. This was like drinking out of a fire hose for emotional, spiritual, and consciousness issues." These "unitive experiences," as one participant described them, healed and transformed the research participants in significant ways, which they referred to as:

- Learning how to "reconnect to that authentic self"
- Realizing that we are all "part of oneness, a greater whole"
- Developing the ability to understand their "own consciousness," the "collective consciousness," and how we "are part of that greater human consciousness and then beyond"
- Understanding the "dimensions and interconnectedness of body, mind, and spirit" up to the point where there was "absolutely no fear of death," as a well-known serial-entrepreneur-turned-investor stated after his out-of-body experience
- Becoming more "rounded [and] balanced"
- Receiving "structure and specific knowledge" on how to continue to grow on the path to self-actualization

In short, the research participants moved from an egocentric approach to life toward a more world-centric one. Their transpersonal experiences led them all to ask essential questions such as "Who am I?" "Why am I here?" "Is this it?" and "Why do I let the mob psychology [of Wall Street] tell me whether I am having a good day or not?" Their new mindset encouraged them to question more deeply the status quo of their lives and the world as a whole. Eventually, they not only noticed the "collective insanity" of the "money game" and questioned whether the "standard operating procedure" for a "successful" person was still the game they wanted to play, but also recognized that (a) they were not "manifesting" their raison d'être, (b) the values they had "adopted" were not "self-selected," and (c) they were "following a script that was not authored" by them.

As they "looked into the future" and saw the "endless stream of closing quarters" as the essential driving force in the business world with its short-term operational approach, they detected the "almost mind-numbingly impossible monotony" around their future lives. They understood that the rewards "were running out" and the next

[79]See Alexander and Langer (1990); Commons et al. (1984) & (1990); Cook-Greuter (2005) & (2008); Gardena et al. (Eds.) (2000); Goleman (2000); Goleman et al. (2002); Kegan et al. (1990); Koplowitz (1984) & (1990); Senge et al. (2005); Wilber (2000b).

"gold ring" was a less and less tempting reward for a job well done. They saw that there were "fewer [attractive] jobs left" in the world and that "maximizing shareholder value" was no longer enticing. Their value systems shifted from their need to control the future to being more present in the *now*.

One investor described his transformational shift from an egocentric view to a world-centric view in the following way in an interview with me[80]: "At the time, I had no clue what was going on. Basically, I was being rewired. Everything I used to think was important was no longer important to me. It was me, me, me and my fabulous career and how do I help create more money for the company so I can create more money for me and more success for me and more power for me? I was never a bad guy, but it was just a small game. It felt like a big game. I thought it was the biggest game in town. But suddenly, when I was rewired, it felt like the smallest game in the universe. When you really make that shift and you start playing for an idea bigger than yourself and you start sensing into what is that divine creative impulse that's seated within me that is my gift to the planet? Within that surrendering was recognizing that there's something unique within me that I was born to become and that by surrendering to that, by paying attention to that, by allowing that to emerge within myself, that I could play a much bigger game, a much more fulfilling game, a much more meaningful game in terms of being able to create from that space in service to a much deeper and broader concept."

All the investors who participated in the research confirmed after their Initiation that they were "less concerned with material things." While taking care of their own personal needs was still important, they noted that they did not "need as many things as" they used to. In fact, "things sometimes get in the way" of what they were now "trying to do." Furthermore, they seemed to not "care about showing off" or "accumulating things" anymore. After their transformation, they also "saw the hollowness" of their previous money and material orientation. They realized there are "a lot of problems that money doesn't solve" because "it's not all about the money" but also about "freedom of expression and creativity," "creating social enterprises and different financing mechanisms that are behind that," and getting rid of the "ideology of rampant consumerism."

Outfitted with *The Ultimate Boon, as* Campbell calls this stage of development, and which includes the acquisition of new instruments, new skills, and a much deeper understanding of their "unlimited potentials," the "interconnectedness, the oneness, and the holistic nature of things," the research participants were ready for the next step in their lives: the *Return* phase of the Hero's Journey.

---

[80]Bozesan (2010).

2.2.4 Showing Up: Entering the Market with Helping Hands

After their life-changing transformations and mind shifts, the research participants viewed their new life purpose as bringing the unity consciousness mindset into the domain of investing, finance, and business "in a way that creates sustainable change relative to the human beings and the planet." They had not abandoned their ambition but had instead redirected it. They were determined to have an even "bigger impact" in the finance and business worlds than before—but in a much more integrated manner. They began to see investing, economics, and business as an "incredible laboratory of consciousness" in which the integration of the interior with the exterior dimensions of life is of utmost significance. They began:

- Expressing a desire to "move capitalism beyond the pure maximizing of profits" by establishing parity between profits, the people, and the planet
- Designing ways to make an "impactful contribution to sustainability, holistic sustainability"
- Wanting to explore, to lead, and to "show different ways of creating social enterprises and different financing mechanisms that are behind that"
- Regarding "societal analysis [as] a spiritual discipline"
- Viewing active participation in and management of the economy as a "deep spiritual practice"
- Realizing the unity of our collective consciousness, that we are truly all one, and the importance of "engaged spirituality" in investing, finance, and business
- Desiring to work on "different governance models and different business models" to start integrating their mission with their evolving "human condition"
- Making sure they were "taking care" of themselves and their "community at the same time"

In short, they now sought to lead a "purposeful life" in which they could use their talents and the process of "consciousness development" to make an impactful contribution to "integral" and "holistic sustainability." They realized there was "no going back" and "change became unavoidable."

2.2.5 Remarkable Waves of Evolution

As a result of their personal transformations, and their realization that they wanted to make an even "bigger impact" in the investing and business world than before and in a much more integrated way, the participants now viewed investing, economics, and business as an "incredible laboratory of consciousness" in which the integration of the intrinsic and extrinsic dimensions of life is of utmost significance. Their newly acquired skills enabled them to have an impact on both their own corporate culture and their broader social environments. They became better relationship people because they were now able to connect on a personal level, rather than seeing relationships only in terms of business opportunities, and to build a bridge between the mind and the heart, between the intrinsic and the extrinsic, between having an "enjoyable business as well as make[ing] money." They became venture philanthropists in addition to or instead of investing because they now viewed "business as a service" to humanity and the planet. Over time, they became involved with the creation of sustainable investing, economic, and business models by, for example:

- Promoting long-term thinking through the realization that it "was not necessarily the shorter-term end state you are working toward but the greater good, the greater end state"
- "Creating social enterprises and different financing mechanisms that are behind that"
- Ceasing to support the "ideology" of "rampant consumerism"
- Getting involved with social justice activism and seeking a more integral "political leadership" to name only a few tactics

As the participants evolved, they uncovered deeper truths about life that liberated them. It was "a liberation from the distortions, lies, and delusions that were constructed to hide the truth"[81] about their true nature. Subsequently, they developed more trust in themselves as well as in other people. This resulted in an increase not only in their authenticity but also in their self-esteem. Yes, you read that correctly. Their "self-esteem," which had been a driving force for their previous success, actually increased because, as they evolved away from their previous superficial, ego-driven state to a trust-driven state, they could now authentically trust in themselves, who they were and what they had to offer the world. They became more self-confident. Concurrent to this they developed a deeper understanding of the "interconnectedness" between people, planet, and profit as well as their own life's purpose, and their personal passions could now be manifested. In a modest way, their mission in life had become more important to them than personal achievement and extrinsic success.

Their significant mind shift led to these investors realizing that they must take a new investing approach, one based on the integration and equality, or parity, of people, planet, and profit rather than prioritizing just one of these (guess which one) at the expense of the other two. They saw that without a comprehensive understanding of global problems, no sustainable solutions to those problems are possible. They realized that social and environmental sustainability were just as important as financial sustainability. They understood that reality comprises subjective, intersubjective, objective, and interobjective aspects. Their transformation attuned them to how crucial the interior aspects of the individual and the collective are in determining a full-spectrum investing philosophy and portfolios. They saw that we do not only have ecological, financial, water, or poverty crises; we also have interior human crises that must be given equal consideration. They realized that their actions in the

---

[81]Wilber (2000a/1995, p. 578).

world must be grounded in the quintessence of life as a whole, its interior as well as exterior reality.

It would seem that a number of business leaders are ready to move up to later stages of consciousness, or a more world-centric view of the world. A brief look at current market dynamics indicates that a new paradigm in investing, philanthropy, business, and leadership is emerging. Moreover, ultra-high-net-worth individuals such as Warren Buffett, Bill Gates, Al Gore, and George Soros are apparently using investing as a *self-actualizing* and legacy-building vehicle with the intention of making the world a better place.[82] But why? One possible explanation may be rooted in the developments of the nineteenth century and reflected in part in the writings of philosopher Karl Marx. Marx hypothesized that the *forces* of production—such as land, natural resources, and technology—develop faster than the *relations* of production—that is, the technical and social relationships and interconnections that people develop while using the forces of production.[83] The fact that the forces of production can move ahead of the relations of production also speeds up the development of culture, techno-economics, and socio-economics, because they co-arise. That can in turn, as we have seen in the rise of socialist movements, produce major disruptions in society and force the development of different levels of consciousness in people. Marx's hypothesis could mean that the significant exponential tech evolution of the past decades can be viewed as a major *force of production* that has run well ahead of the *relations of production* or the *social crisis.*

But the current social crisis is not new. It is the old one, but exacerbated and, unfortunately, not alone this time around. We now also have an environmental crisis that, in a global example of something good coming from something bad, has given birth to the green movement. In his comparative analysis of Marxism and the Green movement, Wilber identifies *reductionism* as a common thread. He suggests that Marxism disregarded people's interiorities and reduced their "higher cultural endeavors in the economic or material realm" to "material productions and material productions and material means."[84] Similarly, "the Greens tend to reduce all concerns to the ecological exchanges of the biosphere," never mind their "integrative potential for a planetary federation of world citizens."[85]

If there is *one* lesson learned that all my research participants have in common and that seems to have accelerated their mindset change to later stages of consciousness, it is that they should honor their interiorities. Imagine if we collectively began to do that in a systematic way. What would the outcome be? Could this inner work be the foundation of an Enlightenment 2.0, as discussed earlier?

In support of such transformation, Thomas Friedman argued in his 2005 book *The World Is Flat*[86] that in the early years of the twenty-first century, humanity reached a

---

[82]Giving Pledge (2020); Gore (1992) & (2006) & (2020); Kelly (2011); Soros (2008).

[83]Marx (2016/1867).

[84]Wilber (2000a/1995, p. 200).

[85]Ibid.

[86]Friedman (2005).

tipping point. Certainly, several significant components of production—led by the Internet as an exponentially growing technology—converged around that time and created a breeding ground for change. Friedman posited that the fall of the Berlin Wall in 1989, the launch of the Internet browser Mosaic, and the growth of global outsourcing, offshoring, open-sourcing, insourcing, supply-chaining, in-forming, and so on all reinforced both the effects and the impacts of each other. The net result of this convergence, he claims, was the emergence of our current global, Web-enabled playing field that allows for multiple forms of collaboration—the sharing of knowledge and work—in real time, without regard to geography, distance, or, in the near future, possibly even language. If Friedman is correct, it would be reasonable to conclude that the current "flattening" of the world, and all the consequences of that flattening, could indeed be considered as the result of a massive mind shift or evolution of human consciousness from a previously more ethnocentric view of the world to a more world-centric one, hence the rise of impact investing.[87] Whether this new way of thinking is a true evolutionary stage that affects humanity as a whole or simply an anomaly affecting a specific group, only the future will determine. What we do know is that at later stages of development, some individuals become able to:

• Understand not just the contexts but also the systems within which they operate
• Generate social transformations through the integration of material, spiritual, and societal factors
• Care a great deal about self-development
• Embrace paradoxes
• Create shared visions that allow both personal and organizational transformation across different developmental levels
• Understand the interconnectedness of life systems on the planet, a fact that enables them to authentically and responsibly become a harmonic part of the whole
• Put theory and principles into practice[88]

On a personal level, as investors and company builders who believe in holistic sustainability, in the late 1990s Tom and I began looking for an investment model that would reflect our personal and professional experience, was rooted in research, and would both allow and facilitate the integration of the various aspects of our work. That search led us to *Integral Investing*.

---

[87]Bozesan (2016).

[88]See, for example, Cook-Greuter (2013); Maslow et al. (1998); Rooke and Torbert (2005).

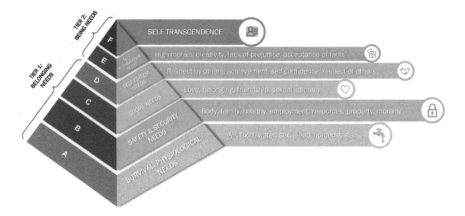

Fig. 2.2   Maslow's pyramid of needs

2.2.6   The Spectrum of Consciousness Evolution

Researchers appear to be unusually united in their assessment of human evolution.[89]
This section looks at some of the more frequently cited researchers on this topic.

The Human Needs Line of Development
Abraham Maslow, a familiar name to anyone who has studied business or management, stressed the importance of focusing on the positive qualities in humans instead
of their psychopathologies. His mentor was Alfred Adler, a colleague of Sigmund
Freud, the founder of analytical psychology, but Maslow questioned the old
methods, believed in human potential, and developed his own ideas about the
human mind, which led to the foundation of two new disciplines: first, humanistic
psychology and later, transpersonal psychology (also called integral psychology,
The Fourth Force).[90] He was convinced that people are inherently good and have a
strong desire to achieve their full potential, and he spent his entire life trying to find
out which circumstances influence the ability to do so.

   Maslow's pyramid (or hierarchy) of needs (Fig. 2.2), a visual representation of
the needs we must meet in order to achieve fulfillment, almost needs no introduction,
given its ubiquity in management and human resource manuals—and of course, it is
not the only valuable resource for finding out more about this topic—but it is always
worth revisiting.

   The pyramid of needs contains six successive stages of development:

- Survival, physiological

---

[89]See, for example, Commons et al. (Eds.) (1984) & (1990); Cook-Greuter (2004) & (2005) &
(2008); Gardner (1993) & (2004); Gebser (1984); Kohlberg and Ryncarz (1990); Wilber (2000b) &
(2000c).
[90]Grof (2006).

- Safety and security
- Social
- Self-esteem
- Self-actualization
- Self-transcendence

The Moral Line of Development and Its Stages

Whereas Maslow focused on the line of development dealing with human *needs*, Carol Gilligan,[91] for example, researched and complemented Kohlberg's[92] *moral* development model. She identified three stages of women's moral development, which she labeled:

- Selfish/preconventional
- Care/conventional
- Universal care/postconventional

Gilligan suggested that as individuals move through these stages, they begin to take a more global view of life and adopt higher moral standards.

The Stages of Sociocultural Evolution

Jean Gebser,[93] to offer another example, identified fives waves of consciousness awakening as it relates to the sociocultural evolution—or forms of realization, thought, and world views—that he called archaic, magic, mythical, mental, and integral.

It is generally agreed that at later stages of development, individuals appear to be in a much better position to take a high moral stance and to apply Kant's categorical imperative,[94] resulting in more compassionate decisions based on higher ethical standards.[95] If individual transformations affect a certain percentage of the population and reach a certain critical mass, a tipping point will be reached whereby, from a collective perspective, the evolution of entire social systems and cultural structures can occur.

Cultural world views are intimately correlated with socio-techno-economic structures because they happen concurrently and influence each other. In accordance with the infrastructural and techno-economic base of society, the labeling and existence of evolutionary periods such as the foraging, horticultural, agrarian, industrial, and informational stages of development are widely accepted as being part of our shared knowledge base.[96] We sometimes refer to them simply as premodern, modern, and postmodern stages of development. To better understand the correlation between the

---

[91]Gilligan (1993/1982).

[92]Kohlberg and Ryncarz (1990).

[93]Gebser (1984/1949, p. 269).

[94]Kant (1993/1949).

[95]Baier (1996/1994); Dalai Lama (1999); Pope Francis (2015).

[96]Pinker (2018) & (2011).

socio-techno-economic and market structures in which an organization operates and the potential risks associated with an investment performed in such a context, I would like to highlight Clare Graves's pioneering work on human nature and values development, now called *Spiral Dynamics*[97] (see also the discussion of the due diligence and de-risking process in Chap. 3).

The Stages of Ego Developmental Line: Spiral Dynamics

Graves, a contemporary of Maslow, was interested in our varying responses and reactions not only to change but also to the increasing complexity of our world. His work challenged the universality of Maslow's hierarchy of needs, and his main conclusion was that human evolution is both social and psychological, in addition to the overwhelmingly accepted notion that it is physical. As Sharon Ede explains, "Graves observed that as certain thresholds of complexity were reached, the mind's ability to make sense of the world became overburdened, and to cope, the mind must create more complex models of reality to deal with the new problems of existence."[98] Graves was among the first theorists to call for the integration of social and cultural aspects within the context of human development. His model became known as the biopsychosocial system of human development and was later used by his student Don Beck in his efforts to support South Africa as it transitioned from apartheid, the Palestinians with their peace activities with Israel, and the creators of the new Icelandic constitution.[99]

Beck was so impressed with Graves's model that he left his tenured academic career as a professor at Northern Texas University and worked with Graves until his death in 1986. Afterward, Beck continued to work on Graves's theory together with his colleague Christopher Cowan, and in 1996 they published their new evolutionary model of flexible intelligence, which they called *Spiral Dynamics*.[100]

According to Beck and Cowan, *Spiral Dynamics* uncovers the hidden programs that characterize human nature, produce diversities, and drive evolutionary transformations offering a "unifying framework that makes genuinely holistic thinking and actions possible."[101] *Spiral Dynamics* foresees two major tiers of human development (Fig. 2.3).

Tier 1 contains six stages of human development from egocentric, to ethnocentric, to world-centric. Tier 2 is Kosmos-centric and contains higher stages of development that have not yet emerged. As we take a closer, bottom-up look at each stage of development, keep in mind that development is not a linear process; instead, it is fluid and flows in waves, whirls, and torrents, sometimes even regressing to earlier stages. (The flowing stages of development in their spiral are color-coded.) Beck and Cowan refer in their work to "tribes," but I acknowledge that this term has negative connotations in certain regions of the world:

---

[97]Beck and Cowan (1996).

[98]Ede (2013).

[99]Beck and Cowan (1996) and personal communications with Don Beck.

[100]Beck and Cowan (1996).

[101]Beck and Cowan (1996, p. 30).

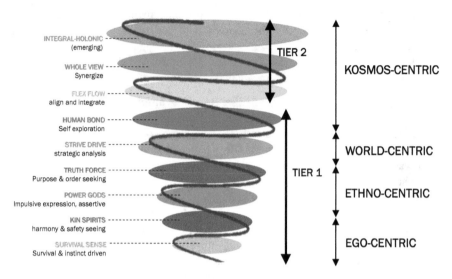

Fig. 2.3 The *Spiral Dynamics* model (adapted after Beck and Cowan (1996) and Wilber (2000))

- *Beige: Survival sense: survival and instinct driven.* This represents a state of nature and human instincts at the level of basic survival in which humans are concerned with mundane things such as food, shelter, and procreation. It is not much different from how things are in the animal kingdom.
- *Purple: Kin spirits: harmony and safety seeing.* At this level, people build ethnic tribes dominated by mysterious, magical, and superstitious thinking as well as curses and spells. This type of behavior can be found in gangs and sports teams.
- *Red: Power gods: impulsive expression, assertive.* This is the first level of development at which there is an emergence of an individual separate from the tribe. Life is hard and rough, and one has to fight to survive. This tends to be the foundation of feudal empires, which are dominated by archetypal gods and goddesses and see existence as "here and now" with the understanding that there is nothing before or after life. Examples for this meme are feudal landlords, gang leaders, wild rock stars, and epic heroes.
- *Blue: Truth force: purpose and order seeking.* At this memetic wave, life is purposeful and divinely controlled, but its outcome is determined by a central authority that is paternalistic, has rigid social hierarchies, and must be obeyed. This authority determines guiding principles for a society, law and order, and the collective understanding of what is right or wrong. Any violation of this order creates a sense of guilt in the perpetrator, will be judged by others, and has significant repercussions for the perpetrator, ultimately severe punishment either here on Earth or elsewhere (e.g., in Hell). This memetic code rewards the faithful. Examples of this are Puritan America, Confucian China, Dickensian England, totalitarian regimes including communism and Nazism, codes of chivalry and honor, patriotism, and religious fundamentalism of all dominations.

- *Orange*: *Strive drive: strategic analysis.* At this level, the laws of science rule a society that thinks for itself and has broken free of the group mentality of the preceding meme. It is achievement-oriented and materialistic. In this meme, the world is viewed rationally; it is mechanistic, deterministic, objective, and guided by scientific experiments. There are plenty of alternatives and opportunities, as thinking is dominated by science and the scientific world view with its natural laws, which can be learned, mastered, and manipulated for one's own purposes. Scientific law rules politics, the economy, human life, nature, and the universe. Society is oriented toward achievement and success as well as materialistic gains in a world divided into winners and losers. The world is viewed as a global marketplace controlled by an invisible hand and the goal is to build business and political alliances in order to manipulate Earth's resources for one's own strategic gains. Examples of such an approach can be found in the Enlightenment, Cold War, emerging middle class, corporations, colonialism, self-interest, and Wall Street.
- *Green*: *Human bond: self-exploration.* This meme characterizes a world-centric society that is community-oriented and has Awakened to the reality that we all share the same habitat on Earth. The meme is socially and ecologically conscious, and its caring facet supersedes the selfish rationality of its predecessor. The world is regarded as our only home, which we must save from destruction. Thinking is dominated by consensus; it is egalitarian as well as pluralistic and detests hierarchy. The aim of this meme is to free the human spirit from greed, doctrine, and divisiveness. The cold rationality of the previous meme is superseded by feelings of belonging to the global community, a sense of sharing common resources, human bonding, ecological sensitivity, and networking. Examples include Greenpeace, animal rights advocacy, ecofeminism, political correctness, and human rights advocacy.

According to *Spiral Dynamics*, the first three stages—beige, purple, and red—are considered to be egocentric in that at these stages people care only about themselves and their own survival. The next two stages—blue and orange—are considered to be ethnocentric, because at these levels people are concerned with the wellbeing (Note: In earlier publications, I used the two words spelling, well-being, but here I decided to use wellbeing in one word to demonstrate the need for a more integral approach of its definition and usage.[102]) of their own groups (tribes) and are often willing to go to war against other groups or social orders in order to defend their point of view.

Only with the onset of the green meme does the world-centric view begin to emerge. Through this meme, people begin to regard the entire world as their home, a home that they need to preserve and treasure.

As with all evolutionary models, it is important to note that every newborn baby begins at the bottom of this model and grows over time into higher stages of development until they reach their own center of gravity, at which point they stop growing. That center is often predetermined by their family and friends, but their own drive also plays a pivotal role. In other words, no one meme is better than another, for we are all born at square one and stand on the shoulders of those who

---

[102]Fiorini et al. (2016).

came before us. Every stage both includes and transcends the previous one. No stage can exist without its predecessor.

However, each of the Tier 1 memes thinks its world view is the correct one or has the best perspective on reality. Therefore, it reacts negatively when challenged and lashes out to defend the position with which it identifies. A sweeping generalization of the differences would look something like this: People at the blue level are rather uncomfortable with both the red impulsiveness of the previous meme and the orange individualism of the next. Orange individualists consider the blue order representatives conservative and backward absolutists, and the green egalitarianists weak and prone to spiritual woo-woo. Green egalitarianists struggle to accommodate excellence and value rankings, big pictures, hierarchies, or anything that appears authoritarian, including science. Therefore, green reacts strongly to blue, orange, and anything post-green. But all this starts to change with Tier 2 thought and perspective.

Tier 2, which is still in the emergent phase, contains the next waves of evolution, with only the yellow (flex flow: align and integrate) and turquoise (whole view: synergize) memes having already been identified. With Tier 2 consciousness, we can, for the first time, vividly grasp the entire spectrum of interior development, and thus see that each level in Tier 1 is crucial for the health of the overall spiral of evolution. Again, each wave both transcends and includes its predecessor. All the Tier 1 characteristics can and will be activated as needed, but people who have reached Tier 2 have their center of gravity there:

- *Yellow: Flex flow: align and integrate.* At this stage, people have arrived at the understanding that all previous stages of Tier 1 are important, and no one meme should be preferred over another. In fact, they see that life is made of natural holarchies, systems, and forms that depend upon each other and must be flexible, aligned, and integrated in a healthy way to enable the emergence of a wholesome yellow meme. In this meme, there is consensus that dissimilarities and pluralities can be integrated into interdependent, natural flows, and egalitarianism can be complemented with natural degrees of ranking and excellence. It is believed that knowledge and competence must supersede power, status, and group sensitivity, and good governance must support the emergence of entities at levels of increasing complexity.
- *Turquoise: Whole view: synergize.* At this universal and holistic level, life manifests as a delicate balance of interwoven forces where we are able to honor our feelings and combine them with the knowledge to create one holistic and conscious system for the benefit of all sentient beings. People believe in a universal order of life that evolves in an organic, conscious manner, one that is not based on external rules, as in the blue meme, or group bonds, such as those imagined in the green meme. Cognitively, people at this level are able to easily navigate the entire spiral; they simultaneously see, honor, and integrate multiple levels of interaction.

In summary, *Spiral Dynamics* offers a natural growth model of value development in which each stage of development includes and transcends the preceding one. Each higher level contains and transcends the one below, just as a cell includes and transcends molecules, which in turn transcend and include atoms, which transcend and include quarks, and so on.

The Leadership Development Framework

While Maslow focused on the development of human potential by fulfilling one's needs and Graves focused on how human values change in tandem with life's circumstances, Harvard scholar and leading developmental theorist and methodologist Susanne Cook-Greuter focused her research on the evolution of self-identity.[103] Her framework was a refinement of, but goes well beyond, Loevinger's ego development model and widely used WUSCT (Washington University Sentence Completion Test of Ego Development).[104] In Cook-Greuter's model, and the sentence completion test (SCT) she refined, she considers both the horizontal—the acquisition of new skills and knowledge at a certain stage or level—and the vertical, or structural, transformation in human evolution to later stages of consciousness. She posits that an interior individual transformation in consciousness does not occur through learning or knowledge acquisition alone. Instead, long-term practices and deep self-reflection are required for lasting, structural, vertical transformation. David Rooke and Bill Torbert who collaborated with Cook-Greuter to build the Leadership Development Framework (LDF), wrote in a *Harvard Business Review* article titled "Seven Transformations of Leadership" that "leaders are made, not born, and how they develop is critical for organizational change."[105]

The LDF is a quantitative instrument based on the SCT. It is designed to measure and assess the various stages/levels of vertical development over time, including adult ego development from egocentric to world-centric action logic. Rooke and Torbert used the LDF over 25 years to understand how thousands of executives in Fortune 500 companies perceived their own actions and behaviors as well as their immediate environment. Participants are categorized according to seven stages of consciousness (linked with dominant action logics), noted below with the proportion of leaders who fall into each one:

- *Opportunist and below*: 5% of participant leaders. Characterized as must-win, self-oriented, and manipulative but good in emergency situations and sales positions.
- *Diplomat*: 12% of participant leaders. Characterized as conflict avoiders but helpful when it comes to unifying people.
- *Expert*: 38% of participant leaders. Characterized as ruled by logic and expertise and good as individual contributors.
- *Achiever*: 30% of participant leaders. Characterized as mostly meeting strategic goals and being good team leaders who are action- and goal-oriented.
- *Individualist*: 10% of participant leaders. Characterized as having the ability to successfully balance competing personal and professional goals and who are effective in the venture and consulting positions.

---

[103]Cook-Greuter (2004).

[104]Loevinger (1977).

[105]Rooke and Torbert (2005, p. 1).

- *Strategist*: 4% of participant leaders. Characterized as very effective at initiating and generating both organizational and personal transformations.
- *Alchemist and above*: 1% of participant leaders. Characterized as integral leaders who excel at both bringing about and leading social transformation through the integration of what are considered to be the most important aspects of life.

According to Cook-Greuter, "only about 10% to 20% of adults demonstrate postconventional action logics. Transpersonal [post-post-conventional] ways of meaning [making] are even rarer."[106] The transformational process of investors and business leaders into leaders with a world-centric action logic, beyond postconventional, is of special interest within the context of this book. The terminology differs—other developmental models also use the terms preconventional, conventional, postconventional, and transpersonal or post-postconventional to describe the full-spectrum trajectory of human development—but the principles are consistent.

I will refer to these levels of development again in Chap. 3, when I discuss the application of the Theta Model and look at how the presented tools can be applied to de-risk investments and to identify leaders who can build sustainable companies and assess the potential of companies to become sustainable and make the *transformation feasible*.

2.3   Mind Shift as a Trend?

What emerges from the research related to various developmental models could be viewed as a common story of mind shift evolution that has been corroborated by various empirical studies on leaders and leadership. Some of those studies were performed at Stanford University and focused on the evolving definition of success from the perspective of accomplished human beings.[107] My theory is also corroborated by research performed by Robert Eccles and Svetlana Klimenko, John Mackey and Raj Sisodia, and Sisodia et al. on "firms of endearment," companies that uphold a culture of strong ethics and sustainability.[108] The data show that corporations with a culture based on sustainability and higher ethical values have also performed well financially—on average, eight times better than S&P 500 companies. The financial information tends to be a good way to convince people empirically of the value of such an approach, letting the figures speak for themselves, as it were.

Drawing on case studies from numerous organizations in the finance, nutrition, health, education, and political sectors, Sisodia et al. strongly suggest that there is a

---

[106]Cook-Greuter (2004, p. 5).

[107]Porras et al. (2007).

[108]Eccles and Klimenko (2019, May–June); Mackey and Sisodia (2013); Sisodia et al. (2007).

genuine ongoing search for meaning and a change of mindset in today's organizations. The Conscious Capitalism movement, started in 2005 by John Mackey, who founded US food retailer Whole Foods, is one manifestation of this trend.[109] In their book *Conscious Capitalism*, Mackey and Sisodia refer to several of the models discussed above and say they "believe that the vision and values of Conscious Capitalism ... are consistent with their [Graves, Beck, and Cowan's] articulation of second-tier memes in *Spiral Dynamics*, as well as Ken Wilber's work on integral consciousness."[110] Under the leadership of Mackey, Whole Foods had a 40% higher ROI than organizations that are not classed as firms of endearment over a period of 10 years.[111] The shareholder value for investors in Whole Foods, which was sold to Amazon in 2017 for US$13.7 billion,[112] grew between 1995 and 2006 to more than 1800%. This could be viewed as confirmation that "culture eats strategy for breakfast," a quote attributed in 2006 to celebrated management consultant Peter Drucker by Ford CEO Mark Fields.

Cultural Creatives and Conscious Capitalists
Like John Mackey, my husband and I are part of the Cultural Creatives generation. We seek the integration of sound financial, economic, environmentally responsible governance criteria with geopolitical sustainability for the benefit of all—and we can make this happen through our business and investment activities as well as through our philanthropic and venture philanthropy activities. Unfortunately, neither the traditional philanthropic, economics, finance, or investing models in general nor the venture capital models in particular gave us the necessary framework to invest with the wellbeing of both our values and our money in mind. Having been part of the human potential movement for decades, we knew that trusting others begins by trusting ourselves. We also knew that more trust and a stronger feeling of security could not come from higher profits at the expense of people or the planet. We knew that they could only come from our heart and soul, and from what we were willing to give to the world rather than we want to receive from it. Hence, we looked for an integration vehicle that would let us honor all our values. In the words of Maslow, we felt the need to *self-actualize* through an integration of all our activities, not just the financial, business, or philanthropic ones. We did not want to make money at the expense of other people or the environment. We did not want to make money during the day within a for-profit-only-oriented context and spend our evenings or weekends at fundraising events, donating money for various causes to fix the social

(continued)

---

[109]https://www.consciouscapitalism.org/

[110]Mackey and Sisodia (2013, p. 204).

[111]Sisodia et al. (2007).

[112]https://tinyurl.com/ya3k2j27

injustice and/or environmental degradation caused by mindless investing or business activities. We wanted to prevent all of that from happening in the first place, and we saw investing and company building as a unique vehicle to pursue our goals. Our investment motto was therefore built on the six Ps: Parity of People, Planet, and Prosperity—with Passion and Purpose.

In the fall of 2001, Tom and I attended a personal development seminar led by Tony Robbins in a tent village in the Moroccan desert, and it was there that we discovered our ideal theoretical framework to integrate our investment and company building activities, as well as our philanthropic endeavors: Ken Wilber's Integral Theory.

In an effort to essentially make sense of the world and integrate a wide variety of systems into one theory of everything, Ken Wilber analyzed hundreds of developmental theories and models, including those discussed above, and developed a simple, elegant, full-spectrum framework he called an integral operating system.[113] It has since become known as Integral Theory or the AQAL framework. Since its inception, the theory has undergone at least five major iterations and has been applied in more than 50 disciplines, including business, education, ecology, and economics.[114]

I will introduce Integral Theory *very* briefly as it relates to investing in the next chapter because for the past 20 years it has been the foundation of our integral investment framework (see Chap. 3).

2.4   Theoretical Foundations of Integral Investing

Let us say you want to travel from Munich to Beijing. Depending on your budget in terms of money, time, or levels of courage and taste for adventure, you can travel by air, train, car, or boat, or you can even hitchhike. No matter what means of transportation you chose, you would better have a good map, or you may never reach your destination. You must be prepared to cope with various surprises arising from differences in the cultures, social and environmental infrastructures, and people you encounter along the way. You will also need to be ready for anything, as the landscape and the people on the ground will all be changing very fast. Buildings are being torn down, new ones are being constructed, people pass away and are born, and change is the only constant.

What if it were possible to find a composite and far-reaching framework that would enable you to navigate the world on the outside and empower you to better

---

[113]Wilber (2000a/1995).

[114]Arnsperger (2010); Esbjörn-Hargens et al. (2010); Esbjörn-Hargens and Zimmerman (2009); Mackey and Sisodia (2013).

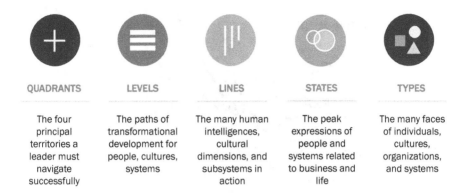

QUADRANTS	LEVELS	LINES	STATES	TYPES
The four principal territories a leader must navigate successfully	The paths of transformational development for people, cultures, systems	The many human intelligences, cultural dimensions, and subsystems in action	The peak expressions of people and systems related to business and life	The many faces of individuals, cultures, organizations, and systems

Fig. 2.4 Five key elements of Wilber's integral framework

understand it on the inside, including traditions, cultures, and societies and how they have evolved throughout the centuries? What if this framework could help you better understand the evolution of life, including the development of human knowledge from science to mathematics to developmental growth? What if there were a map that could help you gain a better perspective not only on yourself and your purpose and place in the world but also on humanity by helping you simplify your decisions and getting a broader perspective and greater insight into the future? Tom and I found Wilber's integral framework to be just such a map—a veritable theory of everything that condenses all major components of reality into five simple elements: quadrants, levels, lines, states, and types.[115] These five elements (Fig. 2.4) also give the integral framework its common name, the AQAL (pronounced ah-qwul): all quadrants, all levels, all lines, all states, and all types.

2.4.1 Quadrants and Levels

The starting point for the integral framework is the understanding that Plato's *value spheres of humanity*—the *Beautiful* (art/self), the *Good* (morals/culture), and the *True* (science/nature)—are ever present, are constantly co-arising, and cannot be divided whether we are consciously aware of them or not.[116] In other words, everything that occurs has three dimensions, or points of view: an individual, or subjective view; a collective-subjective, cultural view; and an objective, provable-facts view. Figure 2.5 shows the Big Three, as these value spheres are also called, embedded in William James' Great Chain of Being[117] in relation to Wilber's integral framework.

---

[115]Wilber (2000a/1995).

[116]Plato (1961/1938).

[117]James (2017/1890).

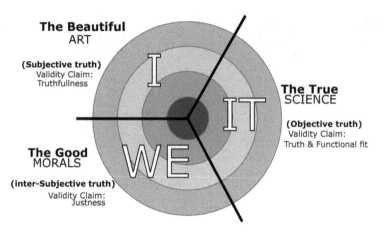

Fig. 2.5 The big three value spheres of humanity (adapted after Wilber (2000))

Wilber associated the first-person singular pronoun—the *I*, also referred to as the *self*, or subjective truth—with Plato's *Beautiful*. The first-person plural pronoun, *WE*, represents the intersubjective truth, morals, and the culture in which we live and is associated with Plato's *Good*. And the third-person singular gender-neutral pronoun *IT* is correlated with Plato's *True* value sphere or objective truth. To achieve a higher differentiation and be more inclusive with respect to additional exterior aspects of reality such as the social and the environmental aspects, Wilber expanded the Big Three and added a fourth quadrant, the exterior collective. This is the lower-right quadrant as seen in Fig. 2.6.

The fourth, lower-right quadrant, which Wilber associated with the pronoun *ITS* (used as a third-person plural gender-neutral pronoun, rather than a possessive, in this context), represents the exterior collective quadrant and refers to the social, global, and ecology realms. This quadrant can be best understood from a systems theory perspective.[118] Being an interdisciplinary field of science, systems theory studies complex systems such as nature, society, and science and provides a framework through which complex systems can be better understood, analyzed, and influenced.

All four quadrants are equally important within our context of Integral Investing, but the fourth is particularly significant because it includes the financial, geopolitical, ecological, and environmental impacts of our collective actions. Wilber's irreducible, all-quadrant, all-level framework lends itself as a theoretical foundation for Integral Investing because it provides an integrating platform to address the current grand global challenges. It allows and encourages multiple world views and perspectives, which are crucial for making decisions in general and investment decisions in particular. Its content-free framework encourages us to take the

---

[118]Von Bertalanffy (2006/1969).

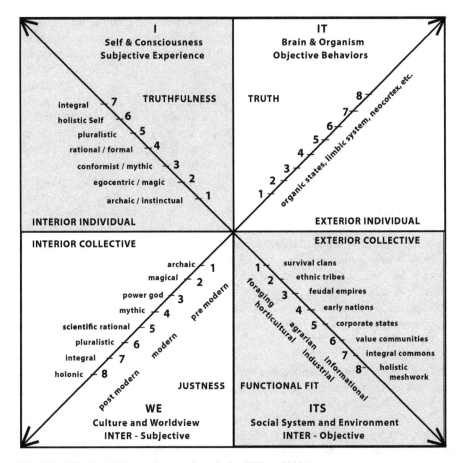

Fig. 2.6 Wilber's AQAL quadrants (adapted after Wilber (2000))

evolutionary—and contextual—attitude that is so desperately needed in today's global finance, investing, business, and economic systems.

The upper-left quadrant refers to the *interior individual* domain or the *terrain of personal/individual experience*. It represents the personal subjective area as it relates to the inner life of an individual. In it, you will find your feelings, sensations, thoughts, and spiritual awakenings. It "includes the entire spectrum of consciousness as it appears in any individual, from bodily sensations to mental ideal to soul and spirit."[119]

The upper-right quadrant refers to the exterior, or more objective, states of being, the *terrain of behavior* that can be seen and registered from the outside (the "IT"), also called the *individual exterior/objective domain*. It is what you look like from the outside. This terrain is more easily measurable with the scientific methods available

---

[119]Wilber (2000b, pp. 62–63).

today and includes "the brain mechanisms, neurotransmitters, and organic compu-
tations that support consciousness."[120] The objective perspective at this level permits
the examination of *exterior behavior* and the structure of each individual phenomenon from humans to animals to insects. This is traditionally the home of natural
sciences, including cognitive science, mathematics, financial theory, chemistry,
physics, biology, biochemistry, neurophysiology, and empiricism. From "the inside,
you find not neurotransmitters but feelings, not limbic systems but intense desires,
not a neocortex but inward visions, not matter-energy but consciousness, all
described in 1st-person immediateness."[121] The interior and exterior dimensions
are equally important, and both must be honored within a holistic world view.

The lower-left quadrant, the *terrain of culture*, enlarges the perspective of reality
through the intersubjective areas of culture such as collective (the "WE") beliefs,
norms, justness, and goodness. Wilber defined this quadrant as "the values, meanings, worldviews, and ethics that are shared by any group of individuals"[122]—the
cultural context in which investing, business, and politics occur. This cultural
context helps give our existence meaning. In fact, we become almost inseparable
from it, because it becomes what we perceive to be our reality. Behavioral economics and scientific psychology only came into existence as academic disciplines after
the birth of modern economics.[123] Thus, within the parameters of the prevailing
neoclassical economics paradigm,[124] the two *territories of felt experience* and
culture—that is, the interior aspects of both individuals and the collective—have
been excluded because of scientific reductionism. In other words, their existence and
influence were difficult to prove in a scientific manner.[125] Consequently, neoclassical economics was reduced to profit and utility maximization, called here *exterior
territories*. Based on the prevalent collective center of gravity at that time, the notion
of the *self-interested homo economicus* was born. The 2008 financial crisis was the
culmination of this application, and Integral Investing is attempting to demonstrate
how this is currently changing within business and economics.

The lower-right quadrant is the *territory of systems theory and analysis*. This
quadrant is the area in which traditional institutions, businesses, and geopolitical
organizations usually interoperate in an objectively measurable and systemic way.
Similar to the upper-right quadrant, this is also the domain in which science has
normally been active, and it is the home of economics, business, civil, and environmental engineering, ecology, astronomy, astrophysics, sociology, and other systemic and infrastructural contexts. This interobjective perspective warrants,
moreover, the configuration and exterior behavior analysis of collective phenomena,
including economic and financial systems, ecological and social systems, and legal

---

[120]Wilber (2000b, p. 63).

[121]Wilber (2006, p. 22).

[122]Wilber (2000c, p. 63).

[123]Kahneman and Tversky (1982); Tversky and Kahneman (1974).

[124]Aspromourgos (1986).

[125]Camerer and Loewenstein (2004).

and political systems. However, neither the objective perspective in the upper-right quadrant nor the interobjective view of the lower-right quadrant are in and of themselves able to effectively move individuals or collectives, of any description, to significant action. Change occurs when individuals and/or collective groups are not only cognitively but also, and more significantly, emotionally impacted, i.e., when their interiors are touched in a deep way. Hence, we need both the interior and exterior dimensions.

The quadrants are also subject to evolutionary development. Depending upon their position on the evolutionary ladder, the *stage* or *level* of development—individually or collectively—will lend itself to a different view of reality. In other words, an average businessperson or investor, e.g., who lives in a postmodern society such as Western Europe will most likely have a different view of the world, and therefore a different investing behavior and portfolio, than an investor from an emerging economy such as one of the BRIIC states. Thus, the application of Wilber's integral model allows for a much more differentiated view of individual and collective investment patterns depending upon the vertical position in each quadrant and how well the horizontal integration of the quadrants has occurred.

2.4.2   Lines, Levels, and States of Development

The upper-left quadrant is the home of individual interiority evolution and contains several lines along which our interior development occurs (see "*Waking Up*: The Hero's Journey"). The lines of development determine our individual psychograph, a form of which is represented in Wilber has identified several different lines of development that he distinguishes as multiple intelligences, including cognitive, esthetic, moral, emotional, and ego development (Fig. 2.7).[126]

According to a wide range of leading developmental psychologists, we as individuals are also subject to an evolutionary process of personal development. This development occurs in *stages* or *levels* as seen in *Spiral Dynamics*, Maslow's hierarchy of needs, and Loevinger's model of ego development. Anyone who has ever tried to lose weight, eat fewer candies, do more sports, stop smoking, or change any unwanted behavior knows how difficult change can be. If we have such a hard time influencing ourselves to change an unwanted behavior when we are in theory in direct control of what we eat, when we eat, and how we behave, imagine how difficult it is to change entire cultures, societies, and dysfunctional systems. In other words, change always starts with us, within our interiors. This is why the aphorism "*you* must be the change you want to see in the world," generally attributed to Mahatma Gandhi, resonates with so many of us. Yet, what people are *willing* to do and what ultimately determines what they will *end up doing* appears to be, according

---

[126]Wilber (2006).

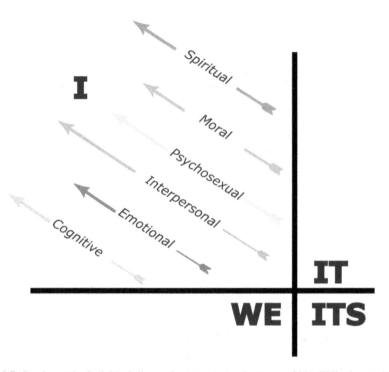

Fig. 2.7 Psychograph: individual lines of personal development within Wilber's quadrants (adapted after Wilber (2000))

to Harvard professor Robert Kegan,[127] a function of their *meaning-making* ability as well as their own *levels* of consciousness evolution.[128]

All the lines associated with interior or personal growth are significant, but within the context of this book, we are interested in the *cognitive, emotional, moral, values, needs,* and *self/ego* lines of development. Why? Because the people we associate with in our business-building activities and investments ought to be integrally informed, integrally developed, and, most of all, integrally acting, whether they use, or are even aware of, these terms or not. In other words, if we look at the research in the context of our own experience over the past three decades, we could reasonably assume that people whose center of gravity is world-centric (Fig. 2.3)—not only cognitively, but also emotionally and morally—would most likely be in a better position to *understand and address* climate change, ethical AI, biotech, and nuclear threats than those whose center is not world-centric.

The psychograph example in Fig. 2.8 can help us identify where our greatest capabilities, talents, and intelligence are; focus on them for the greatest possible

---

[127]Kegan (1982) & (1994).

[128]See, for example, Commons et al. (Eds.) (1984) & (1990); Cook-Greuter (2004) & (2005) & (2008); Gebser (1984); Gilligan (1993/1992); Goleman (1995) & (2000).

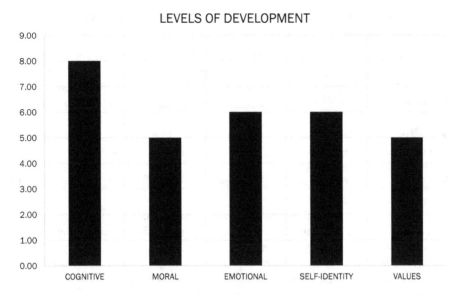

Fig. 2.8 Integral psychograph (adapted after Wilber (2000))

outcome; and thus, avoid wasting our time. In the science-driven Western world, the cognitive line of development tends to lead, followed by the emotional and the moral lines of development. Exploring the evolution of these components of development is important because it could help construct the missing link between the interiority, subjective aspects of the individual transformation, and the exterior impact, including behavior. Both of these points are important in terms of mind shift as it relates to this book. Thus, as we grow internally, our understanding and our level of consciousness also seem to grow. As a result, our behavior is affected. In other words, external transformation appears to be a function of the internal transformation, and it is all reflected in our psychograph. Harvard professor and author of *Changing Minds: The Art and Science of Changing Our Own and Other People's Minds* Howard Gardner considers thinking or cognitive intelligence to be only one of nine different intelligences that influence our decision-making and meaning-making processes.[129] Beyond the logical-mathematical intelligence, to which we mostly refer when we discuss IQ-related intelligence, Gardner identified linguistic intelligence, musical intelligence, special intelligence, bodily kinesthetic intelligence, naturalist intelligence, interpersonal and intrapersonal intelligence, and existential intelligence. He posits that we are made up of all of these and that they all influence human development and behavior. In each individual, these lines are more or less developed—which makes each one of us unique—and no one line is to be preferred over another, just as no stage or level is to be preferred over another. Wilber

---

[129]Gardner (1993) & (2004).

associated each line of development with fundamental life questions and ground-breaking developmental scientists as follows[130]:

- The *cognitive* (logical-mathematical IQ) intelligence/line of development is the most popular in the Western world, dominated as it is by science. It was discovered, researched, and further developed and popularized by Jean Piaget and Robert Kegan.[131] It helps respond to life questions such as *What am I aware of?*
- The *emotional* intelligence/line of development addresses *how we feel* and was popularized through the work of Daniel Goleman, who developed the notion of EQ, the emotional quotient.[132]
- The *needs* line of development represented the core of Maslow's work, discussed earlier (see Fig. 2.2).
- The *values* line of development deals with what is most valued within human evolution as life's circumstances change. I discussed this line earlier in the context of the *Spiral Dynamics* model (see Fig. 2.3).
- The *self/ego-identity line* of development is a major line of development of individual ego/identity evolution, discussed above in the context of the work of Susanne Cook-Greuter (see also its application in Chap. 3).
- The *moral* line of development deals with *what should be.* This is why, in an effort to entice people to adhere to ethical norms in their daily lives, the world's major religions all have their own form of a set of moral guidelines, although their format and wording vary. For example, Christianity has the Ten Commandments, or Decalogue, Buddhism has the Eightfold Path, and Islam has the Islamic Decalogues.[133]

In *A Brief History of Everything*, Wilber argued that the evolution of consciousness has a direction, evolves along various lines, tends to occur generally toward "greater depth and less span," and takes place within "nested spheres, with each higher level transcending and including its predecessor."[134] These are Stages of Growing Up, an actualization holarchy (see also Chap. 3) in which each stage unfolds and then enfolds its predecessor in a nested fashion. Within this actualization holarchy, it is important to differentiate between the "ladder, climber, and view." Wilber used the ladder as a metaphor to represent the *level*, or "basic rungs of awareness," which, once developed, remain in existence as "basic building blocks or holons of consciousness" at various developmental levels/stages of the individual. Wilber argued that the AQAL elements of consciousness "emerge in fairly discrete *stages*," development "enfolds" within certain spheres, and "each higher stage does not actually sit on top of the lower stage." The presented developmental models

---

[130]Wilber (2017).

[131]Kegan (1982); Piaget (1976/1972).

[132]Goleman (1995) & (2000).

[133]Armstrong (2001a/1944) & (2001b/2000) & (1993); Smith (1995/1958); Wilber (2017).

[134]Wilber (2000b, pp. 128–129).

characterize the *climber* of the ladder, who can evolve from the (small) egoic *self* to a higher, world-centric, or even Kosmos-centric *Self*. This "nuclear self," as Heinz Kohut[135] calls it, grows along various lines of development, including, in Wilber's words, "self-identity, self-need, [as well as] moral sense."[136] As discussed in the section about the Hero's Journey, stage development was often triggered through state experiences, or Waking Up, within the context of what Maslow called transcendent or *peak* experiences, meditative or contemplative experiences, *near-death experiences*, or *out-of-body experiences*; and what Mihaly Csikszentmihalyi[137] called *flow* state or unity consciousness experiences, exceptional human experiences, transpersonal experiences, or other spiritual emergencies. Furthermore, at each step of the ladder, the climber faces a fulcrum or three-step process of personal growth— Growing Up—that contains "(1) fusion/identification; (2) differentiation/transcendence; (3) integration/inclusion." Therefore, we need vertical growth within each quadrant as well as horizontal integration at each level of development.

In our culture, the notion of perpetual growth is so deeply ingrained that people tend to gravitate toward believing that later stages are somewhat better than earlier ones. However, this is not necessarily true. Why? Well, think about it: Is a brilliant scientist who devotes their career to developing a lethal weapon that could potentially kill hundreds of thousands of people better or more advanced than someone with no tertiary education who works in an animal shelter? I should say they are not. Cognition development tends to occur first within our education system, but ethics and moral development must be our guiding force if we want to address the challenges that life inevitably throws at us. In order for healthy vertical growth, growth that is rooted in healthy ego development, we need a healthy horizontal integration of our self-identity, because only a healthy ego-identity can be of service to the group and later the world. Therefore, the horizontal integration at each stage of development across all four quadrants (see also Fig. 2.6) is the premise for healthy vertical growth (Fig. 2.9).

Horizontal integration takes care of the skillset development at the same level of consciousness across all four quadrants—individual, culture, society, and the environment. It can help achieve a well-grounded and highly developed sense of self-identity whereby people identify their own place in culture and society. At each level, we develop both functional knowledge and behavioral skills. People can enhance their know-how and technical expertise as well as improve their problem-solving techniques and overall competences.

Vertical development, on the other hand, helps the mindset transformation toward later stages of development from ego- to ethnocentric to world-centric and even Kosmos-centric views of the world. It helps us achieve not only higher cognitive intelligence (IQ), but also higher emotional intelligence (EQ), moral, and inter- and intrapersonal intelligences. Work at this level helps to accelerate our

---

[135]Kohut (1985, pp. 10–11).

[136]Wilber (2000b, p. 132).

[137]Csikszentmihalyi (1990).

VERTICAL GROWTH	HORIZONTAL INTEGRATION
Mindset transformation toward	Skillset development at the same level of consciousness horizontally across all four quadrants
• Later stages of development from ego to ethno-centric to world-centric and even Kosmos-centric	• Well-grounded and developed sense of self-identity and own place in culture and society
• Higher cognitive (IQ), emotional (EQ), moral and inter- and intra-personal intelligences	• Developing functional knowledge and behavioral skills
• Accelerating self-actualization toward wisdom and global caring	• Enhancing know-how and technical expertise
• Developing awareness, multiple perspectives across all quadrants	• Improving problem solving techniques and overall competences
• Enhanced ability to handle and navigate complexity quickly	• Enhancing leadership toolbox
• Increased ability to handle uncertain situations	

Fig. 2.9 Vertical growth versus horizontal integration across the AQAL

self-actualization toward wisdom and global caring and to develop awareness and multiple perspectives across all quadrants. The result can be an enhanced ability to handle and navigate complexity quickly as well as an increased ability to handle uncertainty. In *Changes of Mind*, Jenny Wade explains this increased ability as "higher stages of consciousness comprehend lower stages, but the reverse is not true."[138]

Confessions: Forty Years of Meditation

During my own journey toward personal development over the past four decades, I have noted how easy it has become to live with ambiguity and let go of the need to control. This changed mindset and attitude can be attributed, of course, to the myriad self-development and leadership seminars I have attended over the years, the hundreds of books I have read, my postgraduate psychology studies, and daily exercise and healthy nutrition; in short, my integral practice. Personally, I attribute great merit to my daily meditation practice of approximately 2 hours every morning. However, truth be told, not every meditation practice delivers lasting results. I began meditating in 1980, and over the years I have studied many different techniques with well-known and lesser-known teachers. From attending meditation seminars at the Esalen Institute to teachings with His Holiness the Dalai Lama, I have gained vast

(continued)

---

[138]Wade (1996, p. 267).

insights and experience in this field. However, when I began meditating in the Mahamudra tradition,[139] I realized I had found the right technique for me. It allowed me to experience first-hand its influence on my own growth, and I was aided by the fact that I connected with the teacher. I had the good fortune to be instructed by Harvard professor Daniel P. Brown, an integral thinker with an ability to adapt Tibetan meditation techniques and communicate them to the Western mind, unlike any other teacher I had worked with before. Tom had the same experience.

2.4.3   The Perception of Bias

Tom and I chose the AQAL framework because it offers what is "arguably the first truly comprehensive or integrative world philosophy."[140] For two decades, AQAL has helped us navigate not only exponential growth in technology but also the world and evolution in general. From our perspective, AQAL is particularly fitting because it serves as a holding tank for the abundance of available consciousness models that can not only help us steer our own personal development and contribution to a better world but also guide us toward a more complete de-risking model for our business building and investment activities. More important, as we Wake Up to our current existential threats and become increasingly aware of the importance of our personal biases, we *must* address the interiority of all participating agents from investors, to business people, product developers, politicians, and other decision-makers.

Within the context of AI-based products, the interiority of the programmers has a particular importance since their biases and mindsets influence the computer software they are building. A recent report by the AI Now Institute attributed most bias-related issues to lack of employee diversity,[141] but this is only *one* aspect of the problem. We continue to be oblivious to interior aspects of personal development, and so we must make a collective concerted effort to bring that into the spotlight. While bringing in more women programmers, more programmers of color, and more trans-programmers, for example, would help significantly, it would not address the questions of Growing Up, Cleaning Up, or Waking Up to later stages of human development. For example, a programmer of any gender, any color, any sexual tendency whose center of gravity is ethnocentric could have a nationalistic bias and thus build an AI that would give their fellow citizens a privileged status over citizens of other countries. We must, therefore, ensure all participating agents begin to Wake Up to not only their personal raison d'être in the world but also the potential impact of their work on humanity and the planet. To achieve this—and it is crucial that they

---

[139]Brown DP (2006a).

[140]See https://integrallife.com/five-elements-aqal

[141]West et al. (April 2019).

do—they must begin to Clean Up their biases by Growing Up to later, world-centric stages of development.

According to the PriceWaterhouseCoope and CB Insights *Money Tree Report*, venture capital funding for AI and machine-learning startups for the first three quarters of 2019 was US$12.1 billion, exceeding the 2018 investments of US $10.2 billion, which already represented a 72% increase from 2017.[142] As global spending on AI is projected to grow 28.4% p.a. to US$97.9 billion, according to IDC research,[143] we must become extremely vigilant and begin to take responsibility for addressing the bias issue sooner rather than later before it spirals out of control.

2.5   On Becoming an Integral Investor

Our use of the AQAL model is what led Tom and me to call ourselves integral investors in the disruption era. We see it as equipping us with the right tools to lay claim to that title, especially within the context of exponential investing through AI, and other exponentially growing technologies. In "6 Tools Entrepreneurs Must Master to Succeed in an Accelerating World,"[144] Peter Diamandis defined "six mindsets and tools that every exponential entrepreneur needs to master" in order to succeed:

- "You must understand exponentials" and the 6Ds (see Chap. 1) by becoming an exponential thinker in a global world rather than a linear thinker in a local world.
- "You see the world as abundant (vs. scarce)," as data from the past 200 years demonstrate.[145]
- "You leverage exponential technologies," from AI to 3D printing to synthetic biology.
- "You have an MTP [(massively transformative purpose)] and a moonshot"[146] and subscribe to Google's eight innovation principles.[147]
- "You tap the crowd for expertise, solutions and capital" by maximizing the human and fiscal potential of crowdsourcing options.
- "You launch your vision, experiment and disrupt yourself" by embracing change and new ideas, and following the advice of Reid Hoffman: "If you're not embarrassed by the first version of your product, you've launched too late."

---

[142]Money Tree Report by PriceWaterhouseCoopers Q4 2018. Viewed 20 June 2019 at https://tinyurl.com/y4llqyox and 11 March 2020 at https://tinyurl.com/y5bk4my6

[143]IDC "Worldwide Artificial Intelligence Spending Guide." Viewed 12 March 2020 at https://www.idc.com/getdoc.jsp?containerId=IDC_P33198

[144]https://tinyurl.com/yxb3vnra

[145]https://www.diamandis.com/data?p=data

[146]https://tinyurl.com/y9c6lbnb

[147]https://www.diamandis.com/blog/googles-8-innovation-principles

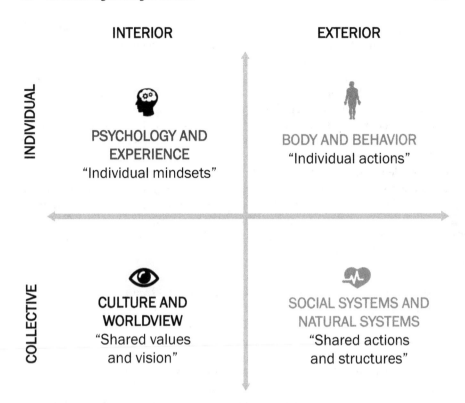

INTERIOR   **EXTERIOR**

INDIVIDUAL

**PSYCHOLOGY AND
EXPERIENCE**
"Individual mindsets"

BODY AND BEHAVIOR
"Individual actions"

COLLECTIVE

**CULTURE AND
WORLDVIEW**
"Shared values
and vision"

**SOCIAL SYSTEMS AND
NATURAL SYSTEMS**
"Shared actions
and structures"

Fig. 2.10 Quadrant view of the AQAL framework

All six points can be used—and in Chap. 3 I explain how Tom and I apply them—to help you be an exponential investor, someone who invests in exponential entre-preneurs who develop exponential technologies and build exponential organizations (see below).[148] But as integral investors, that is not enough for us. Why? Because we are exponential investors who apply the integral framework to *self-actualize* and to address the global grand challenges and ensure that humanity thrives within the planetary boundaries (to make *transformation feasible*). Without an explicit mandate to do that, we believe that regular exponential investors would probably not move fast enough. Why? Because we can only achieve what we focus on and what we measure. If our mind is not set on solving the existential climate problems within the required time frame, for example—that is, before 2030—we will most likely fail. Basically, we must consciously decide what we are aiming to do and give ourselves hard deadlines for doing it.

However, this still may not be enough. Why? Because it would still only be a lower-right, collective-exterior (social and environmental) quadrant view (Fig. 2.10) of the world.

---

[148]Ismail et al. (2014).

As noted earlier, the AQAL quadrants co-arise and cannot be reduced to one another. They must all be applied in order to give a fully comprehensive overview of all the factors that make up a physical or abstract entity. Barrett C. Brown articulates this in a report titled *Four Worlds of Sustainability: Drawing upon Four Universal Perspectives to Support Sustainability Initiatives.*[149] The report is based on his application of the lens of Integral Theory to perform an all-quadrant view of eight bestselling books on sustainability.[150] In his research, he took an ontological approach without an epistemological interpretation and analyzed every sentence in each book, categorizing the sentences according to the quadrant on which they focused. He examined each sentence to assess whether it was taking (a) an interior or exterior view, and (b) an individual or collective perspective of reality. He determined that the lower-right (LR) quadrant perspective dominated. The following list shows the breakdown by quadrant for each book, listed here in the same order that Brown lists them (UL = Upper Left, LL = Lower Left, UR = Upper Right, and LR = Lower Right) (see Fig. 2.6):

- *Cradle to Cradle: Remaking the Way We Make Things*, William McDonough and Michael Braungart: UL: 8%, LL: 9%, UR: 10%, LR: 73%
- *Natural Capitalism: Creating the Next Industrial Revolution*, Paul Hawken, Amory Lovins, and Hunter Lovins: UL: 2%, LL: 7%, UR: 1%, LR: 90%
- *The Ecology of Commerce: A Declaration of Sustainability*, Paul Hawken: UL: 4%, LL: 16%, UR: 5%, LR: 75%
- *Walking the Talk: The Business Case for Sustainability*, Charles O. Holliday Jr., Stephan Schmideiny, and Phillip Watts: UL: 4%, LL: 14%, UR: 3%, LR: 79%
- *The Natural Step for Business: Wealth, Ecology and the Evolutionary Corporation*, Brian Nattrass and Mary Altomare: UL: 11%, LL: 22%, UR: 4%, LR: 63%
- *Plan B 2.0: Rescuing a Planet Under Stress and a Civilization in Trouble*, Lester Brown: UL: 1%, LL: 2%, UR: 6%, LR: 91%
- *Our Common Future*, World Commission on Environment and Development: UL: 1%, LL: 4%, UR: 1%, LR: 94%
- *Ecovillage Living: Restoring the Earth and Her People*, Hildur Jackson and Karen Svensson (Eds.): UL: 11%, LL: 19%, UR: 6%, LR: 64%

All eight books describe and address reality using a primarily social and environmental/systems view. The interior aspects such as the culture, collective intersubjective, shared values, and vision, as well as the individual interior perspective, individual mindsets, or individual external behaviors and actions were represented in only a very small way. Brown agrees that the lower-right quadrant is the strongest and most powerful influencer for change in society—but he also shows why there is little chance of success if we do not take an integral sustainability approach, one that

---

[149]Brown (20 February 2007, pp. 19–28).

[150]Brown LB (2006b); Hawken (1993) & (2017); Hawken et al. (1999); Holliday et al. (2002); Jackson and Svensson (2002); McDonough and Braungart (2002); Nattrass and Altomare (1999); World Commission on Environment and Development (2009/1987).

uses the entire AQAL and not just one particular quadrant. He enumerates successful integral sustainability approaches such as Marilyn Hamilton's for integral cities, Anne Caspari's for the Roman waterway rehabilitation program, and Tam Lundy's integral community development in British Columbia, Canada.[151]

2.5.1   Self-Actualizing Through Investing

As we look around us, Tom and I see more and more investors and company builders like us, people who appear to be self-actualizing through investing. We are aware of more and more peers who are shifting their mindsets toward embracing a more holistic understanding of the world. Investor friends confide in us every day how committed they are to interior development—not to be confused with narcissism, which is concerned only with the ego-self. We see again and again friends who have grown over the years from an egocentric mindset toward a world-centric one and appear to be living a more holistic life—whether they are familiar with Integral Theory or not. In our experience, they are Awakened and have a holistic under-standing of reality. They also have a well-developed sense of humor, live joyous lives, and recognize the need for self-care as a premise for caring for others. We do not need to look at formal research to see how people like Whole Foods founder John Mackey, Generation Investment Management founder David Blood and its chairman Al Gore, Salesforce founder Mark Benioff, or Toniic founders Lisa and Charly Kleissner, to name only a few well-known representatives, are obviously committed to making the world a better place by building more progressive investment and company structures. We call this type of investor an integral investor, and we have a theoretical framework for identifying them (Fig. 2.11).

In our definition, integral investors have a value system rooted in a world-centric level of consciousness or later. As a whole, they seem drawn toward holistically sustainable investing models through which they intend to self-actualize while making sure that financial sustainability is inseparable from a strong social, envi-ronmental, cultural, and highly ethical outcome. Integral investors intend to fully experience life in all its magnitude by:

- *Creating integrally sustainable wealth* through "actively seeking to balance the need for financial return with the yearning to make life a little better for others, themselves, and the Earth"[152]
- *Embracing* "the principles of conscious capitalism, a business approach that emphasizes creating extraordinary outcomes for all stakeholders. We believe

---

[151]Brown (20 February 2007, pp. 37–41).
[152]Brill (2020, p. 1).

Fig. 2.11 Simplified
representation of an integral
investor based on AQAL

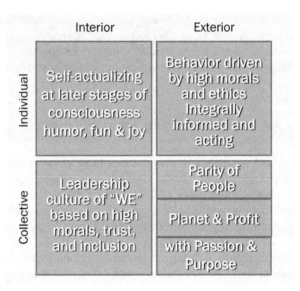

conscious businesses are more innovative, less risky, and better positioned for growth"[153] or

- *Adopting* an "investment process that fully integrates sustainability analysis into our decision-making and is focused on long-term performance"[154]

In more succinct terms, they have the ability to balance the needs of people and the planet with financial sustainability, along with their newly detected purpose and passion for life. They also have a massively transformative purpose (MTP), whether they use that term or not.

2.5.2   The Massively Transformative Purpose

At the January 2019 conference of Abundance Digital, Peter Diamandis showed a video in which the late Stephen Hawking addressed humanity. His words were truly inspiring and touched me deeply, and I would like to share a few of them with you: "How will we feed an ever-growing population, provide clean water ... and slow down global climate change?... let us work together to make [the] future a place we want to visit. Be brave, be determined ... It can be done."[155]

Hawking's call to action should be an inspiration for all of us. We saw earlier that integral investors are mission-driven. Some of them like to refer to their purpose as a

---

[153] http://satoricapital.com/

[154] https://www.generationim.com/generation-philosophy/

[155] Abundance Digital, 2019 A360 Archive Tribute to Stephen Hawking-Flying into Zero-G.

"massively transformative purpose" (MTP). Your MTP reflects you and your belief system; it is inspiring and connects your heart with your mind. It is independent of technology; it is neither too wide nor too narrow; and you can speak with confidence about what it means and why it is your MTP.

Diamandis's personal MTP is to "inspire and guide the transformation of humanity on and off the Earth,"[156] and one MTP of PHD Ventures, one of his organizations, is to "empower entrepreneurs to generate extraordinary wealth while creating a world of abundance."[157] Elon Musk's personal MTP is to have a positive impact on the future through "sustainable energy, [the] Internet, ... making life interplanetary... and AI ... and rewriting genetics."[158] Tesla's MTP is "to create an entire sustainable energy ecosystem ... a unique set of energy solutions ... enabling homeowners, businesses, and utilities to manage renewable energy generation, storage, and consumption ... [and to] ultimately accelerating the advent of clean transport and clean energy production."[159]

Google's MTP is to "organize the world's information" and TED's is "ideas worth spreading." My personal MTP is "to love and to be loved; to inspire and to guide people to awaken to their full potential to serve themselves and the greater good."

2.5.3 The Moonshot

Like many of our Integral Investing peers, Tom and I also have a moonshot. Peter Diamandis cites Astro Teller, head of X, when he explains a moonshot as "going 10X bigger, while the rest of the world is trying to grow 10%."[160] For Tom and me, our moonshot is the investment turnaround (in German, *die Investmentwende*): using investing to implement integral sustainability, the next paradigm in investing. This new paradigm is rooted in culture, values, and morals (intrinsic reality) as well as the material world (extrinsic reality). We are using the investment turnaround to counteract current investment, finance, banking, and economic systems, which have brainwashed us into believing that the only measure of success is money and that investing is all about generating a profit, at the expense of and with no regard for people, the planet, or personal joy and happiness. Our moonshot is allowing us to pave the way toward the implementation of the UN SDGs within the planetary boundaries (see Chap. 3). But how do we do that?

---

[156]https://www.diamandis.com/blog/transformation-of-humanity

[157]https://www.diamandis.com/blog/tech-future-of-food

[158]Starting with minute 1:34, see YouTube video https://tinyurl.com/y4744cnj, and Musk and Neuralink (16 July 2019).

[159]See https://www.tesla.com/about

[160]https://peterdiamandis.tumblr.com/post/164961004383/what-is-a-moonshot

2.5.4 Keeping the Wheel of Your Life Balanced

In *AI Superpowers*, Lee explains the terms 995, 996, and 997. They represent the number of hours employees in China would be working when they joined a certain company: 99 refers to 9 am to 9 pm—the hours between which the employees work—and the 5, 6, and 7 represent the number of working days in a week. The three figures are essentially a code that represents how hard Chinese people are willing to work to nurture national economic development. Lee compared this work ethic with the prevailing work ethic in Silicon Valley. He describes rather cynically how difficult it was to find anybody in the Valley who was willing to meet with a visiting Chinese delegation on a weekend. It is understandable that people are willing to work hard to become successful. However, we need to find a balance between work, personal health, and relationships—otherwise known as work–life balance. Tom and I understand that. We work constantly on our personal growth; we take time to relax and to access deeper dimensions of our own being as well as collective wisdom.

In *Mindset: The New Psychology of Success*, Carol Dweck compares and contrasts two radically different mindsets that she encountered in her research: the *fixed* mindset, which is characterized mainly by the urgency to prove yourself over and over again, and the *growth* mindset, which is rooted in the fundamental belief that your basic talents can be cultivated through your own efforts. In other words, we have a choice about whether we grow and become smart or not, which, to my mind, basically means that a mindset is essentially a belief system.

We have adopted a *growth* mindset and therefore discarded scarcity thinking. We espouse a mentality of abundance with the intention of empowering ourselves and people with whom we work and build companies to act wisely rather than out of fear, which is ultimately destructive.

While it is true that a certain level of financial independence can induce a certain degree of happiness, we have also realized that wealth begins in the head and not in the wallet. Therefore, we have grown to see personal growth as an opportunity to use our skills and talents to address challenges by anticipating them and getting ready to solve them. We have also recognized that, in order to achieve our mission in life, we need a daily routine and regular life practices that help us stay healthy, upbeat, emotionally empowered, and on course. Figure 2.12 shows the integral wheel of life that is at the foundation of our personal growth routine. It was inspired by and derived from Wilber's AQAL.

The individual wheel of life (Fig. 2.13) represents the eight most important aspects of my own life:

- The *interior* aspects are *psychology*, *spirituality*, and *physical health*; the *collective intersubjective* components include *relationships*, both intimate and extended, as well as cultural activities including political or other types of activism.
- The *exterior individual* aspects include play and celebration as well as *career* and *finances*.

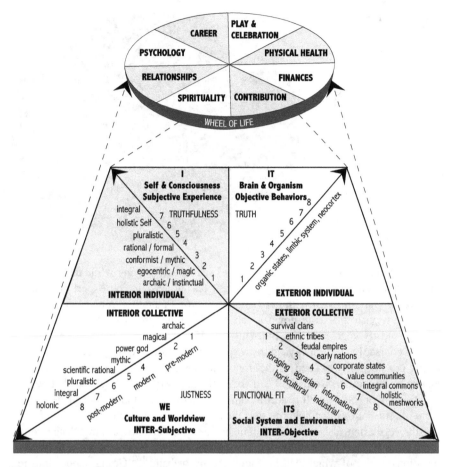

Fig. 2.12 The integral wheel of life practice derived from Wilber's AQAL

- The *collective interobjective aspects* include my *contribution* to the environment and society.

You will find an example of my personal and professional categories of improvement on my website.[161] For each category, I use a host of details that describe my overall strategy and the tactics that help me achieve my goals. I revise every one of them once a month and adjust them if I veer off track or arrive at a different understanding over time. Describing each and every one of my personal and professional categories in detail from vision to daily tactics is well beyond the scope of this book, so the table shows only the barest outline. When it comes to my physical and emotional health and fitness, for example, I establish the vision I have for my physical and emotional health. I then note my motivation for

---

[161]For my own *Personal and Professional Categories* see https://tinyurl.com/ycjmocem

Fig. 2.13 Individual wheel of life

implementing this vision and list the roles I see myself playing while taking care of this personal category (for example, weight loss and wellbeing expert and trusted advisor, woman in touch with her femininity, proud marathon runner). To help me achieve my vision, I write down a variety of routines that I follow (for example, eating a mostly vegetarian diet, enjoying five 45-minute cardio workouts per week). And of course, I adhere always to my own code of conduct. Using my integral wheel of life practice, I try to keep all the important aspects of my life well balanced. For example, I meditate from 3:30 am to 5:30 am every day. I follow that with a 40-minute workout, which is accompanied by audio i-can-tations, a self-developed form of affirmations that help me start the day on a positive note. I eat healthily in a mostly vegetarian fashion with sustainably caught fish on occasion. When something bothers me, I meditate and find emotional stability by asking myself essential questions, some of which can be found on my website.[162] Going deeper into my daily integral life practice would go well beyond the scope of this book. However, if you are interested, it is discussed in more detail in my *Diet for a New Life* book.[163]

2.6   Summary of Chapter 2

Drawing on my personal journey from being a young communist to becoming a high-tech investor, I have argued that we are currently witnessing an extraordinary evolution of consciousness within a certain population of investors and business-people. Using Joseph Campbell's Hero's Journey as a metaphor and Ken Wilber's Integral Theory, AQAL, as a navigation aid, I have presented research to support my

---

[162]See my *Power of Questions* poster at https://aqalgroup.com/extra-materials/
[163]Bozesan (2007).

hypothesis that these individuals appear to have Awakened and evolved to later stages of human evolution and are now challenging the current financial systems and impacting the investing paradigm from that new perspective. They have grown from an egocentric self to a world-centric self and now have multiple and more holistic perspectives on the world.

The studies I cite corroborate neuroscientific research that indicates that such exceptional human experiences can contribute to people achieving higher levels of personal integration and moving on to later stages of ego development. Through their newly acquired value and moral systems, these integrally informed and acting investors—integral investors, as I like to call them—seem drawn toward more sustainable investing and business practices that are now beginning to change the investment, business, and economic paradigms. They seem to want to *self-actualize* through their investing and business activities and ensure that financial sustainability becomes inseparable from the social, environmental, cultural, and behavioral impact of those activities. Furthermore, they appear to have developed a more world-centric understanding of the world in which they view themselves as global citizens who take care of the planet as well as themselves. Therefore, they are using their wealth and influence to also address our grand global challenges. In fact, they now seem to measure their success in life by their contributions toward the achievement of these criteria by adopting models that also include characteristics such as beauty, individual self-actualization, joy, and happiness. To stay physically and mentally healthy and on track, they continue their journey of transformation through daily routines such as the integral wheel of life practice. And they are achieving all of this without turning their backs on technology. In fact, they have successfully leveraged technology to continue moving forward.

They embody my belief that change is possible and that protecting the planet, self-actualizing, and investing are not mutually exclusive. In Chap. 3, I will demonstrate how to implement all that we have discussed so far in the real world to the shared benefit of people and the planet.

References

Aburdene P (2005) Megatrends 2010. Hamptonroads, Charlottesville, VA

Adams JD (ed) (2005) Transforming leadership. Cosimo on Demand, New York

Alexander CL, Langer EJ (eds) (1990) Higher stages of human development: perspectives on adult growth. Oxford University Press, New York

Armstrong K (1993) A history of God: the 4000-year quest of Judaism, Christianity and Islam. Ballantine Books, New York

Armstrong K (2001a/1944) Buddha. Penguin, New York

Armstrong K (2001b/2000) Islam: a short history. Random House, New York

Arnsperger C (2010) Full-spectrum economics: toward an inclusive and emancipatory social science. Routledge, New York

Aspromourgos T (1986) On the origins of the term 'neoclassical'. Camb J Econ 10(3):265–270

Baier AC (1996/1994) Moral prejudices. Harvard University Press, Cambridge, MA

Balandina JJ (2011) Guide to impact investing: managing wealth for impact and profit for family offices and high net worth individuals. Self-published by the author

Balandina JJ (2016) Catalyzing wealth for change: guide to impact investing. Self-published by the author

Beauregard M, O'Leary D (2007) The spiritual brain: a neuroscientist's case for the existence of the soul. HarperCollins, New York

Beck DE, Cowan CC (1996) Spiral dynamics—mastering values, leadership, and change. Blackwell, Malden, MA

Blanchflower DG, Oswald AJ (2004) Well-being over time in Britain and the USA. J Public Econ 88:1359–1386

Bostrom N (2005) A history of transhumanist thought. J Evol Technol 14(1), April 2005. Reprinted (in its present slightly edited form) in Rectenwald M, Carl L (eds) Academic writing across the disciplines. Pearson Longman, New York, 2011. Viewed 16 May 2019 at https://nickbostrom. com/papers/history.pdf

Boyatzis R, McKee A (2005) Resonant leadership. Harvard Business School, Boston

Bozesan M (2007) Diet for a new life: an 8-step integral solution to weight loss and well-being. Sageera Institute, Palo Alto

Bozesan M (2010) The making of a consciousness leader in business: an integral approach. Published Ph.D. Dissertation, ITP Palo Alto. SageEra, Redwood City, CA

Bozesan M (2013) Demystifying the future of investing: an investor's perspective Part 1 & 2. J Integr Theory Pract 8(1 & 2):19–56

Bozesan M (2016) Integral sustainability of how evolutionary forces are driving investors' trust and the integration of people, planet, and profit. In: Lehner OM (ed) Routledge handbook of social and sustainable finance. Routledge, London, pp 296–321

Brill H (2020) Quote viewed 11 March 2020 at https://www.naturalinvestments.com/what-is-sri-investing

Brill H, Brill J, Feigenbaum C (1999) Investing with your values: making money and making a difference. Bloomberg Press, Princeton, NJ

Brill H, Kramer M, Peck C, Cummings J (2015) The resilient investor: a plan for your life, not just your money. Berrett-Koehler, Oakland, CA

Brodwin E (2017) Silicon Valley is obsessed with meditation, and there is new evidence it changes the brain for the better, 24 August 2017. Viewed 12 March 2020 at https://tinyurl.com/v6yc6mg

Brown DP (2006a) Pointing out the great way: the stages of meditation in the Mahamudra tradition. Wisdom Publications, Boston

Brown LB (2006b) Plan B 2.0: rescuing a planet under stress and a civilization in trouble. W.W. Norton, New York

Brown BC (2007) Four worlds of sustainability: drawing upon four universal perspectives to support sustainability initiatives. Integral Sustainability Center, 20 February 2007. Viewed 16 August 2019 at http://nextstepintegral.org/wp-content/uploads/2011/04/Four-Worlds-of-Sustainability-Barrett-C-Brown.pdf

Bugg-Levine A, Emerson J (2011) Impact investing: transforming how we make money while making a difference. Jossey-Bass, San Francisco

Camerer CF, Loewenstein G (2004) Behavioral economics: past, present, future. In: Camerer CF, Loewenstein G, Rabin M (eds) Advances in behavioral economics. Princeton University Press, Princeton, pp 3–51

Campbell J (1968/1949). The hero with a thousand faces. Princeton University Press, New York

Clark C, Emerson J, Thornley B (2015) The impact investor: lessons in leadership and strategy for collaborative capitalism. Jossey-Bass, San Francisco

Collins JC (2001) Good to great: why some companies take the leap and others don't. HarperCollins, New York

Collins JC, Lazier WC (1992) Beyond entrepreneurship: turning our business into an enduring great company. Prentice Hall, Englewood Cliffs, NJ

Commons ML, Richards FA, Armon C (eds) (1984) Beyond formal operations: late adolescent and adult cognitive development. Praeger, New York

Commons ML, Armon C, Kohlberg L, Richards FA, Grotzer TA (eds) (1990) Adult development: models and methods in the study of adolescent and adult thought. Praeger, New York

Cook-Greuter SR (2004) Making the case for a developmental perspective [Electronic version]. J Ind Commer Train 36(7):275–281

Cook-Greuter SR (2005) Ego development: nine levels of increasing embrace. Viewed 4 October 2008 at https://tinyurl.com/yamt5w8j

Cook-Greuter SR (2008) Mature ego development: a gateway to ego transcendence? [Electronic version]. J Adult Dev 7(4):227–240

Cook-Greuter SR (2013) Nine levels of increasing embrace in ego development: a full-spectrum theory of vertical growth. Viewed 15 August 2019 at http://www.cook-greuter.com/Cook-Greuter%209%20levels%20paper%20new%201.1%2714%2097p%5B1%5D.pdf

Csikszentmihalyi M (1990) Flow: the psychology of optimal experience. Harper Perennial, New York

Dalai Lama (1999) Ethics for the new millennium. Riverhead Book, New York

Damasio A (2006) Descartes' error: emotion, reason and the human brain. Vintage Press, London

Davis SF, Palladino JJ (2005/1995) Psychology. Pearson, Upper Saddle River, NJ

Dawkins R (1976) The selfish gene. Oxford University Press, Oxford

Dawkins R (2006) The God delusion. Haughton Mifflin, Boston

Dennett SC (2006) Breaking the spell: religion as a natural phenomenon. Penguin, New York

Descartes R (1998/1637) Discourse on method and meditations on first philosophy. Hackett, Indianapolis

Dörner D (2008/1998) Blueprint for a soul. Rowohlt, Hamburg

Eccles RG, Klimenko S (2019) The investor revolution. Harvard Business Review, May–June 2019. Viewed 11 March 2020 at https://hbr.org/2019/05/the-investor-revolution

Ede S (2013) Spiral dynamics: a way of understanding human nature. Viewed at https://www.cruxcatalyst.com/2013/09/26/spiral-dynamics-a-way-of-understanding-human-nature

Eisler R (2007) The real wealth of nations: creating a caring economics. Berret Koehler, San Francisco

Esbjörn-Hargens S, Zimmerman ME (2009) Integral ecology: uniting multiple perspectives on the natural world. Integral Books, Boston

Esbjörn-Hargens S, Reams J, Gunnlaugson O (2010) Integral education: new directions for higher learning. SUNY Press, Albany

Fiorini RA, De Giacomo P, L'Abate L (2016) Wellbeing understanding in high quality healthcare informatics and telepractice. In: Mantas J, Hasman A, Gallos P, Kolokathi A, Househ MS (eds), Studies in health technology and informatics, vol 226. IOS Press, pp 153–156

Friedman T (2005) The world is flat: a brief history of the twenty-first century. Farrar, Straus and Giroux, New York

Fromm E (1983/1976) Haben oder Sein: Die seelischen Grundlagen einer neuen Gesellschaft. DTV, Berlin

Gardena E, Lynn SJ, Krippner S (2000) Varieties of anomalous experience: examining the scientific evidence. American Psychological Association, Washington, DC

Gardner H (1993) Multiple intelligences. Basic Books, New York

Gardner H (2004) Changing minds: the art and science of changing our own and other people's minds. Harvard Business School Press, Boston

Gebser J (1984/1949) The ever-present origin. Ohio University Press, Athens, OH

Gilligan C (1993/1982) In a different voice: psychological theory and women's development. Harvard University Press, Cambridge, MA

Giving Pledge (2020) Forty U.S. families take giving pledge: Billionaires pledge majority of wealth to philanthropy. Viewed at http://givingpledge.org

Godeke S, Pomares R, Bruno AV, Guerra P, Kleissner C, Shefrin H (2009) Solutions for impact investors: from strategy to implementation. Rockefeller Philanthropy Advisors, New York

Goleman D (1995) Emotional intelligence: why it can matter more than IQ. Bantam Books, New York

Goleman D (2000) Leadership that gets results [Electronic version]. Harvard Business Review, March–April, 78–91. Reprint No. R00204. Viewed 11 March 2020 at https://hbr.org/2000/03/leadership-that-gets-results

Goleman D, Boyatzis R, McKee A (2002) Primal leadership: realizing the power of emotional intelligence. Harvard Business School Press, Boston

Göpel M (2016) The great mindshift: how new economic paradigm and sustainability transformations go hand in hand. SpringerOpen, Berlin

Gore A (1992) Earth in the balance: ecology and the human spirit. Dove Audio Cassettes, Santa Monica, CA

Gore A (2006) An inconvenient truth: the planetary emergency of global warming and what we can do about it. Rodale, New York

Gore A (2020) Generation Investment Management official website. http://www.generationim.com/sustainability/investing.html

Grof S (2006) When the impossible happens: adventures in non-ordinary realities. Sounds True, Boulder, CO

Hawken P (1993) The ecology of commerce: a declaration of sustainability. HarperBusiness, New York

Hawken P (ed) (2017) Drawdown, the most comprehensive plan ever proposed to reverse global warming. Penguin Books, New York

Hawken P, Lovins A, Lovins LH (1999) Natural capitalism: creating the next industrial revolution. Little Brown, New York

Hendricks G, Ludeman K (1996) The corporate mystic: a guidebook for visionaries with their feet on the ground. Bantam Books, New York

Holliday C Jr, Schmidheiny S, Watts P (2002) Walking the talk: the business case for sustainable development. Greenleaf, Sheffield

Investors' Circle (2020) Official website. http://www.svcimpact.org

Ismail S, Malone M, van Geest Y (2014) Exponential organizations: why new organizations are ten times better, faster, and cheaper than yours (and what to do about it). Diversion Books, New York

Jackson H, Svensson K (2002) Ecovillage living: restoring the earth and her people. Green Books, Devon

James W (2017/1890) The principles of psychology, vol 1 & 2. Pantianos Classics, Harvard

Jaworski J (1996) Synchronicity: the inner path of leadership. Berret Koehler, San Francisco

Kahneman D, Tversky A (1982) On the study of statistical intuitions. In: Kahneman D, Slovic P, Tversky A (eds) Judgment under uncertainty: heuristics and biases. Cambridge University Press, Cambridge

Kant I (1993/1949) The philosophy of Kant. The Modern Library, New York

Kegan R (1982) The evolving self: problem and process in human development. Harvard University Press, Cambridge, MA

Kegan R (1994) In over our heads. Harvard University Press, Cambridge, MA

Kegan R, Lahey LL, Souvaine E (1990) Life after formal operations: implications for a psychology of the self. In: Alexander CN, Langer EJ (eds) Higher stages of human development. Oxford University Press, New York, pp 229–257

Kelly E (2011) Exercising leadership power: Warren Buffet and the integration of integrity, mutuality, and sustainability. In: Weir D, Sultan N (eds) From critique to action: the practical ethics of the organizational world. Cambridge Scholars, Newcastle, pp 315–337

Kelly EE, Crabtree A, Marshall P (eds) (2015) Beyond physicalism: toward reconciliation of science and spirituality. Rowman & Littlefield, Lanham, MD

Klein E, Izzo J (1999) Awakening corporate soul: four paths to unleash the power of people at work. Fair Winds Press, Beverly, MA

Kofman F (2006) Conscious business: how to build values through value. Sounds True, Boulder, CO

Kohlberg L, Ryncarz RA (1990) Beyond justice reasoning: moral development and consideration of a seventh stage. In: Alexander CN, Langer EJ (eds) Higher stages of human development: perspectives on adult growth. Oxford University Press, New York, pp 191–207

Kohut H (1985) Self-psychology and the humanities: reflections on a new psychoanalytic approach. W.W. Norton, New York

Koplowitz H (1984) A projection beyond Piaget's formal operations stage: a general system stage and a unitary stage. In: Commons ML, Richards FA, Armon C (eds) Beyond formal operations: Late adolescent and adult cognitive development. Praeger, New York, pp 272–296

Koplowitz H (1990) Unitary consciousness and the highest development of mind: the relationship between spiritual development and cognitive development. In: Commons ML, Armon C, Kohlberg L, Richards FA, Grotzer TA (eds) Adult development: models and methods in the study of adolescent and adult thought. Praeger, New York, pp 105–112

Krugman P (2012) End this depression now! Norton, New York

Lee K-F (2018) AI Superpowers. China, Silicon Valley and the new world order. HMH, New York

Loevinger J (1977) Ego development: conceptions and theories. Jossey-Bass, San Francisco

Mackey J, Sisodia R (2013) Conscious capitalism: liberating the heroic spirit of business. Harvard Business Review Press, Boston

Marques J, Dhiman S, King R (2007) Spirituality in the workplace. Personhood Press, Fawnskin, CA

Marx K (2016/1867) Das Kapital. Nikol, Hamburg

Maslow AH (1999/1968) Toward a psychology of being. Wiley, New York

Maslow AH, Stephens DS, Heil G (1998) Maslow on management. Wiley, New York

McCraty R (2001) Science of the heart: exploring the role of the heart in human performance. Institute of HeartMath, Boulder Creek, CA

McDonough W, Braungart M (2002) Cradle to cradle: remaking the way we make things. North Point Press, New York

Mitroff II, Denton EA (1999) A spiritual audit of corporate America: a hard look at spirituality, religion, and values in the workplace. Jossey-Bass, San Francisco

Moustakas C (1990) Heuristic research: design, methodology, and applications. Sage, London

Musk E, Neuralink (2019) An integrated brain-machine interface platform with thousands of channels. White paper, 16 July 2019. Retrieved https://tinyurl.com/y5kd42fu

Nagel T (2012) Mind & cosmos: why the materialist new-Darwinian conception of nature is almost certainly false. Oxford University Press, Oxford

Nattrass B, Altomare M (1999) The natural step for business: wealth, ecology and the evolutionary corporation. New Society, Gabriola Island

Newberg AB, Lee BY (2005) The neuroscientific study of religious and spiritual phenomena: or why God doesn't use biostatistics. Zygon 40(2):469–489

Piaget J (1976/1972) The child and reality. Penguin, New York

Pinker S (2011) The better angels of our nature: the decline of violence in history and its causes. Allen Lane, London

Pinker S (2018) Enlightenment now: the case for reason, science, humanism, and progress. Viking, New York

Plato (1961/1938) The collected dialogues of Plato: including the letters. Princeton University Press, Princeton, NJ

Pope Francis (2015) Laudato Si' on care for our common home. Our Sunday Visitor, Huntington, IN

Porras J, Emery S, Thompson M (2007) Success built to last: creating a life that matters. Wharton School, Upper Saddle River, NJ

Ray P, Anderson SR (2000) The cultural creatives: how 50 million people are changing the world. Three Rivers Press, New York

Ray M, Rinzler A (eds) (1993) The new paradigm in business: emerging strategies for leadership and organizational change. Jeremy P. Tarcher/Pedigree, New York

Ricard M (2003) Happiness: a guide to developing life's most important skill. Little, Brown, New York

Rooke D, Torbert W (2005) Seven transformations of leadership. Harvard Business Review OnPoint Article, 1–11, April. Reprint No R0504D

Russel MJ, Kanik I (2010) Why does life start, what does it do, where will it be, and how might we find it? J Cosmol 5:1008–1039, 30 January 2010. Viewed 11 March 2020 at http://journalofcosmology.com/SearchForLife121.html

Scharmer O (2010) Seven acupuncture points for shifting capitalism to create a regenerative ecosystem economy. Oxford Leadersh J 1(3), June 2010. Viewed 18 June 2019 at https://tinyurl.com/y32cospb

Scharmer O (2013) Leading from the emerging future: from ego-systems to eco-systems economies. Berrett-Koehler, San Francisco

Schoenberg PLA, Ruf A, Churchill J, Brown DP, Brewer JA (2018) Mapping complex mind states: EEG neural substrates of meditative compassionate awareness. Conscious Cogn 57:41–53. Viewed 31 August 2019 at https://www.pointingoutthegreatway.org/wp-content/uploads/neuroawakening.pdf

Scotton BW, Chinen AB, Battista JR (eds) (1996) Textbook of transpersonal psychiatry and psychology. Basic Books, New York

Secretan L (2006) One: the art and practice of conscious leadership. The Secretan Center, Caledon, ON

Senge P, Scharmer CO, Jaworski J, Flowers BS (2005) Presence: an exploration of profound change in people, organizations, and society. Currency Doubleday, New York

Sisodia R, Sheth J, Wolfe DB (2007) Firms of endearment: how world-class companies profit from passion and purpose. Wharton School, Upper Saddle River, NJ

Smith H (1995/1958) The illustrated world's religions: a guide to our wisdom traditions. Harper, San Francisco

Smith A (2007/1759) The theory of moral sentiments. Cosimo, New York

Smith A (2008/1776) An inquiry into the nature and causes of the wealth of nations. Oxford University Press, Oxford

SOCAP (2012) Official website. http://www.socap.org

Social Venture Circle (2020) Official website. www.svcimpact.org

Soros G (2008) The new paradigm for financial markets: the credit crisis of 2008 and what it means. PublicAffairs, New York

Strong M (2009) Be the solution: how entrepreneurs and conscious capitalists can solve all the world's problems. Wiley, Hoboken, NJ

Stückelberger C, Duggal P (2018) Cyber ethics 4.0: serving humanity with values. Globethics.Net, Geneva. Viewed 23 May 2019 at https://tinyurl.com/y5kt7ffe

Toms M (1997) The soul of business. HayHouse, Carlsbad, CA

Torbert W, Kelly E (2013) Developing transforming leadership: the case of Warren Buffett. Revised paper originally presented at the Integral Theory Conference, San Francisco, July 2013. Viewed 23 August 2019 at http://www.williamrtorbert.com/wp-content/uploads/2013/09/EKellyWRTBuffett.pdf

Tversky A, Kahneman D (1974) Judgment under uncertainty: heuristics and biases. Science, New Series 185(4157):1124–1131. Viewed 22 March 2011 at http://www.math.mcgill.ca/vetta/CS764.dir/judgement.pdf

Vaughan F (2000) The inward arc: healing in psychotherapy and spirituality. IUniverse, Lincoln, NE

Vaughan F (2005) Shadows of the sacred: seeing through spiritual illusions. IUniverse, Lincoln, NE

Vollmann T (2018a) No immediate danger. Volume one of carbon ideologies. Viking, New York

Vollmann T (2018b) No good alternative. Volume two of carbon ideologies. Viking, New York

von Bertalanffy L (2006/1969) General systems theory: foundations, developments, applications. George Brazillier, New York

Von Weizsäcker EU, Wijkman A (2018) Come on! Capitalism, short -termism, population and the destruction of the planet – a report to the Club of Rome. Springer Nature, New York

Wade J (1996) Changes of mind: a holonomic theory of the evolution of consciousness. State University New York, Albany

Walsh R, Vaughan F (1993) Meditation: royal road to the transpersonal. In: Walsh R, Vaughan F (eds) Paths beyond ego: the transpersonal vision. Jeremy P. Tarcher/Pedigree, Los Angeles, pp 47–55

West SM, Whittaker M, Crawford K (2019) Discriminating systems: gender, race, and power in AI. AI Now Institute, April 2019. Viewed 11 March 2020 at https://ainowinstitute.org/discriminatingsystems.pdf

Wilber K (1998) Marriage of sense and soul. Random House, New York

Wilber K (2000a/1995) Sex, ecology, spirituality: the spirit of evolution. Shambhala, Boston

Wilber K (2000b) Integral psychology: consciousness, spirit, psychology, therapy. Shambhala, Boston

Wilber K (2000c) A theory of everything: an integral vision for business, politics, science, and spirituality. Shambhala, Boston

Wilber K (2006) Integral spirituality: a startling new role for religion in the modern and postmodern world. Integral Books, Boston

Wilber K (2017) The religion of tomorrow: a vision for the future of great traditions. Shambhala, Boston

World Commission on Environment and Development (2009/1987) Our common future. Oxford University Press, Oxford

Chapter 3
Integral Investing in the Disruption Era

3.1 The Foundations of a Paradigm Change

I think it would be fair to pronounce 2015 one of the most important years in the history of humanity to date. That year, several significant efforts to secure the future of humanity were made. For example, on September 27, the 2030 Agenda for Sustainable Development was adopted by all UN member states. The intention was to collaborate globally to work toward the implementation of the 17 SDGs, which include the eradication of poverty and climate change, and the provision of inclusive prosperity, good health, and good economic development on a stable planetary system. On December 12, the Paris Agreement was adopted by consensus between 196 nations. Its long-term goal is to keep the increase in the global average temperature to well below 2 °C above preindustrial levels and ideally to no more than 1.5 °C.

As with any reporting, of course, it is important that we read critically, looking beyond the headlines and scrutinizing the data. Scientific communities like the IPCC, for example, are not telling us the whole story in their reports—not because they are actively trying to deceive us but because they are working within the parameters of the scientific method.[1] If you take the time to read the fine print and the footnotes in the IPCC special report on climate change,[2] you will discover that the human-caused increase in greenhouse gases since 1880—from 280 ppm to 410 ppm—is contributing not only to the rise in the global temperature of Earth and the oceans but also to the significant rise in sea levels because of polar glacier melting *and* the subsequent release of methane from permafrost,[3] which amplifies global warming with all its attendant consequences. What does that mean in real terms? Well, even if we stopped adding CO_2 to the atmosphere right now, it might

---

[1]https://plato.stanford.edu/entries/scientific-method/#DisSciMet
[2]See, for example, https://report.ipcc.ch/sr15/pdf/sr15_spm_final.pdf
[3]Gray (20 August 2018).

© Springer Nature Switzerland AG 2020
M. Bozesan, *Integral Investing*, https://doi.org/10.1007/978-3-030-54016-6_3

still be too late to turn things around. The heat produced by the existing greenhouse gases in the atmosphere is equivalent to the heat that would be generated by the explosion of an atomic bomb comparable in size to the one dropped over Hiroshima every couple of seconds.[4] Because the oceans absorb the heat, the polar caps are melting, which means that sea levels will continue to rise alongside the overall increase in temperature on Earth. Our only real option at this stage may be damage control because, with increasing warming, oceans are losing their ability to absorb carbon dioxide and heat. In the September 24, 2019, special IPCC report on oceans and ice, *The Oceans and Cryosphere in a Changing Climate*,[5] more than 100 scientists from 30 countries warn that the oceans' warming rate since the early 1990s has doubled. This is caused by increasing CO_2 absorption, which leads to more frequent and more intense heatwaves, which in turn (1) promote more potent storms and flooding, (2) change underwater ecosystems, thus threatening the survival of fisheries (that could decrease by up to 25%), underwater biomass (marine animals whose population could shrink by 15% by 2100) and biotopes including coral reefs, and (3) a projected sea-level rise of up to 1.1 m by the end of the twenty-first century (and up to 5.4 m in the twenty-third century). It is important to note that these predictions are actually rather cautious and *conservative* because they depend to a large extent on what happens in the planet's cryosphere—that is, the frozen parts of Earth's system, including its mountainous areas with their glaciers, permafrost, Greenland, and the Arctic ice, to name a few. For example, it is expected that global warming levels will determine the rate and extent of further Arctic sea ice loss.

The UN's SDGs are ambitious, transformational goals for global prosperity within planetary boundaries. However, as I noted in Chap. 1, they are also inherently contradictory, which increases the risk that achieving one goal will come at the expense of failing to achieve others. For example, if we pursue goal number 8—good jobs and economic growth—by burning fossil fuels such as coal,[6] it will be impossible to achieve goal number 14—life below water—because we will still be emitting destructive CO_2 into the atmosphere, literally fueling the existing vicious cycle. These contradictions could explain why we have made so little progress toward implementing either the Paris Agreement or Agenda 2030 since 2015.

As is so often the case, though, bad things give rise to good things. The apparent lack of political will to date seems to have served as a catalyst for young people to step up and take widespread action. In 2019, following the lead of 15-year-old Greta Thunberg of Sweden, schoolchildren from developed nations throughout the world joined the Fridays for Future movement[7] and called in no uncertain terms for emergency climate action. In Germany, a computer science student and YouTuber named Rezo posted a video in which he urged young voters to vote green and against the sitting coalition government, which appears to have done nothing to address

[4]Zanna et al. (7 January 2019).
[5]IPCC (24 September 2019).
[6]See, for example, https://tinyurl.com/y7ehbjn2
[7]https://www.fridaysforfuture.org/

current existential threats during its time in power. Rezo attracted support from dozens of other YouTubers, and his video subsequently went viral.[8] Perhaps the upcoming generations will prove to be better planetary caretakers than we have. On September 23, 2019, Greta Thunberg issued an appeal to world leaders to act on scientific data and to stop stealing her "dreams and [her] childhood."[9] Her appeal was answered on December 11, 2019 by the European Parliament's communication on a European Green Deal[10] to significantly increase its climate action and environmental policies. On March 4, 2020, the European Commission went further and proposed the first European Climate Law with the intention to "write into law the goal set out in the European Green Deal—for Europe's economy and society to become climate-neutral by 2050."[11] For the sake of the planet and the future of humanity, let us hope that the COVID-19 crisis marked a significant turning point. Agenda 2030 and the Paris Agreement are both incompatible with conventional economic growth, but there is hope—and investors can play a major role in turning that hope into reality through concrete action starting *today*.

3.1.1 Transformation Is Feasible

When it comes to the urgency of addressing climate change and making available the tools, technology, and resources required to mitigate it, the scientific community is not only united but also has support from other sectors. A coalition of researchers and scientists—currently composed of 70 Drawdown Fellows with an advisory board of 120 prominent geologists, engineers, economists, policymakers, climatologists, agronomists, and businesspeople—has both expressed and offered hope through the publication of *Drawdown: The Most Comprehensive Plan Ever Proposed to Reverse Global Warming*,[12] which contains 80 proposed solutions to our current biggest problems. The solutions, all of which are possible to implement today, are ranked by impact.[13] The top five, as classified in *Drawdown*, are: refrigerant management, wind turbines (onshore), reduced food waste, plant-rich diet, and tropical forests (a superficially ambiguous term that refers to rethinking restoration approaches for tropical forests). My personal favorites are ranked at number 6—educating girls—and number 7—family planning. Why is girls' education singled out? *Drawdown* cites research that "the difference between a woman with no years of schooling and with 12 years of schooling is almost four to five

---

[8]https://tinyurl.com/y89sjqnc; https://tinyurl.com/y9znn3qn

[9]https://tinyurl.com/y4pamvpg

[10]https://ec.europa.eu/info/sites/info/files/european-green-deal-communication_en.pdf

[11]https://ec.europa.eu/info/sites/info/files/commission-proposal-regulation-european-climate-law-march-2020_en.pdf

[12]Hawken (2017).

[13]See also https://tinyurl.com/y7npu6d7

children per woman."[14] This suggests that increasing girls' access to education and birth control will result in a significant population reduction and thus a smaller human footprint on the planet. The *Drawdown* authors calculate that, by taking steps toward universal education and investing in family planning in developing nations, the world could eliminate 120 billion tons of CO_2 emissions by 2050.[15] (Note that they also acknowledge a need to improve access to family planning resources and birth control in certain developed countries). According to 2014 figures, this is the equivalent of roughly 10 years' worth of China's annual CO_2 emissions.

So, with the October 2018 and September 2019 IPCC warnings ringing in our ears and only one decade left to fulfill the Paris Agreement (and, at time of writing, with the USA still indicating its desire to withdraw from it), the big question remains: Can we implement Agenda 2030 with its 17 SDGs within the planetary boundaries?

In *Transformation is Feasible*,[16] Jorgen Randers et al. say that we can achieve our goal of implementing Agenda 2030, but only if we act now *and* stay within planetary boundaries (see Chap. 1). For the report, Randers et al. worked with a team of scientists to produce four potential scenarios for future development. Johan Rockström, one of the leading scientists involved, explained at a talk I attended that, to do this, they built a complex system dynamics model,[17] using socioeconomic data collected over the past decades. This allowed them to test, build, and simulate their four future scenarios up to 2050 with the aim of testing "four different answers to our overarching question: 'How can the world achieve the Sustainable Development Goals within planetary boundaries?'" The four scenarios, named *Same* (business-as-usual), *Faster, Harder,* and *Smarter* (see Fig. 3.1), "are all based on the same historic facts but are shaped by different policy and investment choices made in the coming decade(s)."

Each scenario is therefore named for its predominant underlying formative policy:

- *Same* (red): Where will business as usual take the world toward 2050?
- *Faster* (orange): Will accelerating economic growth help?
- *Harder* (yellow): What if both governments and industry try even harder to deliver on SDGs?
- *Smarter* (green): What if governments and industry actually choose transformational actions?[18]

On the vertical axis are the nine planetary boundaries (PB), the nine factors that regulate the stability of Earth's operating system. They include, for example, biosphere integrity, freshwater use, ocean acidification, ozone depletion, and climate

[14]Hawken (2017, p. 81).
[15]Hawken (2017, pp. 78–79).
[16]Randers et al. (2018); https://tinyurl.com/y9epzlmk
[17]https://en.wikipedia.org/wiki/System_dynamics
[18]Randers et al. (2018, p. 13).

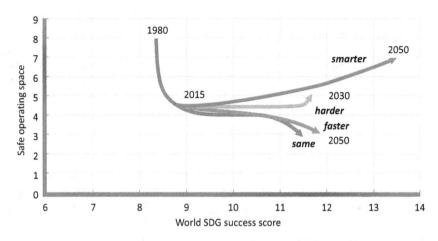

Fig. 3.1 Transformation is feasible: four scenarios for implementing the SDGs within planetary boundaries (Source: own graph adapted after Per Espen Stoknes, BI Norwegian Business School)

change. The figure 9 on the vertical axis means all PBs are in harmony with one another (the green area); the figure 1 means life on Earth as we know it is practically impossible (that is, humans would still exist, but life would be extremely challenging—the red area). The horizontal axis represents the number of UN SGDs that would be implemented collectively at any one point in time, with the intention being to realize as many of the 17 as possible, moving consistently toward the green zone. The figure 6 on the left of the *x*-axis means that 6 of the total 17 are being implemented at any one time, and the figure 14 on the right of the *x*-axis means that 14 of the 17 are being implemented at any one time. In order to successfully implement *all* the SDGs within planetary boundaries, humanity must operate within the green areas on both axes.

Looking at the *red* curve, representing the *Same,* business-as-usual, scenario, we see that in 1980, while the world was fulfilling only eight SDGs, it was still operating within the green zone of planetary boundaries. We moved fast, lifting millions of people out of poverty and hurtling toward lavishness, despite continued exponential population growth. Unfortunately, all the lavishness came at the expense of the planetary boundaries: by 2015 we had fallen into the red zone. The result as per the last IPCC report: global warming of more than 1 °C, moving fast toward 3 °C or even 4 °C. If we continue with the *Same,* twentieth-century-type of politics and outdated economics ideas, we will be able to deliver up to 11 SDGs by 2050, the *Same* scenario tells us, but the price we will pay is the compromised stability of Earth's operating systems. The consequences for humanity would include severe global warming, costly weather events, and social instability with increased political insecurity, rising nationalism, and growing inequality and social unrest.

The second scenario, *Faster*, represented by the *orange* curve, simulates what would happen if we moved faster in a conventional way to realize the SDGs by increasing the average global economic growth from 2.8% per annum in 2018 to

3.5% per annum in 2050. With slightly less than +1% GDP growth per person per year until 2050, we would risk significantly destabilizing the planet without significantly moving forward with our aim of achieving the SDGs. The SDG success score would move only from 9 in 2015 to 11.5 in 2050, despite increased efforts to focus on this particular goal. We would increase investments, trade, and new technology development, but that in turn would increase social inequality, affect a much larger ecological footprint by weakening responsible consumption, and harm life both on land and in water.

A similar outcome would result if we tried *Harder* (yellow curve) at green and inclusive growth by increasing our ability to deliver on our promises by 30–50% across all global sectors of society, from climate to trade agreements. We would address each SDG separately with certain trade-offs whereby we would favor one goal over another (for example, education over sustainable agriculture or clean water over clean energy). Unfortunately, this scenario would not get us out of the danger zone with respect to planetary boundaries, and we would deliver unsatisfactory results on the SDGs, which would remain at 11.5, as in the *Faster* scenario.

But there is a *Smarter* scenario (green curve) that could solve the problem by 2050. However, in order to get there, we as a species need to undergo a radical transformation—starting with a significant mind shift. And to do that, we must disrupt ourselves by acting daringly and thinking outside the box.

Based on the approximately 100,000 data points provided by their real-world research data, the scientists working with Randers et al. identified five transformational actions that could lead to all 17 SDGs being achieved while keeping us in the green zone of the planetary boundaries:

1. *Energy: Accelerated renewables growth.* We would double our investments in renewable energy by scaling up solar and wind power through dispersed energy storage, electric vehicles, and distributed energy infrastructure. Existing power grids would be replaced by digitized and integrated smart grids to help replace fossil fuels with renewable energy sources. Renewables would begin to deliver higher profitability than fossils and be supported by governments pushing through stronger regulations. These measures would lead to emissions being halved every decade from 2030 onward and a global energy democracy being created.

2. *Differentiated growth: Rolling out new development models in the developing countries.* South Korea, Singapore, and China have all quadrupled their GDP per person in the past three decades through sustained economic growth. South Korea, China, Ethiopia, Japan, and Scandinavia are all identified in the Randers et al. report as "role models" for economic growth. Identifying and replicating the factors behind their successes would help deliver differentiated economic growth and stability with higher growth in developing countries. The authors insist that the problem is not GDP growth per person but humanity's overall footprint growth.

3. *Food: Accelerated shift to sustainable food chains.* Sustainable agriculture would be achieved by "linking production to better logistics," encouraging local food

production, reducing food waste, and reducing reliance on herbicides and pesticides. People would adopt plant-based diets and so lower their meat consumption. Embedded intelligence through new technology, digitalization, sensors, satellite monitoring, and the Internet of Things would make real-time big data available for better monitoring of food production areas, weather patterns, and water usage. The combined effects of these changes "would lower the footprint of the food chain by an extra 1% per year, relative to *Same*."

4. *Active inequality reduction.* This would include addressing extreme unfairness created by wealth inequality, introducing "fairer wages and more progressive taxation," increasing unemployment benefits, shortening the working year, creating more jobs in the face of growing automation and AI, and redistributing total output and wealth.

5. *Investment in education for all, gender equality, health, and family planning.* Radically increasing investment in girls' and women's education, gender equality programs, health, and family planning would lead to the stabilization of the world's population. That in turn would improve general wellbeing and, in the words of Randers et al., "a sense of security" that would contribute to reducing the overall ecological footprint of humankind. And by empowering women to become world leaders, we would empower women in general to strive to attain leadership positions, thus setting in motion a self-reinforcing positive spiral that would benefit both developing and developed countries.

Randers et al. insist that these five actions hold "the promise of achieving (nearly) all 17 SDGs within (nearly all) the 9 PBs by 2050, although it takes some time before the Earth's safety margins is back at acceptable levels, from its low of 4.5 in 2015."[19] As investors, we can—we must—take action to redirect humanity from our current path toward destruction back toward the safe zones of our biosphere. We can and must overcome the extant barriers of corruption, nationalism, mistrust, skepticism, lack of global cooperation, and the idea that "free markets" work best without government oversight. *Transformation is Feasible* outlines *how* we can redirect ourselves, but it relies on our changing our current economic system, which is so backward it is not even financially sustainable in the long term. For as long as any of us can remember, making money has been used as the only measure of success—but this has come at the expense of the needs of people and the planet. Fortunately, as we saw in Chap. 2, investors are Waking Up to a world-centric reality and realizing that life is not all about becoming a billionaire.

We cannot eat, drink, or breathe money, diamonds, gold, or pieces of paper with dead notables printed on them (aka banknotes). We came into this world naked and we will leave it naked. It is time to push back against current economic norms. And the first step is a twofold one: to build a system that honors our very source of life, our beautiful blue planet, and the societies and cultures in it and to cultivate a unity mindset. Figure 3.2 shows how the economy could begin to support society and the

[19]Randers et al. (2018, p. 39).

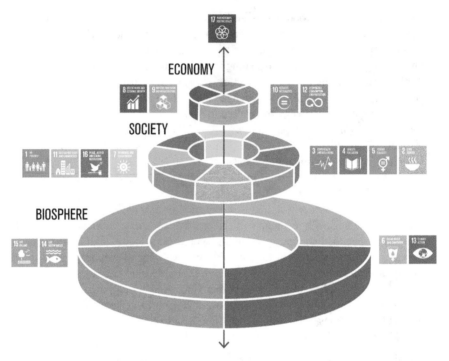

Fig. 3.2 The economy must serve society and the biosphere (Source: Printed with permission by ©Azote Images for Stockholm Resilience Centre; https://tinyurl.com/y7m64bwb)

biosphere within the context of the SDGs. In order to do that, it must reverse its current course and put the biosphere at its foundation so it can serve society, not the other way around. It all starts with us, the people.

3.1.2   The Investment Turnaround: Our Moonshot

Tom and I had been seeking an investment model with appropriate metrics for integral sustainability since the beginning of the twenty-first century. When we first embarked on our search, we quickly realized that no matter how much we invested or what we did in our family office, little would change without political backing and collective action to trigger a paradigm shift in the overall economic, financial, business, and investing models. To this day, the brown economy persists because it is supported by market-distorting subsidies. Fossil fuel subsidies alone totaled US$5.3 trillion in 2015—that is 6.5% of global GDP.[20] Additional subsidies for water, agriculture, and transportation also incentivize pollution habits and the

---

[20]Coady et al. (2017).

abuse of natural resources. Tom and I believe that governments must abolish such dangerous subsidies and introduce both pollution taxes and carbon pricing because they would not only benefit global health and the environment but also stimulate sustainable growth, especially among small to medium enterprises (SMEs), which are a significant economic force in both developing and developed nations—with a contribution of "about 90% of businesses and more than 50% of employment worldwide. Formal SMEs contribute up to 40% of national income (GDP) in emerging economies"[21] and in Germany, for example, their "contribution towards Germany's economic strength, [represents] approx. 35% of total corporate turnover... In terms of their contribution to GDP, these companies even account for close to 55%."[22]

This is why, encouraged by members of the Club of Rome, the Desertec Foundation, and a dozen other caring organizations, in December 2012 I sent a positioning paper to Chancellor Angela Merkel requesting an investment turnaround.[23] I am still awaiting a response. Undeterred by the deafening silence, Tom and I launched our moonshot, the investment turnaround (in German, *die Investmentwende*), together with various other family offices, the Club of Rome co-presidents and members, and organizations such as the Toniic network of impact investors. When the Paris Agreement was signed in 2015 and the 193 Member States of the United Nations approved the 2030 Agenda with its 17 SDGs,[24] we knew that something significant had occurred and that it would support our own endeavors. The world's most demanding list of universal requests ever posed to the global community had been formulated, and we knew that the world was moving on up. The SDGs apply to every nation, every sector, every business, and every profession. They address everything we value collectively, and their successful implementation requires an integral approach to transforming what we do and how we do it.

The SDGs present the ultimate investment challenge, and we realized with delight that the SDG signatories and heads of state had given investors and businesspeople an enormous opportunity—and, of course, a huge responsibility. We accepted the challenge and began investing in and building companies to build an integrally sustainable economy. We did not have all the answers, of course, but we know that you only get the right answers when you ask the right questions.

The investment turnaround uses investing to implement integral sustainability, the next paradigm in investing. Integral sustainability fulfills Gro Harlem Brundtland's call for sustainability by meeting "the need of the present without compromising the ability of future generations to meet their own needs"[25] and is rooted in the essence of all existence, both the interior, such as culture, values, ethics, and exterior realities, the material world. It is a reality in which financial

---

[21]World Bank (n.d.).

[22]Federal Ministry for Economic Affairs and Energy (2020).

[23]See *Positioning Paper* at https://tinyurl.com/y9snzb4x

[24]https://sustainabledevelopment.un.org/sdgs

[25]World Commission on Environment and Development (2009/1987, p. 43).

sustainability is inseparable from a positive environmental, social, cultural, and ethical impact, as well as individual self-actualization, joy, and happiness.

Our Moonshot: The Investment Turnaround
Our moonshot is the implementation of the investment turnaround. It is the specific application of exponential technologies toward achieving Integral Investing, the next paradigm in investing, namely integral sustainability.

It aims at implementing an investing paradigm rooted in the essence of all existence, the exterior reality, the material world, as well as interior realities such as culture, values, ethics, and morals. It is a reality in which financial returns are inseparable from environmental, social, cultural, and ethical impact, including individual joy and happiness. Our first goal is the integrally sustainable implementation of the UN SDGs within planetary boundaries by 2050.

We are also fully aligned with, endorse, and support the implementation of the Club of Rome Planetary Emergency Plan[26] launched on September 24, 2019, during the Climate Summit of the United Nations in New York City. The plan calls for "10 commitments for our global commons" to "stabilize the climate at 1.5 °C above pre-industrial temperatures, halt the loss of biodiversity, slow polar ice sheet melt and glacier retreat, protect critical biomes and store more carbon in soils, forests and oceans," and "10 urgent actions for the transformation" to secure the health and well-being of people and the planet.

The 10 massive commitments are the following:

- Declare critical ecosystems as Global Commons by 2030.
- Set a universal global moratorium on deforestation by 2020 and triple annual investments in forest conservation and restoration by 2025.
- Sign an immediate moratorium on further Arctic oil and gas reserves exploitation by 2020 and develop a Cryosphere Preservation Plan.
- Massively upsurge public and private finance flows for the restoration of critical ecosystems by 2020.
- Stop the current decline of vulnerable ocean ecosystems and secure a New Ocean Treaty in 2020.
- Launch an ongoing public–private Planetary Emergency fund for the global commons in 2020.
- All sovereign wealth funds stop funding deforestation by 2020.
- By 2025 all companies shift to green investments and commit to science-based disclosures and reporting practices.
- Halt all conversion of wetlands, grasslands, and savannahs into agricultural lands and triple the annual investments in their protection by 2025.

---

[26]Club of Rome (24 September 2019, p. 4).

- Introduce financial mechanisms and regulations in 2020 to support local farmers to secure their livelihood through sustainable practices.

The 10 immediate transformative actions are geared toward (a) transforming energy systems, (b) shifting to a circular economy, and (c) creating a just and equitable society grounded in human and ecological wellbeing. They are summarized as follows:

- Halt fossil fuel expansion and fossil fuel subsidies in 2020.
- Double the wind and solar capacity every 4 years, and triple annual investments in renewable energy, energy efficiency, and low-carbon technologies for high-emitting industry segments before 2025.
- Introduce a global floor pricing and taxation on carbon ($<$US$30/t CO_2 and rising) immediately and no later than 2025.
- Halve consumption and production footprints globally by 2030.
- Introduce taxes and regulations to internalize externalities in unsustainable and high-carbon production and consumption by 2025.
- Develop global roadmaps to accelerate regenerative land use and circular economic policies.
- Introduce economic progress indicators for socio-ecological and human health and wellbeing by 2030.
- Provide legal tools that allow indigenous people to secure their land rights by 2025.
- Shift taxation from labor to the use of natural resources by 2020.
- Establish clear funding and retraining programs for displaced workers by 2025.

3.2 Integral Investing at Work

The COVID-19 crisis presents the most recent example of how the individual mindset (our own but also that of our leaders) and the collective mindset of whole populations are influencing our actions in response to the pandemic. It makes it obvious in the context of ethics and morals when contemplating the value of a human life compared with the financial impact caused by the virus. In *The Great Mindshift*, Maja Göpel, Secretary-General of the German Advisory Council on Global Change, shows how existing economic systems undermine not only communities and life on Earth, but also individual happiness and the ability to achieve a sense of fulfillment.[27] To facilitate a mind shift, Göpel introduced the Socio-Ecological-Technical-System (SETS) as a foundation for transformative literacy. The foundation of SETS is five Ps: Paradigms, People, Purpose, Processes, and the Planet.

These represent three types of literacy:

---

[27]Göpel (2016, p. 157).

- *Futures literacy*: Facilitates the understanding of the sources of reason behind systems and their transformation.
- *Institutional literacy*: Enables a multidimensional view of the drivers behind system dynamics.
- *Environmental literacy*: Regards human activity as part of the total web of life on Earth.

Including the entire "web of life on Earth" was Tom's and my intention when we developed Integral Investing with the 6Ps as its motto, the Parity of People, Planet and Prosperity—with Passion and Purpose. A great mind shift is its foundational premise. We too considered it crucial to go well beyond the reductionism of current economic models and to honor complexity in its entirety by including consciousness evolution with its hidden dimensions of life (see the section on Integral Theory (AQAL) by Ken Wilber discussed in Chap. 2). Christian Arnsperger, Professor of Sustainability and Economic Anthropology of the University of Lausanne, Switzerland, is another adherent of Integral Theory. He built his full-spectrum economics framework using it, driven by his belief that today's economics has robbed us "of our ability to reflect on ourselves and our economy" and has therefore become "a truly dangerous discipline."[28] Inspired by Ken Wilber's Integral Methodological Pluralism (IMP),[29] the methods of inquiry embedded in AQAL, Arnsperger argued that in order to fix economics, we must combine at least eight methodologies of knowing, namely, "structuralism and phenomenology for the study of consciousness, ethnomethodology and hermeneutics for the study of culture, brain science and autopoiesis for the study of organisms and brain, and systems theory and social autopoiesis for the study of social systems."[30]

Confessions: On Becoming a Serial Entrepreneur

The squeaking door woke me up as my mother entered the bedroom, and I realized that I had only been asleep for 10 minutes. I was sick with the flu and so had lain down for a few minutes. It was only 4:30 in the afternoon, but the sun had already set over the snow-covered cornfields of the Bavarian Chiemgau. My mother handed me my seven-month-old son, Albert, who started nursing noisily and with undisguised delight the second I took him in my arms, making us laugh. He had arrived relatively late in our lives—I was now in my late thirties and my parents in their mid-sixties—and had given us all a new raison d'être, especially my parents, who loved helping my husband, Tom, and I raise him. His arrival also heralded a turning point in our professional lives.

(continued)

---

[28]Arnsperger (2010, p. 229).

[29]Wilber (2006).

[30]Arnsperger (2010, p. 4).

Back in 1994, Tom and I had left California—and our corporate jobs—to pursue a more meaningful life through entrepreneurial endeavors while riding the Internet wave. Little did we know what we were letting ourselves in for. It all started well enough. We convinced fools, friends, and family to lend us money, and in December 1995, Tom started Cybernet, the first German ISP, and I established Infobahn International as a technology transfer company from Silicon Valley to Europe to start the digitalization process by bringing companies onto the Internet. But by the end of 1997, we were still struggling to pay our bills. At that time, few people in Germany knew what the Internet was, and the situation looked unlikely to change any time soon. A few days before Christmas 1997, work-related stress had led to my contracting flu, forcing me to take some much-needed time off. In addition to being physically sick, I was also experiencing anxiety because I had not made any sales that month, which meant my parents, Tom, and I were all living off my parents' pension. That month, I had used my personal credit card to pay our employees' salaries. But that afternoon, as I lay in bed mulling over our precarious financial situation, the phone rang. I smiled when I heard the pleasant voice of Aziz, the project manager from Andersen Consulting, now Accenture. I had been trying without success since September to persuade him to buy a license of NetDynamics, an Internet building application tool that Infobahn distributed from Silicon Valley. We had met several times, and my programmers had shown him that our Java-based Application Server was perfect for his project, but he had yet to commit to anything. Now he was calling with yet another technical question for me. At the end of my rope and feeling I had nothing to lose, I suddenly heard my croaky voice asking him to finalize a deal. He said, "Oh, yeah, I just signed the purchase order and you should find it in your fax machine before the end of the business day today." And with those words, so began a turnaround in our fortunes. Six months later, Cybernet went public on the German stock exchange and our financial worries were eased for the time being—although we were both painfully aware that that could change at any given moment.

As I saw investing evolve from traditional to impact investing, I realized that IMP could also provide the processes needed in Integral Investing, and it became a fundamental aspect of my own dissertation research. (See the section on The Hero's Journey in Chap. 2.) Thus, the *Theta Model* of Integral Investing was born.

3.2.1 The Inception of Integral Investing

Tom and I started our investment career as angel investors in the mid-1990s. To be successful, we joined first the Munich Business Angel Network and later the Silicon

Valley-based Angels' Forum[31] (TAF for short). Like most players in this field, we looked for (a) "hot" and disruptive ideas that would ideally be patent-protected and eventually revolutionize their particular industry; and (b) highly successful, brilliant, and preferably serial entrepreneurs who wanted to take their company public in less than 5 years. We knew that the venture capital industry existed due to the structure and regulations of the capital markets, which charged higher rates than those applied to traditional bank loans that required hard assets to secure the debt and were usually not available for entrepreneurs. We were young, well-educated, and dynamic. We took risks, the timing was right, and we became financially successful, returning an average investment multiple of 6.8 over almost three consecutive decades.

Yet, after a while, playing the financial-only game ceased to be fulfilling, especially as we could no longer overlook the increasing environmental degradation, loss of biodiversity, overpopulation, and other indications of a world gone slightly mad. We were building financially successful companies while simultaneously supporting more than 38 philanthropic organizations worldwide. On the one hand, we worked very hard to fulfill our dreams through the application of exponential technology. On the other, we felt a moral need to make a difference in the world, reduce humanity's carbon footprint, and help the less privileged escape poverty through philanthropy and venture philanthropy. The disparity between traditional investing—with its regulated and legally mandated fiduciary responsibility to maximize profits—and philanthropy—which aims to do good and fix the damage inflicted by traditional investing—eventually became too difficult to ignore.

Ever since my emigration from Romania I have lived to give back and to make a difference in the lives of the less fortunate than I was. This was no different in Tom's life whose parents barely escaped from East Germany prior to the construction of the Berlin Wall in 1961. Yet, we both realized early on that traditional philanthropy needs just as much reforming as traditional investing does if it is to respond to the needs of our time. Change is not a one-way street. If modern philanthropists are to fulfill their mission of making a difference, they must:

- Reconsider outdated risk-aversion tendencies in their endowment investments that sometimes act against the mission of the charitable organizations they are supporting
- Reevaluate their inertia and, perhaps most important, tendency to compete against each other even as they acknowledge their shared aims
- Learn how to address challenges in effective and efficient ways
- Enable an impartial transition for all
- Call for major reform at a legislative level, including the revision of existing legal structures that are occasionally abused by wealthy individuals in order to bypass tax regulations[32]

---

[31]http://angelsforum.com/
[32]Fulton et al. (July, 2010).

Fig. 3.3 From traditional investing and philanthropy via impact investing to Integral Investing

Tom and I initially turned to impact investing as an alternative approach, but we soon realized that even within that field, investors are quite divided between those who are "financial-first" investors—that is, they will invest only if the financial return is appealing—and those who prioritize impact over ensuring that financial criteria are met (Fig. 3.3).

In order to respond to the growing imbalance between competing, contradictory needs, organizations such as Warren Buffett and Bill Gates's Giving Pledge of Philanthropy, the United Kingdom's Big Society Capital, the United States' Overseas Private Investment Corporation, the Australian Government's Social Enterprise Development and Investment Funds, and various other venture philanthropy initiatives, such as the LGT Impact Venture Fund and Toniic, were formed to show by example how traditional capital, government funds, and philanthropic capital could be integrated.[33] They offer in part mixed investment structures to shrink the seemingly opposing differences between traditional capital, venture philanthropy, and philanthropic donations. The Acumen Fund,[34] to offer another example, invests what it calls "patient" capital: "capital that provides startups with the flexibility and security to grow their business and reach as many poor customers as possible."[35] Their approach is nontraditional in as much as they do not expect high returns from their investment, but they do expect to have their capital returned. This hybrid concept has been shown to be much better at mitigating risk than using investment funds from the very beginning of a new enterprise's life.

---

[33]Ebrahim and Rangan (16 September 2009); Koh et al. (April, 2012); Saltuk et al. (2011); Toniic (2018).

[34]Ebrahim and Rangan (16 September 2009).

[35]See https://acumen.org/approach/

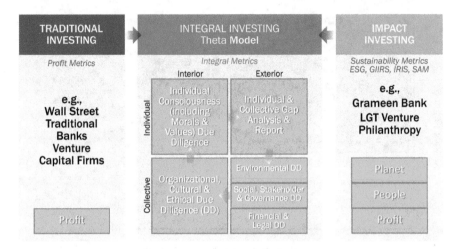

Fig. 3.4 Integral investing facilitates the integration of traditional and impact investing

However, the more we explored these various approaches, the more confident we felt that our own Integral Investing philosophy was the way ahead. The future of investing, we thought, ought to be embedded in the authentic integration of traditional and impact investing and be measured appropriately (see Fig. 3.4).

Before you read any further, please note that what follows is a deep dive into our own application of Integral Theory in investing, company building, and our own lives. Some segments of our approach have been published previously in various forms,[36] and I have included feedback from those publications here.

3.2.2 The Theory of Change

Wilber's Integral Theory provides a post-postmodern framework of life that is based on the theory of evolution and integrates humanity's irreducible value spheres, described by Plato as the *True*/science, the *Good*/morals, and the *Beautiful*/art (Fig. 2.5). It also draws on Immanuel Kant's Big Three critiques: The Critique of Pure Reason, Critique of Practical Reason, and Critique of Judgment or subjective reality. Furthermore, it honors Jürgen Habermas's indivisible three Worlds: the Objective, the Subjective, and the Cultural.

Having been informed by Wilber's integral model, however, Tom and I could not help but notice that current efforts at creating a more sustainable financial system are rather one-sided and draw heavily from Wilber's lower-right quadrant (Fig. 2.6)[37] (see Sect. 2.4.1). This appears to be the case whether we consider traditional

---

[36]Bozesan (2010) & (2013) & (2016), to name only three.

[37]Brown (2007, 20 February, pp. 19–28).

investing or more progressive forms of investing, such as impact investing, triple bottom line investing (TBLI), mission-related investing, Sustainable and Responsible Investing (SRI), value investing, blended value investing, or even venture philanthropy.

Integral Investing: Honoring the Truth in All There Is
The meta-theory and practice of integral investors based on Integral Theory, AQAL (pronounced ah-qwul), by philosopher Ken Wilber.

A closer look at traditional investing, business, and financial systems also reveals that not only are the evolutionary aspects completely missing, so too are the drivers behind the behavioral dimensions (shown in Wilber's upper-right quadrant). Further interior dimensions such as human intelligences (upper-left quadrant) and cultural aspects (lower-left quadrant) are also hard to find. From economics and finance to neuroscience and psychology, the world of science appears to agree, however, that our behavior is influenced by our psyche.[38] The various dimensions of consciousness are consistently co-arising and deeply influencing us and our decisions, whether or not we are aware of them.[39]

This is why Tom and I have aggregated assessment tools, which integrate the AQAL dimensions, for our own due diligence process. Integral investing contributes to the future of investing by (1) honoring the truth in *all* there is, including people, planet, and prosperity; (2) appreciating diversity in culture and society; and (3) seeing reality as an indivisible whole. In this reality, every *exterior*—in not only the individual but also the social, political, and environmental contexts—has an *interior*, a hidden dimension, such as individual behavior and also culture and ethical norms that influence that behavior. So, if we are asking ourselves whether we need a new enlightenment or not, we do not have to go far to see that the integration of the interior dimensions of higher levels of consciousness—that is, a new mindset—could provide a much-needed framework for a more holistic paradigm.

Our Motto: The 6Ps
The Parity of People, Planet and Prosperity—with Passion and Purpose

From an early-stage investment perspective, we saw how our motto, the six Ps—the parity of people, planet, and prosperity—with passion and purpose all driven by the need to implement the UN SDGs within planetary boundaries—could be holistically integrated into the entire value chain creation shown in Fig. 3.5.

---

[38]Camerer and Loewenstein (2004); Yazdipour (2011).

[39]Beauregard and O'Leary (2007); Kahneman and Tversky (1982); McCraty (2001); Newberg and Lee (2005).

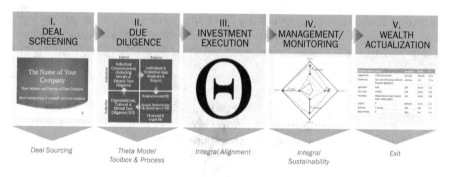

Fig. 3.5 The value chain creation in early-stage investing using Integral Theory

As you will see, we apply an AQAL lens every step of the way, from deal sourcing and screening, all the way through to wealth actualization. (Please note that the entire process described below refers to early-stage investing as a particular asset class. Moreover, I assume readers are already familiar with traditional methods of venture capital and angel investing. My intention is to highlight the differences between Integral Investing and existing venture capital and angel investing models and not to write yet another book on early-stage investing.)

3.2.3   Deal Sourcing and Screening

The first phase in investing always begins with deal sourcing, identifying a potential investment opportunity (Fig. 3.6).

We have been in the investment market since the mid-1990s and receive several hundred investment requests (business plan, executive summary, pitch presentation,[40] etc.) per year through various channels, including word-of-mouth, investment platforms, emails, conferences, and pitch-events. As soon as we receive an investment opportunity it gets registered, receives a ticket, and is entered in the deal pipeline (Fig. 3.7).

Our screening team evaluates the opportunity against the AQAL criteria and decides whether or not to pursue it further. Tom calls our initial laundry list for screening the "inevitable success criteria." He compiles the list from answers to the following questions:

- Does the idea solve a real-world problem? Is it a solution looking for a problem or the other way around? Does the idea work? Is there proof of concept?
- Do the entrepreneurs *own* the idea(s)? Do they own patents? Have they licensed the idea(s)? What about exclusivity? Is the idea free of claims by others? Do they

---

[40]For AQAL Generic Start-up Pitch Template, see https://aqalgroup.com/extra-materials/

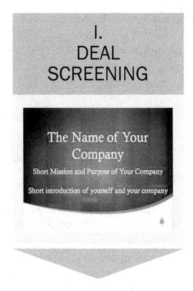

Deal Sourcing

Fig. 3.6 AQAL deal sourcing and screening

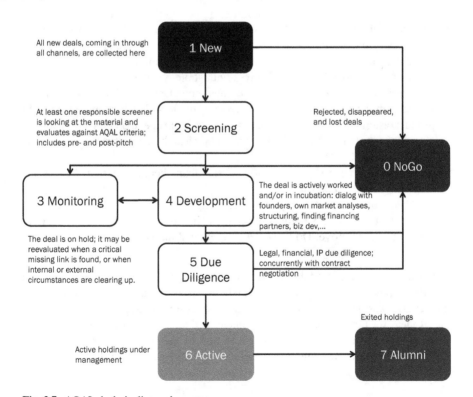

Fig. 3.7 AQAL deal pipeline and process

have "freedom to operate," to build products based on the idea and then sell them?

- Does the idea/solution align with evolution (i.e., singularity/exponential growth)?
- Does the idea/solution align with possible responses to the world's fundamental problems and global grand challenges (e.g., UN SDGs within planetary boundaries)?
- Does someone's career or reputation depend on their finding a solution to the problem?
- How quickly do potential customers need to solve the problem? Do they have a budget to solve the problem? Will the problem become bigger and worse if they do not solve it? How bad can it get?
- Do they have an *"unfair," defendable advantage* with their solution?
- Is there an underlying long-term mechanism that leads inevitably to success (e.g., Internet, AI, synthetic biology, etc.)? If so, what is it?
- Do they have a fundamental business strategy? What about cost advantage, unique technology, differentiation, network/platform effects, economies of scale?
- Are they among the top three in their industry? (Observe the power law of unfair distribution of gains—"the winner takes all").
- Do they have a massively transformative purpose (MTP)?
- Moonshot test: Is the new product/service 10× better? 10% does not cut it, because over time entropy will have shrunk the initial advantage. After repeated hardships, the business proposition must still be significantly interesting.
- Execution ability test: Can they execute? Do the founders bring intrinsic motivation, personal development history, and industry and personal experience?
- Is there a team? Does the team explicitly develop a team culture?
- Do they systematically apply resources with strategy, tactics, and discipline?
- Is there a strong sense of urgency? Will they move fast? How "hungry" are they?
- Is their implementation capital efficient? Can they develop and make their product faster, more efficient, more attractive, and cheaper than their competitors?
- Can they distribute their product faster, more cheaply, and more efficiently than their competitors? How?
- Can they become cash-flow positive faster than their competitors? Does the financial market support it?
- Are there competing financing sources available for this particular asset class?
- Would regulations and regulators let them be successful? Do NOT wait for regulations to improve. Do NOT bet on regulated markets, for they may change overnight.

Once the deal has passed the AQAL screening process, it goes into the monitoring and development phases. A dialog with founders is initiated alongside our own market analyses, potential structuring, search for co-investing partners, brainstorming of ideas for further business development, and so on. If a critical success factor such as a CEO or CFO is missing, the status of the deal switches to on-hold/monitoring until the relevant circumstances have changed or the decision to drop

Fig. 3.8   AQAL fact-finding criteria (See detailed *Fact-Finding Checklist* at https://aqalgroup.com/ AQAL-Integral-Investing-Fact-Finding-Checklist)

the case is taken. If the in-depth screening results are positive, we issue a term sheet, and then due diligence through the Theta Model is initiated.

As integral investors, we search, of course, for deals that are in line with our values and philosophy. Remember, integral investors are *self-actualizing* individuals who have Awakened to a unity-consciousness mindset at later stages of human development. We use AQAL as a map to help us navigate the exponentially growing complexity of the world and have an MTP and a moonshot. We walk our talk and have a daily integral wheel of life practice (see Sect. 2.5.4) that keeps us physically and emotionally healthy, focused, and on track. We are looking for exponentially growing technologies with the intention of building integrally sustainable organizations to successfully address humanity's global grand challenges (GGCs), including achieving the UN SDGs within planetary boundaries. We have been investing for almost three decades now and have a rather long list of screening criteria (Fig. 3.8 shows a small selection of them), as well as a remarkable pool of potential candidates for our deal sourcing.

Our objective is, of course, to get access to an integrally impactful investment opportunity as early as possible, before the entrepreneurs have had the opportunity to present their idea to large investor audiences for fundraising purposes. Ideally, we are introduced to the new deal by a close and trusted friend and expert who has already prescreened the idea. We want to invest early and be leading edge, but not too early, which could take us to the bleeding edge. In order to identify an investment that fits our requirements, we start with negative screening. Our criteria, positive and negative, are dynamic and thus evolve regularly.

One example of negative screening, our exclusion criteria at this point in time, involves cryptocurrencies such as Bitcoin: On the one hand, cryptocurrencies have the potential to positively influence grassroots democracies, individual freedom, accountability, trustworthy authentication processes, and decentralized proof of work. On the other, their issuing process entails a shocking waste of energy. In a

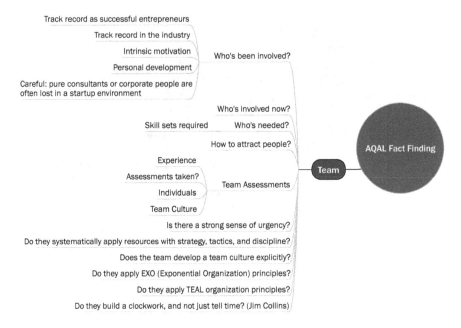

Fig. 3.9 AQAL team screening and fact-finding

research brief titled *The Carbon Footprint of Bitcoin,* published by the MIT Center for Energy and Environmental Policy Research, Stoll et al. show that as of November 2018, the annual energy consumption of Bitcoin was around 48 TWh.[41] They call for regulatory intervention not only because of reasons associated with monetary control but also because of the huge carbon emissions associated with Bitcoin mining. They calculate that annual carbon emissions from Bitcoin production range between 21.5 Mt. and 53.6 Mt. of CO_2, equivalent to the annual CO_2 emission levels of cities such as Hamburg, Vienna, or Las Vegas. Such factors clearly violate not only our decision to not invest in ideas that require major regulatory interventions but also, and more importantly, our moonshot. Moreover, we do not see how Bitcoin actually offers today a significantly better solution to any real-world problem than existing options. In other words, as long as we do not see a *positive* correlation between, in this case, the benefits of Bitcoin outweighing the damage associated with the CO_2 emissions created in mining it, we will invest somewhere else.

If a potential investment passes our negative screening, we then look at the potential for positive impact, which usually addresses, in no particular order:

- The need for integral sustainability of the deal
- Our informal screening/assessment of the team and the individual founders and their biographies (Fig. 3.9)

---

[41] Stoll et al. (2018).

- Our intention to have fun in the process

> **AQAL Screening: A Tool for Value Alignment**
> For us, screening is a nonlinear, fluid, very dynamic, and evolutionary process.
> We are not simply looking for a company into which we want to invest. We are
> looking for partners, people who want to join us in making the world a better
> place through their ideas, and a long-term relationship through building a
> lasting company that serves the greater good. We want to connect with the
> investees, and we want to see if our values align. We are interested in building
> a partnership that serves us collectively.

If the screening is positive, we issue a term sheet and move on to due diligence.

3.2.4   De-risking with the Theta Model

We named the process through which our Integral Investing philosophy is applied in
the due diligence stage the *Theta Model*. It involves applying the tools and methodologies of Integral Theory, AQAL, to de-risk integral investments with the intention
of building integrally sustainable companies from the very beginning (Fig. 3.10).

Fig. 3.10 Integral investing
due-diligence process

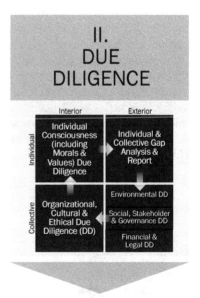

Theta Model

The Theta Model is the due diligence process of Integral Investing. It integrates (a) traditional investing due-diligence criteria (financial, legal, sales due-diligence) with (b) sustainability criteria and impact investing metrics (UN SDGs within planetary boundaries, as well as Social, Environmental, and Governance (ESG) of the UN PRI) and (c) cultural, behavioral, and consciousness criteria as defined in Wilber's integral framework.

The Theta Model makes the AQAL theory applicable within the context of direct investing in early-stage companies. It provides the necessary tools and processes to analyze, measure, and assess potential risks that could prevent us from achieving our target outcomes. The intention is to make sure that the intended goals are attained in all quadrants, levels, lines, structures, types, and other dimensions contained in the AQAL framework (see Chap. 2). Thus, the Theta Model navigates the entire AQAL and functions as a powerful de-risking tool that facilitates a differentiated view not only of investees as individuals and in terms of company culture but also of the context of investing, the exterior reality. This reality is composed of a complex web of interrelated and intra- and interconnected *ecological* structures, *social* and *cultural* systems, and *behavioral* determinants, all of which are subject to *evolution*.

For example, a start-up located in a postmodern society such as France or Germany has to deal with a different employee, or labor, legislation, environmental constraints, resources, and suppliers than one located in South Africa, and its founders and employees will, most likely, have a different view of the world, and therefore different behaviors and leadership skills, than players from an emerging economy such as Indonesia.

The cultural reality with its embedded and active world views, the interior dimensions, are intimately correlated with the social techno-economic structures, the exteriors because they occur together and influence each other. They are different sides of the same coin. Understanding and appreciating differences helps us invest much more sustainably and compassionately, because it acknowledges, honors, and celebrates diversity. The Theta Model helps us integrate the following de-risking characteristics of the due diligence process (Fig. 3.11):

- *Traditional criteria* that ensure financial sustainability and include financial due diligence as well as legal, sales and marketing, and other metrics
- *Sustainability criteria* including impact investing metrics such as the UN SDGs within planetary boundaries, and the social, environmental, and governance (ESG) of the UN Principles for Responsible Investment (PRI)
- *Cultural aspects*
- *Behavioral criteria*
- *Individual interior criteria* as defined in the upper-left quadrant of Wilber's integral framework

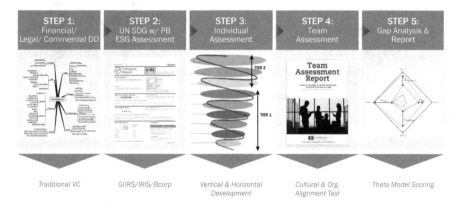

Fig. 3.11 The theta model: de-risking steps of the AQAL due diligence process

The Theta Model is an accelerating process for decision-making as well as a vehicle for the speedy formation of integrally sustainable companies from the very beginning. It offers a five-step de-risking process that includes traditional due diligence and expands it with sustainability measurements as well as with integral investment performance measurements born out of Integral Theory.

Step 1: Financial Due Diligence

The first step of any due diligence process involves traditional financial, legal, and commercial assessments and reflects the lens of the lower-right quadrant of the AQAL. It requires a high degree of granularity and due diligence expertise in identifying as many unknown factors as possible and assessing the greatest potential risks. The purpose of validating a business plan is to uncover missing pieces and determine the financial and legal risks, as well as other risks associated with the market, competition, and intellectual property (IP) issues, to name only a few (Fig. 3.12).

There are plenty of books, systems, websites, consulting services, advice, and training options on traditional due diligence processes in VC investing, so at this point, I will say no more about them than that we hire experts to help us with this important process. Because Tom and I have lived in Germany since 1999, we observe German law. If you want to find out more about due diligence in traditional VC investing, we recommend *Venture Deals* by Brad Feld and Jason Mendelson,[42] and, from a German perspective, Wolfgang Weitnauer's *Handbuch Venture Capital*.[43]

---

[42]Feld and Mendelson (2019).

[43]Weitnauer (2019).

Fig. 3.12 Theta Model
financial, legal, commercial
due diligence (See our
Financial Due Diligence list
at https://aqalgroup.com/
Financial-Due-Diligence-
Pack-Structure-and-
Checklist)

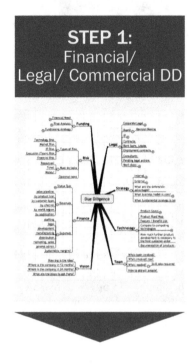

Traditional VC

Investment Example: Protection Through an Anti-dilution Clause

Experienced early-stage investors know how the extremely high risk in the seed and early stages can translate into low valuations. Founders do not like that, of course. However, new and inexperienced investors continuously enter the investment market, which enables founders to consistently find investors who will buy shares at overly high company valuation figures. Sometimes this can lead even experienced investors into a fear-of-missing-out (FOMO) situation where they either pay to play in a start-up that is overvalued or never get a deal at all. An anti-dilution clause can help reduce potential losses. We learned this the hard way.

Tom and I invested early on in Zonare Medical Systems, an ultrasound diagnostic imaging manufacturer, with our Angels' Forum friends. Unfortunately, we were inexperienced at the time and thus did not pay enough attention to the valuation or the anti-dilution clause. Zonare did not grow as fast as projected, and new rounds of funding were needed at down-rounds. The later investors were issued stock at a lower price than we had originally paid because we were not protected enough through an option or the anti-dilution provision. Lesson learned.

It is important to note too that we see Step 1 as being just as important as the following four steps of the Theta Model. The reality is that without financial sustainability there is no overall sustainability. Every aspect of an investment affects the other aspects. It is no accident that our motto starts with "Parity"; it is there to highlight the equal importance we give to People, Planet, and Prosperity—with Passion and Purpose. If even only one of the six Ps were missing, it would indicate a world without sustainability. This is why we use the term *integral sustainability*.

Step 2: Sustainability Due Diligence
In the earlier discussion about the *Transformation is Feasible* report, I noted that there are five important action items that must be addressed in order to ensure our future. From the lower-right quadrant perspective of the AQAL framework, this is the purpose of Step 2 in the Theta Model. It uses various measurement criteria to assess to what degree the implementation of the UN SDGs within planetary boundaries is being addressed.

At this stage in the due diligence process, investees have the opportunity to show how they contribute directly to the achievement of the global sustainability goals. The intention in Step 2 is to:

- *Reduce the risk* associated with the potential violation of climate neutrality laws through their business activities.
- *Create an integrally sustainable company* from the very beginning.
- *Increase transparency.*
- *Identify the sustainability metrics* that apply to the particular business.
- *Prepare for sustainability reporting.*
- *Generate sustainability compliance* as defined by the Sustainable Stock Exchanges (SSE) Initiative of the United Nations Global Compact.[44] Awareness of the SSE could help steer the efforts of the start-up and eventually lead to its receiving a good rating in the event of an exit through an initial public offering (IPO).

We are finding that the investment industry is still in the very early stages of providing quantitative and qualitative evidence and measurements of positive impact criteria that we require in Step 2 (Fig. 3.13). Yet, there are already several tools and/or key performance indicators (KPIs) that can be used to good effect. The Global Impact Investing Network (GIIN), for example, provides the IRIS catalog of metrics "designed to measure the social, environmental and financial performance of an investment"[45] and Toniic, the "global action community for impact investors,"[46] has even developed a direct correlation between GIIN/IRIS and UN SDGs. In order to contribute toward the further development of appropriate metrics, Tom and I became rather active on multiple levels. In 2012, I contributed at the Rio+20 Earth Summit in

---

[44]https://www.unglobalcompact.org/take-action/action/sustainable-stock-exchange-initiatives

[45]https://iris.thegiin.org/metrics/

[46]https://www.toniic.com

Fig. 3.13 Theta model
sustainability criteria

GIIRS/IRIS/Bcorp

Rio de Janeiro,[47] joined the consultations of the International Integrated Reporting
Council (IIRC),[48] and became involved in 2013 with the Social Impact Investment
Taskforce, launched at the G8 meeting in London by the British prime minister at the
time, David Cameron. The initiative was led globally by Sir Ronald Cohen,[49] Big
Society Capital and APAX founder, and comprised a selection of working groups
and national advisory boards. The German advisory board was chaired by
Dr. Brigitte Mohn, chairwoman of the Bertelsmann Foundation, who invited me to
become a member of the national board.[50] The Social Impact Investment Taskforce's
successes were down to its using its publications to establish a baseline for current
developments and steering the future direction of social impact investing worldwide.
It was replaced in 2015 by the Global Steering Group (GSG). Contributing to and
being aligned with such work is important and lead Tom and I to became also active
members of Toniic. Their report, *Powered Ascent: Insights from the Frontier of
Impact Investing*, compares and contrasts investing practices and measurements that
applied GIIN metrics with Toniic member investing practices that used mixed

---

[47]https://tinyurl.com/y8mpajnz & https://tinyurl.com/ycr7zpaq
[48]https://integratedreporting.org/
[49]Cohen (2018).
[50]National Advisory Board (NAB) Deutschland (2014); https://tinyurl.com/nkdb6lx

methods and tools. Both GIIN and Toniic respondents "report that their investments have either met or exceeded their expectations for impact (GIIN: 98%, TONIIC: 87%) and financial performance (GIIN: 91%, TONIIC: 82%)."

Investment Example: The Energy Turnaround

Out of our concern for climate change, and as our professional contribution to the *Energiewende* (energy turnaround) invoked by Chancellor Merkel after the 2011 Fukushima Daiichi accident, Tom and I invested in Entelios AG. It became another success story in our portfolio. Germany's commitment to the Energiewende was an ambitious plan to shift its reliance from nuclear and fossil fuels to renewables. Feeding renewable energy sources such as wind and solar into the existing power grid is cumbersome, though, because these energy sources are not continuous like traditional energy sources. In order to guarantee a reliable and inexpensive energy supply in the future, new solutions are required. Thus, Tom and two of his friends started Entelios AG. It became Germany's first demand-response aggregator and was acquired by EnerNOC in 2014.

Another aspect of metrics that is less commonly used, but which we find very important particularly with respect to carbon markets and the UN SDGs, is the concept of *additionality*. In our view, an investor cannot simply buy a field of solar panels or windmills, for example, and then credibly call themselves an impact investor. Shifting capital from one asset owner to the next (and pocketing the fees) does not change anything. *Additionality* helps identify and *measure* the exact increase in social (people), environmental (planet), and other values that would have not occurred without this particular investment. As integral (impact) investors we must significantly increase the progress made through the investment and be able to measure the real change in form—for example, carbon offsets, increased number of employees, or increased capital invested in additional sustainable assets and/or environmentally protected real estate.

Investment Example: Social Impact and Mission Investing

Two designers, moms who shared common interests in fashion, travel, and children, developed a plan in 2004 to create a new kind of clothing company for children that makes a difference. Tea Living,[51] as the company was named, was concerned with ethical material sourcing and driven by the mission to ensure children live in a safe and prospering world. The company became successful and kept its promises. To this day, it gives 10% of the profits to "ensure a better world for kids everywhere" including children's education.

(continued)

---

[51]https://www.teacollection.com

We believe that the founders' professionalism paired with their mission and purpose made this company integrally successful. We are very proud to be early-stage investors in this company that turned out to be a financial success as well.

For our early-stage investments, we often work with the GIIRS-based (Global Impact Investing Rating System) self-assessment offered by B Corp.[52] We recommend it for the time being because it helps start-up companies get a deeper understanding of what is possible and what to prepare for while building integrally sustainable businesses. Therefore, we encourage our investees to perform a self-assessment. Doing so gives them an opportunity to select, and eventually commit to, certain criteria that they would like to measure and deliver.[53] This could later become the foundation for the governance criteria of the company and part of the articles of association, the social contract between investors and investees.[54]

An additional global framework that can be applied in Step 2 comes in the form of the 232 UN SDG indicators[55] pertaining to the 2030 Agenda for Sustainable Development and adopted by the General Assembly of the UN. As we saw before, we need to implement the UN SDGs within the planetary boundaries in order to live the *Smart* scenario outlined in *Transformation is Feasible*. Therefore, we are looking forward to receiving the proper taxonomy and measurements that could help us as investors achieve these goals. We may also benefit soon from the European Green Deal[56] of the European Commission and its sustainable finance efforts.[57] In recognition of the role that the financial system can play in mitigating the current threats to the planet, the Commission created a 10-step action plan for implementing sustainable finance systems to transform the economy of the European Union to meet the goals of the Paris Agreement and implement the UN SDGs. This long-term strategy, which intends to achieve carbon neutrality by 2050, includes three points of particular note:

- *A green, unified classification system, or taxonomy*, described as "a list of economic activities assessed and classified based on their contribution to EU sustainability related policy objectives" and published in June 2019 by the Technical Expert Group (TEG) on Sustainable Finance, is designed to help assess an economic activity in environmental terms within planetary boundaries. To qualify as green, an investment has to "1. Contribute substantially to one or more of the [six] environmental objectives [laid out in the regulation]; 2. Do no

---

[52]https://bimpactassessment.net/
[53]See a live example of a Bcorp Impact Assessment at https://aqalgroup.com/extra-materials/
[54]See the example application of Governance Criteria at https://tinyurl.com/ycjmocem
[55]https://unstats.un.org/sdgs/indicators/indicators-list/
[56]https://tinyurl.com/vlplq5l
[57]https://tinyurl.com/ydhxzkp6

significant harm to any other environmental objective; 3. Comply with minimum social safeguards (under the draft regulation, these are defined as ILO core labour conventions); 4. Comply with the technical screening criteria."[58]

- *Sustainability-related disclosures* ensure that investors are fully informed by manufacturers and distributors of financial products about the impact of sustainability on investment decisions and financial returns.
- *Climate benchmarks and ESG disclosures* are two new benchmark categories that help inform and orient investors who want to adopt climate-related strategies.

The sustainable finance policy benefits investors by offering a greater choice of green finance products and projects and benefits businesses via new sources of funding from global capital markets and the global financial sector.

By following Step 2 as outlined in our due diligence process, traditional investors can get ready for change, all while benefiting from the green movement and contributing to making a difference to the planet and ensuring the future of life, albeit through an Integral Investing lens. From that perspective, we find the Anderson and Brown integral stakeholder analysis tool[59] useful. It provides invaluable information on objectives, needs, resources, and potential opposition, helps give stakeholders a sense of ownership, and fosters healthy engagement between stakeholders.

Investment Example: Good Ideas, Bad Timing

Sometimes we did the right thing—picked the right investment, with an integrally informed and acting team—but the timing was off. This was the case with BioCee. It developed advanced biocatalytic reactor solutions for the production of clean fuels and chemicals based on a proprietary biocoating technology platform. At the time, we lived between California and Bavaria, but the company was based in Minnesota, in the heart of the United States and several hours away by air from San Francisco. This taught us to be very careful about choosing investments that are close to our home base—no more than a 1-hour flight away.

As fracking and other fossil fuels began filling the energy gap, clean fuels such as those produced by BioCee became too expensive to be viable. The company's operations recently closed, although it still owns invaluable patents.

Step 3: Individual Assessment

As so often happens in life, we learned our first lesson regarding the eminent importance of people over ideas the hard way. It happened in 1994. Tom had finished his MBA at Stanford in 1993 and soon realized that staying with BCG, a

---

[58]EU Technical Expert Group on Sustainable Finance (2019, p. 10).

[59]Anderson and Brown (2013).

consultancy, would not give him the professional fulfillment he sought. BCG had given him a sabbatical and paid part of the cost of his MBA, and Tom had gone back to the company to honor his side of the agreement. We lived in Palo Alto, the heart of Silicon Valley, but his work assignments at BCG were rarely related to technology. Thus, his particular expertise in computer science and AI was not being put to use and he was quite reasonably feeling frustrated. After seeing the Mosaic browser in early 1994, we felt compelled to ride the exhilarating Internet wave and looked for an opportunity to do so. We did not have to look far or for long. During a party hosted by some longtime friends of ours, Gabe and Kristy, the idea to bring real estate listings online was born. Gabe told us about a friend of his, Joe, whose wife was a real estate agent and made the necessary introductions. Joe and his wife decided the idea was worth trying, and the first presentation at Cornish and Carey, the leading real estate broker in the Valley at the time, was soon scheduled. Cornish and Carey also liked the idea and were willing to try it out by giving us a diskette (remember those?) with the data containing the new listings that were going to be published in the weekend editions of the local newspapers. All three friends put some money together to implement the idea. They needed a computer and a Web server that would be connected to the Internet 24/7 so people from around the world would be able to view Cornish and Carey's listings. Tom bought a PC, installed Berkeley Unix (or BSD Unix, as it was known at the time),[60] and began developing automatically generated, static HTML pages in the garage of our College Terrace home in Palo Alto, California.

Investment Example: Team, Team, Team Makes Up 80% of the Risk
BayNet World was a typical Silicon Valley start-up, founded by three people with an idea and a PowerPoint presentation. When Cornish and Carey made its first online sale of a house to a Japanese man who found it on the BayNet Internet platform, we all knew we were onto a good thing. The company was incorporated on October 28, 1994, with Gabe as the VP of Sales and Joe as the CEO. However, personal differences began to surface before too long, and soon after the launch of BayNet World, it became obvious that the team was not in sync. In fact, there was very little team coherence. The founders were very different from each other, and soon those differences began to cause problems. Tom's idea was to get VC funding in order to grow quickly, but his partners wanted to go slowly by bootstrapping. The dissonance between the founders began intruding on our personal relationship with Gabe, and we decided that our friendship was more important than BayNet. Tom and I

(continued)

---

[60]At the time it was called BSD Unix and was an operating system developed at Berkeley University based on the original Unix born at Bell Labs that later became the foundation of various Unix dialects. See https://tinyurl.com/6aqforj

Fig. 3.14 Theta model
individual assessment

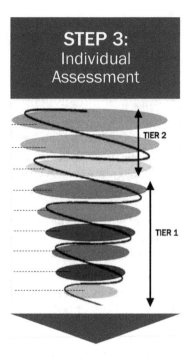

Vertical & Horizontal
Development

eventually moved back to Germany to ride the European Internet wave. That
had also a positive impact on our long-term relationship with Gabe and Joe.
   BayNet World still exists,[61] but it missed the dot.com boom completely.
We exited in 2019 with a multiple of 240× and an IRR of 8% over 25 years. It
was a financial success but an entrepreneurial failure.

We had learned a valuable lesson: *People are more important than ideas*. But
how do you find the right people for your company? This is the purpose of Step
3 (Fig. 3.14).
   In our experience, few investors use formal tools to assess individual investees.
The reason for that maybe that formal tests are rather expensive and take time and
effort to perform and evaluate. But when people are willing to risk their money in an
investment, what is a few extra dollars? We believe that the importance of a formal
test is generally, and erroneously, underestimated, even though such scientifically
proven tools have emerged from elite universities including Stanford, Harvard, and

---

[61]http://www.baynet.com/about-us

MIT. When we ask our peer investors what they base their investment decisions on, most of them refer to a "gut feeling" derived from personal meetings, interviews, and observations rather than the application of scientifically proven instruments. However, Tom and I are not alone in electing to rely on science rather than instinct. David Gladstone and Laura Gladstone, for example, describe their due diligence process, including their assessment of their entrepreneur of choice, in their book *Venture Capital Investing*.[62] During their individual due diligence process, they focus on and try to assess the following aspects of a potential investee:

- *Physical appearance* and *behavioral aspects* such as "determination, resourcefulness, a sense of urgency to get things done, and a realistic approach to facts," as well as "energy level, a better than average ability to speak and communicate, and mental stamina"; and
- *Mental factors* and *moral character traits* including "the need for achievement, need for power, belief that one is control of one's own destiny, and risk preferences" but also "honesty, partnership orientation, and a desire for fair play."

Traditionally, the assessment process for early-stage companies comprises individual interviews and discussions, background checks, personal history evaluations, and observations of body language before and during the due diligence process. "Personality or psychology tests, [occur] but this is not frequently done"[63] by traditional venture capitalists, notes Lin Hong Wong in *Venture Capital and Fund Management*. This is unfortunate for both investees and investors because they share an interest in achieving a successful and fruitful affiliation. Wong points out the importance of not rigidly following standard checklists when assessing a CEO of a start-up, but instead customizing checklists to reflect the type of business, the company strategy, and the other team members as individuals. In addition to the mandatory domain and entrepreneurship expertise, he sees the most important prerequisites as integrity, total commitment to the company shown through an entrepreneur's own cash injection and willingness to accept pay cuts if needed, and adaptability in terms of willingness to grow and take on other roles as required. It is also crucial to delineate certain functions in a start-up. For example, the nature of technology start-ups is such that more often than not there is no CEO in the beginning; instead, the CTO often fulfills that role. Therefore, the due diligence process must assess the suitability of the CTO to function as a CEO. Similar assessments must be made for the roles of CFO, COO, and so on prior to the investment, otherwise they could create a great source of contention and bring the company down. I speak from experience.

But if you can have due diligence processes that are less costly and produce the same reliable results, why would anybody want to spend more money on written psychographs? The rather simple answer has to do with the complexity of being human.

---

[62]Gladstone and Gladstone (2004, p. 30).

[63]Wong (2005, p. 157).

These tests' results can help assess the starting point of a relationship; help define individual and team coaching programs, and the road ahead; and serve as the foundation for the future success that both parties desire. They are instrumental in the building of a robust structure for and the culture of the start-up. According to research by Susanne Cook-Greuter,[64] only 10–20% of adults demonstrate high standards of ethics and high levels of ego development. Identifying those people in a start-up setting would help ensure that what is being promised on the outside is authentically true on the inside.

Beginning with Step 3, the Theta Model goes beyond the due diligence process of both traditional and impact investing. It includes additional aspects of reality—for example, interior, evolutionary, behavioral, interobjective, and intersubjective—that are constantly co-arising and affect us whether we are aware of them or not. The fundamental premise of Integral Theory is that leaders can be developed through vertical learning. Key to vertical learning is identifying the psychological baseline of an individual through the psychograph (see Chap. 2). Vertical learning is currently the number one trend in leader development because it plays a very important role in the success, or otherwise, of early-stage companies in particular. Although the main thread of this discussion concerns vertical growth through vertical learning, I would like to emphasize the equal importance of healthy *horizontal* growth and integration across all four quadrants of the AQAL model.[65] The intention here is not to imply that later stages of human development are better. As we will see in the discourse on hierarchy and the notion of holons, a healthy evolution presupposes both a healthy vertical growth *and* the healthy horizontal integration of the cultural, social, environmental, behavioral, and experiential perspectives/lines at *each* evolutionary altitude/level in all AQAL quadrants (see Chap. 2).

But let us get back to vertical learning. Growth occurs naturally through the evolutionary process when the circumstances are right, but within the context of a company, Barrett Brown states that under the right conditions it can be accelerated significantly.[66] Implemented correctly, self-development work undertaken through vertical learning can broaden our world view and heighten our awareness. Leaders with vertical development skills are perceived as more effective, more complex thinkers, and more capable of addressing complex challenges. Brown's research and hands-on consulting expertise shows that leaders who have mature skills and work on their vertical development appear to:

- Develop a more complex mindset that helps significantly expand their world views.
- Perform better across several mission-critical domains.
- Inspire vision and better lead transformational change.
- Think better strategically, systemically, and contextually.

---

[64]Cook-Greuter (2004).

[65]Bozesan (2013, June).

[66]Brown (2018, p. 19).

- Build better relationships and become better collaborators and problem solvers.
- Make better decisions, reframe challenges, and create more innovative solutions.
- Have an enhanced capacity to tolerate ambiguity and navigate complexity.

In our portfolio companies, as well as within our own investment team, we have applied various tools as we worked through Step 3 of the Theta Model. LDMA (Leadership/Lectical Decision-Making Assessment), for example, is a leadership development tool that focuses on three aspects of decision-making. It grew out of research performed at Harvard University Graduate School of Education, and was created by Kurt W. Fisher and later enhanced by Stein et al.[67] Lectica,[68] an organization with which we worked closely describes these three aspects as:

- *Collaborative capacity*: the ability to integrate diverse perspectives with the intention of developing all-encompassing, pioneering, and successful solutions.
- *Contextual thinking*: the ability to reflect on and analyze problems in terms of the larger systems and contexts to which they belong.
- *Cognitive complexity*: the ability to think in a multi-perspectival manner about complex issues.

In their evaluation forms, these three wide-ranging skills are evaluated through eight lenses:

- Developmental level
- Perspective-taking skill
- Perspective-seeking skill
- Perspective coordination
- Collaborative capacity
- Contextual thinking
- Cognitive coherence
- Decision-making process

When Not to Invest

Several years ago, we applied the LDMA individually to a leadership team in a hydrogen fuel car start-up. The results showed beyond doubt that the CEO and CTO would not be able to work together to help the start-up succeed. While the CTO claimed otherwise, he was neither willing to grow personally nor ready to let go of his "baby" and allow the CEO to do his job. This reality was revealed via the LDMA test, and the results confirmed that the differences between the CEO and CTO were insurmountable, a fact pointed out by other members of the leadership team prior to the LDMA tests, although they had "tried" for more than 12 months to make it work. We ended up not investing,

(continued)

---

[67]Stein et al. (2010).

[68]https://lecticalive.org/about/assessments

and several other potential investors also opted out, although the business idea was both brilliant and timely.

We have also successfully applied Cook-Greuter's Sentence Completion Test (SCT) (see Chap. 2), which has since evolved to become the Maturity Profile (MAP).[69] Cook-Greuter's seminal work is based on her research on adult development and the recognition that the language people use is potentially a direct reflection of their level of consciousness. In her work, she addresses the phenomenon of comprehensive language awareness and analyses the ability of individuals to reflect on the language they use habitually. The SCT is a collection of 30 or so sentence stems—such as "I am. . .," "my father. . .," "work is. . ."—for the testee to complete. The evaluator can then determine an individual's leadership style based on how each stem is interpreted and responded to. In our investment practice, we assess language usage not only through formal tests such as the SCT but also in regular conversation with investees and/or each other. After some practice, your awareness of your own awareness and that of your counterparts will increase. But only a formal scientifically robust test can help identify the disconnect between what people say and how they actually behave. As integral investors, we invest only in people whose mindset is at the world-centric level of development and beyond because, in our view, only at that level of consciousness is there the necessary understanding to make *transformation feasible.*

Step 4: Team Assessment
Anyone who has ever rented or purchased a piece of real estate would agree that "location, location, and location" are the three most important aspects of a good real estate investment. Similarly, any experienced early-stage venture capitalist or angel investor would agree that the quality of a company's management team is arguably the best indicator of the potential future success of a start-up. A high-quality management team is also key for a successful partnership between all stakeholders, including investors, employees, the community at large, suppliers, and other stakeholders. This is why we maintain that more than 80% of the investment risk could be addressed by conducting an integral due diligence assessment of the team. This is beneficial not only for the team itself but also for investors and other stakeholders (Fig. 3.15).

Barrett Brown, a global authority on Integral Theory, coaching, and academic testing, has both coached us and performed numerous assessments for us and our portfolio companies since 2012. During one of our last workshops, he drew my attention to research by Marcial Losada and Emily Heaphy. Losada and Heaphy discovered that one of the best predictors of team performance is the ratio between positive interactions—mutual support, encouragement, and appreciation—and

---

[69]http://www.verticaldevelopment.com/

Fig. 3.15 Theta model
team assessment

negative interactions—disapproval, sarcasm, and even cynicism.[70] In other words,
teams who care about one another work well together, which makes sense, really.

Possessing this type of data about the entrepreneurs in whom you plan to invest
could significantly increase mutual trust and the likelihood of success and reduce the
investment risk related to the team. Fortunately, there are myriad tools for
conducting team assessments. The five dysfunctions of a team tool, for example,
based on the 2002 book of the same name by Patrick Lencioni,[71] is one that we have
successfully applied at various times. The eponymous five dysfunctions identified by
Lencioni are the absence of trust, fear of conflict, lack of commitment, avoidance of
accountability, and inattention to results.

We were once approached by a young Austrian entrepreneur who had developed
a rather interesting software application using AI technology. After several screening
activities during which we performed preliminary due diligence including several
discussions with the founders about the company story, vision, market environment,
business plan, reference calls, and industry interviews; and verification of the

---

[70]Losada and Heaphy (2004, p. 759).

[71]Lencioni (2002).

business model and other document reviews, we invited the entire team of six to our offices in Munich. They were all very capable men and women, and all well prepared. However, during the first meeting, the founder dominated every conversation we initiated with each of his team members as if he did not trust them. For example, we would ask the CFO a question about a detail in the Excel spreadsheet but the founder, the CTO, would step in and answer instead. A second meeting unfolded in the same way. All three of our screening people were united in their opinion that we should drop the deal because the CTO would continue to disempower his team and we did not want to invest in a "king."

In a 2008 *Harvard Business Review* article titled "The Founder's Dilemma,"[72] Noam Wasserman writes about the dilemma of every entrepreneur in search of capital: overcoming the fundamental tension that arises from a founder's wish to be simultaneously "king" and "rich." Investors do not invest in "kings" for two main reasons: they do not want to be his vassals and the attitude of the "king" makes investors fear that it will be difficult to recover their investment.

Investments Examples: Why Culture Eats Strategy for Breakfast

SafeView is a good example of an investment we made in exponential tech and security that suffered from cultural misalignment. In 2003, exponential development in semiconductor manufacturing and computing power made it possible to capture and analyze microwaves in a way not thought possible before. A founder team from a government research facility spun off their idea to build a security body scanner that would be able to detect weapons, even if they were made of ceramic rather than metal. In fact, anything worn on the skin, hidden under clothing, would be visible to security inspectors. It signaled a big improvement in the effectiveness of scanners used in airports, border checkpoints, prisons, and public arenas. The team made great progress in developing the technology into a marketable product. However, they reacted negatively when the first customer feedback from trials came in: The device displayed a picture of the person who was scanned. On a purely functional level, it worked, as anything worn underneath the clothing was clearly visible, but airline customers felt their privacy was being violated and that the body in the scan looked "awful." The engineers wallowed in denial for quite some time. Instead of changing their target market and selling to less customer-oriented markets such as prisons and the military, the founders continued to promote their product to airports and in doing so wasted valuable years. In time, a software was developed that displayed a generic stick figure with the potentially dangerous objects marked on it, and the airports started buying. The company was eventually exited to a global security company and the product is now used at airports worldwide. The delay of 1 or 2 years in market ramp-up

(continued)

---

[72]Wasserman (2008).

Fig. 3.16 Theta model gap
analysis and report

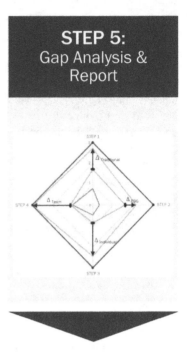

Theta Model Scoring

costs the investors a lot. Fortunately, there was still a financial return, but it
could have been a major success if the engineers had listened to customer
feedback and addressed the "cultural misfit" earlier.

It Infobahn Romania, a technology transfer company we founded in the late
1990s, is yet another example of a start-up company that was perfect in terms
of technology, timing, and market need but failed due to cultural misalignment
of various international teams involved across various countries and continents. At the time, we unfortunately lacked the proper individual and team
development tools and skills to fix these cultural misalignments.

Step 5: Decide: Gap Analysis and Report
Step 5 represents the summary of the integral due diligence process of the Theta
Model (Fig. 3.16).

It offers a gap analysis and report and makes the final recommendation for the
investment.

The integral radar (Fig. 3.17) is the result of the due diligence process and
signifies the differences in terms of integral outcomes along the entire value chain
creation. The yellow line marked with "0" defines the absolute no-go area and

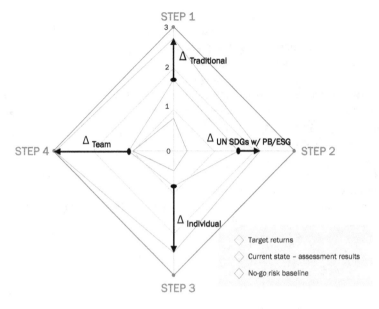

Fig. 3.17 Theta model integral radar

contains characteristics that we do not want to deal with in an investment—for example, the entrepreneurs do not care about sustainability, the focus is on making money only, there is no team, and the mindset of team members is egocentric or ethnocentric. The blue line marked with "1" describes the current state of the investee in all areas of the due diligence process, including the traditional due diligence aspects such as financial, legal, business plan, sales and marketing, GIIRS or other sustainability metrics, individual psychographs, and team assessment. The green line ("2") represents our due diligence team's assessment of the potential to grow in all areas. We also look at the additionality factors that determine what would happen if we did not invest. The decision to invest or not takes time and effort, but skimping on the process invariably leads to failure.

Investment Example: The Power of Market Forces
In 2004, we invested in an exponential tech start-up called Clairvoyante. The founders had a background in the physiology of vision and came up with a very clever way of optimizing computer displays. They discovered that the conventional method of placing small red, green, and blue rectangles (pixels) on a screen is not the best way to produce a high-quality picture. Instead, they patented a new technology to create a brighter, sharper image without increasing the energy consumption or production costs. We were so excited about the

(continued)

exponential drivers in technology growth that we completely underestimated the market forces that often resist change.

What was the problem?

There are only a handful of display manufacturers in the world, and they are heavily invested in expensive manufacturing plants. When a new technology comes along, it must wait in line for the next investment cycle. New entrants, like Clairvoyante, must still battle Porter's five forces[73] and have little negotiation power over a few large potential customers. For an early-stage investor, that can mean the difference between success and failure.

Eventually, Clairvoyante brought its technology to market through Asian manufacturers, but it took much longer than projected. Luckily, we recovered our investment, but we learned not to invest again in a monopolized market with relatively few potential clients.

3.2.5   Investment Execution

The investment execution, Phase III in the value chain creation (Fig. 3.5), is largely a traditional investment activity for which we hire professional lawyers, accountants, and other experts. The details of this particular aspect are beyond the scope of this book, but in summary, the deal execution contains three steps geared at the formal legalization of the integrally sustainable alignment identified during the due diligence process of the Theta Model:

- *Deal negotiation*, which includes pricing, risk reward, and structuring the deal to reduce risk as much as possible.
- *Writing commitment letters and investment memoranda*, which include the terms of commitment and investment, as well as security and collateral, representation aspects, and so on.
- *Legal closing* (Fig. 3.18).

To execute the closing, we work with experienced lawyers, accountants, and partners who can help us navigate the intricacies of local law. Important aspects of AQAL that may deviate from traditional processes are highlighted in Fig. 3.19.

Within the application of the AQAL model at this stage, it is important to make sure that the investee commits legally to the implementation of the Integral Investing criteria previously discussed. This includes the governance aspect of the company. In other words, how do we make sure that the investee company will, for example, truly implement the UN SDGs within planetary boundaries to reduce CO_2 emissions while the team continues to grow collectively and individually? The answer to that is that we can only achieve what we measure. This is why these criteria must be part of

---

[73]https://en.wikipedia.org/wiki/Porter%27s_five_forces_analysis

Fig. 3.18 Integral
investment execution

Integral Alignment

the company's governance documentation and remuneration of its leaders must depend fully, or even in part, upon these criteria being met.[74]

Coming up with integrated measurement criteria (multiple bottom lines) (see Step 2) is the premise for a successful investment. However, an organization will only stay on track with this via meaningful integrated reporting based on the multiple bottom-line metrics. The International Integrated Reporting Council (IIRC), a "global coalition of regulators, investors, companies, standard setters, the accounting profession and NGOs . . . that shares the view that communication about businesses' value creation should be the next step in the evolution of corporate reporting" has been working on this for several years now.[75] The European Commission's sustainable finance strategy discussed earlier should bring us multiple bottom line reporting guidelines relatively soon.

3.2.6   Investment Monitoring

To be successful, a good investor must also have access to and be able to monitor and influence key company decisions, create milestones for the raising of future capital rounds, and stay close to the investee until the exit point (Fig. 3.20).

---

[74]See the example application of Governance Criteria at https://aqalgroup.com/extra-materials/
[75]IIRC (2013).

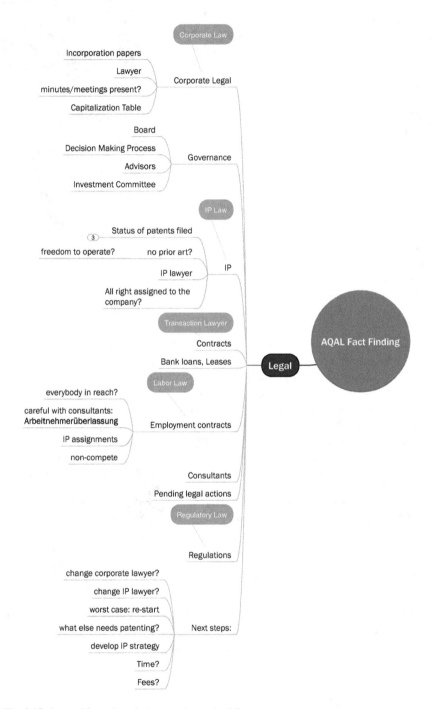

Fig. 3.19 Integral Investing closing top-down checklist

Fig. 3.20 Integral
investment monitoring

*Integral
Sustainability*

From an Integral Investing perspective, the core goal of monitoring, Phase IV of
the value chain creation (Fig. 3.5), is to help build an integrally sustainable company
from the very beginning. But what exactly does that mean?

The components related to building integrally sustainable businesses are manifold and include aspects connected with hierarchical or network/matrix organization
models, management style, conflict resolution models, modes of communication,
leadership models, feminine versus masculine principles, sustainability, and so
on. But what is the governance structure? And more importantly, what role do
people play in such organizations?

Hierarchy, Holarchy, Heterarchy?
Throughout our pre-investor careers, Tom and I experienced organizational structures that were mostly hierarchical but also showed matrix or networking tendencies.
Therefore, we were looking to invest in and build more integral and holistic
organizational frameworks that would support our Integral Investing framework,
including an organizational, leadership, and cultural style based on later stages of
consciousness as described in Chap. 2. We soon learned that hierarchies and
heterarchies/non-ranking structures each have their raison d'être and are an integral
part of reality.[76] Nature is full of self-organizing hierarchies—quarks, atoms, molecules, cells, and organisms—that build on one another to create increasing levels of
complexity. You cannot destroy a cell, as a biological construct, without destroying

---

[76]Wilber (2000a/1995, pp. 22–39).

a molecule and an organism, and any change in an organism will affect all its component parts. Subsequently, Wilber argues that *"reality as a whole is not composed of things or processes, but of holons* [my italics]".[77] "Holon" is a term coined by Arthur Koestler, which Wilber explains as being used to "refer to that, which being a *whole* in one context, is simultaneously a *part* in another [my italics]".[78] This gave rise to the term "holarchy," which Wilber uses interchangeably with hierarchy.

If such hierarchies are so important in nature, why do people sometimes reject them? As a generalization, when people reject hierarchies, they often refer, of course, to pathological social hierarchies such as "ontological fascism (with the one dominating the many)"[79] as experienced in Nazi Germany, former Eastern Bloc countries, or traditional corporate structures.

In some modern hierarchical organizations, we can find inside one level of a hierarchy—for example, within the sales and marketing department—so-called matrix/heterarchical structures. In those, we find players who co-operate with each other, with no element seeming to be more important than another. Think about biology: All the cells in an organism, say the leg, contribute, under normal conditions, to keep the leg healthy. When the brain wants to move the leg, all the cells support the move; but the reverse is not true: a single cell cannot decide to move the whole leg. In a simplified way, we can say *within* each level of a biological hierarchy, we find a heterarchy, and *between* each level we find hierarchy.

Pathological heterarchies can, of course, also happen when fusion—where some people lose their own identity—instead of union and indissociation instead of integration occur. In social structures of this type, for example, all values become regulated in a "flatland devoid of individual values or identities; nothing can be said to be deeper or higher or better in any meaningful sense; all values vanish into a herd mentality of the bland leading the bland." This pathological hierarchy "is a type of ontological totalitarianism (with many dominating the one)".[80] We can see the results of this for ourselves today. As technology has made it easier for us to express our opinions to a global audience with little oversight and few boundaries, a privilege that was previously restricted to the chosen few, so too has it become easier to disseminate hatred and nourish populism, which will, ironically, ultimately challenge the very notion of democracy that made it possible. In a 2014 article in the *New York Times* titled "How Social Media Silences Debate," Claire Cain Miller looked at how user behavior on many social media platforms can render people with dissenting opinions reluctant to express those opinions for fear of backlash.[81] In

---

[77]Wilber (2000a/1995, p. 43).

[78]Wilber (2000a/1995, p. 26).

[79]Wilber (2000a/1995, p. 32).

[80]Wilber (2000a/1995, p. 32).

[81]Miller (2014, 26 August).

summary, "systems theorists tend to say: *within* each level, heterarchy; *between* each level, hierarchy."[82]

But what in the world does this analysis have to do with investing in and building integrally sustainable organizations? Everything, because we can learn from nature, including human nature. In many ways, companies represent a micro-cosmos of our societies and how successfully we govern ourselves. This does not mean that we have to reject or favor one structure over another, but that we must realize that both are important and together can safeguard the health of an organization if properly implemented. Business organizations operate like complex organisms with a brain. While the brain exerts a leading function within the body, each organ and tissue has its own intelligence and ability to communicate and to adapt and control its own function. This occurs in correlation and coordination with the brain, the CEO of the human body. All cells support and work in total unison with and support each other because every "cell transcends but includes molecules, which transcend but include atoms."[83]

As Tom and I continued building integrally sustainable organizations riding the wave of exponentially growing technologies, we kept applying our Integral Investing framework and the Theta Model. At the same time, we stayed alert for other forms of building progressive organizations that we could model. In 2014, we came across two emerging organizational models that have inspired us and whose models we have adopted in part: the exponential organization and the teal organization.

Exponential Organizations

The term *exponential organization* (ExO) was popularized by Salim Ismail, Michael Malone, and Yuri Van Geest via their book of the same name, in which they define an ExO as "one whose impact (or output) is disproportionately large—at least 10× larger—compared to its peers because of the use of new organizational techniques that leverage accelerating technologies."[84] Note that the word "impact" in this definition is understood in terms of the overall *output* of a company and not in terms of the social and/or environmental *impact*, or effect, a company has, which we discussed earlier within the context of impact investing. ExOs are relevant because of the speed with which exponentially growing information technologies are driving companies all over the world to grow and to gain billion-dollar valuations within a short period. Some tech start-ups such as Uber, WhatsApp, and Airbnb have achieved "unicorn" status, with valuations higher than US$1 billion.[85] As of January 23, 2019, an extraordinary avalanche of capital had funded about 310 unicorns that have been collectively valued at US$1052 billion and have raised a combined total

---

[82]Wilber K (2000a/1995, p. 28).

[83]Wilber (2000b, p. 11).

[84]Ismail et al. (2014, p. 113).

[85]Erdogan et al. (May, 2016).

of close to US$257 billion.[86] In 2018 alone, 112 new unicorns joined the global Unicorn Club, a 58% increase from 2017. Fifty-three of them came from the USA, 37 from China, and 14 from various European countries. Within this investor landscape, WhatsApp, whose annual revenue was worth about US$20 million in 2014, had been valued at a jaw-dropping US$19 billion by Facebook, which acquired it in October 2014. The US$19 billion represented 0.03% of the world economy and was more than Iceland's GDP in the same year.[87]

In our view, something has really gone wrong if the value of a messaging company such as WhatsApp, which at the time of its acquisition employed 55 people, is almost double that of Fiat Chrysler, a US motor company that employed 225,587 people in 2014, and almost half the market capitalization of BMW, a German motor company that employed about 116,324 people in 2014.[88] Regardless of how we feel, though, we need to deal with this trend, because it is real. How did it happen? It is the result of many factors, the most important of which is exponentially growing information technologies. Ismail et al. note that they found major overlaps between unicorns and ExOs. While it took a regular Fortune 500 company more than 20 years to reach a market capitalization of US$1 billion, it took the unicorns less than 3 years from their founding date.[89] They posit that the basic metric of ExOs is related to the speed with which management has learned to scale not only the technology but also the organization so they can achieve a minimum of 10× the results of traditional organizations—from an idea to a ready-made product—with a fraction of the resources. An ExO is characterized by 10 points in particular:

- It has a massively transformative purpose (MTP).
- It has an MTP peer group and community.
- It has an exponentially thinking and acting founding team.
- It has a breakthrough idea that delivers an improvement of more than 10× over traditional ones.
- It has a simple but powerful business model and delivery process that is able to compete with traditional businesses (e.g., Netflix vs. Blockbuster).
- It has a minimum viable product (MVP) that can get to market quickly.
- It has a quick validating system for marketing and sales.
- It has an exponentially thinking and acting culture.
- It has a core mission-critical team that questions everything regularly but resides outside the organization in order to avoid attacks by the organization's immune system.
- It is building an entire platform (compare Amazon's success in this area versus Yahoo's).[90]

---

[86]See https://www.cbinsights.com/research/unicorn-startup-market-map/

[87]See https://www.tradingeconomics.com/iceland/gdp

[88]See https://www.bloomberg.com/quote/FCAU:US

[89]Ismail et al. (2014, p. 15).

[90]Ismail et al. (pp. 147–180).

Let us take a brief look at the *external* and *internal* characteristics of an ExO.

The *external* characteristics are summarized as SCALE, an acronym that stands for five key tools or success factors: **S**taff on demand, **C**ommunity and crowd, **A**lgorithms, **L**everaged assets, and **E**ngagement. In a global world driven by exponentially growing technologies, SCALE is key to staying lean, moving fast, and developing smart products quickly. It makes it possible for organizations to modify their workforce to accommodate particular requirements for niche knowledge and skills that may not be otherwise immediately accessible to them, thus enabling organizations to train their core team; increase learning, loyalty, the flow of fresh ideas, and a sense of playfulness; and contribute significantly to the goals of the company—all without managing additional assets or straining the bottom line.

The *internal* characteristics of an ExO are summarized by Ismail et al. as the IDEAS framework: **I**nterfaces, **D**ashboards, **E**xperimentation, **A**utonomy, and **S**ocial Technologies. **I**nterfaces are "algorithms and automated workflows that route the output of SCALE externalities to the right people at the right time internally."[91] **D**ashboards manage, measure, and optimize the capability of the organization to handle and address the huge amounts of information and data that flow into it. **E**xperimentation keeps internal processes aligned with constant change and ensures the organization remains lean and flexible. It tests potential risks, as well as the organization's ability to handle failure, in a controlled manner. **A**utonomy is the process through which "self-organizing, multi-disciplinary teams [are] operating with decentralized authority,"[92] have higher morale and increased agility and are more accountable vis-à-vis their customers. As an example of the application of **A**utonomy, the authors refer to holacracy,[93] a self-management organizational method that empowers its employees to take decisions that are in line with the overall purpose of their organizations. Among the 1000+ companies[94] that have successfully adopted the holacracy's self-management practice are online retail unicorn Zappos.com,[95] game developer Valve Corp,[96] and agribusiness Morning Star Company.[97] The term *holacracy* was coined by Brian Robertson, a brilliant integral thinker whom I met in 2013. Brian was a software developer who took the Agile programming methodology[98] and applied it to create holarchy-based organizations (see "Hierarchy, Heterarchy, and Holarchy"). Holacracy "is a new way of structuring and running your organization that replaces the conventional management hierarchy"[99] whereby the top-down, command, and control power is

---

[91]Ismail et al. (2014, p. 86).

[92]Ismail et al. (2014, p. 102).

[93]Robertson (2015).

[94]https://www.holacracy.org/resource/holacracy-adoptions/

[95]https://www.zappos.com/

[96]https://www.valvesoftware.com/en/

[97]https://www.morningstarco.com/

[98]https://en.wikipedia.org/wiki/Agile_software_development

[99]https://www.holacracy.org/what-is-holacracy

distributed throughout the various levels of the organization. The Social technologies characteristic of ExOs aims at increasing social interactions in organizations by nurturing team stability during periods of rapid growth, encouraging faster decision cycles, and leveraging the community to further develop ideas.

In summary, Ismail et al. have drawn on in-depth research to develop a blueprint for creating ExOs that enable companies to ride the wave of exponentially growing technologies. These ExOs are characterized by having an MTP and implementing five internal attributes (IDEAS) to successfully SCALE five external characteristics to achieve exponential growth.

Can you imagine what would happen if ExOs decided to make their MTP addressing GGCs such as climate change? Can you imagine what would occur if they decided to measure their success not by their financial bottom line alone but by a multiple bottom line (for example, the 6Ps)? What if they decided to set their sights on implementing the UN SDGs within planetary boundaries by 2030? What kind of world would we have?

Investment Examples: Rethinking Measures of Success

In addition to investing in exponential information technology, biotechnology, and clean technology, we continue to invest in other megatrends such as innovation, lifestyle, and medical devices. Penumbra, for example, is a medical device company that develops and manufactures innovative and minimally invasive medical devices for patients who have had strokes or various neurovascular diseases. Penumbra exited after 11 years and delivered a rather successful integral return not only financially but also impact-wise. We are thrilled about the technology of course, which addresses a huge medical need, but we are especially thrilled with the main founder, a serial entrepreneur and former founder of Smart Therapeutics (now Boston Scientific), and his team. Even if Penumbra, or any other of our still-active medical portfolio companies, never returns our investment, we are proud to be part of such medical advances.

NeoGuide is an example of an investment whose story we like to share although it was a complete financial loss. The founders came up with the idea of building a colonoscopy device that would make the procedure easier, faster, and less painful. They wanted to use the latest technologies in robotics in order to build a "camera on a snake" that could follow the bends of the colon. Since the snake would know how to bend itself, it would not exert pressure on the colon walls. Great idea—but too early. The company tried long and hard to make the complicated mechanics work, and after a while, they changed their approach completely, but the tech just did not work out well enough in clinical trials. We still like to talk about the team and their idea, though.

Now let us take a closer look at teal organizations, an organization form that is much more aligned with our own Integral Investing framework.

Teal Organizations

The term *teal organization* was introduced to the world in 2014 by former McKinsey consultant Frédéric Laloux in his book *Reinventing Organizations.*[100] Drawing on research performed on 12 organizations, ranging from nonprofits to businesses, healthcare organizations, and schools, Laloux concludes that there is a new shift in company "consciousness evolution" that has given birth to what he called the teal organization. Why teal? It references the color used by Ken Wilber in his AQAL model, as Laloux built his entire teal organization model on Wilber's Integral Theory. It is embedded in the second tier of the AQAL framework (see the "Spiral Dynamics" section in Chap. 2 and for a direct comparison between Wilber's stages of development with the stages of development identified by the *Spiral Dynamics* model, see Altitudes of Development, on Jeff Salzman's Daily Evolver website, at https://tinyurl.com/y5eogejt).

All the case studies Laloux presents reveal three major breakthroughs in their organizational structures and cultures that are very much in line with the characteristics of the integrally sustainable companies Tom and I are building:

- *Self-management*: The first breakthrough is the creation of structures that go beyond the constraints of traditional hierarchical, command and control power structures and are able to operate, even at large scale, as flexible, collaborative, and self-organizing systems. They have interlocking sets of structures and practices that:

  - Are based on trust
  - Encourage effective and individual decision-making and problem-solving
  - Support progressive ways of sharing information so it is universally available
  - Make self-management possible through proper training and coaching of teams and individuals
  - Lead to quick conflict resolution
  - Assign responsibility and accountability to both individuals and the collective

- *Wholeness*: Showing up fully and as a whole human being, not just as a rational and emotionless individual, is highly encouraged and represents the second major breakthrough of teal organizations. Wholeness means that people in such companies can let go of the traditional "professional masks" that must obey top-down chains of command and control strategies and tactical implementation plans and instead bring in their full emotional, intuitive, and spiritual manifestations of themselves and contribute to innovation, creativity, and nourishing wholesome relationships at work. They honor diversity, are invited to create safe and caring workplaces, overcome feelings of fear and separation, and create a culture of learning and holistic growth. Feedback and respectful confrontation, requests for accountability, and a can-do attitude are explicitly encouraged.

---

[100]Laloux (2014).

- *Evolutionary purpose*: The collective purpose of a teal organization is developed through the people by the people. It is a direct manifestation of their own levels of consciousness and is maintained through integrally informed corporate practices rather than being imposed and determined by top-down strategies, plans, and budgets. Individual purposes are as highly regarded as the collective purpose. The evolutionary purpose of the organization includes profit but *is not limited to it*, because there are no trade-offs between people, planet, profits, and purpose. The teal organization is rooted in the belief that "everything will unfold with more grace if we stop trying to control and instead choose to simply sense and respond."[101]

The Integral Investing framework both includes and transcends models such as ExOs and teal organizations. We build teal organizations that implement exponentially growing technologies, Ismail et al.'s ExOs, with the intention of making the transformation toward addressing the global grand challenges within planetary boundaries feasible.

Teal Organization or Exponential Organization (ExO)?

It is interesting but not at all surprising to find an overlap between companies that are categorized as teal organizations and have also been identified as ExOs by Ismail et al. (2014) (e.g., Zappos, Morning Star, Favi).

Companies represent structures and do not have a consciousness of their own, of course. However, as the people in an organization evolve both individually and as a team, they appear to create organizational structures that reflect the later stages of consciousness evolution discussed in Chap. 2. In applying several developmental models from Clare W. Graves, Don Edward Beck, Chris Cowan, Susanne Cook-Greuter, and Ken Wilber, Laloux comes to the conclusion that organizations, as a living system, also evolve to later stages. He assigns the teal stage, the second tier, to the ones he analyzed.

3.2.7 Wealth Actualization: The Exit

Phase V of our value chain creation is the exit or wealth actualization, which is what we like to call it in reference to the integral return and not only the financial one (Fig. 3.21).

By applying the Integral Investing philosophy in early-stage investing, we not only achieve a significant integral return (as measured by the 6Ps) but also reduce our investment risk.

When our investments have been successful it was because we invested in the best teams, we knew what we were doing and were close to them, the technology

---

[101]Laloux (2014, p. 232).

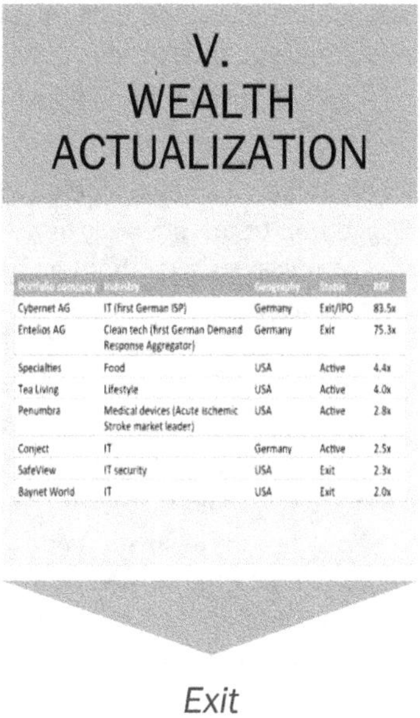

Fig. 3.21 Integral investing wealth actualization/exit

V.
WEALTH
ACTUALIZATION

Portfolio company	Industry	Geography	Status	ROI
Cybernet AG	IT (first German ISP)	Germany	Exit/IPO	83.5x
Entelios AG	Clean tech (first German Demand Response Aggregator)	Germany	Exit	75.3x
Specialties	Food	USA	Active	4.4x
Tea Living	Lifestyle	USA	Active	4.0x
Penumbra	Medical devices (Acute ischemic Stroke market leader)	USA	Active	2.8x
Conject	IT	Germany	Active	2.5x
SafeView	IT security	USA	Exit	2.3x
Baynet World	IT	USA	Exit	2.0x

Exit

was perfect, and the timing was right. In short, we applied the integral investment framework to the letter—and we were lucky. The most important component, however, was the team. By "the team," I mean the whole team of stakeholders including co-investors, suppliers, start-up teams, coaches, and other contributors. Together we built a structure and culture based on trust, integrity, transparency, caring, passion, and fun in addition to the desire to implement integral sustainability. And it paid off.

Investment Example: A Tale of Success
Cybernet AG, a German ISP, went public and became the first Internet stock traded on the German stock exchange before PSINet acquired it at the end of 2002. Its founders and the visionary and progressive culture they built personified the characteristics of higher ethical values.

In Germany, it is relatively easy to implement high standards with respect to environmental, social, and ethical governance (ESG) criteria. Many ESG criteria are mandated by law and are therefore relatively easy for any investor to measure and any start-up company to implement and report.

Some of our portfolio companies did an IPO, such as Cybernet, or were exited in less than 4 years, such as Entelios (see Box "Investment Example: The Energy Turnaround"). Others took more than a decade to become wildly successful, such as Penumbra (see Box "Investment Examples: Rethinking Measures of Success"). But they all had one thing in common: They built a culture based on higher values and aimed to serve the world.

When an investment failed, the reasons were manifold and included a selection of the following:

- We failed to see the lack of team alignment, including a lack of common values, early on or arising over time.
- The investees were both geographically and culturally too far from our circle of influence.
- The technology was the bleeding edge.
- The company ran out of money before it could become successful. Undercapitalization is a common problem for German start-ups, for example. The venture capital market in Germany is significantly underdeveloped compared to the USA and China.
- We were too idealistic and invested in a regulated market in hopes of changing the regulations before running out of funds.
- We invested in "kings": the founder(s) did not want to exit and so we could never retrieve our investment.
- We were too hands-off.
- We did not have an anti-dilution clause to protect us and lost out even though the companies became eventually successful.
- We invested against our intuition and gut feeling and found out too late about formal assessments and tests.
- We did not have the proper scientific tools to assess the entrepreneurs' morals and ethics and so took them at face value.
- We underestimated the importance of proper legal advice and paperwork.
- Perfection became the enemy of the good: alternative solutions caught up faster and came to market before our investees did.
- The timing of our investment coincided with global crises.

Early-stage investing is not a science, it is an art. Yes, there are all kinds of tools and lists, and ways to make sure you cross all the Ts and dot all the Is, but in the end, it is your track record that speaks the loudest. If you measure success in an integrally sustainable way like we do, there are many ways to be fulfilled by your investment activities, including the financial return. In conclusion, Tom would like to share with you one more secret about Integral Investing based on a Bayes-informed strategy on screening.

3.3   The 360-Degree Track Record

As we have seen, being a seed and/or early-stage investor (business angel or VC) is like fishing in a muddy pond. There are a lot of fish but very few of them are worth catching. The probability that a new start-up will develop and eventually provide a large, integrally profitable exit to its investors is minuscule. In our experience, only

Fig. 3.22 The 360-degree
track record matrix

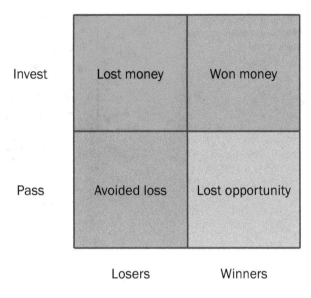

Invest

Pass

Losers   Winners

about 10% of start-ups in a fund portfolio have a chance of becoming successful exits. Investors, therefore, use assessment tools to screen investment opportunities that are presented to them. These tools, in our case the Theta Model, try to predict "winners" and "losers." The essence of the Theta Model strategy is to identify the losers as early as possible by identifying the winners with a high sensitivity and exposing the losers with a *high specificity*. Let us explore this in more detail.

Figure 3.22 shows a 2×2 matrix that represents our process, which we call the 360-degree track record. The matrix shows four possible investment cases, all of which begin with the same likelihood of succeeding or failing (represented through the equal size of the quadrants):

- *Lost money* (upper left, in red) represents an unsuccessful investment.
- *Won money* (upper right, in green) represents a successful investment.
- *Avoided loss* (lower left, in dark gray) represents a passed investment that would be an unsuccessful investment.
- *Lost opportunity* (lower right quadrant, in light gray) represents a passed investment that would have been a successful investment.

When assessing a track record, it is important to include the entire pool (360 degrees) of investments, not only the true positives (green) and false positives (red), but also the true negatives (lower left) and the false negatives (lower right). As we will show, the true negatives (lower left) in particular are often neglected; that is, money not invested, and resources saved. When applying the Theta Model with its five de-risking steps discussed earlier, the 360-degree matrix (Fig. 3.22) translates into Fig. 3.23.

In terms of expected financial return, the passed investments would have no impact, the false-positive investment would lead to a 100% loss, and a true positive

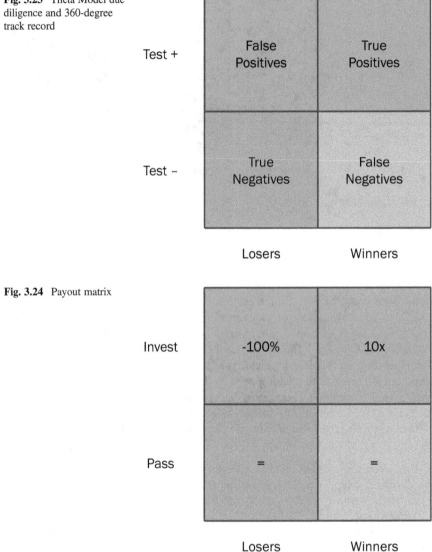

Fig. 3.23 Theta Model due diligence and 360-degree track record

Fig. 3.24 Payout matrix

investment would return a 10× ROI (because it would have to compensate for all the other statistically failed investments) (Fig. 3.24).

In a world where winners are very rare (Fig. 3.25) the investment scenario is similar to that of medical testing and diagnosis.

Fig. 3.25 Winners are rare

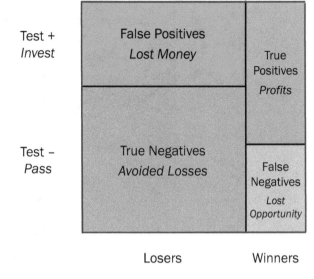

Losers   Winners

To grasp the analogy, let us see how Bayes' theorem[102] can be applied for both drug testing and investing. For example, in a world where only maybe 0.5% of the population are using illicit drugs (or using drugs illicitly), a drug test with 99.0% sensitivity and 99.0% specificity is almost useless, because a positive drug test would only label 33% of the tested people correctly as drug users. However, 67% of positive testers would be false positives (not drug users)! In order to avoid false positives, the test must be extremely specific—for example, 99.9% or 99.99%.

The question then becomes: How can both the *sensitivity and* the *specificity* be enhanced? In other words: How can the track record be improved?

3.3.1   How to Improve the Track Record

There are many ways to improve the track record, but here are four that we find helpful:

- *Fishing in a better pond* (increase the overall prevalence of winners) by, for example, making sure you get access to a higher-quality deal flow (increase the true positives (Fig. 3.26).
- *Developing better ways to pick the winners* (Fig. 3.27): Increase test sensitivity, reduce the false negatives by, for example, adopting better testing methods for team selection (see Steps 3 and 4 of the Theta Model discussed earlier).

---

[102]https://en.wikipedia.org/wiki/Bayes%27_theorem

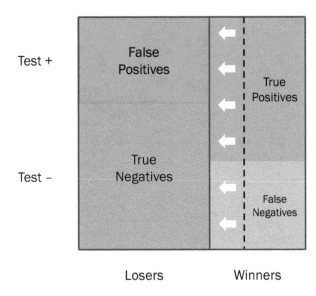

Fig. 3.26 Increase access to a better deal flow

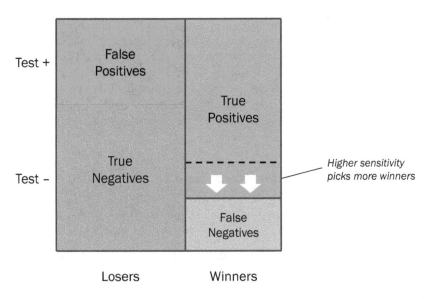

Fig. 3.27 Picking winners

- *Finding better ways to avoid the losers* (increase test specificity, reduce the true negatives, Fig. 3.28) by, for example, applying Step 2 of the Theta Model to avoid risks associated with negative environmental and/or social impact.
- *Optimizing payouts* (chasing unicorns, Fig. 3.29) by, for example, riding the wave of exponentially growing technologies and investing early in climate adaptation (using the *Smart* scenario presented in *Transformation is Feasible*).

Fig. 3.28 Avoiding losers

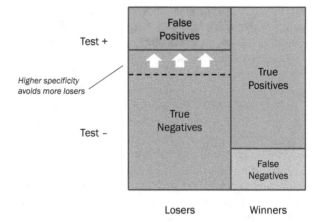

Fig. 3.29 Chasing unicorns

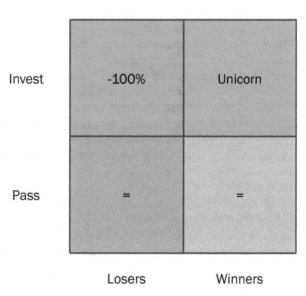

On a per deal basis, losses are limited (you cannot lose more than the investment), but payouts, especially for unicorns, can be huge in integrally sustainable terms. However, in a world where winners are very rare, the investor needs to narrow their focus by improving the quality of the deal flow and applying tests that are extremely high in specificity (see the Theta Model). The latter may seem counterintuitive because success is not so much about finding the winners as it is about avoiding the losers, but it is important.

What has this to do with an investor's track record?

When investors, business angels, VC partners, or asset managers talk about their track record, they are quite selective about what they communicate. They always talk about the winners, rarely about the losers, and *never* about lost opportunities or avoided losses. Experience shows that few angel investors or VC firms have a long-term positive track record, a fact that makes authentic performance statistics rare. This is so for several reasons including the low frequency of winners in the deal flow, and the mediocre accuracy of industry's average prediction. The traditional screening tests and processes are rather unpredictable and muddled, and depend in large part on investors' "gut feelings." Such tests yield only a few successful investments (true positives). Many failed investments (false positives) lose money and occasionally the winners (false negatives) are wasted. In other words, the tests have low *sensitivity* and low *specificity*. However, it is through the avoided losses that a consistent long-term integral investor can shine. It pays to filter out opportunities as early as possible. The Theta Model, with its five steps and assessment tools for individual founders and the team culture, does exactly that: It shines a light on the dark areas, highlights red flags early in the due diligence process, and keeps the screening pipeline thin and the process low-cost.

Early-stage investing is a risky business, but if investors do their homework properly, there should be no regrets. The reality is that we can no longer exclude from investment performance metrics the *interior* dimensions such as cultural values, behavior, joy, and personal happiness. If we choose to ignore the interior aspects, we choose to ignore the fact that reality has both an *interior* and an *exterior*. In investing jargon, this means that financial measurement criteria must be correlated with social, environmental, cultural, and behavioral factors, as well as individual interior development factors (i.e., ego, needs, values, emotions, moral standards). These interior factors can be measured, as we now know. All four AQAL quadrants are tetra-arising; none can be privileged or ignored without repercussions. The Integral Investing practice advocates, and therefore actively encourages, a healthier horizontal integration in terms of cultural, social, environmental, behavioral, and experiential perspectives, no matter which evolutionary altitude is considered.

Within the context of exponentially growing technologies, the next question is: How can we use, for example, artificial intelligence to support the application of Integral Investing to address grand global challenges in the future?

3.4 Scaling Integral Investing with Human-Centered AI

We saw that Integral Investing facilitates the fishing in a better pond which addresses the following three levers of increased prevalence for true positive investments (Fig. 3.30): *integral sustainability*, *scalability*, and *explainability*.

The overall *explainability* of the investment decision can be increased by explicating it using notions that human experts comprehend. For example, "the founder team is missing industry experience, is not complementing each other, and the market opportunity is too small." The overall *scalability* of the investment process can be increased by making the screening and due diligence process more focused, and more efficient.

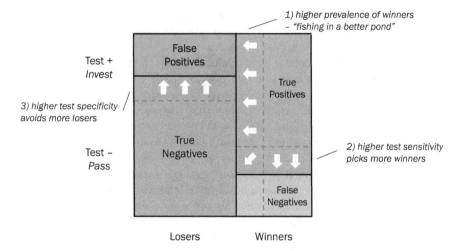

Fig. 3.30 Three levers of increased prevalence for true positive investments: integral sustainability, scalability, and explainability

The main question is one of execution: How can the insights from the 360-degree track record be scaled and accelerated? How can the sensitivity and specificity be increased, while still recognizing a Unicorn when it is showing up? How can better decisions be made more efficiently and how can the process be scaled?

This is where human-centered and collective intelligence AI comes in handy.

One way to improve the decision-making process of investment managers is described by James Surowiecki in his book *The Wisdom of Crowds*.[103] As it turns out, a well-managed group of experts can make better decisions than any single member if certain guidelines are met. These are the following:

- *Diversity of opinions*: Each individual group member must be an expert in his/her field and come from different backgrounds.
- *Independence*: Individual group member looks at the presented information asynchronously, anonymously, and independently from one another in order to form their own opinion. This elicits opinions from every participant including the shyest member of the group and avoids the premature building of herd mentality led by the most dominant individuals.
- *Decentralization*: Groups can collaborate even without meeting in one room (physically or virtually, which presents an advantage in today's post-COVID-19 world).
- *Aggregation*: A designated moderator elicits input from all experts anonymously and summarizes the whole picture. Sometimes this can be as simple as calculating a mathematical mean or average.

---

[103] Surowiecki (2004).

The obvious technology to automate and scale such a process is Artificial Intelligence (AI). However, the current automated learning algorithms need large datasets for their training. And, even if they arrive at a solution, they are often unable to document, explain, or defend their results. Early-stage investing cannot apply such applications of AI because of a lack of data and the difficulties posed by the knowledge acquisition process from experts. Moreover, in order to support a decision-making investment group, an automated tool must be able to document and explain the reasoning behind a decision to "invest" or to "pass."

Because we are dealing with human experts, we need tools that help moderate and manage a group decision-making process in an asynchronous and anonymous manner. We find these in a new branch of Artificial Intelligence called human-centered AI, also known as AI-assisted Collective Intelligence. In our forthcoming paper, *An Integral Approach to Sustainable Investing Using Human-centered AI*, Tom and I, together with Tom Kehler, the inventor of such an application, we describe how that works.[104] Tom Kehler built AI systems already in the 1980s. He was the founder and CEO of IntelliCorp, one of the first commercial AI companies and makers of KEE, an object-oriented Knowledge Engineering Environment, and is an expert in the symbolic, constraint-based flavor of AI. Using modern statistical methods, such as Bayes' Theorem for big data sets, Kehler's latest company, CrowdSmart,[105] built a collective knowledge acquisition method that uses Natural Language Processing (NLP) to generate as output a Bayesian Belief Network that associates propositions and quantitative scores to a predictive score. In the context of a start-up screening, it generates a representation of the collective judgment on whether the asset has the opportunity to create sufficient business results to support future investment and company growth or not. Kehler reports an impressive track record of CrowdSmart with an 85% prediction accuracy compared with the 20–30% prediction accuracy of traditional VC funds.

In conclusion, early-stage investing appears to be the ideal field of application for human-centered AI because:

- There is too little historical data available to train a deep learning algorithm.
- There is too little data available per test case.
- The know-how stands with the human experts and cannot yet be extracted and formalized efficiently.

The screening process is designed to identify innovative solutions, so-called "black swans," and the evaluators must be a diverse group of industry experts, with "skin in the game" who care deeply about addressing the grand global challenges we face. Moving forward, human-centered AI can help accelerate, digitalize, and scale the implementation of Integral Investing and the Theta Model.

---

[104]Bozesan et al. (2020)

[105]https://www.crowdsmart.io

3.5 Principles of Integral Investing

Tom and I acknowledge the severity of humanity's global grand challenges (GGCs), particularly the existential threats such as climate emergency, biological and thermonuclear weapons, and unsafe exponentially growing technologies. The COVID-19 crisis has proven to us that current systems, including the political, economic, financial, and educational, to name only a few, are not well equipped to address the current GGCs in time to save humanity or the planet. This is unfortunate, as time is of the essence. Nonetheless, we believe that *transformation is feasible*, and that the necessary resources, knowledge, technology, leadership, and capital exist to make it happen. A mind shift toward world-centric levels of consciousness is, however, a mandatory requirement and a premise for immediate, united, and adequate global action. We are totally committed to doing our part to ensure the future of life and are guided in doing so by the following 21 key principles. Note that a repetition of what has previously been said is sometimes unavoidable.

Principle 1: Have a Massively Transformative Purpose (MTP)
We take an integrated view of the world and address the grand global challenges (GGCs) through our own integrally sustainable form of investing as described in Chap. 2.

> **Our Massively Transformative Purpose (MTP)**
> Our MTP is to inspire and empower other investors and company builders to join us in ensuring the future of life and wellbeing on our beautiful blue planet.

We believe, furthermore, that the development and deployment of safe and ethically sound exponentially growing technologies are crucial for the future of humanity and invest in those that address GGCs (Fig. 3.31).

What is your MTP? What keeps you motivated and driven? What makes you happy? What gives your life meaning that is uniquely yours? Why do you invest?

Principle 2: Have a Moonshot
We believe in the critical role that investing and company building can play in solving the GGCs. Our current, collective path needs steering in a different direction; we need a turnaround. The Oxford dictionary defines "turnaround" as "a situation in which something changes from bad to good."[106] Although we do not believe that the current investment, economic, and financial systems are bad, we do believe that they must evolve and transform to adequately address the GGCs in a timely manner. This is why we launched the investment turnaround, our moonshot, to achieve the next paradigm in investing.

---

[106]https://tinyurl.com/y288jsj5

- To have fun and to be happy
- To self-actualize through investing
- To be an inspiration and to invite like-minded investors to join us
- To create wealth through financial sustainability and sustainable growth
- To create a conveyor belt for the implementation of Integral Investing
- To create a movement and stewardship for a life worth living on this planet for future generations
- To refocus energy and people in a significant way to solve the global grand challenges (i.e. UN SDG within Planetary Boundaries)

Fig. 3.31 Why we invest

Our Moonshot: The Investment Turnaround

Our moonshot is the implementation of the investment turnaround. It is the specific application of exponential technologies toward achieving Integral Investing, the next paradigm in investing, namely integral sustainability.

It aims at implementing an investing paradigm rooted in the essence of all existence, the exterior reality, the material world, as well as interior realities such as culture, values, ethics, and morals. It is a reality in which financial returns are inseparable from environmental, social, cultural, and ethical impact, including individual joy and happiness. Our first goal is the integrally sustainable implementation of the UN SDGs within planetary boundaries by 2050.

Aside from our Integral Investing model for early-stage investing, another contribution to the implementation of our moonshot is the climate endowment initiative. Originally born out of conversations with members of the Club of Rome, the climate endowment aims to be an "urgent response to the climate crisis and to the European voters' outcry for a green revolution. The aim of the climate endowment is to enable institutional investors to allocate more of their huge capital stock in renewable energy, new mobility, and related cleantech assets."[107]

---

[107]https://aqalgroup.com/climate-endowment-fund/

It is important to keep in mind that the implementation of a moonshot requires a world-centric level of consciousness (see Chap. 2). We remember that according to evolutionary psychologists like Loevinger[108] and Kegan,[109] human beings evolve over the course of their lives from an egocentric level of consciousness to an ethnocentric/tribal, world-centric, or later mindset. At the egocentric level, the individual mindset is focused on the individual's own success and the thinking is either winning or losing. The ethnocentric/tribal mindset is focused on the success of an individual's own group. The world-centric mindset is focused on the healthy development of *all humans* whereby everybody wins. The next evolutionary level of consciousness is the Kosmos-centric mindset, which is focused on the healthy development of all life on Earth and committed to the flourishing of all life everywhere.

What is your perspective, your own world view? What is your own center of gravity? Where do you live most of the time?

Principle 3: Make Transformation Feasible

We are confident that humanity will muster the necessary political will, capital, mind shift, and resources in time to implement the *Smart* scenario outlined in *Transformation is Feasible*.[110] If you look closely at the scientific research presented in that report, it becomes obvious that the implementation of the UN SDGs hinges on the successful return to safe planetary boundaries. As investors, we continue to contribute toward this critical transformation, just as we did with Entelios AG.

The 2011 Fukushima Daiichi nuclear disaster prompted Germany's government to commit to and allocate significant capital toward the energy turnaround (*die Energiewende*). The energy turnaround represents a long-term structural change in energy systems and is a very ambitious plan to shift our reliance on nuclear and fossil fuel energy sources to a reliance on renewables. One major hurdle to moving forward with this is that the existing power grid that supplies our economy was designed to handle continuous energy produced by fossil and nuclear energy sources, rather than renewables, such as wind and solar, which are intermittent in nature. If we are to have a reliable and inexpensive energy supply in the future, we need robust solutions to the problems that are slowing us down. Thus, to provide a software solution to the problem, Tom and some friends started Entelios AG,[111] which became Germany's first demand response aggregator and was eventually sold to global leader EnerNOC, only 4 years after being founded. The climate endowment and our ultra-energy-efficient, sustainable NDC data centers[112] are additional examples of our contribution to making *transformation feasible*.

---

[108]Loevinger (1977).

[109]Kegan (1982).

[110]Randers et al. (2018).

[111]https://www.entelios.de/en/

[112]https://ndc-datacenters.com/

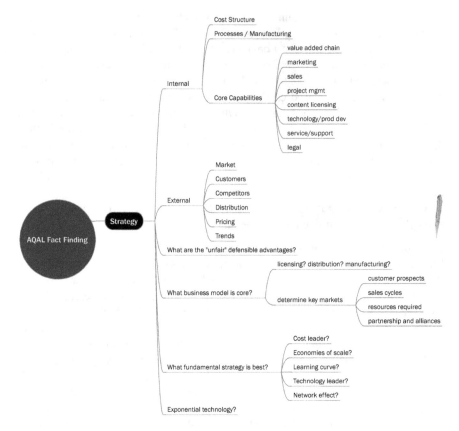

Fig. 3.32 AQAL comparative advantage determination: Strategy selection

What contribution are you making? What contribution *could* you make? We want to hear from you. Join us.

Principle 4: Follow an Investment Strategy
Tom and I are serial entrepreneurs turned investors who continue to build sustainable companies. Drawing on hands-on expertise that has evolved significantly since 1994, we have developed our own investment strategy (Fig. 3.32).

For every action we take and investment we make, we apply in-depth financial, economic, and thorough business know-how. We identify and apply our comparative advantage because we must protect our limited resources from being wasted. We consider financial sustainability to be as important as social and environmental sustainability. This is why we speak about integral sustainability. We have experience; we know what we do and do what we know. We have a stellar track record in investing and company building. We believe that humanity's current challenges also present extraordinary opportunities—which we want to seize for the greater good. We believe in creating abundance through technology by addressing the GGCs and through the implementation of the UN SDGs within planetary boundaries. In an exponentially growing complexity, we use Wilber's AQAL map to simplify complexity in order to better understand and navigate the world. Our collective global challenges can only be addressed collectively and not individually.

What is your core investment strategy? How do you determine your comparative advantage?

Principle 5: Have an Investment Philosophy

When we started our investment and serial-entrepreneurship careers in 1995, we did not have an explicit philosophy for investing. We were excited about life, the future, and the opportunities we saw everywhere around us. We simply wanted to do what we do best and what felt right. We were both sick and tired of corporate life and often disagreed with internal politics and decisions. We also disagreed with the prevailing top-down control and command management styles and did not feel fulfilled in our executive roles. The time had come to move on and do something else. We focused on what would make us happy and started several companies, and the resultant extrinsic markers of success proved us right. Tom and I had been "personal-growth addicts" and "seminar junkies" since our early twenties, and we wanted to continue our path toward *self-actualization*. But this time, we wanted to include our *interior growth* in the process of *exterior growth* through company building and investing. Our exterior investment activities also had to be a direct reflection of our interior, vertical growth, our heart and soul. We wanted to self-actualize through the integration of all our activities, not just the financial, business, or philanthropic ones, but also our consciousness evolution. We called it consciousness leadership. In our investment and company-building activities, we wanted to use technology to fix the existing social and environmental damage and prevent more from happening, and we saw investing in integrally sustainable businesses as a unique vehicle to pursue that goal. Thus, we began investing in and building businesses that were sustainable in all ways: financially, socially, ethically, environmentally, and also in terms of team development and vertical growth.

We believe that the term *work-life balance* is a misnomer in twenty-first-century advanced societies. We are integral human beings, and we believe that we cannot really separate our work from our lives without serious consequences. In our experience, that is a recipe for unhappiness. Thus, we searched for a philosophy that would allow us to integrate all aspects of life and facilitate our individual evolution toward later stages of human development as well as higher stages of consciousness. Lo and behold, during one of the seminars we attended with Tony Robbins, he introduced us to Integral Theory, AQAL, and the work of philosopher Ken Wilber. Our search was over (Fig. 3.33).

We had found our investment philosophy, a *theory of everything*, an integration vehicle for all our endeavors. Rooted in evolution, it helps us integrate *all* of reality—the exterior as well as interior dimensions—in our investment decisions. It is a map that helps us simplify and navigate the complexity of reality while maintaining multiple world views and honoring the evolution of human consciousness from premodern to modern, postmodern, and post-postmodern structures of consciousness.

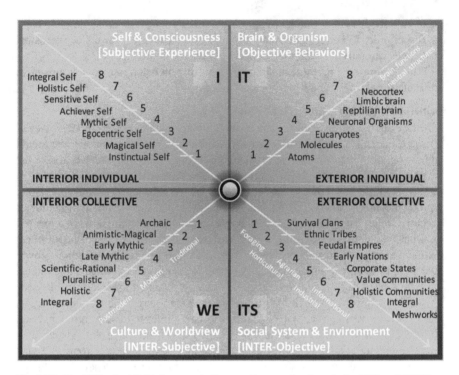

Fig. 3.33 Ken Wilber's AQAL framework (Source: Own graph adapted after Wilber (2000b))

Have you found your investment theory? Does it align with your values and represent all aspects of your lived reality?

Principle 6: Have a Proven Investment Framework

After identifying an investment philosophy, we developed our own investment framework, which we call Integral Investing. This framework both includes and transcends traditional investing, traditional philanthropy, and impact investing alongside their theories, measurements, processes, and practice (Fig. 3.34).

We believe that the Integral Investing framework can provide the next evolutionary step for the future of investing because it provides a meta-theory and practice of investing based on consciousness evolution. It has worked well for us. Our track record speaks for itself.

What is your investment framework? What is your theory of change? What is your logic model? How do you map your theory of change in order to understand the impact of your investments? What is your focus/differentiation? What is your additionality? How is investing serving your own personal growth? How is investing serving the greater good?

Principle 7: Communicate Your Ideals Efficiently

We believe that doing good *and* doing well are not contradictory aims but rather reflections of an indispensable mindset that ensures the future of life and wellbeing in short, integral sustainability. We summarize and communicate this conviction

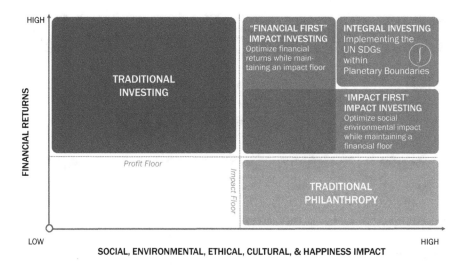

Fig. 3.34 Integral investing as the next paradigm in investing

through our motto, the 6Ps: The *Parity of People, Planet, Prosperity*, all of which we integrate with our own *Passion* for life and in line with our ultimate life's *Purpose*. We believe that *equality*, the parity of all five other Ps, is key to successfully leveraging the power of investing to ensure the future of life. We view ourselves as the custodians not only of financial capital but also, indirectly, of natural and human capital. That includes recognizing interior values such as purpose, joy, and happiness.

Do you have a motto for your investment activities? What is it? Psychologist Paul Watzlawik stated, "You cannot not communicate."[113] How do you communicate your investment thesis? Is it sticky? Is it fun?

Principle 8: Be Smart About De-risking
We de-risk our investment using the proprietary Theta Model that we have developed, refined, and successfully applied since 1995.

The Theta Model
The Theta Model is the due diligence process that applies the tools and methodologies of Integral Investing to de-risk investments with the intention of building integrally sustainable companies from the very beginning.

It is represented in Fig. 3.35 and is described in more detail in Sect. 3.2.4.

De-risking begins with the screening of the investment opportunity. However, once we have issued a term sheet, we begin the due diligence process with in-depth de-risking as described above. Figure 3.36 shows a summary of the risk considerations for each AQAL quadrant.

---

[113]http://scihi.org/communication-paul-watzlawick/

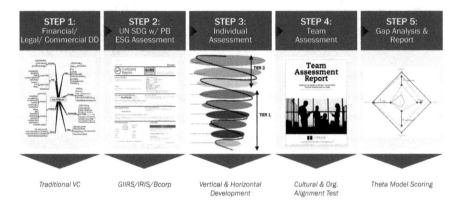

Fig. 3.35 Smart de-risking with the theta model

RISK FACTORS	DESCRIPTION
Financial and legal risks (LR quadrant)	Risks may occur through • Timing (typical early stage/VC risks) • Capital (hybrid sources of capital with different return requirements), currency risks • Technology, market/country risk (political), competition, operational risks, exit risk • Legal, regulatory (incl. political), transference/change of ownership through growth • Combined risk and combined returns, unquantifiable risk
UN SDG within PB Risk (LR quadrant)	The risk criteria include • Lack of standardized criteria for measurement and reporting • Mission drift, reputation loss through failure to meet the impact mission, or • Failure to balance UN SDG in PB/Impact criteria with profit-only criteria, moral hazards
Team Risk/ Corporate Culture (LL quadrant)	Research shows that 80% of the risk is associated with dysfunctional teams including: • Absence of trust • Fear of conflict • Lack of commitment • Avoidance of accountability • Inattention to results
Individual Risk (UL & UR quadrant)	Key people risk associated with personal profiles, levels of consciousness including • Collaborative capacity • Contextual thinking • Handling cognitive complexity and coherence • Developmental risk (perspective-taking, -seeking, -coordination) • Decision-making process and abilities

Fig. 3.36 Risk factors by AQAL quadrants in early-stage investing

How do you de-risk your own investments? What tools do you use to de-risk teams and individual investees? Do you have your own de-risking model?

Principle 9: Invest in the Advancement of Scientifically Proven Technology
During the 2017 Upfront Summit, American investor and entrepreneur Mark Cuban insisted on the role of exponential technologies for our future by stating "Artificial Intelligence, deep learning, machine learning—whatever you're doing if you don't understand it—learn it. Because otherwise you're going to be a dinosaur within 3 years."[114] We could not agree more and this is why we invest

---

[114] min. 9:55 https://www.youtube.com/watch?v=RtZ_H_aSTCI

in scientifically proven solutions to real-world problems. We do not invest in "shoulds," "nice to haves," or "solutions looking for a problem." Instead, we invest in real-world assets (*Realwirtschaft*) and scientifically proven ideas. Moreover, we invest in highly qualified and integrally acting people who advance technology in the service of humanity. We believe in the ingenuity of the human mind to solve critical problems, even if it takes time. And we believe in the evolutionary process that brought the universe and humanity to where we are today, which, as discussed in Chap. 2, humans initially thought was linear and local. As we conquered space and the moon, humanity began thinking and acting globally, supported by exponentially growing technologies. And as more and more of us Awaken to the global impact of human activity, smart *and* wise actions are required. Tom and I are exponential thinkers, yet we act locally for the greater good. We believe that thinking exponentially and globally is crucial for empowering ourselves to address the current existential threats.

As discussed in Chap. 1, exponential growth is rather difficult to comprehend, but we cannot afford to not comprehend it. Our very survival depends on it—the COVID-19 crisis has proven it to us. Another, much more complex example is the rise of sea levels. These levels have risen an average 3.31 mm/year between 1993 and 2017 due to thermal expansion, ocean warming, and melting of the glaciers in Greenland and Antarctica, which trap about 64 meters of sea-level rise.[115] A closer look at satellite data reveals that we are actually dealing with a doubling of the rise in sea levels: from 1.5 mm/year in 1993 to 3.2 mm/year in 2005 and 5 mm/year 2017. This is exponential growth. This means that sea levels could continue to rise by a couple of meters by the end of this century alone even if we stop the emission of greenhouse gasses right away. Bio-hacking and unsafe AI hacking (see Chap. 1) are another example of problems we must address before it is too late. These two examples may seem superficially divorced from each other, but as integral investors, we must leverage scientific proof and technical advancement to address each of them. But those advancements must be safe and beneficial and support the future of life. In short: We must invest in caring cultures and societies.

How do you use scientific proof in your investments? How important are, for example, patented technologies to you? Are you a signatory to the Asilomar AI Principles? How do you protect your privacy, freedom, and your human rights from the unmitigated invasion through unsafe AIs?

Principle 10: Act Boldly Now
We are arguably living through some of the most exciting times in human history, and Tom and I believe that we are very privileged to be alive in this day and age. Conversely, we have never previously faced such pressing challenges. To preserve what we, humanity, have, we must act now. As a species, we have never before faced such necessity or obligation. As investors and company builders, we act boldly now because we feel deeply responsible for the integral impact of our portfolio companies. Therefore, we intend to build integrally sustainable companies that fulfill our MTP from the very beginning and are in line with our moonshot (Fig. 3.37).

---

[115]See https://cnes.fr/fr/climat-laltimetrie-spatiale-scrute-la-montee-des-eaux

- Our actions are meaningful and valuable
- We are authentic, grounded, and realistic
- We interact with integrity, openness, respect, and trust
- We express our joyful passion and inspiration, from the heart with love
- We catalyse growth and progress: Leveraging technology is our main instrument toward significant impact
- We serve as a lighthouse for our industry: We integrate meaningful real economy with sustainable finance by including proven structures and by transcending them into a new paradigm of investing and company building

Fig. 3.37 Our guiding light

Our Integral Investing framework, together with the Theta Model as a de-risking process, helps us act now so we:

- Ensure the future of life on our beautiful blue planet.
- Make the *transformation feasible* by implementing the UN SDGs within planetary boundaries.
- Implement innovative business ideas that solve real-world problems.
- Provide solutions in specific sectors that reflect our expertise, including exponential technologies, climate change, health, wellbeing, lifestyle, cultural innovation, and megatrends.
- Have the ability to massively scale into a worldwide marketplace with a positive impact.
- Attract dedicated, resilient, and integrally acting partners, players, company builders, and management teams.
- Ensure high morals and ethics for the greater good.
- Help create corporate cultures and societies based on higher values and later stages of consciousness.
- Support the development of integrated taxonomies as well as transparent measurement criteria, and integrated reporting.
- Have fun, experience joy, and can self-actualize through our activities.

How do you *act boldly now*? What is your guiding light? What emboldens you to act?

Principle 11: Never, Never, Never Give In

During a 20-minute speech at Harrow School on October 29, 1941, Churchill encouraged his audience to "never give in. Never give in. Never, never, never, never—in nothing great or small, large or petty—never give in, except to convictions of honor and good sense. Never yield to force. Never yield to the apparently overwhelming might of the enemy."[116] The particular enemy Churchill was referring to was Nazi Germany, but Tom and I think his advice applies in general to a life well lived. This is why we have adopted and followed it even when our circumstances were less than ideal. We imagined, believed in our vision, and persevered.

Relatively early in our careers, we worked closely with Larry Ellison, Oracle's founder and a great visionary whose dream was to ultimately sell all Oracle's products via the Internet. Today this is normal; back then it was just a vision. Oracle's German managing director at the time did not share Larry's vision. He not only lacked an understanding of the importance of the Internet for the future of humanity, he also was afraid of cannibalizing his current business. He was not willing to disrupt his own business to make room for the future and did not see that the Internet was inevitable. (This attitude can be seen in many of today's traditional industries, such as the automotive industry, which is transforming too slowly from internal combustion engines to hydrogen or battery-driven ones.) As I had already experienced first-hand the impact of this kind of lack of vision and flexibility with a previous employer, I knew that I had to follow my convictions, my beliefs, my intuition, and my dreams. They pushed me over the edge and were ultimately pivotal in my decision to become an entrepreneur myself. I could never give in, and thus I dived into the Internet wave into which humanity as a whole was eventually catapulted in the twenty-first-century exponential tech era.

Tom and I are convinced that now more than ever, we must believe in our vision, imagine the future, and disrupt ourselves before circumstances or other people do it for us. We can do that by imagining new technologies and how they will create new jobs. In the mid-1990s, few people could have imagined the new jobs that have been created by the Internet—becoming a web designer or an Internet entrepreneur by selling programming skills, books, software, clothing, furniture, etc. over the Internet—the new ways of working created by the Internet—video conferencing with colleagues on the other side of the world or working from home while maintaining contact with clients and colleagues working either from home or in a brick-and-mortar office—or the prevalence and social impact, both negative and positive, of social media, which can both harm and enhance lives. This was all previously possible only in science fiction movies. In a similar way, Tom and I feel a responsibility to continue to imagine, create, and invest in new companies that contribute to addressing our global grand challenges. During a commencement speech at Princeton University in 2010, Amazon founder Jeff Bezos asked his audience if they would follow their passion after graduation or if they would let inertia be their

---

[116]https://www.youtube.com/watch?v=L90BCEVH41U

guide through life.[117] He wanted to know what kind of life they planned to choose. Will it be a life of ease or a life of service and adventure, he asked? Will they guard their hearts against rejection, or will they continue to fall in love no matter what, he inquired? Will they be kind, relentless, and the architects of their own future, or will they play it safe, give up, and be cynical, he wanted to know.

What do you believe in? How do you imagine your future and that of humanity? What will you never give up? What will you never surrender to protect your convictions about "honor and good sense"?

Principle 12: Provide Certainty Where There Is Doubt

As humanity's elites are riding the waves of exponentially growing technologies that are transforming human life as we know it, it is easy to worry about the future. Predicting the future is essentially impossible because there are so many unknowns. The ascent of more oligopolistic market structures could potentially replace the current more liberal economic world order and lead to rising inequality, higher unemployment, and labor displacement at large scale. The truth is, we do not know what will happen or how it will happen. We cannot know. Forecasting the future of work, for example, would be like asking a Neanderthal to predict the profession of a pilot or website developer. And yet, there is so much we can do based on the knowledge and intuitions we already have. As investors and company builders, we are in a position to ease the way into the future by creating not only new technologies and better solutions to global problems but also more employment and new jobs. Research performed for the Obama administration identified four job categories that could be positively influenced by the growth of AI technologies, for example.[118] They include areas where people could:

- Actively *engage* with existing AI technologies to undertake tasks such as cancer detection, communication, and therapy;
- Have the opportunity to *develop* new AI technologies, including training AI systems to conduct liberal arts, social sciences, and ethical evaluations, to name only a few;
- *Supervise* AI technologies at work, including for quality control, evaluations, avoiding AI divergence from original tasks, and resolving competing priorities; or
- *Facilitate* societal shifts that accompany new AI technologies in response to evolving paradigm shifts, including, for example, dramatic shifts in the design of infrastructure and traffic laws.

In all four categories, humans could perform tasks in areas where we are much better than AI systems. As exponential investors and company builders, we invest in entrepreneurs who can solve real-world problems and bring their ideas to life by experimenting, reinventing, and disrupting themselves. Such exponential

---

[117]https://www.youtube.com/watch?v=vBmavNoChZc

[118]https://obamawhitehouse.archives.gov/sites/whitehouse.gov/files/documents/Artificial-Intelligence-Automation-Economy.PDF

entrepreneurs understand the importance of quick action, rapid iteration, and constant experimentation to come up with breakthrough solutions to formerly impenetrable challenges. They push tirelessly to reinvent and disrupt themselves, focusing on the future and leveraging the exponentially growing technologies in the interest of achieving even greater goals.

This is how we try to provide certainty where there is doubt and hope where there is despair. We are mindful optimists, use scientific research, leverage exponential technologies, empower exponential entrepreneurs, and apply our lifelong investment and company-building expertise to show the path to a sustainable and abundance-filled future for us all. We put our money where our collective mouth is. You too have the ability to materialize your dreams.

How do you offer hope where there is only despair? How do you point a way forward?

Principle 13: Recognize the Critical Role of Capital in Transformation
Henry Ford is known for his ambition "to employ still more men, to spread the benefits of this industrial system to the greatest possible number, to help them build up their lives and their homes. To do this we are putting the greatest share of our profits back in the business." His socially oriented attitude was not universally endorsed by his shareholders, least of all the Dodge brothers. They won a suit they brought against him when in 1919 the Michigan Supreme court upheld the order of the lower court that an extra dividend of US$19.3 million be paid to Ford's shareholders. This court decision is often cited in "support for the idea that corporate law requires boards of directors to maximize shareholder wealth." One hundred years later, profit remains the main driver and generally sole measure of success of an organization. But times are changing—and so is our collective mindset, as we saw in Chap. 2.

We believe in the critical role of traditional capital to address the GGCs. However, to achieve that, we work hard at extending our understanding and definition of capital, which is reflected in our Integral Investing framework. Our notion of capital transcends financial capital and includes natural capital, human capital, and social and cultural capital, but also, for example, cognitive, emotional, and psycho-spiritual capital. For example, Sean Esbjörn-Hargens's current research and MetaImpact Framework foresees four types of impact, ten types of capital, three types of data, and four bottom lines all of which could help advance this field in the future.[119]

What is your understanding of capital? How do you apply it to serve yourself and others?

Principle 14: Invest in People, Not Ideas
Bill Joy, co-founder of SUN Microsystems, is attributed with saying "No matter who you are, most of the smartest people work for someone else." This is why attracting brilliant people is critical for anyone starting a successful company. The team is key, and it is one of the main features of our Integral Investing framework (Fig. 3.11).

---

[119]Esbjörn-Hargens (2018); See https://www.metaintegral.com/

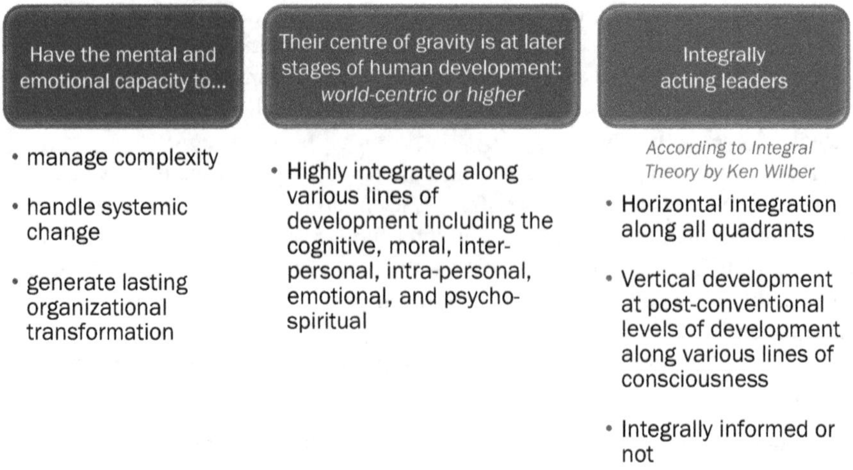

Have the mental and emotional capacity to...	Their centre of gravity is at later stages of human development: *world-centric or higher*	Integrally acting leaders

- manage complexity

- handle systemic change

- generate lasting organizational transformation

- Highly integrated along various lines of development including the cognitive, moral, inter-personal, intra-personal, emotional, and psycho-spiritual

According to Integral Theory by Ken Wilber

- Horizontal integration along all quadrants

- Vertical development at post-conventional levels of development along various lines of consciousness

- Integrally informed or not

Fig. 3.38 Consciousness leaders'/investee's characteristics

Netflix is a good example of an integrally acting organization whose core philosophy supports a culture that values "people over process" and honors "integrity, excellence, respect, inclusivity, and collaboration." They built a culture that encourages "independent decision-making by employees, [who] share information openly, broadly, and deliberately, are extraordinarily candid with each other, keep only our highly effective people, [and] avoid rules.[120] Netflix's philosophy was inspired by Antoine de Saint-Exupéry's *The Little Prince*, in which we are told that someone who wants to build a ship should inspire a longing for the sea in people instead of giving them orders to gather materials and get to work (Fig. 3.38).

In a similar way, Tom encourages our teams "not to tell the time, but to build the clock." He learned that from his professor Jim Collins when he took Jim's class on entrepreneurship at Stanford Business School in 1992/93.[121]

To do that, we invest compassionately and primarily in people, not in ideas. Our experience has reinforced the old adage that "ideas are a dime a dozen" and taught us that 80% of the risk in any endeavor lies with the people involved. Therefore, we invest first and foremost in people because good people can always implement a good idea whose time has come. We identify them using our Theta Model and the tools described in Chap. 2.

How do you define a good team member? How do you find the right people? More importantly, how do you develop a good team member? What about a good team?

---

[120]https://jobs.netflix.com/culture

[121]https://www.jimcollins.com/concepts/clock-building-not-time-telling.html

Principle 15: Build Integrally Sustainable Organizations

The World Economic Forum runs a poll where people can post a video to express their own perspective on some of the most pressing questions associated with current global grand challenges.[122] Some of the questions posted to date are: How do we save the planet without killing economic growth? How do we make sure technology makes life better not worse? Can you be a patriot and a global citizen? How do we create fairer economies?

The suggestions and solutions offered by people like Jacinda Ardern, prime minister of New Zealand; Christine Lagarde, managing director of the International Monetary Fund; and naturalist Sir Richard Attenborough are as diverse as the individuals themselves. As you watch the videos, it soon becomes obvious that the determination, solutions, and resources are available to bring about the necessary change at systemic levels, whether they involve continued growth while addressing inequality, safe AI, or ensuring the future of work. In *A Finer Future*, Lovins et al. show how "an economy in service of life" can be created to enhance human wellbeing and transform our systems—running the gamut from agriculture to transportation to finance—through a circular and regenerative economy, enlightened entrepreneurialism, innovative policy, and, of course, technology.[123]

As investors and company builders, we focus less on macro-economics and top-down systemic change and more on the micro-cosmos of economics. We experiment with and build the progressive types of organizations that get the results Lovins et al. refer to. We build teal-type organizational structures and cultures that use exponentially growing technologies, Ismail et al.'s ExOs, with the intention of making the transformation required to address the GGCs feasible (Fig. 3.39).

Can you imagine what would occur if every start-up or regular company decided to measure their success not only by their financial bottom line but also by a multiple bottom line (for example, the 6Ps) to implement the UN SDGs within planetary boundaries by 2050?

We build integrally sustainable organizations from the very beginning by making sure that the UN SDGs are applied within planetary boundaries to ensure the future of life and wellbeing. We focus on building integrally sustainable companies that are led by integrally informed management teams. We believe that trust and wisdom are foundational to ensuring the future of life. We build integrally sustainable structures, systems, practices, and processes, as well as cultures of trust and wisdom in our investees' and our own organizations.

How do you ensure sustainable abundance creation through your investments? What type of structures, processes, and practices do you build in the organizations in which you invest? What kind of corporate culture do you support? How do you measure success and how do you ensure organizations stay on track?

---

[122]https://www.weforum.org/globalization4/
[123]Lovins (2018).

- We build integrally sustainable companies that have an MTP and make sure the *Transformation is Feasible*

- We measure success through the implementation of UN SDGs within Planetary Boundaries

- We develop and lead the Integral Investing market to ensure the *Future of Life*

- We invest in high-potential companies

- We redirect capital flows into meaningful and valuable endeavors

- We build integrally sustainable organizational structures, systems, practices and processes, as well as cultures of trust (i.e. Teal Organizations, Exponential Organizations)

Fig. 3.39 Building integrally sustainable organizations

Principle 16: Take Pride in Long-Term Investments

The Dutch Golden Age spans roughly the entire seventeenth century, when the Netherlands became one of the most prosperous nations in Europe, if not the most prosperous, after gaining independence from Philip II of Spain. Increased trade development during this time was accompanied by the development of a portrait culture, as wealthy merchants began commissioning painting jobs to painters who had previously struggled to find work. It is estimated that during the Golden Age, between 750,000 and 1,100,000 portraits were painted, with Rembrandt being one of the more famous artists of the time.[124] The culture of portrait painting was eventually disrupted by photography in the early nineteenth century.[125] That in itself rendered many painters jobless, but without the technological advancement of photography, there would be no Van Gogh, no Impressionists, no Picasso, no Expressionists, no modern painters, I dare say. It took a long time, but once photography was producing more accurate representations of reality, painters found themselves surplus to requirement—unless they could transform what they did and how they did it. Art lovers who were open and progressive recognized this change in direction, and those who had the confidence and foresight to purchase a Picasso, for example, in the early days, ultimately made a fortune. In a similar way, we recognize today where the trends are going and invest long term (Fig. 3.40).

In their January 2019 Huffington Post article, "This Could Be the Biggest Scandal of the Climate Change Era," Sandrine Dixon-Declève and Anders Wijkman request

---

[124]Ekkart and Buvelot (Eds.) (2007, p. 228).

[125]https://en.wikipedia.org/wiki/Nic%C3%A9phore_Ni%C3%A9pce

- We invest in high-potential companies
- We build integrally sustainable companies to have a positive impact on people, planet, and profit with passion and purpose
- We develop and lead the Integral Investing market to ensure the future of humanity on Earth
- We redirect capital flows into meaningful and valuable endeavors

Fig. 3.40 In what we invest

that investments be made in order to transform energy systems and "stop excessive waste by promoting reuse, recycling and reconditioning of products and materials, and [to] scale up ways to use land to absorb rather than emit carbon dioxide."[126] Their investment recommendations favor, for example:

- Tripling investments in large-scale reforestation in developing countries
- Incentivizing farmers to sequester carbon in their lands
- Encouraging research, development, and innovation of low-carbon solutions
- Promoting broad-based collaborations between industrial sectors, local and national governments, and investors
- Advocating disruptive technologies that provide solutions "for sectors where emissions are most difficult to eliminate, such as agriculture, aviation, shipping, aluminum, steel and cement"
- Building new infrastructure, retrofitting buildings, and decarbonizing energy grids

This call for investment opportunities is very much in line with programs being invoked by progressive community leaders. By July 29, 2019, for example, more than half of local authorities in the UK had declared a climate emergency.[127] In their investment plans, they state that they intend to:

- Retrofit buildings to make them more energy efficient
- Decarbonize the power grid
- Introduce low-carbon heating
- Electrify transportation

---

[126]Dixon-Declève and Wijkman (2019).

[127]https://tinyurl.com/y4mnfyqu

- Address excessive waste and encourage recycling and overhauling of products and materials
- Use land for carbon sequestration

Needless to say, such investments provide extraordinary business opportunities. According to research by PricewaterhouseCoopers[128] and the Business and Sustainable Development Commission,[129] the implementation of the UN SDGs "opens up US$12 trillion of market opportunities in the four economic systems ... [including] food and agriculture, cities, energy and materials, and health and wellbeing."[130] These industries represent about 60% of the real economy, but in order to make the transition feasible, they would have to implement the UN SDGs within planetary boundaries.

As integral investors acting in the exponential era, we try to unlearn the old; keep an open, beginner's mind; expect big surprises; and put ourselves in a position in which we can identify and harvest the world's best ideas to help us make the transformation feasible. Within this process, we invest long term and look mainly for ideas that:

- Are small but exponentially impactful in an integrally sustainable way
- Have the potential to accelerate change in a significant manner
- Are innovative
- Are disruptive and push institutions and systems to change significantly for the good of all
- Can blend with others to deliver massively compounded solutions that can be distributed in a sophisticated manner
- Have the potential to be applied in new ecosystems as a catalyst for reinventing new institutions such as education, infrastructure, banking, finance, government, healthcare, and other key organizations, etc.

We take pride in making long term, meaningful investments that generate abundance for all and ensure the future of work and the future of life.

What types of investments make you proud? In what do you invest long term?

Principle 17: You Can Only Achieve What You Measure
To fulfill our self-imposed Integral Investing mandate, we measure the activities *and* outcomes of our investments on an ongoing basis. We provide sustainable integration between traditional investing criteria that ensure financial sustainability and impact investing measurements. We have adopted the impact investing definition employed by the Global Impact Investing Network (GIIN): "Impact investments are investments made into companies, organizations, and funds with the intention to

---

[128]See https://tinyurl.com/y2xrk2kz

[129]See https://tinyurl.com/y5jpffxa

[130]See https://tinyurl.com/y5jpffxa

generate measurable social and environmental impact alongside a financial return."[131] They can be made in both emerging and developed markets.

Tom and I use existing measurement criteria and also develop our own metrics as needed. Very early on we began to integrate rigorous financial and legal due diligence criteria with social, environmental, governmental (ESG criteria of the UN PRI) criteria, in addition to cultural, behavioral, ethical, and psychological factors. When the UN SDGs were launched in 2015, we added those too; and following the *Transformation is Feasible* report to the Club of Rome in October 2018, we started focusing on the implementation of its *Smart* scenario. Implementing the UN SDGs within planetary boundaries makes sense on many levels. But finding the best way to measure integral impact is hard work,[132] especially while building integrally sustainable companies that are successful and thrive on a global scale. The current work of the European Commission on sustainable EU policies is a step in the right direction. But it is only a step. We need to move fast and begin to eliminate the current linear, slow response to the exponential threats coming from climate change and exponentially growing technologies including unsafe artificial intelligences.

As we looked more closely at the world through an integral lens, we realized we need multiple bottom-line measurement criteria. What exactly does that mean, you may be asking yourself.

Not too long ago, I spoke at a women investors' conference in San Francisco about measuring and de-risking early-stage investments. The speaker before me had talked about the weak overall performance of angel investing and venture capital in general. She gave a good overview of her own expertise, offered a few tips on the due diligence process, and ended by saying, "I hope you are not scared" while projecting a final slide portraying a frightened-looking comic figure. The audience, made up of mostly novice investors, was very attentive and took lots of notes, but the panic in their eyes was obvious. When I took the stage, I felt compelled to ask the audience: "What if today was the last day of your life? What would you rather do: continue to sit here, or do something radically different from this?" Immediately, the room fell silent. After a short pause, I said, "If you are still sitting here, then I assume that you are living a life of purpose and there is no other place that you would rather be than here. If not, get up and go do what fulfills you, because it is very likely that you will not find your fulfillment here in this context." My own radical departure from traditional investing started with a call for answers to essential questions that are key to measuring success from an Integral Investing perspective. Why? Because these are the hidden determinants for success and they must be brought into the open as early as possible: the *interior* factors, both individual and cultural, are the most important driving forces you will encounter (see Chap. 2) (Fig. 3.41).

---

[131] https://thegiin.org/impact-investing/
[132] So and Staskevicius (2015).

		Traditional Investing	Integral Investing
1	Investment model/ thesis / intention:	Implicit – financial ROI/ algorithm	Explicit – consciousness evolution / integral theory / holon
2	Investor's role:	Refine input into output	Growth enabler/ consciousness leader/ "Spiral wizard"
3	Core measurements:	Financial ROI / IRR	Integral metrics: 6Ps i.e. UN SDG's within PB
4	Selection process:	Unilateral/ mechanistic/ sequential	Interactive / iterative/ dynamic steering
5	Investor/ investee dynamics:	Investor analyses investee	Joint development/Self-actualization growth process/meshwork

Fig. 3.41 Aspects of the paradigm change between traditional investing and Integral Investing

In our view, success is first and foremost an inside job—the only legally acceptable form of insider trading, if you like. Nobody but you can decide whether you are successful or not.

Due diligence in investing starts with *inner due diligence*, which for us is expressed via three questions: (1) Am I having fun with what I am doing? (2) Am I making a difference through my work? (3) Am I creating abundance for all, or am I just making money, which I can neither eat nor drink?

Principle 18: You Cannot Not Invest

As we saw in Chap. 1, daily life appears more complex every day, despite the conveniences of modernity. Between exponentially growing technologies, political polarization, overpopulation, refugee crises, and the climate crisis, we are constantly faced with the need to balance our time between making a living and ensuring we have a life worth living. It can all seem overwhelming, even impossible, and it is easy to fall into the negativity trap set by mass media reports about instability, disasters, and uncertainties, all designed with advertising revenues in mind. Negative news seems to sell better than positive, which makes sense if you are familiar with the concept of negativity bias,[133] and so negative stories form the bulk of daily broadcasts and drive apocalyptic deliberations. Rather ironically, negativity bias evolved as a survival mechanism.[134] In modern times, though, it can lead to psychological disempowerment, fear of the future, hopelessness, aggression, political and economic powerlessness, and eventually assault on democracy. But if we

---

[133]See, for example, Kahneman and Tversky (1982).

[134]Kolb and Whishaw (2003, pp. 238–239, pp. 532).

consciously decide to look at and honor reality, we can circumvent negativity bias and apply a more constructive lens.

After our first IPO, Tom and I, who were in our late thirties at the time, began asking ourselves what we should do with the rest of our lives and we should use the gifts that were bestowed upon us to serve humanity? We decided that the sky was the limit in terms of what we could do, and we knew that we had to make different choices about how to live from then on. We had worked so hard to get to where we were, and changing our old habits was no easy task. Up until that point, we had been driven by a need to make money; now we also wanted to start making a difference. We could no longer compartmentalize our lives into working hard during the week and donating money, outsourcing our philanthropy, at fundraising events on evenings and weekends. But how could we rationalize our dual existence? Remember Watzlawick's assertion that "you cannot not communicate"? Drawing on this, Tom recognized that "you cannot not invest." Investing is very personal: It all starts with the individual. Subsequently, Tom and I believe that everybody is an investor because we all influence the economy through our purchases, votes, work, commitments, knowledge, preferences, love, and caring, etc. Consequently, the market has no intentions—only people do. We are the market. The free market does not really direct or control everything. Concepts and systems like investing, finance, trade, economics, politics, or money have no raison d'être or intrinsic value in and of themselves. They have been created by people for people. They reflect the zeitgeist and what people treasure. And what people treasure changes continuously.

We believe that the GGCs are the result of outdated systems created by outdated mindsets. We believe these systems no longer serve humanity and that Earth needs us to have world-centric mindsets. Because "you cannot not invest," join us and let us together lead the way in creating new investment and business systems that reflect the new zeitgeist. Like Peter Diamandis, we believe that the best way to make a billion dollars is to positively impact "a billion people."[135] Our means to impact a billion people is to pave the way toward integrally sustainable investment and business systems that ensure the future of life and wellbeing for all.

How consciously do you invest to ensure the future of your children, their children, and humanity as a whole?

Principle 19: With Privilege Comes Responsibility
On World Water Day in March 2017, Tom and I participated in the Watershed Conference. It was jointly organized by the Vatican's Pontifical Council for Culture and the international Club of Rome. An audience with Pope Francis was included. Watershed was a global dialog inspired by the Pope in order to secure fresh water for future generations at a time when diminishing safe water supplies threaten economic development, political stability, and public health due to high demand from agriculture, industry, and expanding cities. We all gathered around 6:30 in the morning at one of the main towers of the Vatican and were ushered into the Piazza San Marco,

---

[135]Diamandis (2018); https://tinyurl.com/ya7kbeq5

where we were assigned seats close to the Papal chair. When the popemobile appeared in the piazza, people became very excited. The Pope motioned the driver to stop and stepped out of the vehicle, walking toward a bunch of kids who greeted him very enthusiastically. Pope Francis invited about eight of them into his white popemobile, and the convoy moved on, the people inside the vehicles waving while the crowd continued cheering. Then the Pope stopped again, this time in front of two rows of people in wheelchairs, whom the Pope blessed individually. And so on. Later we learned that much to the horror of his security guards, Pope Francis values connecting with and blessing people more than he worries about the safety of his own life. Why? Because the values that he stands for never die; they only increase. Pope Francis keeps an open heart and an open mind because he knows that his values are as old as humanity and cannot and will not end with his own life. Through our actions, we hope to contribute toward the evolution of consciousness. We believe that higher ethics and morals pave the way for us to do this.

We are part of the post-postmodern generation that seeks to ensure the future of life and to integrate financial sustainability with the ideals of the so-called Cultural Creatives of the late 1960s. The integration of sound financial, economic, environmental, governance criteria with geopolitical sustainability for the benefit of all has thus become a must. But at the dawn of artificial intelligence, we must not lose sight of the need to safeguard our privacy. At a recent conference in Silicon Valley, I heard Peter Diamandis say that "privacy is gone." I reject that and I will fight to protect my human right to privacy until my dying day. Having grown up in communist Romania where "the walls had ears," I struggle greatly with the prospect of my life being laid bare to Alexa, Siri, and their siblings. People must earn the right to be privy to my innermost life. As we saw in Chap. 2 there are various stages of evolution and levels of consciousness. Yet, it appears that any cognitively smart AI programmer can begin to develop AI systems without any due diligence checks on their levels of consciousness or moral and ethical understanding. We must take charge to ensure that a Gandhi, not a Hitler, takes the decisions about humanity's future. Elon Musk has repeatedly stated his worries about the dangers and implications of climate change, a potential third world war that could alienate human civilization, and the negative impact of AI, which he, an intimate insider, considers more dangerous than "nuclear warheads."[136]

I could not agree more, because I know what it means to live in fear. As an emigrant who was born and raised in communist Romania under Ceausescu's dictatorship, I am amazed to be living in a society now where people willingly subject themselves to constant surveillance. Users have allowed Siris and Alexas to listen in through their smartphones and other devices. We have given them the right to listen to our lives. We have agreed to give them our data in exchange for some service we want. Many of us recognized that the only way to improve the technology was to expose it to more and more human conversation. But what we did not know, certainly in the early days, was that not only are they really listening in, but they are

---

[136]https://www.reuters.com/video/watch/idNJw?now=true, min 0:42.

also using our information without our permission. And even now that we do know more about what is going on behind the scenes in terms of surveillance, we are still blithely using the technology.[137]

AI truly has the potential to create an Orwellian system, and we should be very discerning about how we use it. The vast amounts of personal data currently being generated by new medical technology are already challenging the way we think about privacy and data sharing. I demand to be asked whether or not I want to share my data with anyone—or anything. Moreover, if we do decide to share our data with some company or individual, we should be paid for it, because they use it to make money and we should share in that abundance. High ethics and morals take on an unprecedented level of importance if we want to achieve a proper balance between maximizing the potential of these technologies and safeguarding against the privacy and security risks that come with them.

I truly believe that we are living during some of the most miraculous times in human history, but, as we all know, it is not without its challenges. Our biggest task, therefore, is to avoid sliding into contentment and to get involved in co-creating an ethically and morally sound global society in which we all want to live.

What is the biggest global problem that you want to solve, change, and bring an end to because you can? What do you value? How do your investments reflect and support those values? How do you use your talent, resources, and technology to solve the problems that inspire you and give your life a purpose? How do you ensure the highest possible standards of ethics and morals?

Principle 20: Self-Actualize Through Investing
Tom and I have lived in Silicon Valley on and off for more than 30 years since 1984. We began our investment activities with the launch of Mosaic in 1993, with BayNet World becoming our first investment and start-up activity in Silicon Valley. With its multiple of 240× and its IRR of 8% over 25 years until its final exit in 2019, for many reasons BayNet World did not become what it could have, a tremendous dot. com success. It taught us a lot. BayNet World started our investment career in exponential technology. It was a wonderful launchpad for a life well lived in line with our talents and preferences. Today we look at investing not as a profession but as a way of life. We intentionally seek the good in everything. We try to live an integrally informed life guided by an integral life practice (see Chap. 2).

Over the years, we realized, and learned "on the job," that investing is a tricky trade; if done properly and professionally, it can be life-changing and extremely rewarding not only financially, but also in terms of personal growth. Investing and company building can be a wonderful platform for self-actualization, as it has become for us. We love exponential technology and we love to invest in the frontiers of innovation. Investing is a path toward self-actualization, and we seek short-term flow and long-term meaning through our investment activities. This is why we do what we do. We believe that there is always a solution to a problem when you are

---

[137]https://tinyurl.com/y687h4fx

committed to a positive outcome, even if it takes time. The question is how much you want to contribute. Imagine you are 80 years old and reflecting back on your life. What kind of life will you have lived? In the end, we are the sum of our choices. We decided to follow the advice of our dear friend Tony Robbins to make our lives a masterpiece that we will be proud of, regardless of what anyone else thinks of it.

What gets you out of bed in the morning and keeps you up at night? Why do you invest? What makes you happy long term? What gives you pleasure? Who do you want to be at the end of your life? How do you want to be remembered?

Principle 21: Practice Humility

Chinese sage Lao Tse, author of the *Tao Te Ching,* one of the wisest books ever written, wrote that "the more you know the less you understand" and insisted that "not knowing is true knowledge."[138] This is why he taught only three things: simplicity, patience, and compassion. We could not agree more. For example, Einstein demonstrated through his special theory of relativity that mass and energy are interchangeable and formulated it as $E = mc^2$. This theory is one of the most advanced in the history of physics, and yet it has become a symbol for simplicity. In a similar way, Tom and I find Ken Wilber's Integral Theory provides a map of reality that helps simplify its complexity. This is why we apply it within the context of investing and company building. It helps us to understand, navigate, and address investing through a multi-perspectival lens, and to invest patiently in an exponentially evolving universe. If you have ever watched a plant, a tree, or a child grow, you will know that nature is the manifestation of ultimate patience. While witnessing the GGCs and the immense suffering in the world, we cannot help but feel deep sadness and pain in our hearts. Caused by fear and greed, the "suffering seems often cruel, unnecessary, and unjustified—reflecting a heartless universe ... but then our hearts open ... [and] we want to help."[139] This is compassion. This is the willingness to become vulnerable, to open the heart to pain and other sufferings, both our own and others'. And so, Tom and I practice compassion. Not because it is easy, but because it is hard. We believe that living in the unknown keeps the door open to new insights, new developments, and new wisdom. More importantly, while we trust science and scientific research and allow ourselves to be guided by progressive models of the world, we do not follow anyone, because "the moment you follow someone you cease to follow truth."[140] We should be aware that all models, research, and data are fingers pointing at the moon and not the moon itself. And so, moving forward, we practice humility and flexibility. Our intention is to be ready to grow, to shift our beliefs and our activities at any time, should the universe reveal better ways of serving the future of life.

---

[138]Lao-tzu (1988, #47, #71, #67).

[139]Dass and Bush (1992, pp. 3–4).

[140]This quote has been attributed to Krishnamurti. Retrieved 1 August 2019, at https://tinyurl.com/y554peme

How do you open your own heart? How do you show compassion to yourself and others? How do you integrate the wishes of your head with the desires of your heart? How do you remain humble?

3.6 Summary of Chapter 3: A Look at the Future

In a conversation on artificial intelligence with Elon Musk in late 2019, Alibaba's founder Jack Ma stated that he is "quite optimistic" about the future.[141] Ma insisted that only "college people are scared of AI, street-smart people [like him] are not." AI, Ma continued, can help people gain more self-confidence because it will allow them to begin to understand themselves and each other better: When "people know themselves better they will be smarter and will be wiser" and with that they can begin to improve the world and "make life more sustainable." Musk countered by proclaiming Ma's statements to be "famous last words." In spite of Musk's own innate optimism about AI and his "pro-Earth" attitude and action to make life more sustainable through electric cars (Tesla), sustainable energy (SolarCity, Gigafactory), and sustainable housing (Tesla Solar Roof),[142] he also warns that we should not underestimate the future capabilities of AI or the potential impact of those capabilities. He emphasized that humans are failing to fully grasp the full extent of AI's power and ability due to the exponential speed of its development. Musk views humanity as a "biological bootloader for digital superintelligence" in that human biology was essentially the small but crucial piece of code required to jump-start the AI revolution. He also believes that we must take action to ensure the continuation of human consciousness in the future, even if that means humans becoming an interplanetary species.[143] On the surface, their arguments may sound radically different, but in my view, both Ma and Musk basically agree on the fact that we require a shift in mindset if we are to address global challenges—a mindset that has outgrown the current ego- or ethnocentric center of gravity and that operates from a global, world-centric, or even integral view of the world. The COVID-19 pandemic is undoubtedly teaching all of us a hard, and overdue, lesson. Will we heed it?

The Future Is in Our Hands
With or without digital superintelligence and other exponential technologies, it is very possible that we as a species will neither develop a world-centric mindset soon enough to change our damaging behaviors nor have time to begin acting collectively in a SMART way, as *Transformation is Feasible* recommends. Of course, humanity does not have sole control of the fate of our planet. But we do exert significant influence on its continued existence, and to give in to the current grand global

---

[141] See World Artificial Intelligence Conference 2019. Viewed 12 September 2019 at https://tinyurl.com/yxkc6vma (Jack Ma quotes at minute 6:18 and min. 44:20; Elon Musk quote "biological bootloader for digital superintelligence" at min 8:50).

[142] https://tinyurl.com/jxlys59 & https://tinyurl.com/y7ylgxxg & https://tinyurl.com/m86j3hk

[143] https://youtu.be/f3lUEnMaiAU?t=530

challenges without a fight would be irresponsible and ill-advised. That is why this book has been designed to inspire investors—money owners and managers alike—as well as business people, entrepreneurs, company builders, and others who care deeply about the future of our planet to fight back in the way they know best: via their financial and business savvy.

By providing employment, security, wealth, and abundance, investing, company building, and entrepreneurship are essential vehicles for making *transformation feasible*. They also have the potential to contribute to the grand global challenges. Therefore, in this book, I have shared Tom's and my way of making investment an integrally sustainable practice. The investing paradigm I have presented is rooted in the essence of all existence, the *interior* culture—values, morals, and personal joy and happiness—but also the *exterior* reality, the world we see when we open our eyes. In this paradigm, financial returns are inseparable from environmental, social, cultural, and ethical returns, as well as individual self-actualization, joyfulness, and bliss. This translates into a life well lived.

My husband and I choose to abide by the advice of Sir Winston Churchill and to "never, never, never, never—in nothing great or small, large or petty—never give in, except to convictions of honor and good sense."[144] We support Elon Musk's opinion that it is better to be rather "optimistic and wrong than pessimistic and right,"[145] and to do anything and everything we can to contribute in our own way. We call for large-scale, significant action not only because self-actualization and knowing that investments are having a positive impact feels good, but also because Integral Investing helps us act in a SMART way, avoid losses, and protect our investments—and it makes good business sense. For example, a September 2019 report by The Global Commission on Adaptation notes that investments of US$1.8 trillion made between 2020 and 2030 in five areas in particular could result in more than US $7 trillion total net benefits: "early warning systems, climate-resilient infrastructure, improved dryland agriculture crop production, global mangrove protection, and investments in making water resources more resilient."[146]

And remember, these are only five options—there are innumerable other investment options out there with the potential to offer more than simply financial returns.

As we saw in Chap. 1, most of the technologies and resources we need to act are already available, and the current work of the European Commission's high-level expert group on sustainable finance[147] is rather encouraging—if they decide to stick to it and not allow COVID-19 to deter but instead encourage them. Technology is crucial in helping us undo the mess of the Anthropocene whether we use drones to plant trees or undersea robots to plant corals. But given the (double) exponential growth of technology we, the people, need to catch up quickly so it does not become

---

[144]Sir Winston Churchill, https://www.youtube.com/watch?v=L90BCEVH41U

[145]Podcast interview, Joe Rogan Experience #1169 with Elon Musk, minute 47:15. Viewed 31 August 2019 at https://www.youtube.com/watch?v=ycPr5-27vSI

[146]https://cdn.gca.org/assets/2019-09/GlobalCommission_Report_FINAL.pdf

[147]https://ec.europa.eu/info/business-economy-euro/banking-and-finance/sustainable-finance_en#hleg

more intelligent and more powerful than we are. Early in this book, I asked why we need a new Enlightenment and wondered what went wrong with the first one. I do not believe that we need a new Enlightenment. The old one is good enough if applied fully. The original focus of the Enlightenment era on rationality has taken us to the Moon, helped us send probes outside our solar system, and brought us modern medicine, the Internet, smartphones, AI, and biotechnology, to name only a few everyday advances. But now it is time for us as a species to take responsibility for and control over the technology we have invented. It is time for us to "fight for the light of consciousness."[148] Rationality alone will not get us there.

Yes, the denial of scientific facts lives on in some quarters, but evolution *moves on*. This is why we have decided to counteract the regression to the pre-scientific, pre-Enlightenment era and contribute to the elimination of what the *Economist* calls "a severe contest between intelligence, which presses forward, and an unworthy, timid ignorance obstructing our progress."[149]

Yes, it will take time; no, it will not be easy; and yes, there will be massive resistance because change is difficult for most people. But the first step has been taken toward closing a yearly investment gap of almost 180 billion euros in order to achieve EU climate and energy targets by 2030.[150] Our children have already stepped up to the challenge as we saw earlier in the discussion about the Fridays for Future movement. I think it is fair to say that they have finally got us moving through their climate strikes and refusal to go to school on Fridays, by speaking up at conferences such as the World Economic Forum and the United Nations general assemblies, and most recently by supporting the necessary measures to address the COVID-19 pandemic.[151] They give me hope for the future and if there is one thing the COVID-19 pandemic is currently teaching us, it is the need for the application of more wisdom, compassion, love, solidarity, and global collaboration. In short: higher human values harmoniously integrated with scientific achievements. The novel coronavirus is teaching us how to achieve global unity within pluralism—a unity that manifests our humanity, the holistic integration between the head, the heart, and the soul, or in Plato's vision: the True, the Good, and the Beautiful (or Science, Morals, and Art).

The Art and Science of Change
The call for the integration of the Platonic values, the full spectrum of consciousness, is not new and one way to detect it over time is through art. In fact, we can see it embodied in a 1514 painting by Flemish painter Quentin Massys (sometimes spelled Metsys or Matsys): *The Money Changer and His Wife* (Fig. 3.42).

It is possible to interpret this painting as moralizing, satirizing, or as a simple representation of economic activity at the beginning of the sixteenth century in Antwerp, which was one of the richest cities in the world at the time. I have chosen a Platonic interpretation.

---

[148]Elon Musk, https://www.youtube.com/watch?v=f3lUEnMaiAU (min 46)

[149]https://tinyurl.com/ufyzwq4

[150]https://tinyurl.com/yauy94kp

[151]https://www.fridaysforfuture.org/ and https://tinyurl.com/yx845a3v

Fig. 3.42 Quentin Massys (c. 1466–1530): the money changer and his wife, 1514 (Source: Courtesy of Zenodot Verlagsgesellschaft mbH, licensed under the GNU Free Documentation License)

In this symmetrical composition, a money changer and his wife are leaning toward each other, radiating a delicate balance between the feminine and the masculine. Their positions mirror one another, their congruence builds a harmonious unity, and their serene and unassuming expressions inspire trust and peace. The man is counting money, weighing valuables, and appraising rings (a symbol of relationships) and pearls (a symbol of purity, loyalty, generosity, and integrity); his wife is holding a religious text open at a page depicting the Madonna and child. The light falls onto the wife not by coincidence but by design to highlight the religious values (in the form of ethics and morals) that ought to govern the depicted activity, also represented by the man who holds the balance (between valuables and morals) represented by the scale in his left (from the heart) hand. This may also explain why the treasures on the table are in the shade. The convex mirror, albeit tiny, in the front seems to invite us to look at ourselves, while the church tower in the back is a reminder of higher values. The wooden box on the shelf behind the couple symbolizes the Divine, the apple represents the original sin, and the extinguished flame of the candle signifies death. Created at the onset of the Renaissance, this painting is a religious allegory in which Massys is reminding us of the impermanence of things, including our own mortality, and that we will ultimately be judged by our deeds.

Fig. 3.43 Quentin Massys (c. 1466–1530): suppliant peasants in the office of two tax collectors, 1520 (Source: Wikimedia at https://tinyurl.com/y9r3slmz)

Six years later, in 1520, he painted *Suppliant Peasants in the Office of Two Tax Collectors* (Fig. 3.43).

In this painting, the balance has disappeared, replaced by grotesque and disagreeable caricatures of four men surrounded by money and ledgers. The men's wild eyes, anxious looks, and blank faces collectively express greed, anxiety, and mistrust. The toothless, hooded tax collector on the far left appears to be haggling with the two haggard, desperate-looking men on the right. His expression emanates suspicion and avarice, a notion reinforced by his ringed index finger pointing to the pile of coins in front of him, as if he is refusing to give the desperate pair any more time to pay what they owe. In the center of the painting is another tax collector. This one appears to be rather well fed, but I see only emptiness in his eyes. All four men seem totally absorbed by their exchange, albeit for different reasons, and lost in their money-only world dominated by mistrust, angst, and desperation; thus, the need for protection through the tall, stone wall that can be seen on the right. If we look beyond that wall, we can catch a glimpse of a church tower—a reminder of Christian values, but too far in the distance to exert any significant influence.

In *The Money Changer and His Wife*, Massys presented with great subtlety a banking and economic system based on serving the needs of people through higher values, the Platonic values: the *True*, the *Good,* and the *Beautiful.* Only 6 years later, in *Suppliant Peasants in the Office of Two Tax Collectors,* he makes room for money only, and places ugliness at the forefront. Apparently disillusioned with the direction the financial system was taking, Massys let his brush speak out with candor, warning against a financial system that is devoid of human values and detached from beauty, soul and spirit, and moral contemplation.

During the past 500 years, humanity has more or less mastered the requisite balancing act between scarcity and abundance, evolution and regression, and wisdom and folly. The COVID-19 crisis has shown us that we are not ready to handle a "simple" pandemic let alone an existential threat. Climate change, unsafe AI, or nuclear threats are just as real but not in our face just yet.

Moving forward, we could potentially "see a true heaven on Earth for virtually all human beings ... inducing [a] system that results in a full Enlightenment for each"[152] while making the *Transformation Feasible*.

As an investor and/or entrepreneur you can do your part. Will you join us in making this *transformation feasible*?

References

Anderson EU, Brown BC (2013) Integral stakeholder analysis tool for major initiatives. MetaIntegral Academy, Resources Tool No. 18, July 2013. Viewed 12 August 2019 at https://tinyurl.com/wmb4l5v

Arnsperger C (2010) Full-spectrum economics: toward an inclusive and emancipatory social science. Routledge, New York

Beauregard M, O'Leary D (2007) The spiritual brain: a neuroscientist's case for the existence of the soul. HarperCollins, New York

Bozesan M (2010) The making of a consciousness leader in business: an integral approach. Published Ph.D. Dissertation, ITP Palo Alto. SageEra, Redwood City, CA

Bozesan M (2013) Demystifying the future of investing: an investor's perspective Part 1 & 2. J Integr Theory Pract 8(1 & 2):19–56

Bozesan M (2016) Integral sustainability of how evolutionary forces are driving investors' trust and the integration of people, planet, and profit. In: Lehner OM (ed) Routledge handbook of social and sustainable finance. Routledge, London, pp 296–321

Bozesan M, Kehler T, Schulz T (2020) An integral approach to sustainable investing using human-centered AI. Cadmus J 4(2), May 2020. http://cadmusjournal.org/content/cadmus-issues

Brown BC (2007) The four worlds of sustainability: drawing upon four universal perspectives to support sustainability initiatives, February 20. Viewed 16 August 2019 at https://tinyurl.com/ybeporny

Brown BC (2018) The future of leadership for conscious capitalism. Apheno Advisory. Viewed 12 August 2019 at https://tinyurl.com/yb25u6sb

Camerer CF, Loewenstein G (2004) Behavioral economics: past, present, future. In: Camerer CF, Loewenstein G, Rabin M (eds) Advances in behavioral economics. Princeton University Press, Princeton, pp 3–51

Club of Rome, in partnership with The Potsdam Institute for Climate Impact Research (24 September 2019) Planetary emergency plan: Securing a new deal for people, nature and climate. Viewed 30 September 2019 at https://tinyurl.com/y7vgggw7

---

[152]Wilber (2017, p. 608).

Coady D, Parry I, Sears L, Shang B (2017) How large are global fossil fuel subsidies? World Dev 91:11–27. Viewed 10 March 2020 at https://tinyurl.com/y692gdrx

Cohen Sir R (2018). On impact: a guide to the impact revolution. eBook downloaded 21 May 2019 from https://tinyurl.com/yy92urnd

Cook-Greuter SR (2004) Making the case for a developmental perspective [Electronic version]. J Ind Commer Train 36(7):275–281

Dass R, Bush M (1992) Compassion in action: setting out on the path of service. Bell Tower, New York

Diamandis P (2018) The 4 tools making capital more abundant than it's ever been, July 19. Blog on Singularity Hub, viewed 20 July 2018 at https://tinyurl.com/y9xpzqtz

Dixon-Declève S, Wijkman A (2019) This could be the biggest scandal of the climate change era. Viewed 10 March 2020 at https://tinyurl.com/vzcv4cz

Ebrahim A, Rangan V K (2009) Acumen fund: measurement in venture philanthropy (b). HBS Case No. 310-017 Harvard Business School General Management Unit, Harvard Business School Marketing Unit Harvard Business School Paper Nr. 9-310-017, 16 September 2009. Viewed 2 July 2010 https://tinyurl.com/ycclhfoo

Ekkart R, Buvelot Q (eds) (2007) Dutch portraits: the age of Rembrandt and Frans Hals. Mauritshuis/National Gallery/Waanders, Zwolle

Erdogan B, Kant R, Miller A, Sprague K (2016) Grow fast or die slow: why unicorns are staying, May 2016. Viewed 3 August 2019 at https://tinyurl.com/uuhb8m8

Esbjörn-Hargens S (2018) Metaimpact framework introduction, 11 February 2018. YouTube Video viewed 20 July 2018 at https://www.youtube.com/watch?v=oYMgDkhsC3o

EU Technical Expert Group on Sustainable Finance (2019) Taxonomy technical report: Financing a sustainable European economy, June 2019. Viewed 23 April 2020 at https://tinyurl.com/y2qq6syw

Federal Ministry for Economic Affairs and Energy SMEs are driving economic success: facts and figures about German SMEs. Viewed 19 April 2020 at https://tinyurl.com/y3cytbzf

Feld B, Mendelson J (2019) Venture deals: be smarter than your lawyer and venture capitalist, 4th edn. Wiley, Hoboken, NJ

Fulton K, Kasper G, Kibbe B (2010) What's next for philanthropy: acting bigger and adapting better in a networked world. Monitor Institute, July 2010. Viewed 23 December 2010 at https://tinyurl.com/y3nol62q

Gladstone D, Gladstone L (2004) Venture capital investing: the complete handbook for investing in private business for outstanding profits. Prentice Hall, Upper Saddle River, NJ

Göpel M (2016) The great mindshift: how new economic paradigm and sustainability transformations go hand in hand. SpringerOpen, Berlin

Gray E (2018) Unexpected future boost of methane possible from Arctic permafrost, 20 August 2018. Viewed 10 March 2020 at https://tinyurl.com/y68w3uxq

Hawken P (ed) (2017) Drawdown, the most comprehensive plan ever proposed to reverse global warming. Penguin Books, New York

IIRC (2013) The integrated reporting committee. http://www.theiirc.org

IPCC Report (2019) The oceans and cryosphere in a changing climate, 24 September. Viewed 30 2019 at https://report.ipcc.ch/srocc/pdf/SROCC_FinalDraft_FullReport.pdf

Ismail S, Malone MS, van Geest Y (2014) Exponential organizations: why new organizations are ten times better, faster, and cheaper than yours (and what to do about it). Diversion Books, New York

Kahneman D, Tversky A (1982) On the study of statistical intuitions. In: Kahneman D, Slovic P, Tversky A (eds) Judgment under uncertainty: heuristics and biases. Cambridge University Press, Cambridge

Kegan R (1982) The evolving self: problem and process in human development. Harvard University Press, Cambridge, MA

Koh H, Karamchandani A, Katz R (2012) From blueprint to scale: the case for philanthropy in impact investing, April 2012. Viewed 8 May 2012 at https://acumen.org/wp-content/uploads/2017/09/From-Blueprint-to-Scale-Case-for-Philanthropy-in-Impact-Investing_Full-report.pdf

Kolb B, Whishaw IQ (2003) Fundamentals of human neuropsychology. Worth Publishers, New York

Laloux F (2014) Reinventing organizations: a guide to creating organizations inspired by the next stage of human consciousness. Nelson Parker, Brussels

Lao-tzu (1988) Tao te ching: a new English version, with foreword and notes by Mitchell C. Harper & Row, New York

Lencioni P (2002) The five dysfunctions of a team. Jossey-Bass, San Francisco

Loevinger J (1977) Ego development: conceptions and theories. Jossey-Bass, San Francisco

Losada M, Heaphy E (2004) The role of positivity and connectivity in the performance of business teams: a nonlinear dynamics. Am Behav Sci 47(6):740–765. Viewed 19 August 2019 at https://www.factorhappiness.at/downloads/quellen/S8_Losada.pdf

Lovins AL, Wallis S, Wijkman A, Fullerton J (2018) A finer future: creating an economy in service to life. New Society, Gabriola Island

McCraty R (2001) Science of the heart: exploring the role of the heart in human performance. Institute of HeartMath, Boulder Creek, CA

Miller CC (2014) How social media silences debate, 26 August. Viewed at 19 April 2020 https://tinyurl.com/y7c65rv5

National Advisory Board (NAB) Deutschland (2014) Wirkungsorientiertes Investieren: Neue Finanzierungsquellen zur Lösung gesellschaftlicher Herausforderungen. Viewed 19 April 2020 at https://tinyurl.com/nkdb6lx

Newberg AB, Lee BY (2005, June) The neuroscientific study of religious and spiritual phenomena: or why god doesn't use biostatistics. Zygon 40(2):469–489

Randers J, Rockström J, Stoknes PE, Golücke U, Collste D, Cornell S (2018) Transformation is feasible. How to achieve sustainable development goals within planetary boundaries. A report to the Club of Rome, for its 50th anniversary, 17 October 2018. Stockholm Resilience Center. Viewed 20 December 2018 at https://tinyurl.com/y9epzlmk

Robertson BJ (2015) Holacracy: the new management system for a rapidly changing world. Henry Holt, New York

Saltuk Y, Bouri A, Leung G (2011) Insight into the impact investment market: An in-depth analysis of investor perspectives and over 2,200 transactions. J.P. Morgan, Social Finance Research, 14 December 2011. Viewed 14 December 2011 at https://tinyurl.com/y7fxnuvm

So I, Staskevicius A (2015) Measuring "impact" in impact investing. Harvard Business School. Viewed 22 June 2019 at https://tinyurl.com/yxd8jfx2

Stein Z, Dawson T, Fischer KW (2010) Redesigning testing: operationalizing the new science of learning. In: Khine MS, Saleh IM (eds) New science of learning: cognition, computers, and collaboration in education. Springer, New York

Stoll C, Klaaßen L, Gallersdörfer U (2018) The carbon footprint of Bitcoin. Research brief published by the MIT Center for Energy and Environmental Policy Research (CEEPR). Viewed 21 June 2019 at http://ceepr.mit.edu/files/papers/2018-018-Brief.pdf

Surowiecki J (2004) The wisdom of crowds. First Anchor Books, New York

Toniic (2018) T100 power ascent report 2018. Viewed 17 June 2019 at https://toniic.com/t100-powered-ascent-report/

Wasserman N (2008) The founder's dilemma. Harvard Business Review, February 2008. Viewed 12 August 2019 at https://hbr.org/2008/02/the-founders-dilemma

Weitnauer W (2019) Handbuch venture capital: Von der Innovation zum Börsengang. C.H. Beck, Muenchen

Wilber K (2000a/1995) Sex, ecology, spirituality: the spirit of evolution. Shambhala, Boston

Wilber K (2000b) A theory of everything: an integral vision for business, politics, science, and spirituality. Shambhala, Boston

Wilber K (2006) Integral spirituality: a startling new role for religion in the modern and postmodern world. Integral Books, Boston

Wilber K (2017) The religion of tomorrow: a vision for the future of great traditions. Shambhala, Boston

Wong LH (2005) Venture capital fund management: a comprehensive approach to investment practices & the entire operations of a VC firm. Aspatore Books, Boston

World Bank (n.d.) Small and medium enterprises (SMES) finance: improving SMEs' access to finance and finding innovative solutions to unlock sources of capital. Viewed 19 January 2020 at https://www.worldbank.org/en/topic/smefinance

World Commission on Environment and Development (1987/2009) Our Common Future. Oxford University Press, Oxford

Yazdipour R (ed) (2011) Advances in entrepreneurial finance: with applications from behavioral finance and economics. Springer, New York

Zanna L, Khatiwala S, Gregory JM, Ison J, Heimbach P (2019) Global reconstruction of historical ocean heat storage and transport, 7 January 2019. Viewed 11 July 2019 at https://www.pnas.org/content/pnas/116/4/1126.full.pdf

The Manifesto of Integral Investing

We acknowledge humanity's global grand challenges (GGCs), particularly the existential threats such as climate emergency, nuclear capacity, and unsafe exponentially growing technologies. Current systems, including political, economic, financial, and educational systems, are not contrived to handle the GGCs. Nevertheless, we are convinced that *transformation is feasible*, and the necessary resources, knowledge, technology, and capital exist to safeguard humanity and our planet. A mind shift toward world-centric levels of consciousness is a mandatory requirement and a premise for immediate, united, and adequate global action. We are totally committed to doing our part to ensure the future of life. This is our manifesto:

1. *Have a Massively Transformative Purpose*: Our massively transformative purpose (MTP) is to inspire and empower investors and company builders to ensure the future of life and wellbeing. We take a world-centric view of the world and address the GGCs through integral sustainability investing. We believe that the development and deployment of safe and ethically sound exponentially growing technologies are crucial for the future of humanity.

2. *Have a Moonshot*: Our moonshot is the investment turnaround. We believe in the critical role of investing and company building in solving the GGCs. To reverse it, we unleashed the investment turnaround to achieve the next paradigm in investing. This paradigm is rooted in the essence of *all* existence, the exterior reality, the material world, as well as the interior reality, such as culture, values, psychology, ethics, and morals. It is a reality in which financial returns are inseparable from environmental, social, cultural, and ethical impact, including individual joy and happiness.

3. *Make Transformation Feasible*: We believe that *transformation is feasible*. We are confident that humanity will muster the necessary mind shift, political will, capital, and resources in time to implement the *Smart* scenario outlined by Randers et al. in their 2018 *Transformation is Feasible* report to the Club of Rome. The implementation of the UN SDGs must occur within planetary boundaries. We continue to contribute our share of this transformation through

© Springer Nature Switzerland AG 2020

M. Bozesan, *Integral Investing*, https://doi.org/10.1007/978-3-030-54016-6

our integral investments in early-stage, exponential-tech companies, as well as smart grids, ultra-energy efficient, sustainable NDC datacenters, and our efforts toward climate endowments.

4. *Follow an Investment Strategy*: We have an investment strategy and a profound tactical implementation plan based on three decades of hands-on expertise. We know what we do and do what we know. We have a stellar track record in direct investments and company building.

5. *Have an Investment Philosophy*: Our investment philosophy is based on Integral Theory, AQAL (pronounced ah-qwul), by philosopher Ken Wilber, which has been applied in more than 50 disciplines from medicine to economics and business. It is rooted in evolutionary theory and helps us integrate *all* of reality, its exterior as well as interior dimensions, in our investment decisions. It is a map that helps us simplify and navigate the complexity of reality while maintaining multiple world views and honoring the evolution of human consciousness from pre-modern to modern, postmodern, and post-postmodern structures of consciousness.

6. *Have a Proven Investment Framework*: Our proven investment framework is called Integral Investing, a framework that both transcends and includes traditional and impact investing. Integral investing is a meta-theory and practice of investing based on consciousness evolution as described in Wilber's Integral Theory.

7. *Communicate Your Ideals*: We communicate our ideals via our motto, the 6Ps: The Parity of People, Planet and Prosperity with Passion and Purpose. Doing good *and* doing well are not contradictory aims but are indicative of an indispensable mindset that ensures the future of life and wellbeing; in short, integral sustainability. The *equality* of all 6Ps is the key to our future.

8. *Be Smart about De-Risking*: We de-risk our investments using our proprietary Theta Model, the due diligence process of Integral Investing that applies the tools and methodologies of Integral Theory to de-risk investments with the intention to build integrally sustainable companies from the very beginning. We use proven financial due diligence and methods, structures, tools, and metrics to lead the way toward the implementation of the next paradigm in investing. The Theta Model has been developed, refined, and successfully applied since 1995.

9. *Investing in Scientific Proof and Technology Advancement within Planetary Boundaries*: We believe in scientific proof. We invest in scientifically proven solutions to real-world problems. We never invest in "shoulds," but in hard and proven ideas and in highly qualified and integrally informed people. We believe in the ingenuity of the human mind to solve critical problems, even if it takes time. Humanity has arrived at this point in time and space through an evolutionary process that initially looked linear and local. Now it has become obvious that we are subject to an exponentially growing function of evolution that has a global impact. Thus, smart *and* wise action is required.

10. *Act Boldly Now*: We act boldly now and believe that we are living through some of the most exciting times in human history. We are very privileged to be alive in

this day and age, but with privilege comes responsibility. Subsequently, there has never been a better time to act than now, and neither has there ever been a greater necessity or obligation to act.

11. *Never, Never, Never Give In*: During a 20-minute speech at Harrow School on October 29, 1941, Churchill encouraged his audience to "Never give in. Never give in. Never, never, never, never–in nothing great or small, large or petty–never give in, except to convictions of honor and good sense. Never yield to force. Never yield to the apparently overwhelming might of the enemy." The enemy Churchill was referring to was Nazi Germany, but we think that his advice applies in general to a life well lived. This is why we have adopted it.

12. *Provide Certainty Where There Is Doubt*: We provide certainty where there is doubt and hope where there is despair. We are mindful optimists, and we use scientific research and lifelong investment and company-building expertise to clear a path to a sustainable and abundant future for us all. We put our money where our mouth is.

13. *Recognize the Critical Role of Capital in Transformation*: We believe in the critical role of capital to solve the GGCs. However, to achieve that, our systems must move beyond the current understanding of capital as being money and the single measurement of success. We work with and have an extended understanding and definition of capital that transcends the traditional financial capital and includes natural capital, human capital, as well as social and cultural capital, but also, for example, cognitive and psycho-spiritual capital.

14. *Invest in People, not in Ideas*: We invest passionately and compassionately in people, not in ideas. Our experience has reinforced the old adage that "ideas are a dime a dozen" and taught us that 80% of the risk in any endeavor lies with the people involved. Therefore, we invest first and foremost in people, because people at later stages of consciousness are more likely to succeed at implementing a good idea whose time has come.

15. *Build Integrally Sustainable Organizations*: We believe that trust and wisdom are the foundation for the future of life. We walk the talk and work tirelessly toward building a culture of trust in our organizations. We focus on building integrally sustainable companies that are led by integrally informed management teams.

16. *Take Pride in Long-Term Investments*: We choose long-term, sustainable investments over short-term profit at the expense of people and the planet. We take pride in making meaningful investments that generate abundance for all and ensure the future of work and the future of life and wellbeing.

17. *You Can Only Achieve What You Measure*: We believe that we can only achieve what we measure. To fulfill our self-imposed Integral Investing mandate, we measure the activities *and* outcomes of our investments. We use existing measurement criteria for success by applying standards and quasi-standards where they exist and develop our own metrics where needed.

18. *You Cannot Not Invest*. We believe that the market has no intentions, only people do. We think that everybody is an investor, because we all influence the economy through, for example, our purchases, votes, work, commitments,

knowledge, preferences, love, and caring. Like money, the market and our economic systems are constructs made by people to serve people. We believe that our current GGCs are the result of outdated systems created by outdated mindsets that no longer serve humanity. Earth needs world-centric mindsets. We are committed to paving the way toward integrally sustainable investment and business systems that are driven by people rooted in world-centric mindsets to ensure the future of life.

19. *With Privilege Comes Responsibility*: We believe in higher ethics, morals, and unity consciousness. Through our actions we contribute to unleashing the next level of consciousness in human evolution and believe that higher ethics and morals pave the way.

20. *Self-actualize through Investing*: We self-actualize through investing. Investing is not a profession but a way of life for us. We actively seek out the good in everything. We live an integrally informed life guided by an integral life practice and believe that there is always a solution to a problem when you are committed to a positive outcome. We seek short-term flow and long-term meaning through our activities. We think globally and exponentially. We act locally with integral impact to ensure the future of life on earth.

21. *Practice Humility*: We practice humility and seek harmony between head and heart. Chinese sage Lao Tsu wrote in the *Tao Te Ching* that "the more you know the less you understand. . . [and] not knowing is true knowledge." We take those words to heart. While we trust scientific research and allow ourselves to be *guided* by progressive models of the world, we do not *follow* anyone or anything but truth. Moving forward, we practice humility, embrace the unknown, and practice flexibility with the intention to grow, to shift our beliefs and our activities at any time, should the Universe reveal better ways of serving the future of life.

Glossary

Integral Investing The meta-theory and investment practice of integral investors, it is rooted in philosopher Ken Wilber's Integral Theory, AQAL (pronounced ah-qwul).

Integral Investors Self-actualizing individuals who have awakened to a unity consciousness mindset at later stages of human development. They are acting holistically, whether they use AQAL as a guiding map to navigate the exponentially growing complexity of the world or not. Integral investors have a massively transformative purpose (MTP), a moonshot, and a daily integral wheel of life practice. They apply exponentially growing technologies to build integrally sustainable organizations that successfully address humanity's global grand challenges such as implementing the UN SDGs within planetary boundaries.

Integral Map, Framework, or Operating System Synonym for Ken Wilber's Integral Theory, AQAL.

Integral Lens This is the looking glass into the world of investing that uses Integral Theory as its lens.

Integral Sustainability Investing This approach to investing aims to fulfill the call issued in the *Brundtland Report*, named in honor of former Norwegian Prime Minister Gro Harlem Brundtland, who chaired the World Commission on Environment and Development from 1983 through 1987. Brundtland's request for sustainability intends to meet "the need of the present without compromising the ability of future generations to meet their own needs."[1] Integral sustainability fulfills Brundtland's call through investing and the application of Integral Theory, and contends that all investment activity must be rooted in the essence of *all* existence, the *interior* such as culture, values, ethics, and morals as well as *exterior* reality, the material world. It is a reality in which financial sustainability is inseparable from its environmental, social, cultural, and ethical impact, as well as individual self-actualization, joy, and individual happiness.

---

[1] https://en.wikipedia.org/wiki/Brundtland_Commission

© Springer Nature Switzerland AG 2020
M. Bozesan, *Integral Investing*, https://doi.org/10.1007/978-3-030-54016-6

Integral Team The management team, C-levels, in which we invest ought to operate from an integrally informed and/or integrally acting level. The desired center of gravity is second tier with a minimum centered at first tier, orange-level, as defined, for example, by Spiral Dynamics.

Integral Theory Developed by philosopher Ken Wilber, it is rooted in evolutionary theory and honors the truth in all there is. It aims to integrate *all* of reality, exterior as well as interior dimensions. It is a map that helps simplify and navigate the complexity of reality while maintaining multiple world views and honoring the evolution of human consciousness from pre-modern to modern, postmodern to post-postmodern structures of consciousness.

Massively Transformative Purpose (MTP) A term popularized by Singularity co-founder Peter Diamandis. Your MTP reflects you and your belief system; it is inspiring and connects your heart with your mind. It is independent of technology; it is neither too wide nor too narrow; and you can speak with confidence about what it means and why it is your MTP.

Moonshot A moonshot is the intention to achieve something that nobody has achieved before. It means to go "10 times bigger, while the rest of the world is trying to grow 10%."[2] Our professional moonshot is the implementation of the Investment Turnaround (in German, the *Investmentwende*). It is the specific application of exponential technologies toward achieving Integral Investing, the next paradigm in investing, namely integral sustainability. It aims at implementing an investing paradigm rooted in the essence of all existence, the exterior reality, the material world, as well as interior realities such as culture, values, ethics, and morals. It is a reality in which financial returns are inseparable from environmental, social, cultural, and ethical impact, including individual joy and happiness. Our first goal is the integrally sustainable implementation of the UN SDGs within planetary boundaries by 2050.

Theta Factor The result of the Theta Model, AQAL due-diligence process that my husband, Tom, and I use to decide on whether or not to invest.

Theta Model The Theta Model is the due-diligence, de-risking, process that applies the tools and methodologies of Integral Investing to de-risk investments with the intention of building integrally sustainable companies from the very beginning. It integrates (a) traditional investing due-diligence criteria (financial, legal, sales and marketing, etc.) with (b) sustainability criteria and impact investing metrics (for example, UN SDGs within planetary boundaries, as well as Social, Environmental, and Governance (ESG) of the UN PRI, etc.); and (c) cultural, behavioral, and consciousness criteria as defined in Wilber's integral framework.

---

[2]https://peterdiamandis.tumblr.com/post/164961004383/what-is-a-moonshot

Index

© Springer Nature Switzerland AG 2020
M. Bozesan, *Integral Investing*, https://doi.org/10.1007/978-3-030-54016-6